우루과이라운드

제도 및 기타 분야 협상 1

우루과이라운드

제도 및 기타 분야 협상 1

| 머리말

  우루과이라운드는 국제적 교역 질서를 수립하려는 다각적 무역 교섭으로서, 각국의 보호무역 추세를 보다 완화하고 다자무역체제를 강화하기 위해 출범되었다. 1986년 9월 개시가 선언되었으며, 15개 분야의 교섭을 1990년 말까지 진행하기로 했다. 그러나 각 분야의 중간 교섭이 이루어진 1989년 이후에도 농산물, 지적소유권, 서비스무역, 섬유, 긴급수입제한 등 많은 분야에서 대립하며 1992년이 돼서야 타결에 이를 수 있었다. 한국은 특히 농산물 분야에서 기존 수입 제한 품목 대부분을 개방해야 했기에 큰 경쟁력 하락을 겪었고, 관세와 기술 장벽 완화, 보조금 및 수입 규제 정책의 변화로 제조업 수출입에도 많은 변화가 있었다.

  본 총서는 우루과이라운드 협상이 막바지에 다다랐던 1991~1992년 사이 외교부에서 작성한 관련 자료를 담고 있다. 관련 협상의 치열했던 후반기 동향과 관계부처회의, 무역협상위원회 회의, 실무대책회의, 규범 및 제도, 투자회의, 특히나 가장 많은 논란이 있었던 농산물과 서비스 분야 협상 등의 자료를 포함해 총 28권으로 구성되었다. 전체 분량은 약 1만 3천여 쪽에 이른다.

2024년 3월
한국학술정보(주)

| 일러두기

· 본 총서에 실린 자료는 2022년 4월과 2023년 4월에 각각 공개한 외교문서 4,827권, 76만여 쪽 가운데 일부를 발췌한 것이다.

· 각 권의 제목과 순서는 공개된 원본을 최대한 반영하였으나, 주제에 따라 일부는 적절히 변경하였다.

· 원본 자료는 A4 판형에 맞게 축소하거나 원본 비율을 유지한 채 A4 페이지 안에 삽입하였다. 또한 현재 시점에선 공개되지 않아 '공란'이란 표기만 있는 페이지 역시 그대로 실었다.

· 외교부가 공개한 문서 각 권의 첫 페이지에는 '정리 보존 문서 목록'이란 이름으로 기록물 종류, 일자, 명칭, 간단한 내용 등의 정보가 수록되어 있으며, 이를 기준으로 0001번부터 번호가 매겨져 있다. 이는 삭제하지 않고 총서에 그대로 수록하였다.

· 보고서 내용에 관한 더 자세한 정보가 필요하다면, 외교부가 온라인상에 제공하는 『대한민국 외교사료요약집』 1991년과 1992년 자료를 참조할 수 있다.

| 차례

기록물종류	일반공문서철	등록번호	2019090027	등록일자	2019-09-04
분류번호	764.51	국가코드		보존기간	영구
명 칭	UR(우루과이라운드) / 제도분야 협상 그룹 회의, 1991				
생 산 과	통상기구과	생산년도	1991~1991	담당그룹	다자통상
내용목차					

0001

외 무 부

종 별 :

번 호 : GVW-0345　　　　　　　　　　일 시 : 91 0222 1600

수 신 : 장관(통기,경기원,재무,농수,상공,특허청,박수길대사)

발 신 : 주제네바대사대리

제 목 : UR/ 분쟁해결, 최정의정서 주요국 비공식 협의

1. 2.22(금) 12:00 TNC 고위급 의장 자격의 DUNKEL사무총장 주재로 30여개국 참석하에분쟁 해결,최종의정서 분야에 대한 비공식협의가 개최되어, 여타 분야 협의시와 같이 DUNKEL총장이 브랏셀 각료회의시 부여받은 임무(MANDATE) 에 따른 협상 개시를 선언하고 협상의기초, 협상과제, 차기회의 일정(3.20 오전개최) 및 잠정의제를 밝히는 STATEMENT(별첨)를 발표하고, 이에대해 참가국들이 발언없이 묵시적으로 수락함으로써 동 분야에서도 협상 재개에 대한 사실상의 합의가 이루어짐(박공사,민서기관 참석)

2. DUNKEL 총장이 동 STATEMENT 에서 밝힌 주요협상 의제는 아래와같음.

가. 분쟁해결

- MTN/W/35/REV 1 문서의 COMMENTARY 에명기된바와 같이 이사회의 분쟁해결 관련결정절차, 일방조치 억제 및 갓트 비위배 분쟁(NON-VIOLATION COMPLAINTS) 절차등 세가지가 주요현안임

-3.20 차기 협의시에는 현 협상 상황에 대한 평가및 초기단계 협상과제의 선정 문제를 다룸

- 정치적 결정을 요하는 사항이 다수이기는 하나 분쟁해결절차의 최장시한, NON-VIOLATION분쟁절차 등에 관한 규정등 일부사항은 현단계에서 기술적 논의 유용

나. 최종 의정서(FINAL ART)

- UR 협상 결과의 일괄수락(SINGLE UNDERTAKING)여부 및 UR 협상결과 이행을 위한 새로운 기구적측면의 문제가 주요 쟁점이나, 우선은 여타 논의사항 논의에 중점

다. 갓트기능

- 갓트의 기구적 측면 강화 및 세계 경제 정책결정에 있어서의 일관성 제고(GREATER COHERENCE)문제는 정치적 결정을 요하는 사항으로 UR협상 최종단계에 가서야

통상국　　2차보　　국가국(대사)　　경기원　　재무부　　농수부　　상공부　　특허청

　　　　　　　　　　　　　　　91.02.23　03:12 DN

외신 1과 통제관

0002

해결가능하며 현단계에서의 기술적 논의 대상이 아님.

　첨부: 상기 STATEMENT

　(GVW(F)-0076). 끝

　(대사대리 박영우-국장)

PAGE 2

0003

$GVW(A) - 0076 \quad /6222 \ /600$

$"GVW - 0345 \ 첨부"$

22.2.91

DISPUTE SETTLEMENT AND FINAL ACT

Friday, 22 February 1991, p.m.

Note for Chairman

1.   In his closing remarks at the Brussels Ministerial Meeting,
Minister Gros Espiell requested me to pursue intensive consultations with
the specific objective of achieving agreements in all the areas of the
negotiating programme in which differences remain outstanding. These
consultations will, he said, be based on document MTN.TNC/W/35/Rev.1, dated
3 December 1990, including the cover page which refers to the Surveillance
Body and the communications which various participants sent to Brussels.
He added that I would also take into account the considerable amount of
work carried out at the Brussels meeting, although it did not commit any
delegation.

2.   We shall, at this meeting, be taking up Dispute Settlement and the
Final Act. I shall also refer to the FOGS text on Institutional
Reinforcement of the GATT and Greater Coherence in Policy Making.

Dispute settlement

3.   MTN.TNC/W/35/Rev.1 contains a detailed text on Dispute Settlement.
This will be found on pages 289 to 305 of that document. A commentary on
the text identified the three main outstanding issues.

4.   At the next meeting of the group on Wednesday, 20 March starting in
the morning, participants would be given an opportunity to comment on the
present situation in the negotiations on dispute settlement and to identify
work that can usefully be done in the phase of the negotiations that is
just beginning.

7-1

0004

5. It is my judgment that a number of the issues in this area will only be solved when governments are ready to take the political decisions necessary to bring the Uruguay Round to a successful conclusion. I would, however, suggest that there are areas in which technical discussions would be useful at the present stage: for example, the provisions concerning the maximum length of dispute settlement proceedings and the procedures for dealing with non-violation complaints.

Final Act

6. The Draft Final Act will be found on pages 2 to 5 of MTN.TNC/W/35/Rev.1.

7. The two main issues in this area are, in my view, whether the instruments resulting from the Uruguay Round should or should not be accepted as a single undertaking; and the form of the decision to be taken in respect of a new organizational structure to be implemented after the conclusion of the Round.

8. I suggest that delegations are likely to wish to concentrate on other areas of the negotiations before turning to the consideration of these issues.

FOGS text on Greater Coherence

9. Before I close this meeting, I would like to refer briefly to the FOGS texts on Institutional Reinforcement of the GATT and Greater Coherence in Global Economic Policy Making on pages 323 to 325 of MTN.TNC/W/35/Rev.1. An inspection of these texts shows that a number of issues remain to be settled.

3 - 2   0005.

- 3 -

10. I will simply say that these issues seem to me to require political decisions that are unlikely to be forthcoming until the final decisions on the Uruguay Round are taken and that there does not appear to be scope for technical discussions on them at the present stage.

0006

외 무 부

종 별 :

번 호 : GVW-0517　　　　　　　　　　일 시 : 91 0320 1850

수 신 : 장 관(통가, 경기원, 재무부, 농림수산부, 상공부, 특허청)

발 신 : 주 제네바 대사

제 목 : UR/ 분쟁해결 최종의정서에 관한 비공식 협의

　　3.20(수) 10:00-12:15 간 표제비공식 협의가 LINDEN갓트사무총장 특별 보좌관의 사회로 개최된바, 주요 협의 내용 아래 보고함.(본직 및 오참사관참석)

　　1. 분쟁해결 및 최종의정서에 관한 사무국비공식 문서(NON-PAPER)

　　- LINDEN 보좌관은 브랏셀 각료회의시 분쟁해결 및 최종의정서에 관해 주요 국가간 비공식 협의가 진행되었으며 이에따라 갓트사무국이 사무국 책임하에 비공식 문서를 작성하였다고 하고 (3.25.내 각국에 배포 예정)차기회의시 동 비공식 문서에 대해 협의할 것을제의, 이의 제기없이 합의함.

　　2. 기술적인 작업이 가능한 분야에 대한 토의

　　- LINDEN 보좌관은 본 비공식 협의 그룹이 기술적 작업을 진행할 수 있는 가능분야로 아래 4가지 분야를 제시하고 각국의 의견을 문의함.

　　1) 분쟁해결 절차의 시한문제(TIME-LIMIT)

　　2) NON-VIOLATION 분쟁

　　3) 통합문안(SONSOLIDATED-TEXT)

　　4) 타협상 그룹내의 분쟁해결 절차와 23조에 의한 분쟁해결 절차와의 조화문제 (HARMONIZEDTEXT 또는 UNIFIED TEXT)

　　- 대부분의 국가가 통합초안은 기술적인 차원에서 다룰수 있다는 의견을 피력하였으며, HARMORIZED-TEXT 문제는 구체적으로 검토하기에는 아직 시기적으로 이르다는 반응이었고 (인도의 경우본 협상 그룹에서 다룰수 없는 문제라는 점을 명백히함) 시한문제, NON-VIOLATION 분쟁에 대해서는 다소 상이한 반응을 보였음.

　　- 아국은 통합초안에 대한 기술적 작업 진행용의를 표시 하였으며, NON-VIOLATION 문제에 관해서도 기술적 작업을 진행할 수 있을것이라고 하고, 시한 문제는 다소정치적 성격이있고 HARMONZED TEXT 문제는 아직 구체적협의 단계에와 있지 않다고

통상국　　2차보　　경기원　　재무부　　농수부　　상공부　　특허청

본다는 의견을피력함.

　3. 봉합초안 및 HARMONIZED TEXT 문제에 관한 사무국 문서준비

　- 상기 협의에 따라 사무국이 봉합초안 검토를 위해 배경 설명등 관련 자료를 준비키로하였으며, HARMONIZED TEXT 문제에 관해서는 현황자료를 준비 (다소 시간 소요 예정)키로 하였음.

　4. 차기 표제 그룹 회의는 5월 초순경이 될 것이라함.끝.

　(대사 박수길-국장)

※ UR 협상 결과에 관한 검토

1. Lacarte 그룹에서의 논의

- 구성 : 우루과이(Lacarte)대사, 미국, 이씨, 일본, 카나다, 스웨덴, 스위스, 인도, 브라질, 인도네시아대사, 덴켈총장, 린덴 특별고문

- 10.25. 회합 내용
  - Lacarte 대사가 작성한 note for discussion 제시
  - 동 note는 일종의 check list 로서 구체적 협의는 없었으며, 다만 선진국들은 UR 협상의 모든 또는 최대한의 결과가 모든 또는 최대다수의 체약국에 의해 수락되어야 한다는 점을 강조함.

  "of all or most results of the negotiations by a maximum of (if not all) GATT Contracting Parties"

2. Single Undertaking 주장의 논거

- 동경 Round 와 같은 선별 수락 불가

- 25조 (체약국단 결정) 또는 30조 (개정)에 의한 방식도 곤란
  - 참가국간 권리 의무 수준의 균등화 불가능
  - ※ 25조 : 관례상 Consensus에 의한 체약국단의 공동행동
    (Consensus 이므로 이견대립이 없는 분야만 결정 가능)
  - 30조 : 2/3 이상의 동의 필요 (이경우 동의하는 국가에만 구속력) √

0009

3. 미국 입장 (integrated accord approach)

○ 현행 갓트 규정중 UR 협상대상이 아닌 분야

→ 현행 갓트 규정

○ UR 협상 결과 내용이 변경되어야 할 분야

(보조금, 반덤핑, 세이프가드, 농산물, 분쟁해결)

→ 새로운 갓트 규정으로 대체

○ 현 갓트 규정이 규율하지 못하는 분야 (신분야)

→ 새로운 규정 도입

4. EC 입장

○ UR 협상 결과중 이견없이 합의 가능한 분야

→ 25조 결정으로 처리

○ 여타 분야 협상결과

→ 단일 수락 의정서 (Single Protocol of Acceptance) 로 작성

· 모든 분야의 합의 사항을 수락

· 분야별로 수락국이 갓트 규정 개정 정족수가 될 때 관련 갓트
조문 개정 또는 폐기(일정기간 동안 2 원적 갓트체제 존재)

○ 단, 상기 문제는 최종단계에 가서 논의해야 한다는 입장

5. 문제점

○ 개도국의 반발 예상

- 개도국에 대한 갓트 탈퇴 강요 또는 선진국간의 새로운 갓트 창설
결과를 가져올 것으로 부정적 반응

○ 각 협상그룹별 협상결과 처리 방식 상이

○ 세계무역기구(MTO 혹은 WTO) 창설 문제와도 연관.   끝.

0010

※ UR 協商結果의 形態 豫測

1. 갓트 條文 改正 (締約國團 滿場一致)
   ○ 關稅, 非關稅 分野 議定書
   ○ 農産物分野中 議定書 및 國內補助 部分
   ○ 知的所有權 (附隨協定 또는 別途協定도 可能) ── ? Annex Ⅲ ?
   ○ 投資措置 (附隨協定도 可能)

2. 締約國團 決定 (旣存 갓트 規定의 의무 變更이나 새로운 義務創出이 없는 경우)
   ○ 原産地 規定 (附隨 協定으로도 可能)
   ○ 纖維 (別途 纖維協定도 可能)
   ○ 갓트 條文, 갓트 機能, 紛爭解決 節次
   ○ 세이프가드 (附隨協定도 可能)

3. 附隨協定 (동경라운드 結果와 같은 Code 形態)
   ○ 동경라운드 協定改正 (반덤핑, 政府調達, 技術障壁, 輸入許可, 補助金, 相計關稅 協定등)

4. 別途協定
   ○ 써비스 分野

0011

※　동경라운드 結果 (79.4)

o　동경라운드 關稅讓許 議定書와 반덤핑 協定, 補助金. 相計關稅 協定등
　　總 9개의 부속 協定이 合議되고

o　우리나라는 이중에서
　　- 關稅讓許 議定書를 受諾하고
　　- 技術障壁 (80.9), 關稅評價 協定(81.1), 반덤핑 協定(86.2), 補助金.
　　　相計關稅 協定(86.6)의 4개 부속 協定에 각각 加入하였고

o　關稅評價協定 加入 및 同 關稅讓許 議定書 受諾의 경우에는 國會의
　　同意를 받았으나

o　여타 3개 부속 協定은 國會의 同意를 받지 않았음.

0012

감. 조
(심의관시행)

주 제 네 바 대 표 부

제네(경) 20644 - 312   1991. 3. 28

수 신 : 외무부장관

참 조 : <u>통상국장</u>, 경기원, 재무부, 농림수산부, 상공부,특허청

제 목 : UR/분쟁해결·최종의정서에 관한 비공식 협의

    연 : GVW - 0517

    연호 UR/분쟁해결 및 최종의정서에 관한 갓트사무국 비공식 문서

(non - paper)를 별첨 송부합니다.

첨부 : 1. UR/분쟁해결에 관한 비공식 문서 (No. 454)

    2. UR/최종의정서에 관한 비공식문서 (No. 455). 끝.

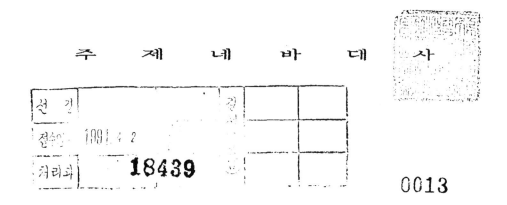

주 제 네 바 대 사

선 견			결		
접수	1991. 4. 2				
처리과	18439				

0013

Secretariat Non-Paper
25 March 1991

Revised Draft Final Act Embodying the Results of the Uruguay Round of Multilateral Trade Negotiations

The attached draft revised text of the Final Act has been prepared by the Secretariat on its own responsibility. It contains changes to the text contained in document MTN.TNC/W/35/Rev.1, which resulted from consultations held in Brussels in December 1990.

It should be noted that dates have been kept as they appeared in the text resulting from the Brussels consultations. They will obviously have to be revised to take into account later developments.

0014

DRAFT FINAL ACT EMBODYING THE RESULTS OF THE
URUGUAY ROUND OF MULTILATERAL TRADE NEGOTIATIONS

1.   Having met at Ministerial level from 3 to 7 December 1990 at Brussels in order to conclude the Uruguay Round of Multilateral Trade Negotiations, the representatives of the Governments and of the European Communities, members of the Trade Negotiations Committee (hereinafter referred to as "participants"), agree that the Agreements, Decisions and Understandings on trade in goods, as set out in Annex I, and the General Agreement on Trade in Services, as set out in Annex II, [the Agreement on Trade-Related Aspects of Intellectual Property Rights, including Trade in Counterfeit Goods, as set out in Annex III[1]] [constitute distinct legal texts] and, together with the institutional provisions set out below, embody the results of their negotiations and form an integral part of the Final Act. They acknowledge that these texts may be subject to rectifications of a formal character that do not affect the substance or meaning of the texts, except as otherwise indicated.

2.   By adopting the present Final Act, participants [agree] [indicate their intention] to submit, as necessary, the legal texts and instruments included in the Annexes for the consideration of their respective competent authorities with a view to seeking approval of these legal texts and instruments in accordance with appropriate procedures of the participant concerned.

3.   Participants agree on the desirability of acceptance of [the] Uruguay Round Agreements by all participants with a view to their entry into force as early as possible and not later than [1 January 1992]. As foreseen in the final paragraph of the Punta del Este Declaration, Ministers meeting also at the occasion of a Special Session of the CONTRACTING PARTIES, to be held prior to the end of 1991, will decide on the implementation of the Agreements, Decisions and Understandings attached hereto, including the possibility of provisional implementation [of some of them], and will fix a date for the entry into force of such instruments.

4.   Participants agree on the desirability of the application by the contracting parties, as from the date of entry into force of the Uruguay Round results, of the General Agreement on Tariffs and Trade on a definitive rather than on a provisional basis.

---

[1]Ministers agreed at the Mid-Term Review that the negotiations on Trade-Related Aspects of Intellectual Property Rights are without prejudice to the views of participants concerning the institutional aspects of the international implementation of the results of the negotiations in this area which is to be decided pursuant to the final paragraph of the Punta del Este Declaration, i.e. by Ministers meeting at a Special Session of the CONTRACTING PARTIES.

0015

5. Participants further agree that in order to provide the administrative infrastructure for the international implementation of the Uruguay Round results, it would be desirable to establish [a new Multilateral Trade Organization] [a new organizational structure] which shall service [, oversee and ensure the operation of] the General Agreement on Tariffs and Trade and the Uruguay Round Agreements, and shall provide the forum for negotiations of agreements [in areas related to trade and development] [in related trade areas].

6. Details of the structure and functioning of an agreement on the matters referred to in paragraph 5 [, including provisions on the establishment of a permanent institutional structure along the lines of the structure established for the negotiations,] should be worked out by an [Interim Committee] in order to enable the Ministers to adopt the agreement on the occasion of the Ministerial Meeting provided for in paragraph 3 in order that it come into effect at the same time as the entry into force of the Uruguay Round Agreements. The [Interim Committee] shall be serviced by the GATT Secretariat and shall be open to all participants in the Uruguay Round that have adopted this Final Act. The Director-General of GATT is requested to establish [such a Committee] within two months after the date of this Final Act.

7. Without prejudice to the measures on special and more favourable treatment in favour of developing participants which appear in the Annexes, the participants agree that least-developed participants [shall] [should] be granted a grace period of [x] years as from the date of entry into force of the relevant legal instruments, during which they will not be required to apply the new commitments negotiated in the course of the Uruguay Round.^{2,3}

8. Participants agree that [all] the Uruguay Round Agreements, enumerated in Annexes [I and II] [I to III] shall be open for acceptance [as a whole] [without exception], by signature or otherwise, by all participants in the Uruguay Round of Multilateral Trade Negotiations.[4] [Participants agree on the desirability of these agreements entering into force only after acceptance by [x].] This is without prejudice to the requirement that such

---

[2] The final form and place of the provisions contained in this paragraph are to be considered in connection with the decision on the implementation of the results of the Uruguay Round, as set out in paragraph 3 above.

[3] The provisions of Part I of the Punta del Este Declaration are relevant.

[4] The question of the acceptance by participants in the Uruguay Round who have not accepted Tokyo Round Agreements and Arrangements, of texts resulting from the renegotiation of such Agreements or Arrangements remains to be considered.

0016

participants who are not contracting parties to the GATT must negotiate their terms of accession to the GATT.

9.   This Final Act and the texts set out in the Annexes shall be deposited with the Director-General to the CONTRACTING PARTIES to the General Agreement on Tariffs and Trade who shall promptly furnish to each participant in the Uruguay Round of Multilateral Trade Negotiations a certified copy thereof.

    DONE at Brussels, this seventh day of December one thousand nine hundred and ninety in a single copy, in the English, French and Spanish languages, each text being authentic.

0017

454

Secretariat Non-Paper
25 March 1991

<u>Draft Revised Text on Dispute Settlement</u>

The attached draft revised text of MTN/TNC/W/35/Rev 1 on dispute settlement has been prepared by the Secretariat on its own responsibility.

Based on the consultations held in Brussels in December 1990, this draft revision contains the following changes:

- an additional sentence added to footnote 1 to the heading of the Understanding, concerning the continuation of existing procedures;

- an amended reference in paragraph A.2 to the principles of international law;

- a clarification in paragraph D.1(a) that the complaining party has a right to the establishment of a panel as of the first Council meeting;

- a clarification of the nature of compensation in paragraph L.1;

- a clarification in paragraph L.7 of the procedure for advanced calculation of retaliation; and

- a revised Section P on non-violation complaints.

In addition, some drafting adjustments of a purely formal character have been introduced in the French and Spanish versions, which do not affect the English text.

0018

Draft Revised Text
25 March 1991

UNDERSTANDING ON THE INTERPRETATION AND
APPLICATION OF ARTICLES XXII AND XXIII OF
THE GENERAL AGREEMENT ON TARIFFS AND TRADE[1,2]

Following the meeting of the Trade Negotiations Committee at
Ministerial level in December 1990, the CONTRACTING PARTIES to the General
Agreement on Tariffs and Trade

Approve the improvements to the GATT dispute settlement rules and
procedures set out in this Understanding.

A. General Provisions

1.   A full review of GATT dispute settlement rules and procedures shall be
completed within four years after entry into force of this Understanding,
and a decision shall be taken on the occasion of the 1994 meeting at
Ministerial level whether to continue, modify or terminate such dispute
settlement rules and procedures.

2.   The dispute settlement system of GATT is a central element in
providing security and predictability to the multilateral trading system.
Contracting parties recognize that it serves to preserve the rights and
obligations of contracting parties under the General Agreement, and to
clarify the existing provisions of the General Agreement in accordance with
the principles of public international law. Contracting parties agree that
recommendations and rulings under Article XXIII cannot add to or diminish
the rights and obligations provided in the General Agreement.

3.   Contracting parties agree that all solutions to matters formally
raised under the GATT dispute settlement system under Articles XXII, XXIII
and arbitration awards shall be consistent with the General Agreement and
shall not nullify or impair benefits accruing to any contracting party
under the General Agreement, nor impede the attainment of any objective of
the General Agreement.

---

[1]A determination has to be made on the entry into force and
application of this Understanding, and on the continuation of the dispute
settlement procedures covered by the Decision of the Council of
12 April 1989 (BISD 36S/61) until the date of application of this
Understanding. It is agreed that existing dispute settlement procedures,
including those contained in the Decision of 12 April 1989, should remain
in effect until the date of application of this Understanding.

[2]It should be noted that existing dispute settlement procedures,
including provisions about full consensus, have not been recorded where
bracketed alternatives appear, even though certain delegations have
expressed a preference for the maintenance of these procedures in some
instances.

failed to settle the dispute within a period of twenty days after the request, the complaining party may request the establishment of a panel.

5.   In cases of urgency, including those which concern perishable goods, the parties concerned, panels and the appellate body shall make every effort to accelerate the proceedings to the greatest extent possible.

C. Good Offices, Conciliation, Mediation

1.   Good offices, conciliation and mediation are procedures that are undertaken voluntarily if the parties to the dispute so agree. They may be requested at any time by any party to a dispute. They may begin at any time and be terminated at any time. Once terminated, the complaining party can then proceed with a request for the establishment of a panel under Article XXIII:2. When good offices, conciliation or mediation are entered into within sixty days of a request for consultations, the complaining party must allow a period of sixty days from the date of the request for consultations before requesting the establishment of a panel. The complaining party may request a panel during the sixty days if the parties to the dispute jointly consider that the good offices, conciliation or mediation process has failed to settle the dispute.

2.   If the parties to a dispute agree, procedures for good offices, conciliation or mediation may continue while the panel process proceeds.

3.   The Director-General may, acting in an ex officio capacity, offer his good offices, conciliation or mediation with the view to assisting contracting parties to settle a dispute.

D. Panel Procedures

1.   Establishment of a Panel

   (a) If the complaining party so requests, twenty days prior to a meeting of the Council, a panel shall be established at that Council meeting, unless at that meeting the Council decides [otherwise] [by consensus] [not to establish a panel].

   (b) The request for a panel shall be made in writing. It shall indicate whether consultations were held, and provide a brief summary of the factual and legal basis of the complaint sufficient to present the problem clearly. In case the applicant requests the establishment of a panel with other than standard terms of reference, the written request shall include the proposed text of special terms of reference.

0021

2.   Standard Terms of Reference

(a)   Panels shall have the following terms of reference unless the parties to the dispute agree otherwise within twenty days from the establishment of the panel:

"To examine, in the light of the relevant GATT provisions, the matter referred to the CONTRACTING PARTIES by (name of contracting party) in document DS/... and to make such findings as will assist the CONTRACTING PARTIES in making the recommendations or in giving the rulings provided for in Article XXIII:2".

(b)   In establishing a panel, the Council may authorize its Chairman to draw up the terms of reference of the panel in consultation with the parties subject to the provisions of the preceding paragraph. The terms of reference thus drawn up shall be circulated to all contracting parties. If other than standard terms of reference are agreed upon, any contracting party may raise any point relating thereto in the Council.

3.   Composition of Panels

(a)   Panels shall be composed of well-qualified governmental and/or non-governmental individuals, including persons who have served on or presented a case to a GATT panel, served as a representative to the GATT or in the GATT Secretariat, taught or published on international trade law or policy, or served as a senior trade policy official of a contracting party.

(b)   The roster of panelists, established through the decision by the CONTRACTING PARTIES on 30 December 1984 (BISD, 31S/9), shall be expanded and improved. To this end, contracting parties may suggest names of individuals possessing the qualifications outlined in paragraph (a) above to serve on panels and shall provide relevant information on their knowledge of international trade and of the GATT.

(c)   Contracting parties shall undertake, as a general rule, to permit their representatives to serve as panel members.

(d)   Panels shall be composed of three members unless the parties to the dispute agree, within ten days from the establishment of the panel, to a panel composed of five members.

(e)   If there is no agreement on the members within twenty days from the establishment of a panel, at the request of either party, the Director-General, in consultation with the Chairman of the Council, shall form the panel by appointing the panelists whom he considers most appropriate, after consulting both parties. The Director-General shall inform the contracting parties of the composition of the panel thus formed no later than ten days from the date he receives such a request.

0022

4. Procedures for Multiple Complainants

   (a) Where more than one contracting party requests the establishment of a panel related to the same matter, a single panel may be established to examine these complaints taking into account the rights of all parties concerned. A single panel should be established to examine such complaints whenever feasible.

   (b) The single panel will organize its examination and present its findings to the Council so that the rights which the parties to the dispute would have enjoyed had separate panels examined the complaints are in no way impaired. If one of the parties to the dispute so requests, the panel will submit separate reports on the dispute concerned. The written submissions by each of the complainants will be made available to the other complainants, and each complainant will have the right to be present when one of the other complainants presents its view to the panel.

   (c) If more than one panel is established to examine the complaints related to the same matter, to the greatest extent possible the same persons shall serve as panelists on each of the separate panels and the timetable for the panel process in such disputes shall be harmonized.

5. Interim Review Stage

   (a) Following the consideration of rebuttal submissions and oral arguments, the panel shall submit the descriptive (factual and argument) sections of its draft report to the parties. Within a period of time set by the panel, the parties shall submit their comments in writing.

   (b) Following the deadline for receipt of comments from the parties, the panel shall issue an interim report to the parties, including both the descriptive sections and the panel's findings and conclusions. Within a period of time set by the panel, a party may submit a written request for the panel to review precise aspects of the interim report prior to circulation of the final report to the Council. At the request of a party, the panel shall hold a further meeting with the parties on the issues identified in the written comments. If no comments are received from any party within the comment period, the interim report shall be considered the final panel report and circulated promptly to the contracting parties.

   (c) The findings of the final panel report shall include a discussion of the arguments made at the interim review stage. The interim review stage shall be conducted within the time period set out in paragraph D.6(e).

0023

6. Various Stages of a Panel

(a) Panel procedures should provide sufficient flexibility so as to
ensure high-quality panel reports, while not unduly delaying the panel
process.

(b) Panels shall follow the Suggested Working Procedures found in the
July 1985 note of the Office of Legal Affairs (annexed hereto) unless the
members of the panel agree otherwise after consulting the parties to the
dispute. After consulting the parties, the panel members shall, as soon as
practicable and whenever possible within one week after the composition and
terms of reference of the panel have been agreed upon, fix the timetable
for the panel process at least until its first substantive meeting.

(c) In determining the timetable for the panel process, the panel
shall provide sufficient time for the parties to the dispute to prepare
their submissions.

(d) Each party to the dispute shall deposit its written submissions
with the Secretariat for immediate transmission to the panel and to the
other party or parties to the dispute. The complaining party shall submit
its first submission in advance of the responding party's first submission
unless the panel decides, in fixing the timetable referred to in the second
paragraph of this section and after consultations with the parties to the
dispute, that the parties should submit their first submissions
simultaneously. When there are sequential arrangements for the deposit of
first submissions, the panel shall establish a firm time period for receipt
of the responding party's submission. Any subsequent written submissions
shall be submitted simultaneously.

(e) In order to make the procedures more efficient, the period in
which the panel shall conduct its examination, from the time the
composition and terms of reference of the panel have been agreed upon to
the time when the final report is provided to the parties to the dispute,
shall, as a general rule, not exceed six months. In cases of urgency,
including those relating to perishable goods, the panel shall aim to
provide its report to the parties within three months.

(f) When the panel considers that it cannot provide its report within
six months, or within three months in cases of urgency, it shall inform the
Council in writing of the reasons for the delay together with an estimate
of the period within which it will submit its report. In no case
[should/shall] the period from the establishment of the panel to the
submission of the report to the contracting parties exceed nine months.

0024

(g) In the context of consultations involving a measure taken by a
developing contracting party, the parties may agree to extend the periods
established in paragraphs B.2 and B.4. If, after the relevant period has
elapsed, the parties cannot agree that the consultations have concluded,
the Chairman of the Council shall decide, after consultation with the
parties, whether to extend the relevant period and, if so, for how long.
In addition, in examining a complaint against a developing contracting
party, the panel shall accord sufficient time for the developing
contracting party to prepare and present its argumentation. The provisions
of paragraph G.4 are not affected by any action pursuant to this paragraph.

(h) Where one or more of the parties is a developing contracting
party, the panel's report shall explicitly indicate the form in which
account has been taken of relevant provisions on differential and
more-favourable treatment for developing countries that form part of the
General Agreement and of the instruments negotiated in GATT under its
auspices, which have been raised by the developing contracting party in the
course of the dispute settlement procedures.

E. Third Contracting Parties

1. The interests of the parties to a dispute and those of other
contracting parties shall be fully taken into account during the panel
process.

2. Any third contracting party having a substantial interest in a matter
before a panel, and having notified this to the Council, shall have an
opportunity to be heard by the panel and to make written submissions to the
panel. These submissions shall also be given to the parties to the dispute
and shall be reflected in the panel report.

3. Such third parties shall receive submissions of the parties for the
first meeting of the panel.

4. If a third party considers a measure already the subject of a panel
nullifies or impairs benefits accruing to it under the General Agreement,
that party may have recourse to normal GATT dispute settlement procedures.
Such a dispute shall be referred to the original panel wherever possible.

F. Panel and Appellate Body Recommendations

Where a panel or the appellate body concludes that a measure is
inconsistent with the General Agreement, it shall recommend that the
contracting party concerned bring the measure into conformity with the
General Agreement. [In cases involving non-violation nullification or
impairment, the panel or appellate body shall recommend that the
contracting party concerned [consider ways and means of making] [make] a
satisfactory adjustment.] In addition to its recommendations, the panel or
appellate body may suggest ways in which the contracting party concerned
could implement the recommendations.

0025

G. Adoption of Panel Reports

1.   In order to provide sufficient time for the members of the Council to consider panel reports, the reports shall not be considered for adoption by the Council until twenty days after they have been issued to the contracting parties.

2.   Contracting parties having objections to panel reports shall give written reasons to explain their objections for circulation at least ten days prior to the Council meeting at which the panel report will be considered.

3.   The parties to a dispute shall have the right to participate fully in the consideration of the panel report by the Council, and their views shall be fully recorded.

4.   Within sixty days of the issuance of a panel report to the contracting parties, the report shall be adopted at a Council meeting unless one of the parties formally notifies the Council of its decision to appeal or the Council decides [otherwise] [by consensus] [not to adopt the report]. If a party has notified its intention to appeal, the report by the panel shall not be considered for adoption by the Council until after completion of the appeal. This adoption procedure is without prejudice to the right of contracting parties to express their views on a panel report.

H. Appellate Review

1.   Standing Appellate Body

    (a) A standing appellate body shall be established by the CONTRACTING PARTIES. The body shall hear appeals from panel cases. The appellate body shall be composed of a pool of seven members, three of whom shall serve on any one case. Members of the pool shall serve in rotation.

    (b) Members shall be appointed by the CONTRACTING PARTIES to serve for a four-year term. Vacancies shall be filled as they arise using the aforesaid procedure.

    (c) Members shall be persons of recognized authority, with demonstrated expertise in law, international trade and GATT matters generally. They shall be unaffiliated with any government. The appellate body membership shall be broadly representative of membership in GATT. Members shall be available at all times and on short notice, and shall stay abreast of GATT activities. They shall not participate in the consideration of any disputes that would create a direct or indirect conflict of interest.

0026

(d) Only parties to the dispute, not third parties, may appeal a panel decision or participate in the appellate review.

(e) As a general rule, the proceedings shall not exceed sixty days from the date a party formally notifies its intent to appeal to the date the appellate body issues its decision. When the appellate body considers that it cannot provide its report within sixty days, it shall inform the Council in writing of the reasons for the delay together with an estimate of the period within which it will submit its report. In no case [shall/should] the proceedings exceed ninety days.

(f) An appeal shall be limited to issues of law covered in the panel report and legal interpretation developed by the panel.

(g) The appellate body shall be provided with appropriate administrative and legal support as it requires.

2. Procedures for Appellate Review

(a) Suggested working procedures shall be drawn up by the appellate body in consultation with the chairman of the Council and the Director-General, and communicated to the contracting parties for their information.

(b) The proceedings of the appellate body shall be confidential.

(c) The appellate body shall address each of the issues raised by the parties to the dispute during the appellate proceeding.

(d) The appellate body may uphold, modify or reverse the legal findings and conclusions of the panel.

3. Adoption of Appellate Reports

An appellate report shall be adopted by the Council and unconditionally accepted by the parties to the dispute unless the Council decides [otherwise] [by consensus] [not to adopt the appellate report] within thirty days following its issuance to the contracting parties. This adoption procedure is without prejudice to the right of contracting parties to express their views on an appellate report.

I. Ex Parte Communications

No ex parte communications are permitted between the panel or appellate body and the parties to the dispute concerning matters under consideration by the panel or appellate body.

0027

J. Time-Frame for Council Decisions

Unless agreed to by the parties, the period from the request under Article XXII:1 or Article XXIII:1 until the Council considers the panel or appellate report for adoption shall not as a general rule exceed twelve months where the report is not appealed or fifteen months where the report is appealed. Where either the panel or the appellate body has acted, pursuant to paragraph D.6(f) or H.1(e), to extend the time of providing its report, the additional time taken shall be added to the above periods.

K. Surveillance of Implementation of Recommendations and Rulings

1.   Prompt compliance with recommendations or rulings of the CONTRACTING PARTIES under Article XXIII is essential in order to ensure effective resolution of disputes to the benefit of all contracting parties.

2.   At a Council meeting held within thirty days of the adoption of the panel or appellate body report, the contracting party concerned shall inform the Council of its intentions in respect of implementation of the recommendations and rulings under Article XXIII:2. If it is impracticable to comply immediately with the recommendations and rulings, the contracting party concerned shall have a reasonable period of time in which to do so. The reasonable period of time shall be:

   (a)   the period of time proposed by the contracting party concerned, provided that such period is approved by the Council; or, in the absence of such approval,

   (b)   a period of time mutually agreed by the parties to the dispute within forty-five days following adoption of the recommendations and rulings; or, in the absence of such agreement,

   (c)   a period of time determined through binding arbitration within ninety days following adoption of the recommendations and rulings.

3.   Except where the panel or the appellate body has extended, pursuant to paragraph D.6(f) or H.1(e), the time of providing its report, the period from the request under Article XXII:1 or XXIII:1 until the determination of the reasonable period of time shall not exceed eighteen months unless the parties agree otherwise. Where either the panel or the appellate body has acted to extend the time of providing its report, the additional time taken shall be added to the eighteen-month period; provided that [in no event shall the total amount of time] [unless there are exceptional circumstances, the total time shall not] exceed twenty-one months.

0028

4. Where there is disagreement as to the existence or GATT consistency of measures taken to comply with the recommendations and rulings under Article XXIII:2, such dispute shall be decided through recourse to GATT dispute settlement procedures, involving resort to the original panel wherever possible. The panel shall issue its decision within ninety days of referral of the matter to it. When the panel considers that it cannot provide its report within this time frame, it shall inform the Council in writing of the reasons for the delay together with an estimate of the period within which it will submit its report.

5. The Council shall monitor the implementation of recommendations or rulings adopted under Article XXIII:2. The issue of implementation of the recommendations or rulings may be raised at the Council by any contracting party at any time following their adoption. Unless the Council decides otherwise, the issue of implementation of the recommendations or rulings shall be on the agenda of the Council meeting after six months following their adoption and shall remain on the Council's agenda until the issue is resolved. At least ten days prior to each such Council meeting, the contracting party concerned shall provide the Council with a status report in writing of its progress in the implementation of the recommendations or rulings.

6.   In cases brought by developing contracting parties, the Council shall consider what further action it might take which would be appropriate to the circumstances, in conformity with paragraphs 21 and 23 of the 1979 Understanding regarding Notification, Consultation, Dispute Settlement and Surveillance (BISD 26S/214).

L. Compensation and the Suspension of Concessions

1.   Compensation and the suspension of concessions or other obligations are temporary measures available in the event that the recommendations and rulings under Article XXIII:2 are not implemented within a reasonable period of time. Compensation is voluntary and, if granted, shall be consistent with the General Agreement.

2.   If the contracting party concerned fails to bring the measure found to be inconsistent with the General Agreement into compliance therewith or otherwise comply with the recommendations and rulings under Article XXIII:2 within the reasonable period of time, such party shall, if so requested, and no later than the expiry of the reasonable period of time, enter into negotiations with any party to the dispute, with a view to developing mutually acceptable compensation. If no satisfactory compensation has been agreed within twenty days after the expiry of the reasonable period of time, any party to the dispute may request authorization from the Council to suspend the application to the contracting party concerned of concessions or other obligations under the General Agreement.

3.   When the situation described in paragraph 2 above occurs, the Council, upon request, shall grant authorization to suspend concessions or other obligations within thirty days of the expiry of the reasonable period of time unless the Council decides [otherwise] [by consensus] [to reject the request]. However, if the party concerned objects to the level of suspension proposed, the matter shall be referred to arbitration. Such arbitration shall be carried out by the original panel, if members are available, or by an arbitrator[1] appointed by the Director-General, and shall be completed within sixty days of the expiry of the reasonable period of time. Concessions or other obligations shall not be suspended pending the outcome of the arbitration.

4.   The amount of trade covered by the suspension of concessions or other obligations authorized by the Council or determined by arbitration shall be appropriate in the circumstances.

5.   The arbitrator shall not examine the nature of the suspended concessions or other obligations, but shall determine whether the amount of trade covered is appropriate in the circumstances. The parties shall accept the arbitrator's determination as final.

6.   The suspension of concessions or other obligations shall be temporary and shall only be applied until such time as the measure found to be inconsistent with the General Agreement has been removed, or the contracting party that must implement recommendations or rulings provides a solution to the nullification or impairment of benefits, or a mutually satisfactory solution is reached.

[7.   The amount of suspension shall, if requested by one of the parties, be determined before expiry of the reasonable period of time, in accordance with the relevant procedures under paragraph L.3 above, and on the understanding that such suspension shall not come into effect before the Council has granted the authorization provided for in paragraph L.3.]

---

[1]The expression "arbitrator" shall be interpreted as referring either to an individual or a body.

0030

M. Strengthening of Multilateral System

The contracting parties shall: (i) abide by GATT dispute settlement rules and procedures; (ii) abide by the recommendations, rulings and decisions of the CONTRACTING PARTIES; (iii) not resort to unilateral measures or the threat of unilateral measures inconsistent with GATT rules and procedures[1]; and (iv) for the purposes of (iii), undertake to adapt their domestic trade legislation and enforcement procedures in a manner ensuring the conformity of all measures with GATT dispute settlement procedures.

N. Special Procedures involving Least-Developed Contracting Parties

1. At all stages of the determination of the causes of a dispute and of dispute settlement procedures involving a least-developed contracting party, particular consideration shall be given to the special situation of least-developed countries.

2. In dispute settlement cases involving a least-developed contracting party where a satisfactory solution has not been found in the course of consultations under Article XXII:1 or XXIII:1, the Director-General shall, upon request by a least-developed contracting party, offer his good offices, conciliation and mediation with a view to assisting the parties to settle the dispute, before a request for a panel is made. The Director-General, in providing the above assistance, may consult any source which he deems appropriate.

O. Arbitration

1. Expeditious arbitration within GATT as an alternative means of dispute settlement can facilitate the solution of certain disputes that concern issues that are clearly defined by both parties.

2. Resort to arbitration shall be subject to mutual agreement of the parties which shall agree on the procedures to be followed. Agreements to resort to arbitration shall be notified to all contracting parties sufficiently in advance of the actual commencement of the arbitration process.

---

[1]This proposed commitment is linked to other parts of this Understanding concerning: (a) an agreement not to oppose the establishment of a panel or the adoption of panel or appellate body reports; (b) an agreement not to retain measures found inconsistent with the General Agreement, or to fail to remedy other measures found to nullify or impair benefits under the General Agreement, beyond the "reasonable period" for compliance; and (c) an agreement not to oppose authorization for the affected party to suspend concessions or other obligations if non-compliance continues after the expiration of the "reasonable period".

0031

3.   Other contracting parties may become party to an arbitration proceeding upon the agreement of the parties which have agreed to have recourse to arbitration. The parties to the proceeding shall agree to abide by the arbitration award. Arbitration awards shall be notified to the Council where any contracting party may raise any point relating thereto.

4.   The provisions on implementation and surveillance shall apply mutatis mutandis to arbitration awards.

P. Non-Violation Complaints[1]

1.   **Option A**

The procedures in this Agreement shall apply, subject to the provisions of paragraphs 2 through 5 below, where a party has recourse to dispute settlement based upon Article XXIII:1(b) in respect of the introduction or intensification of a measure, upsetting the conditions of competition [or] [and] having an [actual or potential] adverse effect on trade, which could not reasonably have been foreseen, and which while not conflicting with the provisions of the General Agreement has frustrated a [legitimate] [reasonable] expectation concerning a benefit accruing to the party [directly or indirectly under the General Agreement] [under a market access concession or other commitment].

Option B

The procedures in this Agreement shall apply, subject to the provisions of paragraphs 2 through 5 below, where a party has recourse to dispute settlement based upon Article XXIII:1(b) regarding the introduction or intensification of a measure not in conflict with the General Agreement, which could not reasonably have been foreseen and which frustrates a [legitimate] [reasonable] expectation of a benefit accruing to the party, [directly or indirectly under the General Agreement] [under a market access concession or other commitment], upsetting the conditions of competition [and] [or] having an [actual or potential] adverse effect on trade.

2.   The complaining contracting party shall present a detailed justification in support of any complaint made pursuant to paragraph 1 above.

3.   Where a measure has been found to constitute a case of nullification or impairment of benefits under the General Agreement without violation thereof, there is no obligation to withdraw [or modify] the measure. However, in such cases, the panel or the appellate body shall recommend that the contracting party concerned make a mutually satisfactory adjustment.

---

[1]Some delegations do not consider that special procedures are appropriate for non-violation complaints.

0032

4. In accordance with paragraph K.2, the contracting party concerned shall inform the Council of its intentions in respect of implementation of the recommendations and rulings under Article XXIII:2. If the parties do not agree, within forty-five days following adoption, that such implementation will result in a mutually satisfactory adjustment, the reasonable period of time for implementation and the value of benefits which have been nullified or impaired shall be determined through binding arbitration[1] within ninety days following adoption, pursuant to paragraph K.2. Upon request by either party, the arbitrator may also suggest ways and means of reaching a mutually satisfactory solution, but such suggestions shall not be binding upon the parties.

5. The provisions of Section L shall apply, except that the arbitrator's decision under paragraph 4 above with respect to the value of benefits shall be in lieu of the arbitration provided for in paragraphs L.3 through L.5.

[6. **Option A**

Other matters raised under Article XXIII:1(b) and those under Article XXIII:1(c) shall be referred to the Council for appropriate action. If a panel needs to be established to address such a case, its terms of reference shall be adopted by consensus.

Option B

Notwithstanding the provisions of paragraphs G.4 and H.3, where a party has recourse to dispute settlement based upon Article XXIII:1(b) involving circumstances other than those outlined in paragraph 1 above, or upon Article XXIII:1(c), Council decisions on the adoption of panel or appellate body reports shall be taken by consensus.]

Q. Technical Assistance

1. While the Secretariat assists contracting parties in respect of dispute settlement at their request, there may also be a need to provide additional legal advice and assistance in respect of dispute settlement to developing contracting parties. To this end, the Secretariat shall make available a qualified legal expert within the Technical Co-operation Division to any developing contracting party which so requests. This expert shall assist the developing contracting party in a manner ensuring the continued impartiality of the Secretariat.

2. The Secretariat shall conduct special training courses for interested contracting parties concerning GATT dispute settlement procedures and practices so as to enable contracting parties' experts to be better informed in this regard.

---

[1] With respect to Sections K, L and P, if the parties cannot agree upon an arbitrator with ten days after referring the matter to arbitration, the arbitrator shall be appointed by the Director-General within ten days, after consulting the parties.

0033

Annex

Suggested Working Procedures

1.   In its proceedings the Panel will be guided by the relevant provisions of the Understanding Regarding Notification, Consultation, Dispute Settlement and Surveillance (BISD 26S/210); of the 1982 Ministerial Declaration (BISD 29S/13); and of the Decisions on dispute settlement procedures adopted by the CONTRACTING PARTIES in November 1984 (L/5718) and in April 1989 (BISD 36S/61). In addition, the following guidelines will apply.

2.   The Panel will meet in closed session. The Parties to the dispute, or other interested Parties, will be present at the meetings only when invited by the Panel to appear before it.

3.   The deliberations of the Panel and the documents submitted to it will be kept confidential. For the duration of the Panel proceeding, the Parties to the dispute are requested not to release any papers or make any statements in public regarding the dispute.

4.   Before the first substantive meeting of the Panel with the Parties, both Parties to the dispute are expected to transmit to the Panel written submissions in which they present the facts of the case and their arguments.

5.   At its first substantive meeting with the parties, the Panel will ask the Party which has brought the complaint to present its case. Subsequently, and still at the same meeting, the Party against which the complaint has been brought will be asked to present its point of view.

6.   As it may be necessary for the Parties to have time to prepare their formal rebuttals, the latter will be made at a second substantive meeting of the Panel. The Party complained against will have the right to take the floor first to be followed by the complaining Party. Both Parties are encouraged to submit, prior to that meeting, written briefs to the Panel.

7.   The Panel may at any time put questions to the Parties and ask them for explanations either in the course of a meeting with the Parties or in writing.

8.   The Parties to the dispute and any third contracting party invited to present its views in accordance with paragraph 15 of the 1979 Understanding (BISD 29S/213) and section F(e) of the April 1989 Decision (BISD 36S/61) are encouraged to make available to the Panel a written version of their oral statements.

0034

9.   In the interest of full transparency, the presentations, rebuttals and statements referred to in paragraphs 5 to 8 above will be made in the presence of both Parties. Moreover, each Party's written submissions, including any comments on the descriptive part of the report and responses to questions put by the Panel, will be made available to the other Party.

10.   Any additional procedures specific to the Panel.

11.   The Panel proposes the following timetable for its work:

(a)   Receipt of first written
      submissions of the Parties: 3-6 weeks

      (1)   complaining Party: _____
      (2)   Party complained
            against: _____   2-3 weeks

(b)   Date, time and place of
      first substantive meeting
      with the Parties: _____   1-2 weeks

(c)   Receipt of written rebuttals
      of the Parties: _____   2-3 weeks

(d)   Date, time and place of
      second substantive meeting
      with the Parties: _____   1-2 weeks

(e)   Submission of descriptive
      part of the report to the
      Parties: _____   3-6 weeks

(f)   Receipt of comments by the
      Parties on the descriptive
      part of the report: _____   2 weeks

(g)   Submission of the final
      report, including the find-
      ings and conclusions, to
      the Parties: _____   2-6 weeks

(h)   Circulation of the report
      to the CONTRACTING PARTIES: _____   2-4 weeks

The above calendar may be changed in the light of unforeseen developments. Additional meetings with the Parties will be scheduled if required.

0035

UR/제도분야 협상 대책

1991. 6. 19.

외   무   부
통   상   국

0036

목   차

0037

1. 분쟁해결

가. 협상 목표

o 분쟁해결 규칙 및 절차의 개선 강화

o 권고 이행 강화를 위한 절차 마련

나. 협상 현황

o 88.12. 중간평가를 통하여 패널설치 시한, 패널보고서 채택 시한, 패널 권고사항 이행에 대한 감시기능 강화등에 합의

o 협상그룹 의장은 그간의 협상 결과를 반영하여 90.10. 자신의 책임하에 결정문 초안(Text)을 작성 하였으며, 동 Text를 토대로 90.11. 그린룸 협의를 거쳐 수정 Text를 브랏셀 각료회의에 제출

o 동 협상 그룹은 기존의 제반 규정(갓트 22, 23조, 79년 양해, 82년 선언 및 '66, '84, '89년 결정)을 통합한 통합문안을 상기 의장안과는 별도로 브랏셀 각료회의에 제출하고, 동 각료회의 이후 91.3.1 이전에 최종합의문을 포함하는 최종 통합문안을 작성할 예정 이었으나, 시간 촉박 및 여타 협상 분야 진전 부진으로 통합문안 도출에 실패

o 91.2. 주요국 비공식 협의에서 Dunkel 사무총장 Statement 수락
  - 하기 세가지 주요 현안등 정치적 결정을 요하는 사항이 다수 있으나, 기술적 논의 유용

1

. 이사회의 분쟁해결 관련 결정 절차

. 일방조치 억제

. Non-violation 분쟁해결 절차

o 91.3. 주요국 비공식 협의 결과

- 브랏셀 회의시 주요국 비공식 협의 결과를 감안한 사무국 작성
  Non-paper를 차기 회의시 논의키로 합의

  . 동 Non-paper는 브랏셀 각료회의에 제출된 Text 내용과 거의 동일

- 기술적 논의 가능한 4개분야 제시

  . 분쟁해결 절차 시한 문제

  . Non-violation 분쟁해결

  . 통합문안 (consolidated text)

  . 타협상그룹 분쟁해결 절차와의 조화문제(harmonized text)

- 상기 4개분야중 대부분의 국가가 통합문안에 대한 기술적 논의는
  가능하나, 조화 문제 논의는 아직 시기상조라는 반응
  (여타 2개분야에 대하여는 계속 상이한 의견)

o 91.3. 주요국 수석대표급 비공식 협의를 통하여 분쟁해결, 갓트기능 및
  최종의정서를 통합한 협상그룹 재구성

다. 합의사항

o 중간평가 합의사항(89.4)

- 패널설치 시한

  . 늦어도 두번째 이사회에서 설치

- 패널 보고서 채택 시한

  . 이해당사국 협의 개시이후 15개월 이내

- 패널 권고사항 이행에 대한 감시기능 강화

  . 보고서 채택후 6개월이후부터 자동적인 감시기능 발동

- 조기 수확분야로 결정하고 그간의 합의내용의 시험적 적용을
  89.5.1부터 개시, UR 종료시까지 적용

2

0039

o 브랏셀 각료회의에 제출한 Text상의 합의사항(중간평가 합의사항
  부분은 제외)

  - 일반규정

    . 본 결정 시행후 4년내 분쟁해결 절차 전면 재검토

    . 1994년 각료급 회의에서 개정 여부 결정

  - 협 의

    . 부패 상품을 포함한 긴급의 경우, 패널과 상소기구는 절차를
      최대한 가속화

  - 패널의 구성

    . 자격있는 정부 또는 비정부 인사로 구성

    . 패널리스트 명부는 확대, 개선

  - 중간검토 단계

    . 패널은 보고서 초안의 서술부분(사실과 주장)을 당사국에 제시

    . 당사국은 패널이 결정한 시한내 서면으로 의견 제시

    . 당사국들의 의견 접수 검토후, Panel은 서술부분과 Panel의
      검토 및 결론을 포함하는 중간보고서를 당사국에 제시

    . 당사국은 패널에 대해 중간보고서를 재검토 할 것을 서면 요청 가능

  - 개도국 특별 우대

    . 패널보고서는 갓트상의 개도국 우대 관련조항이 어떠한 형태로
      적용 되었는지를 명시

  - 제3국 권한

    . 제3국은 Panel 1차 회의에 제출된 문서 접수권 보유

    . 동일 사안에 대하여 제3국은 GATT에 제소 가능하며, 이경우
      가능한한 원래의 Panel에서 취급

  - 상소제도(상설상소기구)

    . 4년 임기를 가진 7명의 구성원으로 상설상소기구 설치

    . 법률, 국제무역 및 GATT 업무에 정통한 비정부 인사로 구성

3   0040

- 상소 검토 절차

  . 상소업무 절차는 상소기구, 이사회 의장, 사무총장이 협의,
    작성하여 체약국단에 통보하며, 상소기구 의사 진행은 비공식

- 이 행

  . 패소국은 보고서 채택후 30일이내 이사회에 권고이행 계획을
    통보하며, 즉각적인 권고사항 이행이 불가능한 경우에는
    합리적인 이행기간을 가짐

  . 합리적인 이행기간은 ①패소국이 제시하고 이사회에서 합의한
    기간, ②이사회에서의 미합의시 권고 채택후 60일이내 당사국간
    합의한 기간, ③또는 당사국간 미합의시 권고 채택후 90일이내
    구속력있는 중재를 통하여 결정한 기간

  . 권고사항 이행을 위한 조치의 GATT 합치 여부에 대한 분쟁은
    가능한한 원래 패널 회부를 통한 기존의 GATT 분쟁해결 절차에
    따라 처리

- 보상 및 양허 중지

  . 보상은 자발적 조치, MFN 원칙 적용

  . 합리적인 기간내에 권고사항 이행이 불가능한 경우 보상에 대해
    상호 합의

  . 미합의시, 승소국은 양허 또는 여타 갓트상의 의무 중지에 대한
    이사회의 승인 요청

  . 패소국이 양허중지의 수준에 반대할 경우, 중재에 회부
    (Ⅰ)중재는 원래의 패널 또는 사무총장이 임명하는 중재자가 수행
    (Ⅱ)중재는 합리적인 기간 종료후 60일이내 완료

  . 당사국은 중재기구의 결정을 최종적인 것으로 수락

- 최빈개도국을 위한 특별 절차

  . 특별고려 제공 및 패널 구성전에 협의 과정에서 사무총장이 중개,
    화해, 조정

4

0041

라. 주요쟁점 및 주요국 입장

o 일방 조치 억제

- 미   국 : 일방조치 억제 공약을 위해서는 분쟁해결 절차의
            매 단계에서 Blockage 요소 완전 제거 필요

- 대다수 국가 : 갓트 위반 일방조치 억제 의무 선행

o 패널 및 상소보고서 자동 채택

- 미   국 : 이사회가 보고서를 채택하지 않기로 결정하지 않는 한,
            자동 채택

- EC, 일본등 : 유보 입장

- 인도등 : 기존의 consensus 방식에 의거, 채택

o 보복 자동 승인

- 미   국 : 이사회가 보복 승인 요청을 거부키로 결정하지 않는 한,
            자동적으로 보복 승인 부여

- EC, 일본등 : 유보 입장

- 인도등 : 기존의 consensus 방식에 의거, 승인

o 본 결정 문안상의 이사회 의사 결정 방식 및 갓트 25조의 적용 가능성

- 미   국 : Blockage 요소를 완전 제거한 자동화된 분쟁해결 절차의
            수립을 위하여 갓트 25조의 적용 가능성 완전 제거 제안

- EC, 카나다, 오지리등 : 본 결정 문안상의 이사회 의사 결정을
            전통적인 consensus 관행에 의할것을 규정한
            문안도 함께 삭제할 것을 제안

o non-violation 분쟁

- EC : 갓트 2조에 국한된 별도의 non-violation 분쟁처리 절차 설정
       방안 제안

- 미, 일본등 대다수 국가 : EC 제안의 의도가 분명치 않다고 지적

5

0042

마. 협상 전망

　○ 갓트 분쟁해결 절차의 매단계에서 blockage 요소를 완전 제거하려는
　　　미국의 입장과 미국의 301조등 일방조치 억제에 대한 공약을 받아
　　　내려는 여타국의 입장이 첨예하게 대립

　○ 따라서, 패널 및 상소보고서 자동채택과 보복 자동 승인 문제는 갓트
　　　위반 일방조치 억제문제와 연계되어 있으므로 미국이 어떤 형태로든
　　　일방조치 자제를 약속하지 않는한 타결이 어려울 것으로 전망

바. 협상 대책

　○ 갓트 위반 일방조치 억제 공약
　　　- 미결쟁점 타결을 위해 일방조치 억제 공약 선행 필요

　○ 패널 및 상소보고서 채택 및 보복승인
　　　- 자동채택 및 승인에는 반대이나, 일방조치 억제 공약이 선행되고
　　　　협상 대세에 비추어 반대 불가시 수용 검토

　○ 본 결정 문안상의 이사회 의사 결정 방식 및 갓트 25조의 적용 가능성
　　　- 갓트 25조의 적용 가능성 완전 제거시, 본 결정 문안상의 이사회
　　　　결정을 전통적인 consensus 관행에 의할 것을 규정한 문안도 함께 삭제

　○ non-violation 분쟁
　　　- non-violation 분쟁을 위한 별도 분쟁해결 절차를 설정할 충분한
　　　　이유가 없는만큼 보다 명확한 EC 입장이 개진될 때까지는 갓트 일반
　　　　분쟁해결 절차에 따라 처리한다는 입장 견지

6

0043

2. 깟트 기능

가. 협상 목표

○ 체약국의 무역정책 및 관행에 대한 감시기능 강화

○ 각료의 참여를 통한 깟트의 효율성 및 의사 결정 기능 개선

○ 국제통화, 금융기구와 깟트의 연계 강화

나. 협상 현황

1) 88.12. 중간평가

○ 국별 무역정책 검토 제도 실시 합의

○ 각료급 참여 확대 문제 합의

- 각료급 깟트 총회 2년 1회 개최

○ 국제통화 및 금융기구와의 관계 강화 방안에 대하여는 계속
  검토키로 합의

2) 90.10.26. (10.9. TNC 비공식 회의에서 설정한 시한)

○ 그룹차원의 협상 종료 및 브랏셀 각료회의에 제출할 각료의
  결정 초안 채택

3) 90.11.2. TNC

○ TNC 수석대표 비공식 협의에서 합의된 협상 기초가 있는 분야로 분류됨.

4) 90.12. Brussel 각료회의시 깟트 기능에 대하여 협의 없었음.

다. 합의사항 (브랏셀 각료회의에 제출한 Text상의 합의사항)

1) 감시 기능 강화

○ 국별 무역정책검토(TPRM)

- 89.4. 중간평가시 합의되어 조기 시행중인 TPRM의 존재 재확인

7

0044

- 장기 검토 일정을 91.6.까지 결정

- 92.10에 TPRM 운용 재평가 검토

o 국제무역 환경 검토

- 89.4. 중간 평가시 합의되어 조기 시행중인 특별이사회에서의
  연례 국제무역환경 검토 제도를 계속키로 재확인

o Domestic transparency

- 각국의 무역정책 결정과 관련한 명료성 (예 : 공청회 개최,
  독립연구기관을 통한 손익분석등)을 제고한다는 권고적인
  성격의 결정문 합의

o 통고 제도 개선

- 통고 의무의 강화 (1979년 양해사항 재확인 및 통고 대상 사항
  목록 합의)

- 중앙통고 기탁소 설치

  . 제반 갓트 규정에 의거한 통고사항 취합, 각국의 통고의무
    준수 여부 주의 환기

- 기존 통고 의무 및 절차를 재검토하여 단순화, 체계화하기 위한
  작업반을 UR 협상 종료 직후에 설치

2) 기구적 측면의 갓트 강화

  o 89.4. 중간평가시 2년 1회의 갓트 각료급 총회 개최에 합의

라. 주요쟁점 및 주요국 입장

1) 기구적 측면의 갓트 강화

o 소규모 각료회의 설치 문제

- 미국, 호주외에 대체로 반대 의견이며, 정치적으로 결정되어야
  할 문제로 인식

  . 인도등 강경론자들은 각료회의 회부에도 반대한 바 있음.

8

0045

- 브랏셀 각료회의 직전 최근 미국은 갓트 관리 이사회(Management
  Board) 설치를 제의한 바, 이는 주요 정책 결정 기관으로서 IMF의
  Interim Committee와 동등한 지위에서 협력하며, 18개국으로 구성
  (4대국은 상설회원, 무역 고순으로 16위 국가까지는 격년제
  참가, 여타 국가는 순번제로 1년씩 교대)

o MTO/WTO 설치 문제

- EC(공식 제안), 카나다(비공식 제기)는 다음 사항을 포함하는
  신기구 설치 협정 체결을 제안
  . 회원국 규정 및 기구적 조직
  . UR 협상 결과의 이행, 특히 모든 협정에 통용되는 분쟁해결
    절차 이행을 위한 법적 근거
  . 사무총장 및 사무국
  . 예산 규정
  . 기타 기구의 법적인 지위, 특권과 면제, 기타 기구와의
    관계등 행정 규정

- 각국 입장
  . 미국은 소극적이었으며, 개도국들은 Cross-sectoral
    retaliation에 우려 소극적 입장
  . 개도국은 UN, UNCTAD 등에서 ITO 설치 거론

2) 통화, 금융, 무역정책간의 일관성 (coherence)

o IMF, IBRD, GATT의 정치적 합동 각료선언

- 당초 EC는 3기구 담당 각료들간의 합동 각료 선언을 채택하여,
  일관성 문제에 대한 정치적 결의를 보여야 한다고 주장

- 이러한 EC의 제의에 대해, 개도국이 동조 하였으나 미국을 위시
  여타 선진국은 반대의사 표명
  . 미국은 각국 정부의 자체적 책임, 개도국의 무역자화 필요성
    등을 강조하는 각료선언안 제안

9

0046

- 이에따라 일단 갓트의 일방적인 각료선언을 각료회의 결정의
  형태로 초안 하였으나 실질문제(환율, 금리, 개도국의
  교역조건, 개도국에 대한 금융지원)에 대한 언급문제와 관련
  다수 미합의사항 존재

○ 사무국간 실용적 협력
- 중소 선진국들이 강력히 추진하는 3개기구 사무국간 인전교류,
  연구협력, 감시기능 관련 협력등 사무국간 협력 강화 차원의
  실용적 접근 방식
- EC가 상기 합동 각료선언과 연계하여 반대함에 따라 합의되지
  못하고, 일단 갓트 사무총장으로 하여금 실용적 협력 방안을
  포함하여 가능한 일관성 강화 방안을 연구하여 91.12.31.까지
  보고토록 요청 내용만 잠정 합의

마. 협상 전망

○ MTO/WTO 설치 문제는 UR이후 구체적인 논의 가능성

○ 소규모 각료회의 설치 및 갓트관리이사회 구성 문제는 참여범위
  설정에 어려움으로 타결 난망

○ 각기구간 MANDATE 차이 및 각기구의 독자적인 결의 절차에 비추어
  실질 협력은 대단히 어려운 작업으로 사료됨

바. 협상 대책

○ 감시 기능 강화
- 과도한 예산 증대, 기구 확장없는한 찬성
- TPRM 설치 목적상 필요한 수준 이상으로 무역 외적 사항에 대해
  감시 기능을 확대하는데는 소극적 입장

10

o 소규모 각료회의

  - 아국의 참여 확보가 최우선의 관심사항

o 갓트 관리이사회

  - 의사 결정기관이 아니고 자문적인 성격을 띤 협의기구로 하는것이
    바람직

o MTO/WTO

  - 원칙적으로 찬성이나 UR 종료후에 논의하는 것이 바람직

  - UR 협상 진전상황 및 EC, 카나다 제안의 구체화 상황을 보아가며
    입장 정립

o Coherence 문제

  - 중.소 선진국들이 제안한 실용적 접근방안이 현실적으로 바람직하나
    아국에 특별한 이해관계 없는 사항이므로 개도국 입장을 고려,
    입장 표명 자제

11

0048

3. 최종의정서

가. 협상 현황

○ 브랏셀 각료회의 이전 논의동향

- 90.10. 제네바에서 Lacarte 우루과이 대사가 비공식 그룹
  (일명 Lacarte 그룹)을 결성하고 UR 협상 결과 처리 문제에 관한
  비공식 문서를 제출, 이에 관한 논의 시작

  . Lacarte 그룹 : 우루과이, 미국, EC, 일본, 카나다, 스웨덴,
    스위스, 인도, 브라질, 인도네시아 대사, 던켈 총장, 린덴 특별고문

  . 논의동향 : 선진국들은 UR 협상의 모든 또는 최대한의 결과가
    모든 또는 최대 다수의 체약국에 의해 수락되어야 한다는
    점을 강조

- 브랏셀 각료회의 직전 주요국 그린룸 협의에서 UR 협상 결과를
  수록할 최종의정서 문안에 관해 협의

  . 선진국들이 Single Undertaking을 주장한데 반해 개도국은
    신분야가 갓트의 일부가 될 수 없음을 주장

○ 브랏셀 이후의 협상 진행 상황

- 91.1.22 및 3.20 두차례 분쟁해결 및 최종의정서에 관한 주요국
  비공식 협의를 개최

  . 최종의정서 분야에 대한 구체적 협의는 없었음.

- 3.25 사무국, 하기 요지의 향후 협의를 위한 비공식 문서 배포

  . 모든 협상 참가국은 가급적 조속한 협상 결과의 시행을 위하여
    UR 협정을 수락

  . 협정의 이행을 위한 1991년말 이전 각료회의 개최

  . 결과 이행을 위한 기구 설립에 합의 및 동 기구 설립을 위한
    임시 위원회 설립

  . 개도국들에게 UR 결과 이행에 대한 일정한 유예기간 부여

12

0049

나. 주요쟁점 및 주요국 입장

    o Single Undertaking 문제

      - 선진국 : Punta del Este 각료선언에 따라 협상 결과를 취사
        선택하여 수락하는 것은 불가

      - 개도국 : 신분야 협상은 GATT 외적인 사항이며, Single
        Undertaking으로 할 경우 다수 개도국의 GATT 탈퇴를 초래할
        가능성을 이유로 반대

    o MTO 설치 문제

      - EC, 카나다 : UR 협상 결과, 특히 신분야 협상 결과의 수용 및
        시행을 위해 새로운 국제무역기구의 설치가 불가피

      - 개도국 및 미국 : UR 협상 종료후에 논의될 사항

    o 잠정 적용 문제

      - 선진국 : UR 협상 결과가 최종 발효될 때까지 희망 국가간 잠정
        적용 필요

다. 협상 전망

    o 협상분야의 성격상 당분간 막후 비공식 협의를 계속하다가 UR 협상
      최종단계에 본격 거론 전망

    o Single Undertaking 문제는 의무 수락 분야와 선택수락 분야의
      2원 구조로 타협안 모색 가능성도 배제 불가

    o MTO 설치 문제는 신분야 협상의 결과에 따라 계속 추진 여부 좌우 예상

13

0050

라. 협상 대책

　o Single Undertaking 관련, 일괄 수락이 불가피할 것으로 예상되며, 협상
　　결과의 일부국가간 잠정 적용 문제는 하기 이유에서 바람직하지 않음.
　　　- 일시적으로 기존 갓트와의 2중 법적 구조 초래 가능성
　　　- 선진국의 아국에 대한 잠정 적용 압력 예상

　o MTO 설치 문제는 원칙적으로 동조 가능
　　　- MTO 설치 문제는 협상 추이를 감안, 대책 수립.　　　　끝.

14

0051

UR/제도분야 협상 대책

1. 협상 동향 및 예상 합의 수준

가. 협상 동향

○ 88.12. 몬트리올 중간 평가 각료회의시 분쟁해결 및 갓트기능 분야에서 상당한 수준의 합의가 이루어졌으며 현재 동 합의사항을 잠정적으로 시행중

○ 현재까지 미합의로 남아 있는 하기 주요쟁점들은 정치적 결단을 요하는 사항들로서 UR 협상 결과의 전체적 윤곽이 드러나는 최종단계에서 본격적인 협상이 이루어질 것으로 전망
- 분쟁해결 관련 이사회 결정시 자동성 인정 여부 및 일방조치 억제 공약 선행 여부
- MTO 설립 문제
- UR 협상 결과의 일괄수락(Single undertaking) 여부

나. 예상 합의 수준

○ UR/제도분야 협상그룹은 분쟁해결 규칙 및 절차의 개선 강화, UR 협상 이후 새로운 국제무역기구(가칭 MTO) 설립, UR 협상 이행 관련 최종 의정서 작성을 주요협상 대상으로 하고 있는바, 여타 협상그룹에서는 참가국간 이해관계에 따른 협상이 이루어지고 있는데 반해 UR/제도분야 협상그룹은 갓트 전반에 관한 제도적 개선을 추구

○ 따라서 갓트의 제도적 측면 강화를 적극 추진하고 있는 선진국 입장이 대부분 반영 될 것으로 전망

1

0052

ㅇ 동 협상그룹이 갓트 전반에 관계되는 사항을 다루고 있으며, 제도적
  개선을 통해 다자간 무역체제를 강화해야 한다는 명분에 반대할 수
  있는 소지가 적으며, 아국 입장에서도 협상의 대세에 따르더라도
  ·별다른 무리없이 수용이 가능한 협상 분야임.

2. 협상 대책 및 대응 논리

가. 전체 협상과 연계, 입장 반영이 필요한 사항

1) 일방조치 억제 공약

ㅇ 대   책

- 이는 분쟁해결 관련 이사회 결정시 자동성(automaticity) 부여
  문제와 연계된 문제로서, 갓트 분쟁해결 절차의 매단계에서
  blockage 요소를 완전히 제거하려는 미국의 입장과 미국의 301조
  발동등 일방조치 억제에 대한 공약을 받아내려는 여타국의
  입장이 대립

- 일방조치 억제 공약선행이 필요하다는 것이 아국 포함 다수국 입장

ㅇ 대응 논리

- 일방조치는 그 자체로서 갓트 분쟁해결.제도 위반이며, 일방조치가
  자행되는 경우 갓트의 분쟁해결 절차가 무의미 해질 것이며, 또한
  일방조치 자체가 다자간 무역체제에 대한 위협이므로 일방조치
  억제 공약 선행이 필수적

나. 계속 반영이 필요한 사항

1) 이사회의 분쟁해결 관련 결정시 자동성 부여

ㅇ 대   책

- 이사회의 분쟁해결 관련 결정시 자동성이 부여되는 경우에 특히
  문제가 되는 것은 패널 및 상소보고서를 채택시 및 패널 권고사항
  불이행시 보복 승인에 대해 결정을 내릴때임.

2

0053

- 아국이 여타국을 제소하는 경우보다는 여타 회원국으로부터
  제소를 당할 가능성이 많은 현재의 상황에서 분쟁해결 관련
  이사회 결정을 기존의 consensus 방식에 의하도록 하는것이
  바람직 할 것이나 분쟁해결 절차를 엄격화 함으로써 제도적
  개선을 모색한다는 것이 협상의 전반적인 분위기임을 감안,
  궁극적으로 이사회의 분쟁해결 관련 결정시 자동성을 부여하는데
  반대하기 어려운 실정
- 다만, 동 문제와 연계되어 있는 일방조치 억제 공약이 선행되어야
  한다는 조건부로 자동성 부여 문제를 수용토록 함.

  O 대응 논리
  - 갓트 분쟁해결 해결 절차의 효율성 제고를 통한 다자무역체제의
    강화에는 동의하나, 갓트체제를 일탈하는 일방조치가 존속될
    경우에는 다자간 분쟁해결 기능강화는 무의미함.
  - 따라서 분쟁해결 절차의 자동화는 일방조치 억제가 선행되어야만
    수락 가능함.

2) 20일이전 패널설치 요구시 첫번째 이사회시 패널 설치 여부
  O 대   책
  - 제소국이 20일이전에 패널설치를 요구하는 경우 첫번째 이사회시
    패널을 설치토록 한다는 사무국 안과 관련, 20일의 기간은 너무
    촉박하므로 중간평가시 합의한대로 패널 설치 시한을 늦어도
    두번째 이사회에서 설치하도록 함.

  O 대응 논리
  - 갓트이사회는 패널설치 여부를 결정하는 장소로서 뿐만 아니라
    패널의 설치가 필요한지에 대한 체약국의 의견 수렴 장소로서도
    의미가 크므로 패널 설치 결정은 늦어도 패널설치 문제가 상정된
    이사회의 다음 이사회에서 결정되도록 하는 것이 바람직.

3) 소규모 각료회의 설치
  O 대   책
  - 협상 대세를 수용할 수 있으나, 우리나라의 참여 확보 필요

3

0054

o 대응 논리

  - 참가범위가 제한적인 소규모 각료회의가 설치되는 경우, 동 기능은
    갓트의 계약적인 성격을 감안하여 자문적인 성격으로 해야하며,
    참가범위는 국제무역상 접유율을 기준으로 결정되어야 함.

다. 협상 대세 수용 분야

  o 분쟁해결 관련사항
    - 분쟁해결 절대적 최대 시한 설정
    - 통합된 분쟁해결 관련 text 작성
    - 타협상분야 분쟁해결 절차와의 조정
    - non-violation 분쟁

  o 갓트 기능 강화 관련사항
    - MTO 설립
    - 국제통화, 금융, 무역정책간의 일관성 확보

  o UR 협상 결과의 일괄 수락 문제
    - UR 협상 결과의 일괄 수락(Single undertaking)과 관련, 아국의
      일괄수락이 불가피 할 것으로 예상되므로, 여타국의 참여를
      확대한다는 측면에서 협상 대세 수용. ··   끝.

4

기 안 용 지

분류기호 서 번 호	통기 20644-	(전화: 720 - 2188)	시 행 상 특별취급	
보존기간	영구 . 준영구 10. 5. 3. 1.	차 관	장 관	
수 신 처 보존기간		전 결		
시행일자	1991. 9.18.			

보조 기관	국 장		협조기관	제2차관보:	기획관리실장: 총무과장: 기획운영담당관:	문 서 통 제
	심의관					
	과 장					
기안책임자		안 명 수				발 송 인

경유 수신 참조	내부결재	발신명의		

제 목   UR 협상 참가 정부대표 임명

스위스 제네바에서 개최되는 UR/제도분야 협상 그룹회의(9.26)

및 UR/서비스와 시장접근 분야에서의 한.미 양자협의(9.23주간 개최)에

참가할 정부대표를 "정부대표 및 특별사절의 임명과 권한에 관한

법률"에 의거, 아래와 같이 임명할 것을 건의합니다.

- 아   래 -

- 1 -

0056

1. 회 의 명 : UR 제도분야 협상그룹 회의 및 UR/서비스

   시장접근 분야에서의 한.미 양자협의

2. 회의기간 및 장소 : 91.9.24-27, 스위스 제네바

3. 정부대표 : 통상기구과장 홍종기

4. 출장기간 : 91.9.24-29

5. 훈   령 : 별   첨

6. 소요경비 :

   가. 항공료 : $2,134

   나. 체재비 : $66X5박 = $330

   다. 일식비 : ($20+$42)X6일 = $372

       총 계 : $2,836

   라. 지변항목 : 경제활동 초외여비

첨 부 : 훈 령.   끝.

- 2 -

0057

훈 령

1. UR 제도분야 협상 그룹회의와 관련 하기 입장에 따라 대처함.

   가. 일방조치 억제

      ㅇ 갓트 위반 일방조치 억제 의무 선행이 필요함.

   나. 패널 및 상소보고서 채택 및 승인

      ㅇ 자동채택 및 승인 문제는 일방조치 억제 공약이 선행되어야
         수용 검토

   다. non-violation 분쟁

      ㅇ 동 분쟁을 위한 별도의 분쟁해결 절차를 선정할 충분한 이유가
         없는만큼 보다 명확한 EC 입장이 개진될 때까지 갓트 일반
         분쟁해결 절차에 따라야 한다는 입장 견지

   라. 최대 시한

      ㅇ 21개월의 절대적 시한 설정보다는 불가항력의 경우 예외를
         인정함이 바람직함.

   마. 통합 text

      ㅇ 절차 명료화를 위해 바람직함.

2. UR/서비스 및 시장접근 분야 관련 한.미 양자협의

   ㅇ UR 협상관련 한.미 양자협의에 대비하여 개최된 UR 대책 실무회의
      결과(시장접근 분야 : 8.30, 서비스 분야 : 9.12)에 의거하여
      미측과의 협의에 임하고 쟁점별 미측 입장을 파악함.

0058

발 신 전 보

분류번호	보존기간

번 호 : **WGV-1254** 910919 1911 FN 종별 : _____

수 신 : 주 제네바 대사. 총영사

발 신 : 장 관 (통 기)

제 목 : UR/제도분야 협상 그룹회의 및 서비스, 시장접근 분야 한.미 양자협의

9.26 귀지 개최 예정인 UR/제도분야 협상 그룹회의(9.26)와 한.미 서비스 및
시장접근 분야에서의 한.미 양자협의(9.23주간 예정)에 참가할 정부대표가 아래와 같이
임명 되었으니 귀관 관계직원과 함께 참석토록 조치바람.

- 아 래 -

1. 정부대표 : 외무부 통상기구과장 홍종기

2. 귀지 도착일시 : 91.9.24(화) 22:30 SR-837편

3. 훈 령 : 본부대표 지참. 끝.   (통상국장 김용규)

			보 안 통 제	

앙고재	91년 9월 18일 통상기구과	기안자 성명 안명수	과 장	심의관 전결	국 장	차 관	장 관	외신과통제

0059

외 무 부

종 별 :

번 호 : GVW-1845 　　　　　　　　일 시 : 91 0927 1100

수 신 : 장관(통기)

발 신 : 주제네바대사

제 목 : UR/분쟁해결 공식회의

연: GVW-517, 제네(경) 20644-312

1. 연호 표제회의가 9.26.LACARTE 의장의 사회로 개최된바, 주요내용 아래 보고함.

(홍과장, 신서기관 참석)

가. 브랏셀 각료회의시 협의 결과를 기초로 작성한 사무국 NON-PAPER(3.25자) 협의

1) 패널 설치 시한(TIME-FRAME) 문제

0 패널 설치 요청이 이사회 개최 20일전에 이루어지면 첫번째 이사회에서 패널을설치할 수 있다는 사무국안에 대해 인도, 브라질이 20일 기간이 너무 촉박하다는 점을 지적함.

2) 갓트 규정에 위배되지 않는 분쟁(NON-VIOLATION) 해결 절차

0 갓트 규정에 위배되지 않는 분쟁해결에 대한 특별절차에 관한 사무국안에 대해미국,일본,아국등 다수국은 상기 분쟁처리에 관한 특별 절차 도입 필요성에 의문을표시하고,구체사항에 대한 추가협의를 요한다고 함.

나. 통합문안(CONSOLIDATED TEXT) 작성

0 브라질,일본등 다수국은 금일 사무국이 작성한 통합문안에 원칙적인 지지의사를 표명하고 기술적 작업진행에 참여할 용의를 피력하였음.

다. 타협상 분야 분쟁해결 절차와의 조정(COORDINATION) 문제

0 23조에 의한 분쟁해결 절차와 타협상분야에서의 분쟁해결 절차와의 조정문제는갓트의 분쟁해결 절차의 일관성 제고를 위해 중요하고 긴급한 문제라는 의장의 발언에 대해,멕시코는 현재 갓트내에 있는 8개의 분쟁해결절차와 관련 FORUM SHOPPING 문제를 방지하기 위해 제도적 장치 보완이 필요하다고 언급함. 한편 인도는

통상국　　2차보

본그룹은상품 분야 협상의 분쟁 해결절차를 다루도록 되어 있으며 서비스, TRIPS 등 신분야에서의 분쟁해결 문제는 동 그룹의 소관분야가 아니라는 반응을 보였음.

2. 의장은 차기 공식회의를 10.24-25간 개최할 예정이며 10월말에는 분쟁해결 분야의 최종안(REV.2)을 완성하기 위해 차주부터 집중적인 비공식 회의를 개최하여 3.25자 사무국안에 괄호로 표시된 미결 쟁점, 상기 금일회의에서 지적된 사항, 최근 비공식 협의과정에서 제기된 아래사항에 대한 협의를 진행하겠다고 함.

- FORUM SHOPPING 억제문제
- 제소의 적격성 판단문제
- 보복
- 패널권고 불이행시 대책
- 패널 구성문제
(대사 박수길-국장)

외 무 부

종 별 :

번 호 : GVW-2037

일 시 : 91 1017 1830

수 신 : 장관(통기)

발 신 : 주제네바대사

제 목 : UR 분쟁해결 비공식 협의

연: GVW-1845

연호 9.26 분쟁해결 공식 회의시 LACARTE의장이 밝힌대로 10.7주간부터 기술적 논의가 가능한 통합 문안 작성, 타협상분야 분쟁해결절차와의 조정문제, NON-VIOLATION 분쟁문제에관하여 잇슈별로 비공식 협의가 진행중인바, 10.16까지의 논의 결과를 아래보고함.(이성주 참사관참석)

1. 통합 문안 작성

0 8.12.자 사무국 NON-PAPER 를 기초로 10.9-11간 3회에걸쳐 협의를 진행, 상기 NON-PAPER 40페이지(58년 절차 부분) 까지 1차 통합 작업을마쳤음.

0 상기 협의 결과에 따라 사무국이 새로운 초안을 작성한후 10.7 비공식 협의를재개하며, 나머지 66년결정 부분에 대한 통합 작업 및 새로운 초안에대한 재검토를추진할 예정임.

0 상기 1차 통합 작업 결과중 주요 내용은 아래와같음.

- 발효후 4년이내 전면 재검토 조항(A1)은 GENERALPROVISION 의 성격이 아니므로 DRAFT DECISION 으로 이전

- 82년 선언 VIII항(권고 및 판정은 분쟁의만족스러운 해결을 목표로 해야 함)을GENERALPROVISION에 추가

- A6항 위치의 적정성 여부가 제기되어 추후 다시 검토키로 합의

- 협의관련 EC, 일본의 제의로 23조 2항 절차에 회부하기에 앞서 22조 2항 절차에 따라 만족스러운 해결책을 강구해야 한다는 79년 선언 6항을 통합 문안에 추가키로합의(이에 대해 미국은동문안이 BLOCKAGE 수단으로 악용될 우려가있으므로 적절한 기회에 문제를 제기할 예정임을 밝힘)

- 8페이지 비고란의 언급사항 관련 미국의 주장으로 협의 절차의 CONFIDENTIALITY

통상국   2차보   경기원   상공부

PAGE 1

91.10.18   09:01 BX

외신 1과 통제관

0062

규정을 신설

- 58년 절차(40 페이지) 2,3,4항을 45일 시한 삭제등 사무국이 필요한 문안조정을 한 후 협의관련 SECTION 으로 전환키로 합의(1,5,6항은 삭제), 동 논의과정에서 동절차가 22조 1항 협의 절차에만 해당되는 것과 관련 23조 협의에까지 확대 적용하는문제가 거론되었으나 일본이 반대입장을 밝힘.

- 패널 구성과 관련, 79년 양해 11항(분쟁당사국인사 배제조항) 추가

- 개도국이 당사국인 패널에 개도국측의 PANELIST포함 조항(79년 양해 ANNEX 6(II)항 일부 문안수정

- 패널절차 관련(미국이 분쟁당사국의 서면 진술시한 설정 조항(84년 결정 B 4항)의 SHOULD를 SHALL 로 수정, 시한 설정을 의무화 할것을 주장한데 대해, 아국,인도,EC등의 D6(F)항의 FLEXIBILITY 유지와의 상충등을 이유로 반대함으로써 D 6(F) 항의BRACKET 처리결과에 따라 조정키로 절충

- 패널 보고서 이행관련 NON-PAPER 31 페이지 우측 비고난에 제기된 패널보고서채택 6개월후 이사회 상정은 대부분의 국가가 당사국의 요청이 없어도 자동 상정되는 것으로 인식을 같이함.

2. 타협상분야 분쟁해결 절차와의 조정문제

0 연호 9.26.공식회의 직후 LACARTE 의장이 주요국과 협의를 갖고 사무국에 요청한바에 따라,사무국이 새로운 토의 문서를 작성 10.16 비공식협의시 배포, 이를 기초로 토의를 진행함.

0 사무국이 작성 배포한 문서는 분쟁해결 절차논의가 진행되고 있는 5개 협상그룹(농산물,섬유, 규범제정, TRIPS, SVC)의장앞 LARCARTE의장의 COVER LETTER, 이에 첨부될 GENERALWORDING, 각 협상 그룹의 분쟁해결 관련조문의 특징 요약문(이상 FAX 송부) 및 각 그룹분쟁해결 조문과 일반 절차와의 대비문으로구성됨.

0 인도가 TRIPS, SVC 협상 최종결과의 지위관련 아무런 협의도 없었으므로 상기양분야와의 조정문제는 검토할 수 없다는 입장을 재차 피력한 반면(브라질 동조), 미국, 캐나다,놀웨이등 선진국은 타협상분야 토의를 예단함이 없이 또한 필요시 상기양분야 포함여부에 대해서는 이견이 존재한다는 점을 명기해서라도 일단 각그룹 참고용으로 각 그룹의장앞으로 상기 문서를전달 할것을 주장함으로써(아국을 포함 다수국동조), 대립을 보였으나, 멕시코의 제의에 따라 <u>사무국이 비공식 협의에서 논의된 내용을 LACARTE 의장에게 보고하고 동의장이 독자적 책임과 판단아래 타그룹</u>

PAGE 2

전달문제를 포함향후에 취할 조치를 결정키로 합의함.

3. NON-VIOLATION 분쟁

O 10.16 동 문제에 관한 1차 비공식 협의가 개최된바, EC 가 3.25.자 사무국 NON-PAPER 상의 OPTION A 와 B를 봉합한 새로운 초안을 배포(FAX 송부)하였으나, 특별절차 도입을 희망하는 EC의 의도, NON-VIOLATION 분쟁의 범위등과 관련 참가국들의 질문에 대해 기존의 답변 이외에 설득력있는 답변을못함으로써 10.18 동 문제에 관한비공식 협의를 재개키로 하였음.끝

(대사 박수길-국장)

PAGE 3

0064

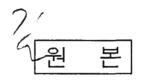

외 무 부

종 별 :

번 호 : GVW-2038

수 신 : 장관(봉기)

발 신 : 주제네바대사

제 목 : UR 분쟁해결

일 시 : 91 1017 1830

연: GVW-2037

연호 분쟁해결 관련 초안을 별첨 전송함.

첨부: 상기 초안(총 6페이지)

(GVW(F)-0425).끝

(대사 박수길-국장)

통상국   2차보

PAGE 1

91.10.18   08:32 DU

외신 1과 통제관

0065

UR(우루과이라운드).제도분야 협상 그룹 회의, 1991   71

GVW(五)-0425   H 017 1830

"GVW-2038 첨부"

Lacarte 의장 cover letter초안

Dear Mr. Chairman,

The Negotiating Group on Institutions pursuant to its mandate has drafted an Understanding on the Interpretation and Application of Articles XXII and XXIII of the General Agreement. The Group has noted that certain dispute settlement provisions have emerged in some other Negotiating Groups. In the course of their deliberations participants have felt that the Negotiating Group on Institutions should ensure consistency and coherence in the dispute settlement rules and procedures which will emerge from the Uruguay Round and prevent eventual conflicts between the various Uruguay Round agreements and arrangements. Having regard to the relevant provisions of the Punta del Este Declaration and the Mid-Term Review Decisions participants in the Group have recognized that ideally there should be dispute settlement procedures generally applicable, even though for very specific reasons special provisions might be contemplated in certain areas. It is felt that in these cases the text should make clear whether the special procedures will be optional or mandatory and whether or not they will have precedence over the general dispute settlement procedures. As a result of consultations carried out within the Group, participants have requested me to convey to the Chairman of other Negotiating Groups a draft text concerning the general applicability of the Understanding on dispute settlement to the various codes or arrangements, together with some comments with respect to the draft dispute settlement provisions of the instruments concerned. These texts are hereby attached.

Sincerely yours,

J. Lacarte-Muró
Chairman
Negotiating Group on Institutions

To: Chairman of
     Negotiating Groups
     on: Agriculture
         Textiles
         Rules
         TRIPS
     Group of Negotiations on Services

0066

/ /

General Wording 초안

[Except as otherwise provided for in this agreement,*] consultations and the settlement of disputes with respect to any matter affecting the operation of this agreement shall be subject to the procedures of Articles XXII and XXIII of the General Agreement, and the Dispute Settlement procedures as adopted by the CONTRACTING PARTIES.

_____

*To be included only if there are differences.

각고물별별 본리해야될략한 통리문술

Agreement	Nature of dispute settlement mechanism - Summary
Rules of Origin	The provisions of Articles XXII and XXIII of the General Agreement, as elaborated upon by the Negotiating Group on Dispute Settlement, are applicable to this Agreement.
Agreement on Import Licensing	Consultations and the settlement of disputes with respect to any matters affecting the operation of this Agreement, shall be subject to the procedures of Articles XXII and XXIII of the GATT, and the Dispute Settlement Procedures as adopted by the CONTRACTING PARTIES (Article 6).
Technical Barriers to Trade	Consultations and the settlement of disputes with respect to any matter affecting the operation of this Agreement shall be subject to the procedures of Articles XXII and XXIII of the GATT, including Dispute Settlement Procedures as adopted by the CONTRACTING PARTIES, and shall take place under the auspices of the Committee on Technical Barriers to Trade (Article 14).
Preshipment Inspection	There are essentially two dispute settlement mechanisms: one for disputes between preshipment inspection entities and exporters and the other for disputes between contracting parties regarding the operation of the agreement. In the former case, disputes are to be settled under independent review procedures outlined in the Agreement.
	Consultations among contracting parties with regard to any matter affecting the operation of the agreement will be conducted under the provisions of Article XXII of the General Agreement as amended by the Uruguay Round (Article 8).
	Disputes among contracting parties regarding the operation of the Agreement shall be subject to the provisions of Article XXIII of the General Agreement, as amended by the Uruguay Round (Article 9).
Safeguards	Contracting parties which consider that their rights under this Agreement are being nullified or impaired have recourse to the dispute settlement provisions of the General Agreement (Paragraph 41).

6-3

0068

- 2 -

Agriculture: Sanitary and Phytosanitary Standards	This decision shall be subject to the provisions of Articles XXII and XXIII and the dispute settlement procedures applicable to those Articles or adopted by CONTRACTING PARTIES.
Textiles and Clothing	This Agreement sets out provisions to be applied during a transitional period for the integration of the textiles and clothing sector into GATT.... (Article 1, paragraph 1).
	A Textile Monitoring Body (TMB) shall be established to supervise the implementation of the Agreement, to examine all measures taken under its provisions and their conformity therewith, and to take actions specifically required of it in the Articles of this Agreement. The TMB will develop its own working procedures. [excerpts from Article 9.] The TMB would serve as a forum for dispute settlement. Pursuant to Articles 3.5 and 8.3, certain matters may be taken up under normal GATT procedures.
Subsidies	Part X of the Agreement states that without prejudice to the provisions of Articles 4, 7 and 9, the provisions governing the settlement of disputes under the General Agreement shall apply, mutatis mutandis, to the settlement of disputes under this Agreement. Article 4 relates to remedies in cases of prohibited subsidies; Article 7 relates to remedies in cases of actionable subsidies while Article 9 relates to special "safeguard" procedures.
Customs Valuation	The comprehensive text of the 1979 Agreement with regard to dispute settlement still stands since it was not the subject of negotiations in the Uruguay Round.
	Paragraph 11 of Article 20 (Dispute Settlement) enjoins parties to a dispute relating to rights and obligations under the Agreement to complete the dispute settlement procedures under the Agreement before availing themselves of any rights which they have under the GATT, including invoking Article XXIII thereof. This implies that dispute settlement will in the first instance be organized under the auspices of the Committee on Customs Valuation before any other GATT body is considered.

6-𝓍

0069

- 3 -

Government Procurement The 1979 Agreement was not renegotiated in the Uruguay Round. The dispute settlement procedures in the existing Agreement remain unchanged. They are organized exclusively under the Committee on Government Procurement with no recourse to GATT procedures.

6-5

0070

Non-비교(수,에 등건멍 관2면 '
10,16 비상석 엽의시 제대된 EC 협안

P.1   The procedures in this agreement shall apply, subject to the
      provisions of paragraphs P.2 through P.5 below, where a
      party has recourse to dispute settlement based upon Article
      XXIII:1(b) alleging that the introduction or intensification
      of a measure not in conflict with the General Agreement, and
      which could not reasonably have been foreseen, frustrates a
      [legitimate expectation of a benefit accruing to the party
      under a market access concession or other commitment under
      the General Agreement] [REASONABLE EXPECTATION OF A BENEFIT
      ACCRUING TO THE PARTY DIRECTLY OR INDIRECTLY UNDER THE
      GENERAL AGREEMENT], upsetting the conditions of competition
      [and] [OR] having an [ACTUAL OR POTENTIAL] adverse effect on
      trade.

      Note: bracketed clauses in lower case are to be read
      together, and bracketed clauses in upper case are to be
      read together.

외 무 부

종 별 :

번 호 : GVW-2075   일 시 : 91 1021 1850

수 신 : 장관(통기)

발 신 : 주제네바대사

제 목 : UR/분쟁해결 비공식 협의

연: GVW-2037

1. 표제 협의가 연호에 이어 10.17-18 양일간 LINDEN 고문 사회하에 계속된바, 동 협의에서는 연호보고와 같이 사무국이 재작성 제시한 안을 기초로 통합 문안을 재검토, 동 작업을 대체로 마무리짓고(8.12. NON-PAPER 41페이지 개도국이 관련된 분쟁에 관한 특별 절차를 규정한 66년 결정의 통합문제는 선.개도국간 첨예한 의견 대립으로 미결), 미국, 카나다, 일본등이 제의한 사무국의 3.25.자 TEXT 에 대한 일부 수정안을 검토확정(일부등 미합의) 하였으나, 예정된 NON-VIOLATION 분쟁에 대한 토의는 EC 의 준비부족으로 10.21(월)로 연기되었고, 타협상 분야 분쟁해결 절차와의 조정 문제도 사무국이 LACARTE의장의 COVER LETTER 초안을 수정 배포하였으나 시간 부족으로 구체토의가 이루어 지지 못하였음. 그밖에 CANADA 가 3.25. 사무국 TEXT 상의 ANNEX(WORKING PROCEDURES)에 대한 UPDATE 안을 제시하였으나 역시 시간 부족으로 토의치 못함.

2. 상기 양일간 사안별 토의 내용은 아래와 같음.

가. 통합 문안 작성

- NOTIFICATION 관련 조항(8.12. 문서 7페이지 첫2개 PARA)은 제도분야 통고문제에 포함, 취급되어야 할 사항이므로 삭제, 분쟁 당사국인사의 패널위원 선임 금지조항에 '당사국이 달리 합의하지 않는한' 이라는 단서 설정(미국제의) 개도국 관련 조항(8.12. 문서 26페이지, 2번째 PARA)은 아국, 미국의 위치 부적절지적으로 이행 감시 관련 항목으로 이전

- 66년 절차(개도국 특별 절차) 통합문제에 대해서는 미국이 중재의 의무화, 패널 설치, 패널보고서 제출, 이행시한등 새로운 절차와 상치되는 사항이 많음을 지적하고 개도국에 대해서 66절차를 인정할 경우 분쟁해결 절차가 2원화(TWO-TIER SYSTEM)

통상국   2차보

되므로 반대한다는 입장(EC, CANADA 동조)을 취한데 대해, MEXICO가 동 절차는 개도국의 기득권임을 들어 동절차의 무효화에 반대하면서 동 절차 전체를 문안조정없이 봉합문안 말미에 별도 항목으로유지함으로써 개도국을 하여금 분쟁발생 초기에 어느절차에 따를 것인지 선택할 수 있록 해야한다고 주장하고, 이에 대히 칠레, 인도, 브라질,알젠틴등 개도국이 동조(아국은 동 절차가유지되더라도 사실상 아국이 활용키를 기대 키어려움을 감안 입장을 표명치 않음) 함으로써 합의점을 찾지 못하고, LINDEN 고문의 제의로 미국, EC, 카나다, 멕시코, 브라질, 칠레 6개국이 참가하는 소그룹에서(1차) 협의한후, 재론키로 함.

　나. 3.25.TEXT 대한 수정 제의 검토

- A 1항(발효후 4년 이내 재검토) 관련 현시점에서 각료회의 개최일정 전망이 불가하므로 '4년내 재검토를 마치고, 동 재검토가 완료된이후의 첫번째 각료급 총회에서 결정'키로 문안수정(카나다 제의)

- FOOTNOTE 1(경과 규정)의 명확화를 위한수정(미국제의)

- B. 3항(협의 요청)및 D. 1(B)항(패널설치)관련 문제되는 조치의 내용 및 법적근거를 협의요청 및 패널 설치 요청시 명시토록하는 내용 추가(미국제의)

- D. 1(A)항 (패널 설치시한) 관련, 일본이이사회 개최 20일전 봉보시 첫번째 이사회에서 패널 설치 가능토록 하는 수정안을 제의하였으나, 아국, 인도, 멕시코, BRAZIL등이 반대하여 합의를 보지 못함.

- D 2항(패널의 TOR) 관련, 미국이 패널은당사국간 협의단계에서 거론된 구체적조치(SPECIFIC MEASURES)에 대해서만 심사해야한다는 내용의 세항 신설을제의하였으나,멕시코가 반대하고, 논의되었는지의 여부에 대한 입증의 어려움등이논란이 되어 합의도출 실패

- 패널 절차 중단 관련 규정(전체 시한에영향없이 12개월 범위내에서 중단가능, 12개월초과시 패널 자동해체) 신설합의(카나다 제안)

- 보고서 채택, 상소기구 결정 채택, 패소국의이행의사 봉보 관련 시한내 이사회개최가예정되어 있지 않을 경우에도 당사국 요청시이사회가 자동 개최되도록 하자는내용의 일본제의에 대해, 현행 이사회 소집 규정(10-DAY-RULE)상 당연한 내용이므로볼 필요하다는 반론도있었으나, 절차를 명확화 한다는 차원에서수용키로 합의

- J,K 항 패널 보고서 채택 및 합리적 이행기간결정까지의 총 기간의 기산 시점을

PAGE 2

협의 요청시점에서 패널 설치 시점으로 변경하는 대신, 총기간을 각각 3개월씩 단축함으로써 당사국이합의하면 총 기간에 구애 받음이 없이협의기간을 여유있게 갖을수있도록 수정(카나다제의)

　다. 타협상 분야 분쟁해결 절차와의 조정 문제

　- 사무국이 (농산물) (섬유,) 규범제정의 3개분야의장앞으로 된 LACARTE 의장의 COVER LETTER수정안을 배포한데 대해 호주가 3개분야에한정하는 것 역시 협상 결과를 예단하는것이라는 지적이 있었고, 동 3개 분야 한정이LUCARTE 의장과의 협의결과에 따른 것이냐는다수국의 문의에 대해 사무국은 아직 협의한바없다고 답변함.

　- 사무국은 동 작업 관련 연호 각 협상그룹 별로작성된 대조표에 대해서는 검토조차 착수치 못하고있는 점에 우려를 표명함

　3. LINDEN 고문은 10.8 협의시 LACARTE 의장요청으로 10.21(월) 오후 동 의장 주재로 비공식협의를 개최할 예정임을 밝히고, 그 이전에 모든미결사항에 대한 처리를마무리 짓기 위해 주말회의개최를 제의하였으나, 다수 대표의 사정으로 10.21.오전협의를 계속키로 하였음.

　4. 이상과 같이 기술적 사항에서도 미결쟁점이다수(66년 절차, 3.25.TEXT 에 대한 수정 제의중일부 미합의 조항, 조정작업 관련 대비표검토작업 NON-VIOLATION 분쟁등) 남아 있기때문에 상기 LACARTE 의장 주재 회의에서10.24-25 공식회의를 대비한 최종 의견 조정이이루어질 전망은 극히 불투명함.끝

　(대사 박수길-국장)

PAGE 3

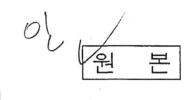

관리	
번호	91-695

외 무 부

종 별 :

번 호 : GVW-2111
일 시 : 91 1023 1750

수 신 : 장관(통기,경기원,재무부,농림수산부,상공부,특허청)

발 신 : 주 제네바 대사

제 목 : UR/협상대책(제도분야)

연: GVW-2083

대호 협상대책중 제도분야 관련 사항을 아래 보고함.

1. 분쟁해결

가. 주요쟁점 사항

일반문서로 재분류(198１ . 12.31 .)

0 일방조치 억제공약, 패널 및 상소기구 보고서 자동 채택, 보복의 자동승인등 분쟁해결 절차의 자동화 문제가 최대 쟁점으로, 이는 최종단계 정치적 결정을 요함

0 그밖에 패널 설치시한, NON-VIOLATION 분쟁, 통합 문안 작성, 타협상 분야 분쟁해결 절차와의 조화 문제등의 과제가 남아 있음.

나. 협상 진전 사항

0 9.26 공식회의 이후(10 월중) 기술적 협의 기능 사항에 대한 비공식 협의만이 진행되었을뿐, 정치적 쟁점에 대한 논의는 전문한 상태임.

0 상기 기술적 협의도 통합 문안 작성 작업 및 브랏셀 TEXT 에 대한 일부 수정 보완 작업만이 비교적 진전을 보이고 있을뿐, 패널설치 시한(첫번째 또는 두번째 이사회)에 대한 의견 대립이 계속되고 있고, NON-VIOLATION 분쟁에 대해서는 EC 가 준비 부족을 이유로 실질 토의를 계속 지연시켜오고 있는 상태임.

0 또한 통합문안 작성 작업에 있어서도 개도국에 대한 특별절차를 규정한 66년 결정의 통합 문제로 선.개도국이 의견대립을 보임으로써 새로운 쟁점으로 부과되었으며, 타협상 분야와의 조화 문제 역시 서비스, TRIPS 분야와의 조화 문제는 최종 협상 단계까지 미결 상태로 남아 있을 전망임.

다. 기존 아국 입장 관철 가능성

0 일방조치 억제 공약

- 절차의 자동화등 분쟁해결 절차의 전반적 강화 문제와 연계되어, PACKAGE 에

통상국	장관	차관	1차보	2차보	경제국	외정실	분석관	청와대
안기부	경기원	재무부	농수부	상공부	특허청			

PAGE 1

91.10.24   05:55
외신 2과 통제관 CD

0075

의하지 않는한 미국의 일방적 양보 기대 곤란

　0 패널보고서, 상소기구 결정 자동채택 및 보복승인 자동화 문제

　- 상기 일방조치 억제 문제와 직접 연계되어 있을뿐 아니라, 협상 분위기상절차
자동화에 더이상 거부하기 어려운 문제

　- 10.22. 비공식 협의시 인도가 패널 보고서 채택관련 60 일까지는 전봉적
CENSENSUS 방식 적용을 주장하는 수정안을 제출했으나, 관철키 어려울 것으로 전망

　0 패널 설치 시한

　- 아국, 인도, 멕시코, 브라질, 칠레등이 두번째 이사회에서의 설치를 선호하고
있으나, 선진국의 첫번째 이사회 설치 입장도 강경하여 관철 가능성 불부명

　0 NON-VIOLATION 분쟁

　- 아직까지 EC 가 구체적 입장 및 의도를 밝히지 않고 있어 쉽게 전망키 어려우나
EC 입장이 상당히 강경한 만큼 적정 수준에서 EC 주장을 수용할 것으로 전망

　라. 향후 대책

　0 일방조치 억제공약

　- 계속 동 공약 선행이 필요하다는 입장에 <u>동조</u>   *더33중 배이다는것이이선저?*

　0 분쟁해결 절차의 자동화

　- 협상 분위기상 반대키 어려우므로 상기 공약과의 TRADE-OFF 를 조건으로 수용

　0 패널 보고서 채택 시한

　- 기존 입장을 표명하되 협상 분위기상 필요할 경우 대세에 따라 대처

　2. 갓트 기능 및 최종의정서

　가. 주요쟁점 사항

　0 경제정책 결정상의 일관성 제고 문제(갓트기능 분야)

　0 MTO 설립, 잠정위원회 설치 문제(최종 의정서와 갓트 기능 분야 중복)

　0 SINGLE UNDERTAKING 문제

　나. 협상 진전 상황

　0 91.3.25. 사무국이 최종 의정서에 관한 NON-PAPER 를 제출한 외에 브랏셀회의
이후 특별진전 사항 없음.

　다. 향후 대책

　- EC 및 개도국의 의욕적 제안 보다는 사무국간 실용적 협력 확대 방안이
현실적이나 아국에 특별한 이해관계가 없는 사항이므로 입장표명 자제

PAGE 2

0076

O MTO 설립문제

- UR 협상 종료시 MTO 설치 필요성에는 동조하되, 구체적 사항은 UR 협상 종료후
협의 추진 주장

O SINGLE UNDERTAKING 문제

- 아국의 일괄 수락은 불가피한 상황이므로 여타국 참여 확대 차원에서 지지하되,
의무 선택수락의 2 원 구조 가능성이 있는 경우 이에 대해서도 신중히 검토.끝

(대사 박수길-국장)

예고:91.12.31. 까지

외 무 부

종 별 :

번 호 : GVW-2121   일 시 : 91 1024 1200

수 신 : 장 관(통기)

발 신 : 주 제네바 대사

제 목 : UR/분쟁해결 비공식 협의

연: GVW-2075

1. 표제 협의가 연호에 이어 10.21-23 간 계속된바(10.21 오후 회의는 예정대로 LACARTE 의장이주재, 여타 회의는 LINDEN 고문이 주재), 동 협의결과 요지 아래 보고함.(이성주 참사관 참석)

가. BRUSSELS TEXT 에 대한 연호 수정 제의중미합의 사항 재검토 및 미국등 일부국의 국가 추가제의를 검토, 이중 일부 제의에 대해 합의 도출

나. 66년 절차 문제를 제외한 통합문안에 합의   내용?

다. REV. 2에 포함할 결정문안 초안(새로운절차의 적용에 관한 경과 규정 및 4년이내재검토 관련)에 대한 대체적 합의 도출

라. NON-VIOLATION 문제는 EC 의 준비 부족을구실로한 지연 전략으로 토의 못함.

아. 타협상 분야와의 조화 문제 역시 추가 진전없음.

2. 이에 따라 명 10.24 오전 개최될 제도 분야 공식회의에서는 상기 1항 '가' 합의 사항을 반영한REVISED BRUSSELS TEXT 2부(CLEAN TEXT 및 변경내용 식별 가능한 ANNOTATED TEXT 각 1부), 통합문안 2부(역시 CLEAN 및 ANNOTATED TEXT 각 1부)및 브랏셀 TEXT 수정 제의중 미합의 사항 LIST를 배포, LACARTE 의장이 그간의 비공식 협의결과를 보고한후, 오후에 공식 회의를 속개참가국들의 의견을 청취키로 하였음.

3. 한편 10.25(금) 공식 회의에서는 제도 문제 및최종 의정서 문제를 검토할 예정이며, 분쟁해결 비공식 협의는 금번 공식 회의 기간 및 그이후에도 계속 미결 사항에 대한 협의를 진행할예정임. REV.2 문안이 언제 나올런지는 전망키어려우나 내주말까지 의장 초안을 작성해야 한다면내주말 경에 공식 회의를 재소집할 가능성도없지 않음.

4. 10.21-23 간 비공식 협의의 분야별 결과는아래와 같음.

통상국   2차보   구주국   정와대   안기부

           91.10.25   01:42 FN

외신 1과 통제관

0078

가. 브랏셀 TEXT 수정안 검토

0 브랏셀 TEXT 및 봉합문안의제목(TITLE)합의

- UNDERSTANDING ON RULES AND PROCEDURES GOVERNING THESETTLEMENT OF DISPUTESUNDER ART 22 AND 23 OF THE GATT

0 B 4,5 항 부패성 상품

- 부패성 상품 판정 주체가 불명한 점을 개선키위해 미국이 수정안을 제시했으나, 동 수정안자체도 완전치 못하고 별다른 대안도 발견할수없어 철회, 원안대로 유지키로 합의

0 D 3(D)항 PANELIST 명부

- 미국의 제의로 비정부 인사만 포함하는 현행ROSTER 를 체약국이 추천하는 정부, 비정부인사의 INDICATIVE LIST 로 대체키로 합의

0 E 4 항, 패널에 기 회부된바 있는 동일 사안처리

- 미국이 기존 문안(정상적 절차)대신 신속한절차(ON EXPIDITED BASIS)를 봉해 처리 하자는 요지의수정안을 제시했으나, EC, 카나다, 일본,홍콩등 다수국이 반대, 합의 도출 실패

0 G 4 항, 보고서 채택- 인도가 이사회의 보고서 채택 과정에 한해서만 새로운 REVERSE CONSENSUS 방식대신 전통적CONSENAUS 방식을 적용하되 60일 내 채택 여부가결정되지 못하면 상소할 수 있도록 하는 내용의수정안을 제시

- 제안국 인도는 자동화된 절차에서 경시될가능성이 있는 제 3국의 권리측면을 제안의이유로 강조하고 브라질, 멕시코가 이사회의 역할강화라는 차원에서 검토해볼 가치가 있다고 하였을뿐 대다수의 국가는 상소의 우려,상소주체의 변경 (승소국이 항소 하게 되는 상황),제 3국이 적극적인 입장을 표시한 전례가 거의없었음 등을 이유로 반대하여 합의 도출 실패

0 H 2(D) 상소 기구의 결정

- 미국이 상소기구가 기존 문안대로 패널의 결정을지지, 수정, 번복 하는데 추가하여 패널에 환송할수 있도록 하자는 내용을 제의

- 전체적 시한과의 관계, 법률 문제 한정 여부등 미진한 문제의 보완 작업을 거쳐 대체로 합의에 이르고 있으나 일본이 입장을 유보함으로써 추후겟고 논의키로 합의

0 K 5 이행감시

- 기존의 보고서 채택후 6개월후 이사회의 자동감시기능 발동을 합리적

PAGE 2

0079

이행기간설정후6개월로 수정 합의(미국 제의)

0 L 1,4,5,6 보상의 규모

- 미국이 기존 TEXT 의 APPROPRIATE IN THECIRCUMSTANCES 를 무효화 및 침해 수준에SUBSTANTIALLY EQUIVALENT 한 수준으로 수정 제의

- 멕시코가 기존 APPROPRIATE 표현은 23조의 내용그대로 이며, 이를 EQUIVALENT로 변경할 경우PUNITIVE NATURE 의 결여로 위반을 촉진하고 제28조 양허 재협상 규정의 존재 가치를 없애버릴우려가 있음을 들어 반대함으로써, 현재양국간에 절충 문안협의중(보상　보복보다　보고서권고　이행　선호, 보상　보복이 이루어진후에도이사회의감시 기능 계속 발동등)

- 아국은 이사회의 감시 기능 계속 발동은 K 5에 이미 규정되어 있음에 비추어 불필요하다는 의견을 개진한바, 미국도 TPRM, 사무총장의 년2회 STATUS REPORT 등 감시 기능이 있어 불필요하다는 데에는 공감하나 멕시코의 우려를 덜어 주기 위해 필요하다는 의견을 개진

0 ART 24조 12항(지방정부)합의 내용 추가

- 카나다가 갓트 조문 그룹 협상 결과를 각각 L 7항뒤 및 B 1 항앞에 추가할 것을 제의

- 대부분의 국가가 24조 12항 합의 TEXT 의 분할이 아니라는 전제하에 지지하였으나, CODE 에의 적용확대에 관한 우려를 염두에 둔 EC 가강하게 반대함으로서 계속논의키로함.

0 0. 4 중재에의 준용

- 기본 이행 조항(SECTION K)에 추가하여 보상관련조항(SECTION L)도 중재에 준용할 것을 내용으로하는 스위스 제안에 대해 EC 가 NON-VIOLATION분쟁과 관련 입장을유보함으로써 미합의

0 부속서(WORKING PROCEDURES)

- 연호 카나다 제의에 대해 PANEL 제 1차회의에의 제 3국 참가 관련 베네주엘라의제안(모든 제 3국이 동시에 출석 의견 개진)을추가하여 합의함.

0 기타 연호 D 2(A)항 (패널은 당사국 협의 단계거론 사항만 심사) 및 D 1(A)항(천번째이사회에서의 패널 설치) 제의는 철회됨.

나. 통합문안 작성

0 66년 절차 통합 협의 소그룹은 동 절차중 일부를통합 문안에 수용하는 방향으로

PAGE 3

0080

원칙적인 의견접근은 이루었으나 세부 사항에 관해서는 계속협의중임.

　다. 새로운 절차의 적용 및 재검토에 관한결정문안

　0 사무국이 비공식 협의 토의 내용에 입각 작성한 초안에 미국이 신절차 발효시이전의 모든 규정을 대체한다는 점을 명시하자고 주장한데 대해 브라질이 66년 절차의 통합 결과를 보고 검토해야 한다는 입장을 표명한 외에는 대체로 원칙적인 합의는 이루어진 상태임.

　라. NON-VIOLATION 분쟁

　0 동 문제에 대한 EC 의 계속된 지연전략에 대해, 미국이 최종 단계에서 기습적제안을 하려는 의도가 아닌가 우려된다고 하면서 강한불만을 제기

　0 이참사관이 개인적으로 접촉한 다수국 대표도 EC의 협상 태도에 대해 강한 불만을 갖고 있었으며, TRIPS, 농산물등과 관련 EC 로서 밝히기 어려운 사정이 있는 것으로만 추측하고있었음.

　마. 타협상 분야와의 조화 문제

　0 연호 각 그룹 의장앞 COVER LETTRE 초안을 LACARTE 의장에게 보고하였으나, 동 처리에 관해동 의장이 어떤 방침을 갖고 있는지 사무국으로서도 알수 없다 함.

　(단 공식 회의가 끝나기 까지는 아무런 행동도 취하지 않을 것이라는 점은 확실)
끝

　(대사 박수길-국장)

PAGE 4

0081

외　무　부

종　별 :

번　호 : GVW-2154　　　　　　　　　　　일　시 : 91 1028 1500

수　신 : 장관(봉기)

발　신 : 주 제네바 대사

제　목 : UR/제도 분야 공식회의

　　연: GVW-2121

　　표제 회의가 LACARTE 의장 주재로 10.24-25양일간 개최된바, 동 결과 아래 보고함.(이성주 참사관 참석)

　　1. 10.24 공식회의(분쟁해결)

　　0 오전 회의시 분쟁해결 관련 연호로 보고한 문서배포와 함께 LACARTE 의장이그간의 비공식협의 경위를 간략히 설명하였음.

　　0 오후 회의에서 각국의 COMMENTS 를 요청하였으나 어느 국가도 발언하지 않음으로써 의장은 각국이 입장을 공약(COMMIT)하지 않는다는 것을 전제로 현 단계에서이에 대한 컨센서스가 있는것으로 간주한다고 하고 회의를 마침.(일방 조치억제,절차의 자동화등 기존 주요 쟁점에 대한 괄호는 계속 남아 있음)

　　2. 10.25 공식회의(최종의정서)

　　0 91. 3.25 사무국 NON-PAPER 에 대한 아국 포함 22개국이 SINGLE UNDERTAKING 및MTO 설립 문제에관한 입장을 표명함.

　　0 SINGLE UNDERTAKING 문제에 대해서는 미국, EC,카나다, 스위스, 호주, 헝가리,스웨덴, 뉴질랜드,일본, 오지리, 알젠틴, 홍콩, 태국이 지지 입장을 브라질, 베네주엘라, 탄자니아, 칠레, 인도가 반대입장을, 이스라엘 및 멕시코가 좀더 두고 보아야한다는 입장을 표명함.

　　0 MTO 설립 문제에 관해서는 EC 가 설립필요성(DESIRABLILITY)에 대한 단순한확인보다, 실제로 설립될수 있도록 최종 의정서에의해 실효적 결정(EFFECTIVE DECISION)이 내려져야할 것이라고 강조하면서, 현 단계에서 상정할 수있는 MTO 의 역할로서분쟁해결 절차의 적용과 TPRM 의 시행의 2가지 예를 들었음.

　　이에 대해 카나다, 호주가 동조 입장을 표명하였고, 일본은 5항 및 6항이

통상국　　2차보　　분석관　　청와대　　안기부

PAGE 1　　　　　　　　　　　　　　　　　　　91.10.29　　03:03 DW

　　　　　　　　　　　　　　　　　　　　　　외신 1과 통제관

　　　　　　　　　　　　　　　　　　　　　　　　　0082

적절히균형이 이루어졌다는 의견을 밝혔으며, 여타 대다수 발언국은 구조,회원, 기능,
UR협상결과,   여타   국제기구와의   관련성등과   관련 추가 검토가 필요하며,
OPEN-MINDED의 입장에서 동 작업에 참여할 의사를 밝혔음.(베네주엘라는 최근 ITO관련
UNCTAD 내논의에 언급하면서 타국제기구의 견해도 아울러 참작해야 할 것이라는
의견을 개진함.)

    0 아국은 SINGLE UNDERTAKING 을 지지하나 이를위해서는 균형된 협상 결과
도출이중요하다는점 및 MTO 설립문제에 관한 논의에 OPEN-MINED 한 입장에서 참여할
용의가있음을 밝혔음.

    0 한편 MTO 의 SCOPE OF RESPONSIBILITY 와 관련GATT 및 UR 결과외에 추가적
임무를 상정하고있는가 하는 LACARTE 의장의 질문 및 SINGLEUNDERTAKING 을
수락하지않는 국가의 회원자격에 관한 말레이시아의 질문에 대해, EC는 UR 협상
결과로 나오는 무역의 모든 측면(ALL ASPECTS OF TRADE EMERGING OUT OF THE UR)이
대상이 되나, 현 단계에서는 특정한 새로운 사항(ANYTHING NEW)를 제시한 것은
아니며, SINGLEUNDERTAKING 불수락 국가는 상당한 문제점이 있을 것이라고만 답변함.

    3. 차기회의 일정
    의장은 당분간 비공식 협의를 계속한후 내주말경 공식회의를 재 소집할
필요가있다고 판단되므로 각국이 이에 대비해 줄것을 요망함.(10.25 분쟁해결 비공식
협의시 LINDEN 고문은 동 공식 회의를 10.31 오후 개최키로 결정하였다고 밝혔음.)끝
    (대사 박수길-국장)

PAGE 2

0083

외 무 부

종 별 :

번 호 : GVW-2155

수 신 : 장관(봉기)

발 신 : 주제네바대사

제 목 : UR/분쟁해결 비공식 협의

일 시 : 91 1028 1500

연:(1) GVW-2121

(2) GVW-2154

1. 연호 (2) 제도분야 공식회의기간(10.24-25)중 계속된 분쟁해결관련 비공식협의(LACARTE 의장 또는 LINDEN 고문 주재, 이성주 참사관 참석) 결과 요지를 아래보고함.

가. EC 가 NON-VIOLATION 분쟁관련 P.1항 기존 문안을 대폭 간소화한 문안을 제시, 이에대한 토의진행

나. 중재자가 합리적 이행기간을 결정함에 있어 기본 GUIDELINE 을 정할 것을내용으로 하는 미국수정안 검토

다. 86년 절차 통합문제 검토

2. 향후 협의 일정관련 사무국은 10.28.주간에도 비공식 협의를 계속하여 미결사항을 논의해나가되, 제도분야 공식회의가 10.31.오후로 확정되었고 동 공식회의이후에는 LACARTE 의장이 자신의 TEXT 를 준비해야 하므로 동일자를 모든 문제에관한 CUT-OFF DATE 로 받아들여야 하며, 따라서 10.28 부터는 이제까지 논의해온사항외에 AUTOMATICITY 문제, 일방조치억제공약 문제(M 항) 및 FINAL ACT 에 관한논의도 추가돼야 할 것이라고 밝힘. LACARTE 의장도 각국이 기술적 사항에 대한 기존입장에 집착하는 점에 불만을 표시하면서 핵심적인 사항(REAL THINGS)에 대한 논의가남아 있음을 상기시켰음.

2. 10.24-25 비공식 협의 결과 상세는 아래와 같음.

가. NV 분쟁

O 10.24. EC 가 23조 1항 B 에 해당되는 모든 NV 분쟁에 특별 절차를 적용할 것을내용으로 하는 수정안(P.1)을 제시하면서, 23조1항 C관련 분쟁(0.6)에 관해서는

통상국   2차보   분석관   청와대   안기부

91.10.29   02:38 DW

외신 1과 통제관

0084

신축적인 입장임을 표명

　- EC 는 동 제안 설명에서 23조 1항 B의 경우 제소국의 입증의무, 해당조치 철폐의무 부재, 패널, 상소기구 판정이후 부터 이행관련 다소 상이한 과정을 거치는 점외에는 일반 분쟁과 다름이 없음을 강조

　O 미국, 일본, 홍콩, 카나다등 대부분의 국가는 상기 EC 의 제의가 이제까지 쟁점이 되어왔던 NV 분쟁의 대상범위 논의를 백지화 하는 처사라고 비난하면서, 일반분쟁과 큰 차이가 없다면서 별도항에 규정하려는 의도를 집중 추구함.(놀웨이만이 전반적차원에서 NV 분쟁과 일반 분쟁을 구분하는 것이 유익할수도 있다는 의견을 개진, EC입장에 다소 동조적 태도를 보임)

　O EC 는 별도항 유지 이유가 상기 3가지 차이점이 있기때문이며, EC 로서는 양보를 많이 했으며, 별도항 유지는 더이상 물러설수 없는 아주 중요한(POLITICAL) 잇슈라는 입장을 반복 피력함(미국은 상기 차이점을 관련 여타 조항에 통합하는 안을10.25 제출)

　O EC 는 또한 패널.상소기구 결정 채택이후 이행절차 관련 TIME FRAME 에 불균형있다고 지적(일반 분쟁의 경우, RPOT 결정 90일, 불이행시 보복승인 30일, 보복규모에 대한 중재 60일, NV 분쟁의 경우, 90일내 RPOT 및보상규모가 동시에 결정)하고150일로 연장을 요구함.

　O LACARTE 의장은 23조 1항 A CASE 분쟁의 경우에도 최종 판정이 NV 로 날 수 있고, 반대로 B CASE는 GATT 위반 사례로 판정이 날 수있으며, C CASE 역시 같은 개연성이 있음을 지적, 23조 1항 B만 언급한 EC안의 문제점을 지적함.

　O P 6항에 대해서는 대부분의 국가가 OPTION B를 선호하고, 스위스가 C CASE 분쟁의 경우 신축성 있는 절차의 필요성을 강조하면서 WORKING PARTY 회부 방안 검토의견을 제시함에따라 EC 가 10.25.SPECIAL W.P 에 회부, 동S.W.P.는 12개월내 보고서제출, 이사회에서의 컨센서스 방식에 의한 보고서 채택을 내용으로하는 문안을 제시했으나, 과거 대부분의 WORKINGPARTY 가 유명무실, 비효율적이었던 점에 비추어호응을 받지 못함.

　O 한편 알젠틴은 P 3항 NV 의 경우 해당조치 철폐의무 없다는 문안과 관련 이는이사회의 기능을 약화시키는 것이라 하여 강한 반대입장을 표명함.

　나. 합리적 이행기간의 GUIDELINE

　O 미국이 10.24.일반적 GUIDELINE 으로서 이행기간을 12개월 이내로 하되, 상황에

PAGE 2

0085

따라서 가감할 수 있도록 하는 내용의 문안을 K 항에 추가할 것을 제의하고 멕시코및 카나다가 이를 지지함(특히 멕시코는 최대기간을 2년으로 한정하고 2년이 넘을경우 양허정지 승인요청을 가능토록하자고 주장하였으며, 인도도 RPOT 가 너무 장기간일경우 MANDATORY COMPENSATION 이 있어야 한다는 입장을 피력함)

0 아국은 각국의 국내제도의 차이, 분쟁사안별 특수성을 무시한 일률적인 최대기간 설정을 받아들이기 곤란하다는 입장을 밝히고, GUIDELINE 설정 문제에 대해서는대부분의 국가가 원칙적인 지지를 하는 대세를 감안 이에 반대치는 않으나 12개월이라는 기간의 적정성 여부에는 의문이 있다고 발언한바, 일본도 같은 견해를 표명하였고, 기타 스위스, 브라질, 놀웨이도 유사한 입장을 표시함.

다. 66년 절차 통합

0 소그룹 회의에서 구체적 진전이 없으므로 10.24.비공식 협의시 LACARTE 의장이동문제를 유도한바, 미국,카나다,뉴질랜드,호주등 선진국이 OPTION 2(일반절차 해당부분에 통합) 선호입장을 표시하였으나 멕시코는 OPTION 1(전체를 별항으로 통합)이동 절차의 INTEGRITY를 깨지 않기때문에 더 선호하며, 동 OPTION이라면 토의 용의있으나 OPTION 2 토의는 본부훈령을 요한다고 답변한후, 89.4월 중간 평가합의는양절차의 공존을 인정(1.10항)하고 있음을 지적함.

0 이에대해 미국은 양절차의 5개 차이점을 구체적으로 열거한 대비표를 제시하고중간 평가합의의 잠정적 성격을 상기시킴

0 10.25. 협의시 미국은 OPTION 1 에 입각 브랏셀 TEXT A 5 대체문안(새로운 절차가 기존의 모든절차를 대체하나, 예외적으로 개도국 제소 분쟁의경우 제소국이 선택할 경우 새로운 절차에 대한 대안(ALTERNATIVE) 로 66년 절차에 불일치 하지않는 한89.4월 중간 평가 합의 절차를 적용)을 제시하였으나, 시간 부족으로 토의치 못하고주말에 소그룹 회의를 계속키로 함.

라. 기타사항

0 보상의 규모(L 1,4,5,6)

- 연호 문안대로 합의

0 동일 사안 처리(E 4)

- 미국이 기존 TEXT E 4 항의 NORMAL 을삭제하고 패널이 동절차를 단축할 수도있다(MAY)는 내용의 양보안 제시

0 상소기구 결정, 패널 환송 (H 2 D)

PAGE 3

0086

- 미국이 연호 제안을 철회

0 패널 및 송소기구의 권고 내용(F)

- 멕시코가 선별적 적용으로 인한 차별을 예방키위해 F 항 마지막 문장(권고사항 이행에관한 방안 제시)의 MAY SUGGEST 를 SHOULD NORMALLY SUGGEST 로 변경할 것을 제의한바, 미국이 거의 선례가 없었다는 점, 패널에 과중한 부담초래 가능성,비현실적 방안 제시 우려등을 들어 강하게 반대하고, 모든 국가가 이에 동조하였으나멕시코는 이 문제는 계속 거론할 예정이라고 말함.

0 보복의 사전 승인(L 7)

- 멕시코가 상기 '나'항 관련 L 7 항의 BRACKET 제거를 주장하였으나, 아국(승소국으로 하여금 합의에 의한 보상액 결정 노력 유인 제거), 스위스(패소국에 대한부당한 압력), 놀웨이(RPOT 내 불이행을 단정), 일본(점진적 이행시 적용방법)등이반대하고, EC도 NV 분쟁과 관련하여 입장을 유보함.(미국은 멕시코에 동조적 입장)

- 10.25 사무국이 RPOT 만료 60일전 요청시 사전승인이 가능토록하는 절충안을제시하였으나, 멕시코는 BRACKET 제거가 안되면 수락할수없다는 입장을 고수함. 끝

(대사 박수길-국장)

외 무 부

종 별 :

번 호 : GVW-2192

일 시 : 91 1030 1730

수 신 : 장 관(봉기)

발 신 : 주 제네바대사

제 목 : UR 분쟁해결 비공식 협의

연: GVW-2155

표제 비공식협의가 LACARTE 의장 주재하에 10.28-29 양일간 계속되어 10.28 협의시에는 연호공식 회의시 배포된 REVISED BRUSSLES TEXTS(91.10.23) 상의 괄호 내용을 1차 검토하였으며, 10.29 협의에서는 최근 제시된 수정 제의를 토의하였는 바, 동결과를 아래 보고함.(이성우참사관 참석)

1. 10.23 TEXT 검토(괄호 쟁점)

가. 패널 설치 시한(D. 1, A)

O 설치시점(첫번째 또는 두번째 이사회) 관련의장이 두번째 이사회로 하되 첫번째와 두번째 이사회의 간격을 30일을 넘기지 않는 절충안을 제시, 각국의 의견을 문의한 바, 적극적인 반대의사가 없었으므로 동 문제에 관해서는 타결 가능성이 보인다고 언급하였으나, 구체적 결론은 보류

O 'OTHERWISE' 또는 NOT TO ESTABLISH'에 관해서는 기존 입장 대립

나. 패널 활동기간(D.6.F.)

O 아국은 예외적 상황에 대비한 신축성 유지가 필요하다는 입장에서 SHOULD 지지, 일본은 SHOULD지지하나 QUALIFIED SHALL 도 검토 용의가 있음을 표명

O 놀웨이는 전체 시한(K.3) 범위내에서 매단계별로는 신축성을 부여함이 바람직하다고하면서 SHALL 을 주장하고 다수국이 동조

O 의장은 전체적인 분위기가 SHOULD 선호임을 파악했다고 언급

다. 패널 및 상소 기구 권고(F)

O NON-VIOLATION 분쟁과 관련된 사항이므로 검토생략

라. 패널 보고서 채택 (G.4)

O EC, 놀웨이가 OTHERWISE 선호 입장을 표명하고, 인도는 G 4 관련 자국의 수정안

통상국   2차보

91.10.31   09:56 WH

외신 1과 통제관

0088

에 대한 절충이 진행중임을 상기 시킴.

　마. 상소기구 시한(HLE)

　0 의장이 상소기구는 패널에 비해 상당히 제한된임무가 부여되는 점을 고려 SHALL 로 합의토록 권유하였으나, 아국, 일본, 카나다, EC, 홍콩등이 반대

　사. 상소기구 보고서 채택(H.3)

　0 기존 입장 대립 계속

　아. 전체 시한(K.3)

　0 의장이 아무리 복잡한 분제이더라도 개선, 강화된 절차하에서는 시한을 지키는데 큰 문제가 없을 것으로 본다는 의견을 제시하고 합의를 유도

　0 상기 '나'항 놀웨이의 의견(전체 시한은 절대시한화, 단계별 시한은 신축성 부여) 관련 호주, 스위스, EC, 브라질, 아국, 일본등이 예외적 상황 발생 가능성을 고려치않고 절대시한화하는데 대한 위험성을 지적하고 둘째 BRACKET를 지지

　0 미국은 예외적 상황임을 누가 판정하느냐 하는 문제에 대한 해결책이 없으면 무한정 지연될 가능성이 높으므로 받아들일수 없다는 입장

　0 뉴질랜드가 ' UNLESS THERE ARE EXCEPTIONALCIRCUMSTANCES AND THE PARTIES AGREE'의 절충안을 제안하고 호주, 홍콩이 고려 가능하다는 의견을 피력하였으나 결론도출 실패

　자. 보복의 자동 승인(L.3)

　0 기존 입장 대립 계속(아국, 브라질은'OTHERWISE', 뉴질랜드, 홍콩, 호주는 'NOT TO'지지 입장 표명)

　차. 보복의 사전 승인(L.7)

　0 RPOT 만료 60일전 요청시 사전 승인이 가능토록하는 연호 절충안 (별첨 1)을 미국, 카나다가 지지

　0 EC, 아국, 일본, 태국, 브라질은 60 일전요청의 단서가 있더라도 BRACKET 유지필요 주장

　카. 일방 조치 억제(M)

　0 미국이 동 조항은 여전히 여타 조항과 연계되있는 정치적 잇슈라고 하고 (III)항 일방 조치에 대한 정의의 불충분 (패널 절차 BLOCKAGE, 권고 불준수도 일방 조치에 해당된다는 입장)

　(IV) 항의 경우 GATT 10 조에 대한 현문안상의 문제점을 지적

PAGE 2

0089

O EC 는 동 조항이 EC 에게도 정치적으로 극히 민감한 잇슈라고 반박하였으며, 기타 아국 포함 거의 대다수 국가가 동 조항의 중요성을 강조

O 의장의 대다수 국가의 견해를 참작, 미국이 동문제를 긍정적으로 검토해 줄것을 촉구

2. 각종 수정제의검토

가. 패널 및 상소기구 권고(F)

O 분쟁해결 절차가 자동화 되면서 패널보고서등이 GATT 가 명시적으로 규정하고있지않은 사항에 대해 새로운 RULE 을 설정하는 효과를 내서는 곤란하다는 미국의 우려가 반영되어 이미 A 2 에 있는 내용과 동일한 문안(당사국의 권리 의무에 변경 초래불가)을F2 로 신설키로 합의(별첨 2)

나. NON-VIOLATION 분쟁(P)

O P6 항 관련 연호 스위스 의견을 반영, EC 가제시한 C 케이스 관련 수정안(별첨6)에 대해WORKING PARTY 는 문제가 많으므로 PANEL 에 회부하되, H.F.L 항을 적용치않기로 하면 해결될수 있을 것이라는 의견을 제시한 바, EC가 동 내용을 미국이 서면제안해 줄것을 요청.

O 홍콩은 상기 미국의 의도가 PANEL 에 회부하되 완화된 절차를 적용하려는 것이라면 89.4월 중간평가 합의 시점까지의 절차를 적용하는 것으로 하면 더욱 간단히 해결 될 문제라는 의견을 제시함으로써, 의장이 미국과 홍콩이 문안을 협의 줄것을 요청

O P 1 항에 대해서는 연호 EC 수정안 (별첨3)에 대해 알젠틴이 대안 (별첨 4)을제시한바이에 대해 EC 가 강력 반대의사를 표명한외에는 별다른 진전없음.

다. 66년 절차 통합 문제

O 연호 이후 이해관계 소그룹에서도 의견 접근을 보지 못함으로써, 동 소그룹은 OPTION 1(개도국이 희망하면 66 절차를 선택토록 하는 TWO TIER SYSTEM)과 OPSTION 2(66 절차를 완전 폐기)를 동시에 담은 PAPER(별첨 7)를 제시

O 미국, EC, 일본이 OPTION 2 를 멕시코, 브라질, 칠레가 OPTION 1 을 주장 합의도출 실패

첨부: 1. L. 7 관련 사무국 수정안

2. F 항 관련 합의문안

3. P 1 항관련 EC 제안

PAGE 3

0090

4. P 1 항 관련 알젠틴 제안

5. P 1,6 항 관련 미국제안

6. P 6 항관련 EC 제안

7. 66 절차 관련 소그룹 PAPER. Q끝

(GVW(F)-462)

(대사 박수길-국장)

- 9 -

25.10.91 (별첨 1)

(p.m.)

VII. Paragraph L.7

[7. The level [amount] of suspension shall, if requested sixty days before the end of the reasonable period of time by one of the parties, be determined before expiry of the reasonable period of time, in accordance with the relevant procedures under paragraphs L.3, L.4 and L.5 above, and on the understanding that such suspension shall not come into effect before the Council has granted the authorization provided for in paragraph L.3.]

0092

(벽.쳡 2)   - 6 -

24.10.91   (US proposal)

5.15 p.m.

<u>IV. Add the following paragraph to section F of Brussels Text:</u>

F.2 In their findings and recommendations, the panel and appellate body
cannot add to or diminish the rights and obligations provided in the
General Agreement.

                        = Agreed =

(벽첨 3)   - 11 -

24.10.91 (5 p.m.)   (EEC proposal)

IX.   P. <u>Non-Violation</u>

P.1 The procedures in this Understanding shall apply, subject to the provisions of paragraphs P.2 through P.5 below, if and to the extent that a panel or the appellate body determines that the case brought before it concerns nullification or impairment of benefits under the General Agreement without violation thereof within the meaning of Article XXIII:1(b).

0094

(별첨 4)

Argentine
28-10-91 P.5

F. PANEL AND APPELLATE BODY RECOMMENDATIONS

Option 1: In the fifth line insert after the words "shall recommend" the following "either the withdrawal or modification of the measure or that the contracting party concerned make a mutually satisfactory adjustment".

Option 2: "the solution it considers appropriate to restore the balance of rights and obligations under the General Agreement, including the withdrawal or modification of the measure".

P. NON- VIOLATION COMPLAINTS

P.1.

After the words "General Agreement" in the fifth line add the following sentence "nullify or impair any benefit accruing to it directly or indirectly or impedes the attainment of any objective under the General Agreement".

P.3.

New text.

"Where a measure has been found to constitute a case of nullification or impairment of benefits under the General Agreement the panel or the appellate body shall recommend that the measure be withdrawn or modify or the contracting party concerned make a mutually satisfactory adjustment".

P.4.

In the second line from the bottom replace "but" for the word "and".
In the last line delete the word "not".

P.5.

Mantain only: "The provisions of Section L shall apply".

P.6.

Delete both options.

(별첨 5)   - 12 -

25.10.91   *Exercise*

                                            (~~US proposal~~)

IX. bis   Non-violation

Insert the following new paragraph between D.6(d) and D.6(e):

(d bis)   If the complaint concerns nullification or impairment of benefits
under the General Agreement without violation thereof, within the meaning
of Article XXIII:1(b), the complaining contracting party shall include a
detailed justification in support of such complaint in its written
submission.

Revise para K.2 to read:

2.   At a Council meeting held within thirty days of the adoption of the
panel or appellate body report, the contracting party concerned shall
inform the Council of its intentions in respect of implementation of the
recommendations and rulings under Article XXIII:2.

(a)   If the panel or appellate body has found that a measure is
inconsistent with the General Agreement, and if it is impracticable with
the General Agreement, and if it is impracticable to comply immediately
with the recommendations and rulings, the contracting party concerned shall
have a reasonable period of time in which to do so. The reasonable period
of time shall be:

   (i) the period of time proposed by the contracting party concerned,
   provided that such period is approved by the Council; or, in the
   absence of such approval;

   (ii) a period of time mutually agreed by the parties to the dispute
   within forty-five days following adoption of the recommendations and
   rulings; or, in the absence of such agreement;

   (iii) a period of time determined through binding arbitration within
   ninety days following adoption of the recommendations and rulings.

0096

- 13 -

(b)   If and to the extent that the panel or appellate body has determined
      that the case brought before it concerns nullification or impairment
      of benefits under the General Agreement without violation thereof,
      within the meaning of Article XXIII:1(b), and if the parties do not
      agree, within forty-five days following adoption, that the
      implementation proposed by the party concerned will result in a
      mutually satisfactory adjustment, the reasonable period of time for
      implementation and the level of benefits which have been nullified or
      impaired shall be determined through binding arbitration within 90
      days following adoption.

Revise section F to read:

Where a panel or the appellate body concludes that a measure is
inconsistent with the General Agreement, it shall recommend that the
contracting party concerned bring the measure into conformity with the
General Agreement. Where a measure has been found to constitute a case of
nullification or impairment of benefits under the General Agreement without
violation thereof, there is no obligation to withdraw [or modify] the
measure. However, in such cases, the panel or the appellate body shall
recommend that the contracting party concerned make a mutually satisfactory
adjustment. In addition to its recommendations, the panel or appellate
body may suggest ways in which the contracting party concerned could
implement the recommendations.

Add following footnote to para L.3:

   [1] In cases concerning nullification or impairment of benefits under
the General Agreement without violation thereof, the arbitrator's decision
provided for in paragraph K.2(b) with respect to the level of benefits
shall be in lieu of the arbitration provided for in paragraph L.3.

0097

(별첨 6)   - 14 -

25.10.91

X. Article XXIII:1(c) Complaints

1.   The Council shall refer any complaint brought under Article XXIII:1(c)
to a special working party. This working party will examine the facts of
the matter in the light of the relevant provisions of the General
Agreement; it will signal any general problems affecting the General
Agreement as a whole;   it will address recommendations for a mutually
satisfactory adjustment to the parties and/or issue general recommendations
to the CONTRACTING PARTIES. The report of the special working party will
be issued within twelve months.

2.   On the basis of the report, the Council may take appropriate action by
consensus.

(별첨7)

29.10.91

OPTION :

Delete section 26, "Special Procedures:" and replace paragraph
1.10 with the following two paragraphs:

1.10 This Understanding shall be applied only with respect to new
requests under Article XXII:1 and XXIII:1 made on or after
the date of entry into force of this Understanding. With
respect to disputes for which the request under Article
XXII:1 or XXIII:1 was made before the date of entry into
force of this Understanding, GATT dispute settlement rules
and procedures in effect immediately prior to the date of
entry into force of this Understanding shall continue to
apply.

1.11 Notwithstanding paragraph 1.10 above, if a complaint is brought by a
developing contracting party, that contracting party may choose to
apply, as an alternative to this Understanding, the provisions of the
Decision of the CONTRACTING PARTIES of 5 April 1966 (BISD 14S/18),
instead of the provisions of this Understanding. In that event, the
same procedures shall apply that would have applied to cases brought
pursuant to the 1966 decision immediately prior to the date of entry
into force of this Understanding, including the procedures contained
in the Decision of the Council of 12 April 1989 (BISD 36S/21).

OPTION 2

Delete section 26, "Special Procedures:" and replace paragraph
1.10 with the following:

1.10 This Understanding shall be applied with respect to all new
requests under Article XXII:1 and XXIII:1 made on or after
the date of entry into force of this Understanding. With
respect to disputes for which the request under Article
XXII:1 or XXIII:1 was made before the date of entry into
force of this Understanding, GATT dispute settlement rules
and procedures in effect immediately prior to the date of
entry into force of this Understanding shall continue to
apply.

0099

외 무 부

종 별 :

번 호 : GVW-2193
일 시 : 91 1030 1730

수 신 : 장관(통기)

발 신 : 주 제네바 대사

제 목 : UR/분쟁해결 비공식 협의

91.10.28 현재 표제 협의 미결 쟁점 사항 LIST 를별첨 송부 함.

별첨: 상기 LIST. (GVW(F)-463)

(대사 박수길-국장)

통상국	장관	차관	1차보	2차보	외정실	분석관	정와대	안기부

91.10.31   08:56 BX

외신 1과   통제관

0100

28.10.91

Outstanding proposals with respect to the revised Brussels text are listed hereunder. The relevant texts are annexed. Further proposals will be circulated separately.

I.   Paragraph A.5   1966 Procedures (US proposal)
I. bis Paragraph A.5   1966 Procedures (Mexican proposal)

II.   Paragraph B.1 (before):   Article XXIV:12 (Canadian proposal)

III. Paragraph E.4:   Measures previously examined by a panel
                                (US proposal)

IV   Paragraph F.2:   Function of panel and appellate body
                                (US proposal)

V.   Paragraph G.4:   Adoption of panel reports (Indian proposal)

VI.   Paragraph K.3:   Reasonable Period Guidelines (US proposal)

VII. Paragraph L.7:   Level of suspension

VII.bis Paragraph L.7 (after):   Article XXIV:12 (Canadian proposal)

VIII. Paragraph O.4:   Arbitration (Swiss proposal)

IX.   Section P: Non-Violation (Article
                                XXIII:1(b))

IX. bis Paragraph D.6(d bis)
        Paragraph K.2
        Section F
        footnote to para L.3: Non-Violation (US proposal)

X.   Section P: Article XXIII:1(c)

Consolidated Text

    The situation of the Decision of 5 April 1966, which appears in Section 26, remains outstanding.

0101

- 2 -

25.10.91   (US proposal)

I.   Paragraph A.5

Replace para A.5 with the following:

This Understanding shall repeal and replace all earlier decisions of the
CONTRACTING PARTIES with respect to dispute settlement rules and
procedures, except as follows:

(a) The Decision of 5 April 1966 (BISD 14S/18) may be applied, as an
alternative to the rules and procedures provided in this
Understanding, to complaints brought by developing countries choosing
to apply the 1966 procedures instead of this Understanding. In such
cases, the procedures contained in the Decision of the Council of 12
April 1989 (BISD 36S/21) shall apply to such disputes to the extent
that the 1989 procedures are not inconsistent with the 1966
procedures.

(b) With regard to disputes for which the request under Article
XXII:1 of XXIII:1 was made before the date of entry into force of this
Understanding, it is agreed that GATT dispute settlement rules and
procedures in effect immediately prior to the date of entry into force
of this Understanding shall continue to apply to those disputes.

0102

- 3 -

25.10.91   (Mexican proposal)
(5.30 p.m.)

<u>I. bis Paragraph A.5</u>

All the points set out in this Understanding shall be applied as a
complement to and without prejudice to any provision on special and
differential treatment for developing contracting parties in previous
instruments on dispute settlement including the CONTRACTING PARTIES'
Decision of 5 April 1966 (BISD 14S/18).

- 4 -

23.10.91   (Canadian proposal)
19.15

II. Provisions Governing All Regional and Local Levels of Government

PLACE AFTER PARAGRAPH L.7

L.7 bis The dispute settlement provisions of the General Agreement may be invoked in respect of measures affecting its observance taken by regional or local governments or authorities within the territory of a contracting party. When the CONTRACTING PARTIES have ruled that a provision of the General Agreement has not been observed, the responsible contracting party shall take such reasonable measures as may be available to it to ensure its observance. The provisions relating to compensation and suspension of concessions or other obligations apply in cases where it has not been possible to secure such observance.[1]

PLACE BEFORE PARAGRAPH B.1

B.1 bis Each contracting party undertakes to accord sympathetic consideration to and afford adequate opportunity for consultation regarding any representations made by another contracting party concerning measures affecting the operation of the General Agreement taken within the territory of the former.

---

[1]Inclusion of paragraphs L.7bis and B.1bis herein are conditioned on inclusion of identical paragraphs in 'The Understanding on the Interpretation of Article XXIV of the General Agreement on Tariffs and Trade'. Should that Understanding be amended, the question of inclusion of the paragraphs herein shall be reconsidered.

0104

- 5 -

(US proposal)

III.   Measures Previously Examined by a Panel

Modify paragraph E.4 of the 25 March 1991 text to read:

"If a third party considers a measure already the subject of a panel nullifies or impairs benefits accruing to it under the General Agreement, and if that party's complaint is limited to the same specific measure identified in the request for the previous panel, that party may have recourse to GATT dispute settlement procedures on an expedited basis."

25.10.91 (12 p.m.)

(US proposal)

Modify E.4

Add a new third sentence:

"Where the panel determines that such a situation is involved, it may shorten the timetable for the panel process originally set pursuant to paragraph D.6(c)."

0105

- 6 -

24.10.91   (US proposal)
5.15 p.m.

IV. Add the following paragraph to section F of Brussels Text:

F.2 In their findings and recommendations, the panel and appellate body cannot add to or diminish the rights and obligations provided in the General Agreement.

= Agreed =

0106

- 7 -

(Indian proposal)

Adoption of Panel Reports

V. Proposal for substituting paragraph G.4

While considering adoption of the panel report, the Council shall follow the traditional practice of consensus. If, within sixty days of the issuance of the report to the contracting parties, the report has not been adopted by the Council, either of the disputants would be free to refer the matter to the Appellate Body.

0107

- 8 -

24.10.91 (5.15 p.m.)   (US proposal)

VI. Reasonable Period Guidelines

Add a new paragraph K.3 and renumber the following paragraphs accordingly:

Paragraph K.3:

In arbitration pursuant to paragraph K.2(c), a guideline for the arbitrator should be that the reasonable period of time to implement panel or appellate body recommendations should not exceed twelve months from the adoption of a panel or appellate body report. However, that time may be shorter or longer, depending upon the particular circumstances.

0108

- 9 -

25.10.91

(p.m.)

VII. Paragraph L.7

or less

[7. The <u>level</u> [amount] of suspension shall, if requested <u>sixty days before</u>
<u>the end of the reasonable period of time</u> by one of the parties, be
determined before expiry of the reasonable period of time, in accordance
with the relevant procedures under paragraph<u>s</u> L.3, <u>L.4 and L.5</u> above, and
on the understanding that such suspension shall not come into effect before
the Council has granted the authorization provided for in paragraph L.3.]

0109

- 10 -

VIII. Arbitration   (Swiss proposal)

Modify paragraph 0.4 to read:

0.4, Sections K and L of this Understanding shall apply _mutatis mutandis_ to arbitration awards.

0110

- 11 -

24.10.91 (5 p.m.)   (EEC proposal)

IX.   P.   <u>Non-Violation</u>

P.1 The procedures in this Understanding shall apply, subject to the
provisions of paragraphs P.2 through P.5 below, if and to the extent that a
panel or the appellate body determines that the case brought before it
concerns nullification or impairment of benefits under the General
Agreement without violation thereof   within the meaning of Article
XXIII:1(b).

0111

- 12 -

25.10.91   (~~US proposal~~)

IX. bis   Non-violation

Insert the following new paragraph between D.6(d) and D.6(e):

(d bis)   If the complaint concerns nullification or impairment of benefits
under the General Agreement without violation thereof, within the meaning
of Article XXIII:1(b), the complaining contracting party shall include a
detailed justification in support of such complaint in its written
submission.

Revise para K.2 to read:

2.   At a Council meeting held within thirty days of the adoption of the
panel or appellate body report, the contracting party concerned shall
inform the Council of its intentions in respect of implementation of the
recommendations and rulings under Article XXIII:2.

(a)   If the panel or appellate body has found that a measure is
inconsistent with the General Agreement, and if it is impracticable with
the General Agreement, and if it is impracticable to comply immediately
with the recommendations and rulings, the contracting party concerned shall
have a reasonable period of time in which to do so. The reasonable period
of time shall be:

     (i)   the period of time proposed by the contracting party concerned,
     provided that such period is approved by the Council; or, in the
     absence of such approval;

     (ii)   a period of time mutually agreed by the parties to the dispute
     within forty-five days following adoption of the recommendations and
     rulings; or, in the absence of such agreement;

     (iii)   a period of time determined through binding arbitration within
     ninety days following adoption of the recommendations and rulings.

0112

(b) If and to the extent that the panel or appellate body has determined that the case brought before it concerns nullification or impairment of benefits under the General Agreement without violation thereof, within the meaning of Article XXIII:1(b), and if the parties do not agree, within forty-five days following adoption, that the implementation proposed by the party concerned will result in a mutually satisfactory adjustment, the reasonable period of time for implementation and the level of benefits which have been nullified or impaired shall be determined through binding arbitration within 90 days following adoption.

Revise section F to read:

Where a panel or the appellate body concludes that a measure is inconsistent with the General Agreement, it shall recommend that the contracting party concerned bring the measure into conformity with the General Agreement. Where a measure has been found to constitute a case of nullification or impairment of benefits under the General Agreement without violation thereof, there is no obligation to withdraw [or modify] the measure. However, in such cases, the panel or the appellate body shall recommend that the contracting party concerned make a mutually satisfactory adjustment. In addition to its recommendations, the panel or appellate body may suggest ways in which the contracting party concerned could implement the recommendations.

Add following footnote to para L.3:

1 In cases concerning nullification or impairment of benefits under the General Agreement without violation thereof, the arbitrator's decision provided for in paragraph K.2(b) with respect to the level of benefits shall be in lieu of the arbitration provided for in paragraph L.3.

0113

25.10.91

X. Article XXIII:1(c) Complaints

1.   The Council shall refer any complaint brought under Article XXIII:1(c) to a special working party. This working party will examine the facts of the matter in the light of the relevant provisions of the General Agreement; it will signal any general problems affecting the General Agreement as a whole; it will address recommendations for a mutually satisfactory adjustment to the parties and/or issue general recommendations to the CONTRACTING PARTIES. The report of the special working party will be issued within twelve months.

2.   On the basis of the report, the Council may take appropriate action by consensus.

0114

외 무 부

종   별 :

번   호 : GVW-2220   일   시 : 91 1101 1630

수   신 : 장 관(통기,경기원,재무부,상공부)

발   신 : 주 제네바대사

제   목 : UR/제도분야 공식 회의

연: GVW-22041.

표제 공식회의가 LACARTE 의장 주제로 10.31.오후 개최되어 연호 비공식 협의시 EC 가 배포한 MTO 의 역할과 임무에 관한 DRAFTOUTLINE 만을 집중 논의한 바, 동 결과를 아래 보고함.(이성주 참사관, 신부남서기관 참석) @ 가. EC는 최종 의정서에 UR 협상 결과의일부로서 MTO 를 설립한다는 결정이 포함되기를 바라며, 각 협상 참가국으로 하여금 이에 대한 국내적 동의를 얻는데 도움이 되도록 최소한의 운곽에 대한 합의(UNDERSTANDING)는 있어야 한다고 보기 때문에 동제안을 제출하는 것이나 동 형태는 현단계에서는 UR 협상의 실질적내용에 전념해야한다는 다수국의 의견을 참가하여 최대한 간략히 하였다고 설명함.

나. 이에 대해 카나다가 EC의 주장은 자국의 견해와 유사하다면서 특히 봉함분쟁해결절차(2항) 관련, 이를 MTO 설립 문제와 관련 시키는 것은 새로운 분쟁해결 절차의 시행지연을 초래할 가능성이 있기 때문에 반대한다고 밝히고, 동 기구 설립을 순수히 기구적(ORGANIZATIONAL) 개념에 의해 추진 하는것이 라면 동 구체 내용을 보아추후 입장을 정립하겠지만, 현재 UNCTAD 내에서 논의되고 있는 것과 같이 개발 개념을 도입하려 하거나 GATT의 계약적(CONTRACTUAL) 성격에 반경을 가하는 것이라면 절대로 찬성할 수 없다는 점을 분명히 한다고 발언

라. 기타 알젠틴을 서두를 페루, 코스타리카, 콜롬비아,튜니시아, 이집트,필리핀, 유고등이 UR 협상결과에 대한 전체적인 운곽이 나오고 동 결과가 만족할 만한 것으로 밝혀지기 전에 동기구 설립에 관한 언질을 할 수 없다는 입장을 표명함(이중이집트중 일부 국가는 TRIPS, SVC 협상 결과의 분리도 언급)

마. 스위스는 EC의 구상을 기본적으로 찬성하나, 분쟁해결 절차 문제에 관해서만은 미국입장에 동조함.

통상국   2차보   경기원   상공부 · 재무부

PAGE 1   91.11.02   08:16 WH

외신 1과 통제관

0115

바. 의장은 FOGS 분야에서는 그간 전혀 협의자체가 없었고, 분쟁해결 분야에 관한 집중적인 비공식 협의가 있었으나 아직도 패널보고서 채택, 양허 정지, NON-VIOLATION 분쟁, 66년 절차 통합 문제등 다수경쟁이 미결상태라고 언급한후 다음주 부터 8-10 일간 FINAL ACT, FOGS,분쟁해결 3개분야 미결쟁점에 관해 집중적인 비공식 협의를 가질 예정이며, 현재로서는 공식회의 날짜를 정할 수 없으나 언제나 소집 가능성이있음을 유념해 달라고 하였음.

2. 내주 비공식 협의는 우선 10.4.FINAL ACT,10.5.COHERENCE 문제를 토의할 전망임.끝

(대사 박수길-국장)

외 무 부

종 별 :

번 호 : GVW-2204   일 시 : 91 1031 1700

수 신 : 장 관(봉기)

발 신 : 주 제네바 대사

제 목 : UR/제도 분야 (최종의정서)

　　　연: GVW-2154

　　　연호 표제 비공식 회의가 LACARTE 의장 주재로 10.29-30 간 개최되어 91.3.25 자 사무국 비공식 문서중심으로 SINGLE UNDERTAKING, MTO 설립 문제등을 논의하였는바, 주요 논의 요지 아래 보고함.

　　1. SINGLE UNDERTAKING 문제

　　- 미국은 최종의정서 1항에 규정된 ANNEX I (상품 무역에 관한 협정)과 ANNEX II (서비스무역에 관한 협정)를 ANNEX (무역에 관한협정)로 봉합, 규정할 것을 제의하였으며, 이에 EC, 북구, 일본이 지지하였음.

　　- 이에 대해 인도, 브라질, 멕시코는 최종의정서는 정치적인 문서로서 가급적 명확한 의미를 가져야한다고 전제하고 상기 제안이 SINGLE UNDERTAKING문제 (특히 봉합분쟁 해결 절차와 부문간 보복문제)를 예단하는 결과가 될수 있다는 점을 지적함. 의장은 동건과 관련 타 협상 분야에서 구체적인 협상 윤곽이 나오면 다시 논의하기로 함.

　　2. MTO 설치문제

　　- EC 가 MTO 의 봉합 분쟁해결 절차, TPRM시행 등 역할 개요를 언급한 문서를 배포하였으며, 카나다가 상기 기능을 다룰수 있는 MTO 의 유용성을 언급하면서, EC 제안을 지지하였음. (상기문서 별첨 FAX 송부)

　　- 이에 대해 인도, 모로코, 말련, 홍콩, 미국이 최종의정서는 기본적으로 정치적인 결정을 규정한 문서로서 동문서에 MTO 설립문제와 같은 구체적이고, 법적 구속력있는 사안을 다루는것은 적절치 않으며, MTO 설립 문제는 UR협상 타결후 구체적으로 논의하는 것이 바람직하다고 하였으며, 미국은 봉합분쟁 해결절차 이행이 MTO설립 필요성과 직접 관련이있는 것은 아니라고 언급함.(미국)

통상국　　　2차보

PAGE 1   91.11.01　　09:19 WG

3. 최저 개도국에 대한 유예기간 부여 문제

 - 최저 개도국을 대표한 방글라데시가 최저개도국에 대한 우대문제는 일정 기간의 유예기간후에도 최저 개도국에서 졸업할수 있다는 보장이 없으므로 상다이간의 유예기간을 부여해줄것을 요청하면서, 현재 '(X)년에서 (XX)년'으로 수정 제의함.

 - 이에 대해 EC, 미국, 카나다가 최저 개발국에 대한 우대 문제는 UR 협상 결과 따른 공약에대해 일괄적으로 유예기간을 부여하는 것 보다는 개별 협상 분야별로 구체적인 해결책을 모색하는 것이 바람직하며, 최종의정서에는 '푼타'선언에 언급된 최저 개발국에 대한 특별규정과 유사한 일반적인 규정을 삽입하는 것이 적절하다고 언급하였음.

북구의 요청에 따라 동건 관련 사무국에서 작성한 문안을 배포하였는바, 별첨 FAX 송부함.

첨부: 상기 문서 각 1부. 끝

(GVW(F)-465)

(대사 박수길-국장

GUW(下)-0465   11/03/ 1700

" GUW-2204 첨부,,

(EC 제안)

DRAFT OUTLINE OF ROLE AND TASKS OF
A MULTILATERAL TRADE ORGANISATION

29. 10. 31

The main elements of an organisational treaty establishing a Multilateral Trade Organisation should be, inter alia:

1) A single Institutional framework for all existing GATT agreements as well as for all results of the Uruguay Round;

2) An Integrated Dispute Settlement procedure applicable to all parts covered by this Institutional framework;

3) A regular Trade Policy Review Mechanism, covering all parts covered by this Institutional framework;

4) Provisions on membership;

5) Establishment of an International Bureau or Secretariat consisting of a Director-General and his staff;

6) Budgetary provisions;

7) Provisions on the legal capacity of the organisation, privileges, immunities, relations with other organisations;

8) Final provisions.

0119

2-1

30.10.91   para. 7

   Participants recognize that in the negotiations special attention has
been given to the particular situation and problems of the least developed
countries and that special and differential treatment has been accorded to
these countries in the instruments and arrangements negotiated in the
course of the Uruguay Round. Participants undertake to keep under review
the problems of the least developed countries and will continue to seek the
adoption of positive measures to facilitate the expansion of trading
opportunities in favour of these countries.

0120

2 —2

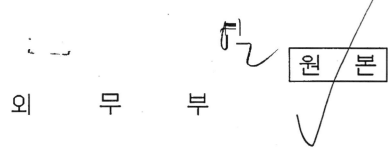

외 무 부

종 별 :

번 호 : GVW-2234
일 시 : 91 1101 2000

수 신 : 장 관(통기,경기원,재무부,상공부)

발 신 : 주 제네바대사

제 목 : UR/분쟁해결 비공식 협의

　　　10.30-31간 진행된 표제 비공식 협의(LACARTE의장 주재)에서는 패널보고서 채택(G4항)에 관한 인도제안 및 NON-VIOLATION 분쟁(P항)문제가 논의된 바, 동 결과 아래 보고 함.(이성주참사관 참석)

　　1. 패널보고서 채택(G4항) 관련 인도제안

　　0 인도가 10.23.논의시 표출된 각국의 1차적의견(GVW2121, 4G 항 '가')을 참작,별첨 1수정안을 제출

　　0 인도는 이사회의 역할 및 패널 계쟁사항에 이해관계를 갖고 있는 제 3국의 권리 측면을 다시 강조하고, 자국안 채택시 상소기구 회부건수가 급증할 것이라는 지적에 대해 브랏셀 TEXT상의 제도하에서도 패소국은 국내정치적이유에서라도 대부분 상소할 것이라는 점을 지적

　　0 브라질만이 다소 긍정적 반응을 보였을뿐, 미국,EC,일본, 홍콩, 호주등이 아래와 같이 문제점을지적

　　- 패널의 결정은 당사국만 구속하며, 선례를 형성하는 것이 아니므로 제3국권리와분쟁당사국 권리간의 분명한 구별 필요

　　- 이사회가 상소기구에 회부시 동 기구의 TOR(재심의 의뢰사항)을 어떻게 결정하는지의 여부등 세부사항 불언급, G4수정안 마지막문장의 'SHALL'의 문제점

　　- 분쟁당사국은 패널 결정에 동의함에도 불구하고 제3국이 반대하여 상소된 경우, 상소기구결정의 당사국에 대한 구속력 문제

　　0 인도는 상기 문제점을 검토 재차 수정안을 제시하겠다 하면서, 패널보고서의 선례 형성여부에 관해서는 사실상 선례형성을 해왔다고 언급하고 , 이점에 대해서는미국도 다소수긍함

　　2. NON-VIOLATION 분쟁(P항)

통상국　2차보　경기원　재무부　상공부

PAGE 1

91.11.02　08:56 WH

외신 1과 통제관

0121

가. 제 23조 1항 'C'분쟁

0 GVW-2192 2항 '나' 에 따라 홍콩이 미국과 협의별첨 2 수정안을 제시

0 카나다도 새절차에 구절차를 언급하는 방식은 바람직하지 않다는 고려에서 별첨 3과 같이 자국수정안을 제시(홍콩제안과의 내용상의 차이점은동 제안이 상소기구회부를 포함하고 있는 점 및이사회에 회부할 수 잇사는 점임)

0 스위스(상소기구 회부반대), 미국이 홍콩안을 지지한 외에는 특별한 논의는 없었으며, 의장이 홍콩, 스위스간 협의 재작성토록 권유

나. 제 23조 1항 'B' 분쟁(P 1-5항)

0 미국은 자국제안(GVW-2192 의 별첨 5)이 10.24-25협의시 다수국이 NV 분쟁 관련 별도항 설정필요성에 의문을 제시했음을 반영, EC 안의 내용에 변경을 가함이 없이 관련항에 봉함을 시도한 것일뿐, 자국 입장을 구속하는 것이 아니라하고 EC 또한 별항 유지입장을 계속 주장함으로써 특별한 진전이 없었음.

0 반면 알젠틴 제안(연호 별첨 4)에 대해서는 다수 국가가 동 제안은 <u>NV 의 경우 해당 조치의 철폐 의무가 없다는 기존 관행(79년 양해 부속서5항 참조)</u>에 변경을 가하게 되므로 받아들일수 없다는 입장 표명

0 P 3항 BRACKET 관련('OR MODIFY' 포함여부)대다수 국가가 ' 상호 만족스러운 해결' 에 해당조치의 수정 여부도 한가지 방안으로 남겨두어야 한다는 점 및 79년 양해 부속서 4항에 MODIFICATION에 관한 언급이 없음등을 이유로 동 문안삭제를 주장한데 대해, EC 와 일본은 유지입장 표명

0 P 4항 관련 RP 및 보상규모 결정을 위한 중재시한을 현 90일에서 150일로 연장하자는 EC의 주장(GVW-2155 3항 '가')에 대해 미국포함 대다수 국가가 반대함으로써의장은 미.EC.간 계속 협의토록 권유(EC 가 90 또는 150일로 BRACKET 을 설치할 것을 제의하였으나, 의장은 더이상의 BRACKET 증가는 허용할 수 없다고 거절)

0 P 1항 EC 제안에 대해서는 미국과 EC 가계속 협의한후 재론키로 함.

별첨: 1. G4항 관련 인도 제안

2. P 6항 관련 홍콩제안

3. P 6항관련 카나다 제안

(GVW(F)-0474).끝

(대사 박수길-국장)

PAGE 2

0122

(박종범1)
GUW(下)-0474 1110/2000 0110191.약
"GUW-2234 첨부"

Paragraph G.4

Within sixty days of the issuance of a panel report to the contracting parties, the report shall be adopted by the Council by the traditional practice of consensus, unless one of the parties formally notifies the Council of its decision to appeal or there are differences of opinion in the Council on the legal interpretations developed by the panel. In the latter event, the Council shall refer the report to the Appellate Body with a view to seeking a confirmation of the legal interpretations developed by the panel.

Paragraph H(d) Add a new sentence

However, the GATT Council may also refer a panel report to the Appellate Body for seeking a confirmation of the legal interpretations developed by the panel in accordance with paragraph G.4

Paragraph H (f)

The Appellate Body shall consider only those issues of law covered in the panel report and legal interpretations developed by the panel.

3-1

0123

(벙접2)

29.10.91
16.40

HONG KONG

Procedures for Article XXIII:1(c)

Notwithstanding any other provision of this Understanding, where a party has recourse to dispute settlement based upon Article XXIII:1(c), the GATT dispute settlement rules and procedures contained in the Decision of the Council of 12 April 1989 (BISD 36S/21), shall apply instead of this Understanding. Similarly, if a panel examining a matter pursuant to the rules and procedures of this Understanding should conclude that the provisions of Article XXIII:1(c) apply to any matter being examined[1], the rules and procedures contained in BISD 36S/21 shall apply, instead of this Understanding, from that point at which the panel so concludes.

---

[1] In the event that a panel functioning under this Understanding finds that provisions of Article XXIII:1(a) or XXIII:1(b) are also applicable in the same case, the panel shall issue a separate panel report addressing only the Article XXIII:1(c) issue for purposes of this different procedure.

3-2

0124

Procedures for Article XXIII:1(c) Cases

Where the parties to a dispute agree, or a panel determines, that any matter falls under the provisions of Article XXIII:1(c), the procedures in this Understanding shall apply, except that:

a) adoption of panel and appellate body reports (G.4 and H.3) shall be by the traditional practice of consensus,

b) the procedures outlined in sections K and L herein shall not apply, and

c) a party to the dispute may refer the matter to the Council for a decision by consensus regarding what action is appropriate in the circumstances.

In the event that a panel finds that other provisions of Article XXIII:1 are also applicable in the same case, the panel shall issue a separate panel report addresseing only the Article XXIII:1(c) isssue for the purposes of this different procedure.

3-3

0125

외 무 부

종 별 :

번 호 : GVW-2291   일 시 : 91 1108 1900

수 신 : 장관(봉기, 경기원)

발 신 : 주제네바대사

제 목 : UR/제도분야(최종의정서)

연: GVW-2220

1. 연호 표제 비공식 회의가 LACARTE 의장 주재로11.6-8간 개최되어 EC 가 배포한MTO 역할개요에 대해 논의하고, 이를 기초로 EC 가차주회의에 MTO 설립에 관한 구체적인 자료를제출키로 하였는바, 회의 참석국들은 MTO설립에 대한 각국의 입장을 밝히기 위해서는 MTO 에 관한 구체적인 내용이 필요함을언급하였음. 주요 논의 요지 아래 보고함.(신서기관참석)

2. EC 는 UR 협상 결과의 일부로서 MTO 를 설립한다는 결정이 포함된 최종 의정서에 대해 협상 참가국들의 국내적 합의를 얻는데 도움이되도록 제출한 MTO 역할 개요에 대한 설명을하였음.

이에 대해 호주, 뉴질랜드, 스위스, 아국등은 MTO설립에 대한 각국의 입장을 밝히고, MTO설립문제를 포함한 UR 협상 결과에 대해 국내적 승인 절차를 받기 위해서는현 단계에서 MTO 에 관한 구체적인 TEXT 가 필요함을 언급하였음.

3. 사무국측(LINDEN 보좌관)은 UR 협상결과와 MTO 설립문제에 대한 국내적 승인을 동시에받기 위하여는 UR 협상 타결에 따라 FINAL ACT서명을 위한 회의전에 MTO 역할 에 관한 실질적 문제를 타결하고 FINAL ACT 서명후 구성된 MTO 설립문제를 논의하기 위해 구성될 잠정위원회(INTERIM COMMITTEE)에서는 기술적인 사항을 마무리 짓는 것이 바람직 하다고 함

4. EC 가 배포한 MTO 역할 개요에 대한 논의요지는 아래와 같음.

(1) MTO 의 단일구조(SINGLE INSTITUTIONAL FRAMEWORK)

SINGLE UNDERTAKING 을 기초로한 모든 갖트 협정과 UR협상 결과를 포함하는 MTO의 단일 구조에대해 이를 찬성하는 선진국과 반대하는개도국으로 의견이 나뉘어짐.(2) 봉합 분쟁 해결 절차 시행

통상국	장관	차관	1차보	2차보	외정실	분석관	청와대	안기부
경기원								

PAGE 1   91.11.09   09:03 BX

외신 1과 통제관

0126

선진국들은 기존 갓트 협정과 UR 협상 결과에적용할 수 있는 봉합분쟁 해결 절차가FORUM-SHOPPING 방지등의 유용성을 지적하며 MTO의 주요기능에 포함되어야 한다고하였으며 개도국들은 부문간 상호보복 문제(CROSS-RETALIATION)의 봉합분쟁해결 절차 와의 관계를들어 입장을 유보함.

미국,일본은 봉합분쟁해결 절차 운용을 위해 반드시 MTO 설립이 필요한 것이 아님을 지적함.

(3) 종합적인 TPRM 시행

대부분 참가국들은 MTO 에서 시행될 TPRM이 현재 갓트에서 시행중인 TPRM 형식을따른다면 상기 제도 시행에 찬성함.

(4) 회원에 관한 규정

선진국들은 SINGLE UNDERTAKING 기초하에 모든 UR결과를 수락한 갓트 체약국이 회원국이 될 수있으며 MTO 가입에 관한 규정을 갓트 관련규정을 준용할 것이라는 EC 견해를 찬성했으나 개도국들은 MTO 는 보편성의원칙에 따라 가급적 모든 국가에 개방되 어야한다고 언급함.

(5) 사무국 설치에 관한 규정

EC, 카나다는 MTO 사무국은 현행 갓트 사무국을 골격으로 한 조직을 상정하고 있다고 언급한데대해 인도, 홍콩등 개도국은 사무국 구조 문제는 UR 협상 결과에 따라결 정할 문제라고언급하였음.

(6) 예산 규정

TO 사무국이 효율적이고 경제적인 예산운영을할 수 있는 명시적인 규정 필요성이언급됨.

(7) 기타문제

0 현행 갓트 규정에 있는 개정, 효력발생,탈퇴, 웨이버 부여에 관한 규정 제정 필요성이언급됨

0 미국, 자메이카, 칠레등은 MTO 설립후 MTO와갓트와의 2원구조에서 오는 문제점특히 양회원국간에 분쟁이 발생하였을 경우 관할패널 결정등 문제점을 제기하였음.

5. 의장은 이번에 논의된 사항을 기초로 EC 가사무국의 지원을 받아 MTO 설립과관련한 구체적인 논의자료를 작성 토록하여, 이를 기초로 차주에 비공식회의 개최하여 MTO 설립에 관한협의를 계속하기로 하였음.끝

PAGE 2

0127

원 본

외 무 부

종 별 :

번 호 : GVW-2294   일 시 : 91 1108 1930

수 신 : 장관(통기, 경기원, 재무부, 농수산부, 상공부)

발 신 : 주 제네바 대사

제 목 : UR/TNC 던켈총장 보고 분야별 분석 평가분석(제도분야)

연: GVW-1514

연호 던켈총장 보고(W/89) 및 ANNOTATED NEOGOTIATING AGENDA(W/89/ADD.1) 관련 제도분야에 관한 당관의 분석, 평가등을 아래 보고함.

1. 분쟁해결 절차

O DUNKEL 의장은 자신의 평가발언중 전체 PACKAGE 의 4 개 기본요소중의 하나로 언급, 동 문제의 중요성을 부각시킴

O 특히 절차의 자동화 문제 및 일방조치 억제문제를 타분야 협상결과에의 적용문제와 함께 3 개 핵심적 미결사항으로 분류하면서, 상기 양문제는 상호연계되어 있음을 지적한바, 절차의 자동화 문제는 세부 기술적 사항까지 대부분 작업이 마무리된 상황과 일방조치 억제 공약이 필수적이라는 모든 참가국의 공통된 의견을 감안할때, 이는 미국을 겨냥한 지적으로 평가됨. 그러나 미국으로서는 국내 제반 사정에 비추어 최종 순간까지도 이문제에 대한 구체적 언질을 줄 수 없는 입장임.

O 새로운 분쟁 해결절차를 UR 협상 결과 전반에 적용하는 문제(조화문제) 역시 개도국이 극히 민감한 반응을 보이는 사항임을 감안할때 최종 순간의 정치적타결 또는 소수 핵심국간 막후절충 가능성을 기대하는 외에는 실무차원에서는 추가 진전을 기대하기는 어려운 것으로 전망됨

- 기타 W/89/ADD.1 에 포함된 NON-VIOLATION 분쟁문제, 66 년 절차통합문제에 관해서는, 최근 EC 가 보여준 진진한 협상 자세와 여타국의 협조적 태도에 비추어 NON-VIOLATION 분쟁에 관해서는 적절한 선에서 절충이 가능할 것으로 예상할 수 있으며, 66 년 절차문제 역시 아직까지도 선. 개도국간 첨예한 대립양상(선진국 OPTION 2 주장, 개도국 OPTION 1 주장)을 보이고 있으나 문제의 성격에 비추어 협상자체에 대한 중대한 걸림돌이 될 것 같지는 않음.

통상국	장관	차관	1차보	2차보	경제국	외정실	분석관	청와대
안기부	경기원	재무부	농수부	상공부				

PAGE 1   91.11.09   07:21

외신 2과 통제관 BD

0128

2. 갓트 기능 분야

- 통고절차강화, TPRM, 국내적 명료성제고등 대부분의 잇슈가 이미 합의 상태에 있으므로, W/89/ADD.1 에서 경제정책 수립상의 일관성 문제만이 미결사항으로 지적되었으나 의장 평가에서는 특별한 언급 없음.

- 동 일관성 문제는 EC 가 강한 관심을 표시하고 개도국이 동조하고 있으나, 사실상 핵심잇슈는 아니므로 향후 협상과정에서도 우선 순위를 부여키 어려울것으로 예상됨.

3. 제도분야

- PARA 19 에는 비교적 간단히 언급되 있으나 역시 의장 평가에 4 대 기본요소로 포함, 정치적 성격이 강한 문제임을 입증

- 최대 잇슈인 SINGLE UNDERTAKING 문제는 결국 최종단계에 가서나 결정될 사항이나, 의장 평가 및 W/89/ADD 1 상의 표현으로 보아 SINGLE UNDERTAKING 방향으로 몰아가려는 의도가 강한 것으로 분석되며, 이는 또한 선진국 및 주요 교역국이 대부분 양승하는 사항이므로 SINGLE UNDERTAKING 될 가능성이 높다고 볼 수 있음.

- MTO 설립 및 동기구의 기본윤곽 합의 문제는 현재 대부분의 국가(특히 미국은 개발개념 도입 및 GATT 의 계약정 성격 변경초래 가능성에 강한 우려)가 소극적 반응을 보임으로써, EC 가 수세에 몰려있는 형편이나, 최종의정서에 이 문제를 담지 않는한 여사한 기구의 설립 가능성은 영원히 상실될 것이라고 보는 EC 로서는 이 문제를 강력히 계속 나갈것으로 예상됨.

(대사 박수길-국장)

예고:91.12.31. 까지

외 무 부

종 별 :

번 호 : GVW-2315　　　　　　　　　　일 시 : 91 1113 1500

수 신 : 장관(봉기,경기원,재무부,농림수산부,상공부)

발 신 : 주 제네바 대사

제 목 : UR 제도분야 비공식 협의(분쟁해결)

연: GVW-2234

1. LACARTE 의장 주재 11.11-12 양일간 개최된 표제협의에서는 분쟁해결 절차 논의를 재개, 연호 10.31 까지의 협의 결과를 기초로 사무국이 작성배포한 11.11 현재 OUTSTANDING PROPOSAL 목록(별첨1) 및 REVISED CONSOLIDATED TEXT 를 바탕으로 논의를 진행한바, 합리적 이행기간의 지침 설정문제(상기 TEXT 10.3 항 BIS, 이하 모든항번호는 동 TEXT 에 입각) 및 1.2 항, 1.4 항관련 경미한 DRAFTING 수정에 대해서 합의를 보고, 기타 8.4 항(이미 패널에서 다루어졌던 동일사안 처리) 관련 미국이 제안 철회 용의를 표명한점, 23.4 항(이행 및 보상 관련 조항의 중재절차에서의 준용)에 EC 를 제외한 모든국가가 수락용의를 표명한 점등에서 다소의 진전이 있었으나, 그밖에는 뚜렷한 진전없음.(이성주 참사관 참석)

2. 의장은 최근 수주간의 비공식 협의 결과 오히려 후퇴하고 있는 인상(지엽적 사항만 거론, 동사항마저도 상당수 핵심쟁점에 연계시키는 협상태도등)이라고 개탄하고, 정치적 쟁점을 포함한 향후 협상 진행에 관한 각국의 견해를 문의한바, 미국은 동쟁점들은 타분야 협상결과를 보기전에 독자적으로 결정하기 어려운 사항이므로 큰 진전을 기대하기 어렵다는 의견을, EC, 일본, 인도는 타분야 결과만을 기다릴수만도없으므로 계속 협상을 진행해 나가자는 의견을, 호주는 정치적 쟁점에 대한 IDENTIFY 를해보자는 의견을, 홍콩은 '전체가 합의되지 않는한 아무것도 합의된 것으로 간주하지않는다'는 대전제를 염두에 두고 우선 일방 조치억제문제(21항)을 토의하자는 의견을제시했으나, 구체적 결론을 내리지 못하고 11.14 비공식 협의시에는 우선 CROSS-RETALIATION문제를 논의키로 하였음.(11.13 및 15에는 MTO문제 논의)

3. 미결사항별 논의 내용은 아래와 갑음.

가. 지방정부 관련 카나다 수정안(별첨 1의 4,10페이지)

통상국　　2차보　　경기원　　재무부　　농수부　　상공부

91.11.14　05:26 DQ

외신 1과 통제관

0130

- 갓트 조문 그룹의 24조 12항 협의 내용을 일정단서(FOOTNOTE)를 조건으로 협의 및 이행관련 항목에 추가할 것을 내용으로 하는 카나다제안 (GVW-2121 참조)에 대해 EC 가 별첨 2의4-1 PAGE 와 같은 추가 FOOTNOTE 설정을 제의

- 이에 대해 카나다는 호의적 고려 가능하다는 입장을 표명하였으나, 미국은 EC요구에 반대 입장 표명

- 카나다는 최근 자국내 지방정부의 발언권 강화 움직임을 언급하고 이들에 대한 중앙정부의 통제 강화를 위해서 자국의 수정안은 꼭 반영되어야 할 입장임을 강조함.

나. 패널에 기회부된, 동일사안 처리(5페이지)

- EC 를 비롯 다수국이 계속 소극적 반응을 보임으로써 미국은 동 제안 철회 의사를 표명하였으나, 베네주엘라가 이를 자국제안으로 대신 내놓겠다고 나섬.(의장이 베네주엘라에 재고를 촉구)

다. 패널 및 상소기구의 권고(6 페이지)

- 알젠틴의 제안에 대해 (GVW-2234참조)대부분의 국가가 NV 처리의 기본 취지 및관행에 어긋난다는 이유로 반대(알젠틴은 동입장 고수)

라. 패널 보고서 채택(7 페이지)

- 제안국 인도의 재수정안(GVW-2234) 참조)이 준비안됨으로써 토의 연기

마. 합리적 이행기간의 가이드라인(8 페이지)

- 미국이 12개월 대신 15개월로 양보한데 대해 10.24 논의시 (GVW-2155) 부정적입장을 표명한 국가(아국포함)들이 이를 수락합의함.(EC 만이 여타 사항과 관련해 입장을 유보한다함.)

사. 보복규모의 사전 승인(9 페이지)

- 멕시코가 내용 자체는 완화되면서 괄호는 그대로 남아 있음에 불만을 표시하고 더 이상 흥미가 없다는 뜻을 시사하였으나, 대신 미국이 자국으로서는 중요한 사항이라고 언급하고 당초 원안에 기초를 두고 계속 협의할 것을 주장

- EC, 스위스는 RPOT 만료 60일전 안에 대해서도 수락 불가 입장 표명

아. 중재에의 준용(11 페이지)

- 대다수 국가가 수락 용의를 표명(EC 만이 NV분쟁관련 입장 유보)

자. NON-VIOLATION 분쟁

1) 23조 1항 B 케이스 (12 페이지)

- EC 가 10.24 자국안에 'THE CONTRACTING PARTYALLEGES' 를 추가한 수정안을

PAGE 2

0131

제시 (12-1페이지)한바, 미국이 이미 23조 1항 CHAPEAU 에 규정된바에 따라 제소국은제소시 A, B, C 중 어디에 해당된다고 적시하게 되어 있는데 구태여 추가할 필요성이 있는지의 여부에 의문을 제기

  - 미국은 또한 제소국은 A 케이스로 제소하였으나 패널이 B 케이스(NV 분쟁)로 결정할수도 있음을 지적

  - 또한 MIXED CASE 의 경우 위반 부분과 비위반부분에 대한 각각 별도의 보고서제출 여부등의 문제가 제기됨.

  2) 23조 1항 C 케이스(16-18 페이지)

  - 10.31 토의결과에 따라 홍콩 및 카나다가 공동작성한 새로운 제안 (18-1 페이지)을 제시하였으나,- EC 는 2 째줄 OR 를 AND 로 수정(상기B 케이스 수정안과 같은맥락), 일본은 카나다원안 (18 페이지)을 지지(구절차 언급이 바람직하지않음), 스위스는 마지막 문장(MIXED CASE 의 경우별도 보고서 제출) 관련 상기 B CASE 와의 일관성 유지 필요등을 제기함.

  - 인도, 호주, 뉴질랜드, 놀웨이는 지지 가능하다는 의견 피력, EC 는 B CASE 합의후로 REVIEW하겠다는 입장.

  3) 알젠틴 제안(15 페이지)

  - 상기 '다' 항과 사실상 동일 내용이므로, 토의생략 (의장이 철회 용의를 문의하였으나 알젠틴은 거부)

  차. 1. 2 항 및 1. 4 항 DRAFTING 개선 (20-21 페이지)

  - 합의

  카. 66년 절차(22 페이지)

  - 더이상의 합의 도출 노력이 현 상황하에서 불가하다고 의장이 OPTION 1 및 2 중 각국의 입장을 문의

  - 멕시코, 베네주엘라, 인도, 칠레, 브라질은 OPTION 1 지지

  - 미국, EC, 일본, 카나다, 호주, 뉴질랜드, 스위스,항가리는 OPTION 2 지지, 아국도 절충이 불가한 상황이라면 OPTION 2 선호 입장임을 표명

  타. 기타

  - 11.11 오후 토의후 의장은 11.12 정오를 DEADLINE으로 하여 더이상의 제안은 접수치 않을 것임을 분명히 함에 따라 미국은 11.12 아래 5가지 사항을제기, (동 제안TEXT 별첨 3)

1) 1.1 항 관련 주석(FOOTNOTE 2)삭제 또는 문안 완화

2) 1.7 항 3-4 째 문장 삭제(23조와 동일 내용, 여타부분과 중복)

3) 1.8 항 2 째 문장 삭제 또는 패널 보고서 채택,상소 보고서 채택, 보복의 승인등과 같이 BRACKET 처리 또는 다른 방법으로 연계성 명기

4) 4.1 항에 현행 이사회 소집 관행(10일 사전요청)을 주석으로 명기

5) 19.4 항 관련 예외적인 상황을 당사국이 합의하는 경우로 국한 √

첨부) 1. 11.11 현재 OUT STANDING PROPOSAL 목록

2. 미국 제기 사항. 끝

(GVW(F)-0505)

(대사 박수길-국장)

GVW(H)-05-1   11/13 1500
"GVW-2315 첨부"   (별첨 1)

11.11.91   Dispute Settlement

Outstanding proposals are listed hereunder. The relevant texts are annexed.

Revised Brussels Text [Consolidated text paragraphs in square brackets]

X Paragraph A.5:	1966 Procedures (US proposal)	
X bis Paragraph A.5:	1966 Procedures (Mexican proposal)	
[Para. 1.10]		
II. Paragraph B.1 (before):	Article XXIV:12 (Canadian proposal)	
[Para. 2.1bis]		
III. Paragraph E.4:	Measures previously examined by a panel	
[Para. 8.4]	(US proposal)	
IV. Section F:	Function of panel and appellate body	
[Para. 17.1]	(Argentinian proposal)	
V. Paragraph G.4:	Adoption of panel reports (Indian proposal)	
[Para. 14.4]		
[Para. 15.4]		
[Para. 15.6]		
VI. Paragraph K.3:	Reasonable Period Guidelines (US proposal)	
[Para. 19.3bis]		
VII. Paragraph L.7:	Level of suspension	
[Para. 20.7]		
VII.bis Paragraph L.7 (after):	Article XXIV:12 (Canadian proposal)	
[Para. 20.7bis]		
VIII. Paragraph O.4:	Arbitration (Swiss proposal)	
[Para. 23.4]		
IX. Section P:	Non-Violation (Article XXIII:1(b))	
[Para. 24.1]		

IX.bis Paragraph D.6(d bis)   )
        [Para. 10.6bis]   )
        Paragraph K.2   )
        [Para. 19.3]   ) Non-Violation (integration proposal)
        Section F   )
        [Para. 17.1]   )
        footnote to para L.3   )
        [Para. 20.3]   )

IX.ter Paragraphs P.1 to P.6:	Non-Violation (Argentinian proposal)	
[Para. 24.1 et seq]		
X. Paragraph P.6:	Article XXIII:1(c)	
[Para. 24.6]		
X.bis Paragraph P.6:	Article XXIII:1(c) (Hong Kong proposal)	
[Para. 24.6]		
X.ter Paragraph P.6:	Article XXIII:1(c) (Canadian proposal)	
[Para. 24.6]		

Revised Consolidated Text [Brussels text paragraphs in square brackets]

XI. Paragraph 1.2:	General provisions (New Zealand proposal)	
[Para. A.2]		
XI bis Paragraph 1.2:	General provisions	
[Para. A.2]		
XII. Paragraph 1.4:	General provisions	
[Para. A.3]		
XIII. Section 26		
Para. 1.10 and 1.11:	Decision of 5 April 1966	
[Para. A.5 and	(Mexican and US proposals)	
Para. A.5bis]		

20 -1

0134

- 2 -

25.10.91   (US proposal)

I.   Paragraph A.5 [1.10]

Replace para A.5 [1.10] with the following:

This Understanding shall repeal and replace all earlier decisions of the CONTRACTING PARTIES with respect to dispute settlement rules and procedures, except as follows:

(a) The Decision of 5 April 1966 (BISD 14S/18) may be applied, as an alternative to the rules and procedures provided in this Understanding, to complaints brought by developing countries choosing to apply the 1966 procedures instead of this Understanding. In such cases, the procedures contained in the Decision of the Council of 12 April 1989 (BISD 36S/21) shall apply to such disputes to the extent that the 1989 procedures are not inconsistent with the 1966 procedures.

(b) With regard to disputes for which the request under Article XXII:1 of XXIII:1 was made before the date of entry into force of this Understanding, it is agreed that GATT dispute settlement rules and procedures in effect immediately prior to the date of entry into force of this Understanding shall continue to apply to those disputes.

66년 절차와 동일기 (p.22 논의도 대체기)

0135

20 - 2

25.10.91 (Mexican proposal)
(5.30 p.m.)

I. bis Paragraph A.5 [1.10]

All the points set out in this Understanding shall be applied as a complement to and without prejudice to any provision on special and differential treatment for developing contracting parties in previous instruments on dispute settlement including the CONTRACTING PARTIES' Decision of 5 April 1966 (BISD 14S/18).

66년과 동세(p.22 논의로 대치)

- 4 -

23.10.91   (Canadian proposal)
19.15

II.   Provisions Governing All Regional and Local Levels of Government

PLACE BEFORE PARAGRAPH B.1 [2.1bis]

B.1 bis Each contracting party undertakes to accord sympathetic consideration to and afford adequate opportunity for consultation regarding any representations made by another contracting party concerning measures affecting the operation of the General Agreement taken within the territory of the former[1].

---

[1] Inclusion of paragraphs L.7bis [20.7bis] and B.1bis [2.1bis] herein are conditioned on inclusion of identical paragraphs in "The Understanding on the Interpretation of Article XXIV of the General Agreement on Tariffs and Trade". Should that Understanding be amended, the question of inclusion of the paragraphs herein shall be reconsidered.

0137

30 — 4

1

A - 1

(EC추가안)
91. 11. 11 (月) 오후.

Inclusion of paragraphs L.7 bis and 8.1 bis are without prejudice to
any obligations resulting from any other agreement or understanding
concluded under the auspices of GATT concerning measures adopted by
regional or local governments or authorities within the territory of a
contracting party.

30 — 5

- 5 -

(US proposal)

III.   Measures Previously Examined by a Panel

Modify paragraph E.4 [8.4] of the 25 March 1991 text to read:

"If a third party considers a measure already the subject of a panel
nullifies or impairs benefits accruing to it under the General
Agreement, and if that party's complaint is limited to the same
specific measure identified in the request for the previous panel,
that party may have recourse to GATT dispute settlement procedures on
an expedited basis."

25.10.91 (12 p.m.)

(US proposal)

Modify E.4 [8.4]

Add a new third sentence:

"Where the panel determines that such a situation is involved, it may
shorten the timetable for the panel process originally set pursuant to
paragraph D.6(c) [10.4]."

30 — 6   0139

- 6 -

28.10.91   (Argentinian proposal)

IV. Section F. [17.1] Panel and Appellate Body Recommendations

Option 1: In the fifth line after the words "shall recommend" insert the following "either the withdrawal or modification of the measure or that the contracting party concerned make a mutually satisfactory adjustment".

Option 2: "the solution it considers appropriate to restore the balance of rights and obligations under the General Agreement, including the withdrawal or modification of the measure".

0140

30 — 7

- 7 -

(Indian proposal)

<u>Adoption of Panel Reports</u>

<u>V. Proposal for substituting paragraph G.4 [14.4]</u>

Within sixty days of the issuance of a panel report to the contracting parties, the report shall be adopted by the Council by the traditional practice of consensus, unless one of the parties formally notifies the Council of its decision to appeal and/or there are differences of opinion in the Council on the legal interpretations developed by the panel. In the latter event, the Council shall refer the report to the Appellate Body with a view to seeking a confirmation of the legal interpretations developed by the panel.

<u>Paragraph H.1(d) [15.4]</u>   Add a new sentence

However, the GATT Council may also refer a panel report to the Appellate Body for seeking a confirmation of the legal interpretations developed by the panel in accordance with paragraph G.4 [14.4].

<u>Paragraph H.1 (f) [15.6]</u>

The Appellate Body shall consider only those issues of law covered in the panel report and legal interpretations developed by the panel.

30 — 8

0141

- 8 -

24.10.91 (5.15 p.m.)   (US proposal)

VI. Reasonable Period Guidelines

Add a new paragraph K.3 [19.3bis] and renumber the following paragraphs accordingly:

Paragraph K.3 [19.3bis]:   *Agreed.*

   In arbitration pursuant to paragraph K.2(c) [19.3(c)], a guideline for the arbitrator should be that the reasonable period of time to implement panel or appellate body recommendations should not exceed ~~twelve~~ months from the adoption of a panel or appellate body report. However, that time may be shorter or longer, depending upon the particular circumstances.

30 — P   0142

- 9 -

25.10.91
(p.m.)

VII.   Paragraph L.7 [Para. 20.7]

[7. The level [amount] of suspension shall, if requested sixty days before the end of the reasonable period of time by one of the parties, be determined before expiry of the reasonable period of time, in accordance with the relevant procedures under paragraphs L.3 [20.3], L.4 [20.4] and L.5 [20.5] above, and on the understanding that such suspension shall not come into effect before the Council has granted the authorization provided for in paragraph L.3. [20.3]]

20 — 10

0143

- 10 -

VII.bis Provisions Governing All Regional and Local Levels of Government

PLACE AFTER PARAGRAPH L.7 [20.7]

L.7bis [20.7bis] The dispute settlement provisions of the General Agreement
may be invoked in respect of measures affecting its observance taken by
regional or local governments or authorities within the territory of a
contracting party. When the CONTRACTING PARTIES have ruled that a
provision of the General Agreement has not been observed, the responsible
contracting party shall take such reasonable measures as may be available
to it to ensure its observance. The provisions relating to compensation
and suspension of concessions or other obligations apply in cases where it
has not been possible to secure such observance.[1]

p.4 諒解와 동일

---

[1]Inclusion of paragraphs L.7bis [20.7bis] and B.1bis [2.1bis] herein
are conditioned on inclusion of identical paragraphs in "The Understanding
on the Interpretation of Article XXIV of the General Agreement on Tariffs
and Trade". Should that Understanding be amended, the question of
inclusion of the paragraphs herein shall be reconsidered.

0144

- 11 -

VIII. Arbitration   (Swiss proposal)

Modify paragraph 0.4 [23.4] to read:

0.4. [23.4] Sections K[19] and L[20] of this Understanding shall apply
mutatis mutandis to arbitration awards.

0145

- 12 -

24.10.91 (5 p.m.)   (EEC proposal)

IX.   P. [24] Non-Violation

P.1 [24.1] Notwithstanding any other provisions of this Understanding, if
and to the extent that a panel or the appellate body determines that the
case brought before it concerns nullification or impairment of benefits
under the General Agreement without violation thereof within the meaning of
Article XXIII:1(b), the provisions of paragraphs P.2 [24.2] through
P.5 [24.5] below shall apply.

0146

|2—|

Section P. Non-Violation

P.1.   The procedures in this Understanding shall apply, subject to the provisions of paragraphs P.2 through P.5 below, if and to the extent that the complaining party alleges, and the panel or the appellate body determines, that the case concerns nullification or impairment of benefits under the General Agreement without violation thereof within the meaning of Article XXIII : 1(b).

0147

- 13 -

25.10.91   (Integration proposal)

<u>IX. bis   Non-violation</u>

Insert the following new paragraph between D.6(d) and D.6(e)
[Para. 10.6bis]: ㄴ ㄱ거셧

(d bis)[10.6bis] <u>If the complaint concerns nullification or impairment of
benefits under the General Agreement without violation thereof, within the
meaning of Article XXIII:1(b), the complaining contracting party shall
include a detailed justification in support of such complaint in its
written submission.</u>

Revise para K.2 [19.3] to read:

2.   At a Council meeting held within thirty days of the adoption of the
panel or appellate body report, the contracting party concerned shall
inform the Council of its intentions in respect of implementation of the
recommendations and rulings under Article XXIII:2.

(a) <u>If the panel or appellate body has found that a measure is
inconsistent with the General Agreement, and if it is impracticable</u>
to comply immediately with the recommendations and rulings, the contracting
party concerned shall have a reasonable period of time in which to do so.
The reasonable period of time shall be:

    (i) the period of time proposed by the contracting party concerned,
    provided that such period is approved by the Council; or, in the
    absence of such approval;

    (ii) a period of time mutually agreed by the parties to the dispute
    within forty-five days following adoption of the recommendations and
    rulings; or, in the absence of such agreement;

    (iii) a period of time determined through binding arbitration within
    ninety days following adoption of the recommendations and rulings.

(b) <u>If and to the extent that the panel or appellate body has determined
that the case brought before it concerns nullification or impairment
of benefits under the General Agreement without violation thereof,
within the meaning of Article XXIII:1(b), and if the parties do not
agree, within forty-five days following adoption, that the
implementation proposed by the party concerned will result in a
mutually satisfactory adjustment, the reasonable period of time for
implementation and the level of benefits which have been nullified or
impaired shall be determined through binding arbitration within 90
days following adoption.</u>

Revise section F [17.1] to read: ㅏ ㅓ 수녕

Where a panel or the appellate body concludes that a measure is
inconsistent with the General Agreement, it shall recommend that the
contracting party concerned bring the measure into conformity with the
General Agreement. <u>Where a measure has been found to constitute a case of
nullification or impairment of benefits under the General Agreement without</u>

0148

- 14 -

violation thereof, there is no obligation to withdraw [or modify] the measure. However, in such cases, the panel or the appellate body shall recommend that the contracting party concerned make a mutually satisfactory adjustment. In addition to its recommendations, the panel or appellate body may suggest ways in which the contracting party concerned could implement the recommendations.

Add following footnote to para L.3 [20.3]:

1   In cases concerning nullification or impairment of benefits under the General Agreement without violation thereof, the arbitrator's decision provided for in paragraph K.2(b) [19.3] with respect to the level of benefits shall be in lieu of the arbitration provided for in paragraph L.3 [20.3].

0149

- 15 -

20.10.91   (Argentinian proposal)

IX.ter   Section P [24] Non-Violation Complaints

Paragraph P.1 [24.1]:

After the words "General Agreement" in the fifth line add the following
sentence "nullify or impair any benefit accruing to it directly or
indirectly or impedes the attainment of any objective under the General
Agreement".

Paragraph P.3 [24.3]:

"Where a measure has been found to constitute a case of nullification or
impairment of benefits under the General Agreement the panel or the
appellate body shall recommend that the measure be withdrawn or modified or
that the contracting party concerned make a mutually satisfactory
adjustment."

Paragraph P.4 [24.4]:

In the second line from the bottom replace "but" for the word "and".
In the last line delete the word "not".

Paragraph P.5 [24.5]:

Maintain only: "The provisions of Section L [20] shall apply".

Paragraph P.6 [24.6]:

Delete both options.

0150

- 16 -

25.10.91

X. Article XXIII:1(c) Complaints

1.   The Council shall refer any complaint brought under Article XXIII:1(c)
to a special working party. This working party will examine the facts of
the matter in the light of the relevant provisions of the General
Agreement; it will signal any general problems affecting the General
Agreement as a whole; it will address recommendations for a mutually
satisfactory adjustment to the parties and/or issue general recommendations
to the CONTRACTING PARTIES. The report of the special working party will
be issued within twelve months.

2.   On the basis of the report, the Council may take appropriate action by
consensus.

0151

- 17 -

29.10.91
16.40   (Hong Kong proposal)

X.bis   Procedures for Article XXIII:1(c)

Notwithstanding any other provision of this Understanding, where a party has recourse to dispute settlement based upon Article XXIII:1(c), the GATT dispute settlement rules and procedures contained in the Decision of the Council of 12 April 1989 (BISD 36S/21) shall apply instead of this Understanding. Similarly, if a panel examining a matter pursuant to the rules and procedures of this Understanding should conclude that the provisions of Article XXIII:1(c) apply to any matter being examined[2], the rules and procedures contained in BISD 36S/21 shall apply, instead of this Understanding, from that point at which the panel so concludes.

---

[2]In the event that a panel functioning under this Understanding finds that provisions of Article XXIII:1(a) or XXIII:1(b) are also applicable in the same case, the panel shall issue a separate panel report addressing only the Article XXIII:1(c) issue for purposes of this different procedure.

0152

- 18 -

1.11.91 a.m.   (Canadian proposal)

X.ter Procedures for Article XXIII:1(c) Cases

Where the parties to a dispute agree, or a panel determines, that any matter falls under the provisions of Article XXIII:1(c), the procedures in this Understanding shall apply, except that:

(a) adoption of panel and appellate body reports (G.4 [14.4] and H.3 [15.13]) shall be by the traditional practice of consensus,

(b) the procedures outlined in sections K [19] and L [20] herein shall not apply, and

(c) a party to the dispute may refer the matter to the Council for a decision by consensus regarding what action is appropriate in the circumstances.

In the event that a panel finds that other provisions of Article XXIII:1 are also applicable in the same case, the panel shall issue a separate panel report addressing only the Article XXIII:1(c) issue for the purposes of this different procedure.

0153

18-1

12. 11.91
QKL

Hong Kong and Canada proposal

Procedures for Article XXIII:1(c)

     Notwithstanding the provisions of this Understanding, where a party has recourse to dispute settlement based upon Article XXIII.1(c), or a panel determines, that any matter falls under the provisions of Article   ⌐— *And (EC)* XXIII.1(c), the GATT dispute settlement rules and procedures contained in the Decision of the Council of 12 April 1989 (BISD 36S/61) shall apply from the point at which the panel report has been issued to the contracting parties for consideration for adoption instead of the rules and procedures of this Understanding. In the event that a panel finds that other provisions of Article XXIII.1 are also applicable in the same case, the panel shall issue a separate panel report addressing only the Article XXIII:1(c) issue for purposes of this different procedure.

0154

- 19 -

(New Zealand proposal)

<u>Revised Consolidated Text</u>

<u>XI. General Provisions</u>

<u>Paragraph 1.2 [A.2]</u>: Add new third sentence

Contracting parties recognise that the prompt settlement of situations in which a contracting party considers that any benefits accruing to it directly or indirectly under the General Agreement are being impaired by measures taken by another contracting party, is essential to the effective functioning of the General Agreement and the maintenance of a proper balance between the rights and obligations of contracting parties.

0155

- 20 -

Revised Consolidated Text

XIbis.   General Provisions

Paragraph 1.2 [A.2]   Agreed

Paragraph 1.2 [A.2] lines 6 and 7: delete "The CONTRACTING PARTIES agree
that".

0156

- 21 -

<u>Revised Consolidated Text</u>

<u>XII. General Provisions</u>

<u>Paragraph 1.4 [A.3]</u>

Agreed

Paragraph 1.4 [A.3] line 1: delete "The CONTRACTING PARTIES agree that".

0157

1991-11-13 18:49 KOREAN MISSION GENEVA 2 022 791 0525 P.15

- 22 -

29.10.91

Revised Consolidated Text

XIII.   1966 Procedures

Option 1   (Mexican proposal)
Delete section 26, "Special Procedures;" and replace paragraph 1.10 [A.5] with the following two paragraphs:

1.10 [A.5] This Understanding shall be applied only with respect to new requests under Article XXII:1 and XXIII:1 made on or after the date of entry into force of this Understanding. With respect to disputes for which the request under Article XXII:1 or XXIII:1 was made before the date of entry into force of this Understanding, GATT dispute settlement rules and procedures in effect immediately prior to the date of entry into force of this Understanding shall continue to apply.

1.11 [A.5bis] Notwithstanding paragraph 1.10 above, if a complaint is brought by a developing contracting party, that contracting party may choose to apply, as an alternative to this Understanding, the provisions of the Decision of the CONTRACTING PARTIES of 5 April 1966 (BISD 14S/18), instead of the provisions of this Understanding. In that event, the same procedures shall apply that would have applied to cases brought pursuant to the 1966 Decision immediately prior to the date of entry into force of this Understanding, including the procedures contained in the Decision of the Council of 12 April 1989 (BISD 36S/21).

Option 2   (US proposal)
Delete section 26, "Special Procedures;" and replace paragraph 1.10 [A.5] with the following:

1.10 [A.5] This Understanding shall be applied with respect to all new requests under Article XXII:1 and XXIII:1 made on or after the date of entry into force of this Understanding. With respect to disputes for which the request under Article XXII:1 or XXIII:1 was made before the date of entry into force of this Understanding, GATT dispute settlement rules and procedures in effect immediately prior to the date of entry into force of this Understanding shall continue to apply.

0158

ぴ号제기사항

백걉 2

(U.S. Proposal)

Footnote 2

Option 1: Delete Footnote 2

Option 2: Move the supernumeral to after the first sentence in paragraph 1.2, and revise Footnote 2 to read as follows:

> "It is noted that Article XXV also affords an appropriate avenue for clarifying the existing provisions of the General Agreement."

1

0159

(U.S. Proposal)

Paragraph 1.7

Delete the third sentence. Articles XXIII:1(b) and XXIII:1(c)
speak for themselves; it is unnecessary to paraphrase them in
this text.

Delete the last sentence. This sentence is repeated in para.
24.2.

2

0160

(U.S. Proposal)

Paragraph 1.8

The second sentence should be deleted. Alternatively, it should
be bracketed or otherwise highlighted in the same way as other
parts of the text for which decisions are related, including
paras. 4.1, 14.4, 15.13, and 20.3.

3

0161

(U.S. Proposal)

Proposed footnote to Paragraph 4.1:

In accordance with past practice, a meeting of the Council
in addition to the Council's regularly scheduled meetings
~~may~~ be convened at the request of any contracting party upon
10 days notice in advance.

4

0162

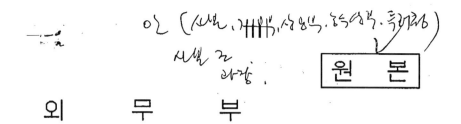

외 무 부

종 별 :

번 호 : GVW-2327 　　　　　　　　일 시 : 91 1114 1230

수 신 : 장 관(봉기, 경기원)

발 신 : 주 제네바 대사

제 목 : UR/제도분야(최종 의정서)

　　　연: GVW-2291

　　1. 연호 표제 비공식 회의가 LACARTE 의장 주재로 11.13 개최되어 EC, 카나다가제출한 <u>MTO설립에</u> 관한 협약안에 대해 논의 하였는바, 주요 논의 요지 아래 보고함. (신서기관 참석)

　　2. MTO 설립에 관한 협약안에 대한 EC 및카나다의 설명

　　가. EC, 카나다는 우선 금일 제출한 MTO설립에 관한 협약안은 양 당사국의 공식제안이아니고 지난주 비공식회의에서 각국이 요청한대로 MTO 설립 관련 구체적인 내용을 논의하기 위해 제출한 자료라고 전제함. (MTO협약안 별첨 FAX 송부)

　　나. MTO 의 구조 (2조)와 관련, MTO 는 갓트협정, 동경 라운드 협정, UR 협상 결과를 포함하는 무역 활동을 위한 공동의 제도적 기초를 제공하도록 규정하고 있는바, 갓트 협정, UR 협상 결과와 동경라운드 협정을 아래 3가지로 구분함.

　　1) 상품에 관한 제협정(ANNEX 1A)

　　2) 서비스에 관한 협정(ANNEX 1B)

　　3) 정부 구매, 민간 항공기, 육우 및 낙농에 관한 협정(ANNEX 1C)

　　다. 회원에 관한 규정(3조)과 관련, MTO 는 UR 협상 및 동경라운드 협상에서 합의 된상품과 서비스에 관한 제협정(ANNEX 1A 와1B)을 수락한 갓트 체약국에 대해 <u>93.1</u> 부터 개방되며, 갓트 체약국이 <u>95.1 까지</u> 상품과 서비스에 관한 제협정을 수락하지않을 경우에는 당사국과 MTO 와 합의된 조건에 따라 MTO협약에 가입할수 있음.

　　라. MTO 의 기능(4조)와 관련 MTO 는봉합분쟁 해결 절차와 <u>TPRM</u> 을 시행하도록 규정하고 있는바, 봉합 분쟁해결 절차는 상품및 서비스 관련 협정에 적용되며, ANNEX 1C 에 규정된 협정에 대해서는 분쟁 당사국이 관련협정 당사국인 경우에만 적용됨.

통상국	장관	차관	2차보	구주국	청와대	안기부	경기원

PAGE 1　　　　　　　　　　　　　　　　　　　　　91.11.15　　02:27 FN

외신 1과　통제관

0163

마. MTO 의 구조(5조)와 관련 각료급회의(격년제 개최), 일반 이사회 (1년 2회 개최),상품 및 서비스에 대한 문제를 각각 다루는 이사회(월별 개최)로 구성

바. EC 는 MTO 협약안의 핵심사항은 MTO구조와 관련된 SINGLE UNDERTAKING 와 봉합분쟁해결 절차임을 강조하고 MTO 를 유엔 전문기구의 하나로 상정하고 있지 않다고 함.

3. MTO 협약안에 대한 논평

가. MTO 회원에 관한 규정과 관련 미국,노르웨이는 MTO 와 갓트와의 관계 문제는MTO 협약등에 규정하는 것보다는 각국에 일임해야 할 사항이라고 언급하였으며, 인도, 콜롬비아, 항가리는 MTO 회원 규정에 유보를 표시함.

나. MTO 의 기능과 관련 미국, 인도는 4조에 규정된 MTO 기능이 제한적이라고 하고, MTO 의구조와 관련, 스웨덴은 상품 및 서비스 협정을 관할하는 이사회가 분리되어 있어, 각 이사회가 유사한 사안에 대해 상반된 결정을 할 가능성을 언급함.

다. 한편 인도, 브라질은 실질적인 문제를 타결해야 할 현 상황에서는 MTO 설립에 관한 구체적인 협의 즉 MTO 설립여부 및 MTO역할에 대한 결정을 내릴 단계가 아니라고 하고,회의 진행방식과 관련 MTO 설립논의가 많은 참여국에 우려를 표명하였음.(필린핀,파키스탄, 콜롬비아, 말련 동조 발언함) 이에 대해 스웨덴, 호주는 UR 협상 타결 목표 시점이 몇주안남은 현 상황에서 MTO 설립문제를 논의하는 것이 시의 적절한 것이라고 언급함.

라. 홍콩은 UR 협상 결과의 이행을 위해 새로운 국제기구를 설립하는것 보다 기존 갓트사무국의 확장이 더 바람직하다고 하였으며, 일본은MTO 설립 협약을 UR 협상 일부로서 국내적 승인을 얻기 위해서는 안전한 협약안이 필요한바, FINAL ACT 서명시까지 MTO 설립에 관한 완전한 협약(FULL TEXT)를 작성하기에는 남은 협상 기간이 촉박함을 지적함.

(싱가폴 동조)

4. 의장은 추후 최종 의정서 분야에서는 MTO문제를 집중적으로 논의하겠다고 하면서 11.15차기 회의를 개최키로 하였는바, MTO 설립관련 EC 가 제출한 협약안과 사무국의 문서를별첨 송부하니, 가급적 구체적인 본부입장 회시바람.

첨부: 1. MTO 설립에 관한 EC, 카나다 제안

2. MTO 설립에 관하 사무국 문서. 끝

(GVW(F)-507)

PAGE 2

0164

GUW (不)- 0507   ////7 1230
" GUW-2327 첨부 "   EC. 가나다 제안

AGREEMENT ESTABLISHING THE MULTILATERAL TRADE ORGANISATION

The Contracting Parties,

Recognizing that their relations in the field of trade and economic endeavour should be conducted with a view to raising standards of living, ensuring full employment and a large and steadily growing volume of real income and effective demand, developing the full use of the resources of the world at sustainable levels, and expanding the production and exchange of goods and services,

Being desirous of contributing to these objectives by entering into reciprocal and mutually advantageous arrangements directed to the substantial reduction of tariffs and other barriers to trade and to the elimination of discriminatory treatment in international trade relations,

Determined therefore, to preserve the basic principles and to further the objectives of the General Agreement on Tariffs and Trade and to develop an integrated, more viable and durable multilateral trading system encompassing the GATT as amended, all Agreements and Arrangements concluded under its auspices and the complete results of the Uruguay Round multilateral trade negotiations,

Agree as follows:

Article I

Establishment of the Organisation

The Multilateral Trade Organisation (herein after referred to as "the MTO") is hereby established. It shall enter into force on the same date as the other Uruguay Round results.

Article II

Scope of the MTO

1. The Multilateral Trade Organisation (MTO) shall provide the common institutional framework for the conduct of trade relations in all matters related to the General Agreement on Tariffs and Trade as amended, the Tokyo Round Agreements and Arrangements and the Uruguay Round results. The detailed list of legal instruments covered by this organisation is set out in Annex 1, as may be amended.

11 — 1   0165

- 2 -

2. The MTO shall provide the forum for further negotiations among its members concerning their multilateral trade relations as may be decided by the Ministerial Conference on the General Council.

Article III

Membership

1. The MTO shall be open for signature as from 1 January 1993 to all GATT contracting parties including the European Communities who have by that date accepted all legal instruments listed in Annex 1A and 1B.

2. A contracting party to GATT which meets the criteria set out in paragraph 1 above, but which has not accepted this Agreement as of 1 January 1995 shall be subject to the provisions of paragraph 3 below.

3. Any other government or government acting on behalf of a separate customs territory possessing full autonomy in the conduct of its external commercial relations and and of the other matters provided for in this Agreement can accede to this Agreement on terms to be agreed between such government and the General Council of the MTO.

Article IV

Functions of the MTO

1. The MTO shall provide an integrated Dispute Settlement procedure as set out in Annex 2 as may be amended. These rules shall apply to all legal instruments listed in Annex 1A and 1B as well as to the legal instruments listed in Annex 1C, to the extent that the parties to a dispute are members of these latter legal instruments.

2. The MTO shall administer a Trade Policy Review Mechanism as set out in Annex 3, as may be amended.

Article V

Structure of the MTO

1. There shall be a Ministerial Conference consisting of the Ministers responsible for international trade relations of all the members, which shall meet every two years, starting for the first time in December 1993. The task of this Conference shall be to review the operation of the organization and all legal instruments administered by it, to launch further negotiations and to decide on the implementation of results that may have been negotiated among and adopted by the members of the MTO.

11-2

0166

- 3 -

2. There shall be a General Council consisting of trade representative of all the members, which shall meet twice a year, starting in June 1993. The task of this General Council will be to supervise the operation of the MTO, in the time between two Ministerial Conferences and decide on all issues conferred upon it by this agreement.

   It shall carry out the functions of the MTO and may, to this effect, establish subsidiary bodies. It shall establish its own rules of procedure and shall approve the rules of procedure of the Specialised Councils and any subsidiary body.

3. There shall be Special Councils for Goods and Services, consisting of representatives of all members responsible respectively for trade in Goods and Services, which may meet on a monthly basis.

   The Council for Goods shall deal with all matters related to trade in goods on the basis of the legal instruments set out in Annex 1A.

   The Council for Services shall deal with all matters related to trade in Services on the basis of the legal instruments set out in Annex 1B.

Article VI

Voting

At meetings of the General Council, each Member of the MTO shall be entitled to have one vote, and, except as otherwise provided for in this Agreement, decisions of the General Council shall be taken by a majority of the votes cast.

Decisions on accession of new members shall require a two third majority in the General Council.

Amendments to this Agreement, or to any of the legal instruments listed in Annex 1 shall be adopted on the basis of consensus among all members.

// -3

0167

역문서

Relationship between Uruguay Round Agreements and previous GATT Agreements

1.   The GATT has so far not entered into force and continues to be applied on the basis of the 1947 Protocol of Provisional Application (-PPA) and subsequent accession protocols.

2.   Paragraph 4 of the Draft Final Act envisages application of GATT on a definitive basis as from the date of entry into force of the Uruguay Round results.   This could be achieved by including into the Implementation Agreement a commitment to apply the GATT, subject to certain changes as agreed in the Uruguay Round and in the Implementation Agreement (e.g. without current GATT Articles XXVI, XXIX, XXXI to XXXIII), on a definitive basis among the parties to the Implementation Agreement.

3.   The relationship between the Implementation Agreement and previous GATT Agreements (PPA, accession protocols, MFA, Tokyo Round Agreements) could be explicitly regulated in the Implementation Agreement.   For instance, a provision similar to Article 16:5 of the 1979 Anti-Dumping Code could provide that "acceptance of this Agreement shall carry denunciation of the ... (PPA, MFA, specified Tokyo Round Agreements) for each party to those Agreements.   Such denunciation shall take effect on the date of entry into force of this Agreement for each such party with due regard to the notification requirements set out in the withdrawal clauses of such Agreements."

4.   But contracting parties might find it more advantageous to leave it to each individual party of the Implementation Agreement to decide for itself whether and when to withdraw from the PPA, the MFA and the Tokyo Round Agreements.   In the absence of any such withdrawals, the relationships between the Uruguay Round Agreements and previous GATT Agreements would be governed by the general principles of international treaty law set out in the 1969 Vienna Convention on the Law of Treaties:

    (a) Among parties to both the Implementation Agreement and earlier GATT Agreements, "the earlier treaty applies only to the extent that its provisions are compatible with those of the later treaty" (Article 30:3, 4(a)).   So the Uruguay Round Agreements would prevail.

    (b) Among parties to both the Implementation Agreement and earlier GATT Agreements and parties to only one or all of the earlier GATT Agreements, "the treaty to which both States are parties governs their mutual rights and obligations" (Article 30:4(b)).   So, for example, the PPA (GATT), MFA and Subsidy Code would continue to apply.   But, pursuant to their withdrawal provisions, any signatory could withdraw from these Agreements upon the expiration of sixty days.

5.   Which ones of the 199 existing GATT legal instruments, listed in the "Status of Legal Instruments" (GATT loose-leaf edition), will be affected by the Uruguay Round Agreements depends on the latters' contents. It would seem neither necessary nor advisable (so as to obviate mistakes and unnecessary disputes) to add to the Implementation Agreement a list of GATT legal instruments affected by the Uruguay Round Agreements.

A—4

사무국 문서

11.11.91

MTO Proposal Item (4):   Provisions on membership

<u>Options</u>:

<u>Membership</u>

The Members of the MTO shall be the contracting parties to the Uruguay
Round Agreements on Trade in Goods, the General Agreement on Trade in
Services and to the Agreement on Trade-Related Aspects of Intellectual
Property Rights including Trade in Counterfeit Goods.

11 - 5

0169

MTO Proposal   Item (5):   Establishment of an International Secretariat

Options:

- The GATT Director-General and the ICITO/GATT Secretariat shall become the Director-General and Secretariat of the MTO. The powers, duties, conditions of service and terms of office of the Director-General and the staff rules shall conform to regulations approved by the MTO Council.

- (Article IX of a 1990 Secretariat Non-Paper on the MTO):

"The General Council shall appoint a Director-General as chief administrative officer of the MTO. The powers, duties, conditions of service and terms of office of the Director-General shall conform to regulations approved by the General Council."

- (Article 7 of the 1955 Agreement on the OTC):

"The Secretariat

(a) The Assembly shall appoint a Director-General as chief administrative officer of the Organization. The powers, duties, conditions of service and term of office of the Director-General shall conform to regulations approved by the Assembly.

(b) The Director-General or his representative shall be entitled to participate, without the right to vote, in all meetings of the Assembly and subsidiary bodies of the Organization.

(c) The Director-General shall appoint the members of the staff, and shall fix their duties and conditions of service in accordance with regulations approved by the Assembly.

(d) The selection of the members of the staff shall as far as possible be made on a wide geographical basis and with due regard to the various types of economy represented by Member countries. The paramount consideration in the selection of candidates and in determining the conditions of service of the staff shall be the necessity of securing the highest standards of efficiency, competence, impartiality and integrity.

(e) The responsibilities of the Director-General and of the members of the staff shall be exclusively international in character. In the discharge of their duties, they shall not seek or receive instructions from any government or from any other authority external to the Organization. They shall refrain from any action which might reflect on their positions as international officials. The Members shall respect the international character of the responsibilities of these persons and shall not seek to influence them in the discharge of their duties."

11 - 6

0170

- (Articles 84,85 of the 1948 Havana Charter):

The Director-General

"1.   The chief administrative officer of the Organization shall be the Director-General. He shall be appointed by the Conference upon the recommendation of the Executive Board, and shall be subject to the general supervision of the Board. The powers, duties, conditions of service and terms of office of the Director-General shall conform to regulations approved by the Conference.

2.   The Director-General or his representative shall be entitled to participate, without the right to vote, in all meetings of any organ of the Organization.

3.   The Director-General shall present to the Conference an annual report on the work of the Organization, and the annual budget estimates and financial statements of the Organization."

The Staff

"1.   The Director-General, having first consulted with and having obtained the agreement of the Executive Board, shall have authority to appoint Deputy Directors-General in accordance with regulations approved by the Conference. The Director-General shall also appoint such additional members of the Staff as may be required and shall fix the duties and conditions of service of the members of the Staff, in accordance with regulations approved by the Conference.

2.   The selection of the members of the Staff, including the appointment of the Deputy Directors-General, shall as far as possible be made on a wide geographical basis.... The paramount consideration in the selection of candidates and in determining the conditions of service of the Staff shall be the necessity of securing the highest standards of efficiency, competence, impartiality and integrity.

3.   The regulations concerning the conditions of service of members of the Staff... shall be fixed, so far as practicable, in conformity with those for members of the Secretariat of the United Nations and of specialized agencies."

B-9

0171

MTO Proposal   Item (6): Budgetary provisions.

Options:

- The Interim Committee shall elaborate the provisions on the MTO Budget
  and MTO Contributions for adoption by Ministers. Such provisions shall
  be based, as far as practicable, on the provisions and practices for
  the GATT Budget.

- (Article XI of the 1990 Secretariat Non-Paper on the MTO, similar to
  Article 9 of the 1955 Agreement on the OTC):

                    "Budget and Contributions

(1)   The Director-General shall present to the General Council the
annual budget estimates and financial statements of the MTO. The
General Council shall approve the accounts and the Budget.

(2)   The General Council shall apportion the expenditures of the
Organization among the Members, in accordance with a scale of
contributions to be fixed by the General Council, and each Member
shall contribute promptly to the Organization its share of these
expenditures.

(3)   The General Council shall decide on administrative measures to be
taken with regard to Members in arrears of their contributions."

- (Article 91 of the 1948 Havana Charter for an ITO):

                    Contributions

'Each Member shall contribute promptly to the Organization its share
of the expenditure of the Organizaton as apportioned by the
Conference. A Member which is in arrears in the payment of its
contributions shall have no vote in the organs of the Organization, if
the amount of its arrears equals or exceeds the amount of the
contributions due from it in respect of the preceding two complete
years. The Conference may, nevertheless, permit such a Member to vote,
if it is satisfied that the failure to pay is due to circumstances
beyond the control of the Member."

0172

MTO Proposal   Item (7):   Provisions on the legal capacity of the
                           organization, privileges, immunities, relations with other
                           organizations

Options:

- (Article XII and XIII of the 1990 Secretariat Non-Paper on the MTO,
  similar to Articles 10 and 11 of the 1955 Agreement on the OTC):

"Status

(1) The MTO shall have legal personality.

(2) The MTO shall enjoy in the territory of each of the Members such
legal capacity, privileges and immunities as may be necessary for the
exercise of its functions.

(3) The representatives of the Members and the officials of the MTO
shall enjoy such privileges and immunities as are necessary for the
independent exercise of their functions in connection with the MTO.

(4) The privileges and immunities to be accorded by a Member to the
MTO, to its officials and to the representatives of its Members shall
be similar to those accorded by each Member to specialized agencies of
the United Nations, to their officials and to the representatives of
their members, under the Convention on the Privileges and Immunities
of the Specialized Agencies, or under similar arrangements.

Relations with other Organizations

(1) The MTO shall make arrangements with intergovernmental bodies and
agencies which have related responsibilities to provide for effective
cooperation and the avoidance of unnecessary duplication of
activities.

(2) The MTO may make suitable arrangements for consultation and
cooperation with non-governmental organizations concerned with matters
within the scope of the MTO."

- See also the more elaborate provisions in Articles 86 - 90 of the 1948
  Havana Charter for an ITO.

0173

MTO Proposal   Item (8): Final provisions

Most final provisions should be included in the Implementation Agreement,
or in the respective substantive Agreements (GATT, GATS, TRIPS), rather
than in an MTO Agreement.

Options:

-   (Articles XIV and XV of the 1990 Secretariat Non-Paper on the MTO):

"Amendments

Decisions on amendments of this Agreement shall be taken by two-thirds
of the Members.

Final Provisions

1.   This Agreement shall be open for acceptance, by signature or
otherwise, by all participants in the Uruguay Round of Multilateral
Trade Negotiations.

2.   This Agreement shall be part of the Uruguay Round results and
shall enter into force on the same date as the other Agreements,
Decisions and Understandings embodying the results of the Uruguay
Round.

3.   Prior to the entry into force of this Agreement, the text of this
Agreement shall be deposited with the Director-General to the
CONTRACTING PARTIES to the General Agreement on Tariffs and Trade, in
his capacity as depositary of the Uruguay Round results. He shall
promptly furnish a certified true copy thereof and a notification of
each acceptance thereof to each signatory of the Agreement on the MTO.
The Agreement shall, upon its entry into force, be deposited with the
Director-General of the MTO.

4.   This Agreement shall be registered in accordance with the
provisions of Article 102 of the Charter of the United Nations."

-   (Article 16 of the 1955 Agreement on the OTC):

"Amendments

Amendments to this Agreement shall become effective, in respect of
those Members which accept them, upon acceptance by two-thirds of the
Members of the Organization and thereafter in respect of each other
Member upon acceptance by it."

8-10

0174

- Accession, non-application and withdrawal provisions may not be necessary in an MTO Agreement if the membership, non-application and withdrawal provisions in the Implementation Agreement, or in the GATT, GATS and TRIPS Agreements, were applicable and "The members of the MTO are the contracting parties to the Uruguay Round Agreements".

- Transitional arrangements may not be necessary if the MTO and its organs were to be established with the entry into force of the MTO Agreement, and the GATT Secretariat and GATT Director-General were to become the MTO Secretariat and MTO Director-General.

- Entry into force could be regulated to the effect that "This Agreement shall be part of the Uruguay Round Agreements and shall enter into force on the same date as the Uruguay Round Agreements."

- The relationship between the Uruguay Round Agreements and previous GATT Agreements (e.g. the PPA, accession protocols, MFA, Tokyo Round Agreements), as well as other "final clauses" (e.g. on waivers, non-application of the Agreement between particular contracting parties) should be regulated in the Implementation Agreement rather than in the MTO Outline Agreement.

- Reservations to the MTO Agreement should not be permitted.

- Other final provisions (e.g. on signature, languages) should be included into the Implementation Agreement in a uniform manner applicable to all Uruguay Round Agreements including the MTO Agreement.

- The relationship to countries applying GATT on a de facto basis could, as in the past, be regulated in Decisions of the CONTRACTING PARTIES.

0175

외 무 부

종 별 :

번 호 : GVW-2338　　　　　　　　　　　일 시 : 91 1115 1030

수 신 : 장관(통기,경기원,재무부,농수산부,상공부)

발 신 : 주제네바대사

제 목 : UR/제도분야 비공식 협의(분쟁해결)

　　1. 11.14. 표제협의(LACARTE 의장주재) 에서는 교차보복 문제가 논의된바, 미국이먼저 교차보복 필요성을 제기하고, EC,카나다,뉴질랜드, 스위스,북구등이 동조 또는 검토 용의를 표명한 반면,아국포함 개도국은 반대입장을 표명한바 동 결과 아래 보고함.(이성주 참사관 참석)

　　가. 미국은 UR 협상이 전분야에 걸쳐 참가국권리.의무가 균형을 이루는 GLOBALLYBALANCED PACKAGE를 추구하고 있는 만큼, 권리침해시 해당분야뿐 아니라 타분야에서도 보복을 허용, 전체적인 권리.의무관계의 재균형(REBALANCING) 도모를 용이하게해야만 협상 결과의 실효적 이행이 가능하다고 하면서, 이에 대한 의지만 있으면교차보복의 규정방법, 특별히 어려운 분야의제외등 관련 법칙, 기술적 문제는 협상을통해 다루어 나갈수 있을 것이라 함.

　　나. EC, 카나다, 스위스, 북구는 동일 분야 에서 보복에 우선을 두되 불가능할경우에 한하여 충분한 정당성(JUSTIFICATION) 입증 조건하에 SECTOR간, 협정간 교차보복을 인정하는HIERARCHY 도입, 문제가 되는 일부 분야는 교차보복대상에서 제외하는 방법등이 고려될 수 있을것이라 하면서, MODALITIES 에 대한 토의 용의를 표명함.

　　다. 아국, 인도, 홍콩, 싱가폴, 브라질, 태국,베네주엘라, 이집트, 말련, 칠레,항가리등은 아래 이유로 반대 입장을 표명함.

　　- 상품협정, 써비스협정, TRIPS 협정은 서로 다른별개의 법체계

　　(아국)

　　- 상품, 써비스, TRIPS 별로 자체적, 내부적으로권리.의무상의 균형을 도모하는것으로 이해

　　- 신분야의 경우 피해수준의 정확한 계량화 및상품분야와 등가관계 산정이 사실상

통상국　　차관　　2차보　　안기부　　경기원　　재무부　　농수부　　상공부

PAGE 1　　　　　　　　　　　　　　　　　　　　91.11.15　　20:44 ED

외신 1과 통제관

0176

불가능(아국)

  - 써비스 분야에 대한 보복 효과는 상품분야보다 훨씬 장기적이고 광범위함(예:은행지점의 폐쇄)

  - 보복력이 제한된 개도국에 대한 선진국의 일방 통행적 보복 무기화 가능성(아국)

  - 예외설정시 협상력이 큰 선진국에 불리한 분야가 우선 제외될 경우 개도국에게 더욱 불리

  - 써비스, TRIPS, TRIMS등은 새로운 분야인 만큼 일정기간 시행해 본 후 검토하는 것이 타당

  라. 상기에 대해 미국은 협상 결과의 균형은 분야별 내부적 균형이 아니라 전체에 걸친(ACROSSTHE BOARD) 균형이라는 점을 재강조하고, 계량화의 어려움은 상품분야 내부에서도 품목분야별로 어려움이 존재하며, 개도국의 보복력이 제한되어있다는 것은 그만큼 양허수준이 낮다는 것을 반증하는 것일 뿐 이라고 반박하고, 교차 보복문제를 계속 토의해 나갈 것을 요청함.

  2. 제도분야 공식협의는 11.15.오후 개최될 예정이며, LACARTE 의장은 동 회의에서 내주회의 일정을 밝히겠다고 하였음.끝

  (대사 박수길-국장)

PAGE 2

0177

외 무 부

종 별 :

번 호 : GVW-2354   일 시 : 91 1116 1100

수 신 : 장 관(통기, 경기원)

발 신 : 주 제네바 대사

제 목 : 제도분야 공식회의

　　1. 금 11.15 개최된 표제회의에서는 LACANTE 의장이 분쟁해결 절차 및 MTO 설립문제를 포함한 FINAL ACT 관련 지난 공식회의 이후의 비공식 협의 결과를 설명에 이어 23개국 대표의 발언이 있었는바, 발언국은 대부분 MTO 설립문제 및 통합분쟁 해결제도 및 CROSS-RETALIATION 등 분쟁해결 절차상의 일부문제점에 대한 견해를 피력함. (본직, 이성주참사관, 신부남 서기관 참석)

　　가. MTO 설립문제

　　0 필리핀(ASEAN 대표), 인도, 유고, 아르헨티나, 아국등은 동 문제가 UR 협상 이행과 관련 중요한 문제이긴 하나 현시점에서는 실질적 문제 논의에 우선을 두고, 구협상 결과가 나온 연후에 각료회의등에서 논의하는 것이 적절하다는 의견을 피력

　　0 멕시코, 브라질등은 각국 정부가 정치적으로 결정해야 할 사항으로 이를 위해서는 동기구에 대한 실질적 내용을 알아야 한다는 의견 표명

　　0 베네주엘라는 UN 에서의 국제무역 기구설립 문제에 대한 논의 결과도 감안해야한다는 의견을 피력

　　0 제안국인 EC 및 카나다는 MTO 설립은 UR협상 결과의 이행을 위해 필수적인 문제임을 재차 강조함.

　　나. 분쟁해결 절차

　　0 의장은 아래 5개 사항이 현재까지의 주요 미결현안임을 언급

　　- 일방 조치 억제 공약(전반적 협상 결과와 연계되어 있음을 부언)

　　- NON-VIOLATION 분쟁.

　　- '66 절차 통합문제

　　- 통합분쟁 해결 제도

통상국	차관	1차보	2차보	구주국	외정실	청와대	안기부	경기원

91.11.16 　　 20:37 FN

외신 1과 통제관

0178

- 교차 보복문제

0 인도, 이집트, 브라질, 베네주엘라 등은 봉합분쟁 해결 제도 도입 및 교차 보복인정에 반대입장을 표명

0 아국도 상기 양문제에는 신중히 다루어져야 할사항이라는 의견 표명

0 반면, 미국은 상기 양문제는 SINGLE UNDERTAKING과 상호 밀접히 연관되어 있는사항이라고 함으로써 이에 대한 미국의 입장이 강경함을시사하였으며, 또한 분쟁해결 절차는 모든 분야의 협상 결과를 보고난 후에나 결정 가능한 사항이라는 11.12 비공식 협의시 밝힌 (GVW-2234 참조)을 되풀이 함으로써 일방조치 억제 관련 쉽게 양보치 않겠다는 자세를 암시함.

다. COHERENCE 문제

0 의장은 이문제도 조만간 비공식 협의에서 다루어져야 할 사항이라고 언급하였으나, 참가국으로부터 구체적 코멘트는 없었음.

라. 기타

0 의장은 TRANSPARENCY 차원에서 비공식 협의가 OPEN-ENDED 임을 강조, 희망국 참여를 권유하고 차기 회의는 MTO 문제, 분쟁해결 분야에서 실질적인 결과가 나오는것을 보아 소집할 예정이라고 언급

2. 한편, 11.15 오전에 열린 최종의정서 비공식회의 에서는 EC, 카나다가 제안한MTO 설립에 관한 협약안을 계속 논의하였는바, 회원에 관한 조항(3조)에 규정된 갓트 체약국에 대한 2년간 가입 유예기간 부여문제, 봉하분쟁 해결절차를 관리할 특별기구 설립 필요성(EC제안),MTO 의 산하 기관 구성문제, 협약간 ANNEX IC 관련 MTO 가입에 필수적이 아닌 MTN 협정의 범위 확대문제등을 논의하였음. 차기회의는 11.21-22간 개최 예정임. 끝

(대사 박수길-국장)

PAGE 2

0179

외 무 부

종 별 :

번 호 : GVW-2375 　　　　　　일 시 : 91 1120 1500

수 신 : 장관(봉기, 경기원, 재무부, 농림수산부, 상공부, 특허청)

발 신 : 주 제네바 대사

제 목 : UR/개도국 비공식 그룹회의

연: GVW-2347

1. 11.19(화) 표제회의가 BENHIMA 의장 주재로 개최되어 제도분야 협상 현황을 협의하였는바, 인도 대표가 신분야를 포함하는 SINGLE UNDER TAKING에 대한 개도국들의참여에 신중을 기할 것을 촉구하고 MTO 설립에 반대의사를 표명한데 대하여, 여타개도국들은 동 문제들이 향후 국제무역 장래에 커다란 영향을 미칠 것임을 감안, 신중한 검토가 필요함을 주장하였으며, 기타일방조치, 분쟁해결 절차의 자동화등에대한협상 현황 설명이 있었음. (김서기관 참석)

2. 인도 대표는 SINGLE UNDERTAKING 문제와 관련, 푼타 델 에스테 각료 선언상의 SINLE UNDERTAKING은 정치적 약속이며, 법적인 약속이 아닌 만큼 개도국들은 각료선언문 제1부 상품 교역 분야의협상 결과만을 수용하는 문제를 검토할 필요가 있다고강조하고, MTO 설립문제와 관련 이는 선진국들이 신분야를 포함하는 SINGLE UNDERTAKING을 기정 사실화하고 통합분쟁해결 절차를 도입함을써 CROSS-RETALIATION 을 개도국들에게 강요하려는 시도라고 발언함.

3. 칠레, 모로코, 알젠틴, 필리핀, 브라질 대표들은SINGLE UNDERTAKING 이나 MTO설립문제등은 다자무역 체제의 장래를 결정하는 중요한 문제이며, 현재 개도국들이 신분야 협상에도 참여하고 있는 만큼 구체적 협상 결과가 나온후 동문제를 검토하는 것이 타당할 것이라는 의견을 제시함.

4. 한편 브라질, 홍콩 대표들은 지난 11.15 자배포된 분쟁해결 절차에 관한 수정봉합문서에 일방조치가 21조에 언급되어 있음을 지적하고 동 문제에 대한 개도국들의 관심을 환기시키면서, 특히 분쟁해결 절차가 자동화 될경우, 동 절차상의 이사회의 역할 약화에 우려를표명함.

5. 의장은 금번 회의에서 거론된 SINGLEUNDERTAKING, MTO 설립, 일방조치 및

통상국　2차보　정와대　안기부　경기원　재무부　농수부　상공부　특허청

PAGE 1 　　　　　　　　　　　　　　　91.11.21　08:53 ED

외신 1과 통제관

0180

분쟁해결자동화등에 대한 개도국 비공식 LDHW의 우려를 적절한 경로를 봉하여
표명키로함, 끝

　　　(대사 박수길-국장)

PAGE 2

0181

외 무 부

종 별 :

번 호 : GVW-2405   일 시 : 91 1121 1930

수 신 : 장 관(봉기)

발 신 : 주 제네바 대사

제 목 : UR/ 최종의정서(MTO)

연: GVW-2327

1. 표제 비공식 회의가 LINDEN 보좌관 주재로 11.20 개최되어 연호 MTO 사무국 구성, 예산규정등에 관해 사무국이 문서로 제시한 옵션안에 대해 논의하였는바, 주요요지 아래 보고함.(오참사관, 신서기관 참석)

가. 사무국 구성에 대한 규정

0 EC, 카나다는 MTO 관련 사무국이 90년 제출한 NON-PAPER 에 사무국 구성에 관한 규정을 논의 기초로 하는데 지지하였으며, 뉴질라니드, 미국, 홍콩,브라질, 호주,아국은 MTO 사무국 조직은 갓트의 현 사무국 체제를 기본적으로 유지하는 것이 바람직하다고 언급함.

베네주엘라는 사무국 고위직 임명시 지리적인 고려 반영등 임명에 대한 규정이 필요하다고 함.

나. 예산 규정

0 미국, 베네주엘라, 일본, EC, 아국은 90년사무국 NON-PAPER 의 예산 규정이 옵션안중에서 가장 적절하다고 언급하였으며, 회원국 분담금은 가급적 갓트 규정을 적용하되 (각국의 무역량을 기준으로 결정) 서비스 및 TRIPS 관련 무역량을 산출하기위한 기준을 마련할 필요성이 제기됨.

다. MTO 의 특권, 면제 및 타국제기구와의관계

0 대체로 90년 사무국 NON-PAPER 의 관련 규정을 선호하였으며, 타국제 기구와의 협력 관계를 설정할수있는 권한은 궁극적으로 MTO 의일반 이사회에 있으며, MTO 가사무국 주재국과의 본부 협정 (HEADQUARTER AGREEMENT)체결 필요성도 언급되었음.

라. 최종 규정(FINAL PROVISIONS)

0 LINDEN 보좌관은 대부분의 실질 협상 분야협정(GATT, GATS, TRIPS)에 최종

통상국   2차보   구주국   청와대   안기부

     91.11.22   06:21 FN

외신 1과 통제관

0182

규정이 포함되어 있기 때문에 MTO 협약에 최종 규정을 포함시키는 것은 바람직 하지 않다고 언급하였으며, 참석국들은 대체로 이에 동조함.

　마. 기타

　페루, 인도는 SINGLE UNDERTAKING 을 전제로 한 MTO설립후 <u>MTO 와 기존 갓트의 2원 구조에서 오는 문제점을 지적하였으며</u>, 탄지니아는 EC, 카나다가 제의한 MTO 협정안은 상품, 서비스 협정이 분리되어 있는 '푼타' 선언 정신에 위배됨을 지적하고 MTO 설립 문제를 현 상황에서 논의하는 것이 적절치 않다고 지적함.

　2. LINDEN 보좌관은 금일 및 지난주 비공식회의에서 논의된 사항을 반영하여 EC및 CANADA 가 MTO 설립에 관한 <u>수정 협약안을 작성, 이를 11.26 비공식 회의에서 논의 하기로 하였음.</u> 끝

　（대사 박수길-국장）

PAGE 2

0183

외 무 부

종 별 :

번 호 : GVW-2418   일 시 : 91 1122 1630

수 신 : 장 관(봉기,경기원,재무부,농수산부,상공부)

발 신 : 주 제네바대사

제 목 : UR/제도분야(분쟁해결) 비공식 협의

　　　11.18-20간 진행된 표제 비공식 협의에서는 사무국이 작성한 11.14.현재의 OUTSTANDING PROPOSAL목록(별첨 1)을 기초로 이들 미결사항 전반에 대한 재검토가 있었으며,그 결과로 패널 설치시한(4.1항) 및 중재 절차에의 준용(23.4항)등에 대한 합의가 이루어졌고, NV 분쟁, 패널보고서 채택(인도제안)등에 대한 장시간의 논의가 진행되는등 다소의 진전을 보였는바, 동결과를 아래 보고함.(이성주 참사관 참석). 한편분쟁해결 분야 차기 비공식 협의는 11.27 속개 예정이며, 경제정책상의 일관성 제고 문제등갓트 기능분야 토의도 내주중 부터 시작될 가능성이 있음.

　　1. 합의 사항가. 패널 설치(4.1항)

　　- 미국이 4.1항 괄호 처리되어 잇는 FOLLOWING THAT을 살려 2번째를 이사회에서의 패널 설치에 동의 하는 대신 10일 사전 요청으로 이사회를 소집할 수 있는 현행 관례를 동항 각주에 명기할 것을 제의하고 , 2번째 이사회에서의 설치를 주장해온 국가(아국포함)들이 이를 수락함으로써 합의(단,주말, 공휴일등에 대비 별첨 2와 같이 15일로 연장 합의)

　　나. 이행 및 보상관련 조항의 중재절차에의 준용(23.4항)

　　- 제안국인 스위스가 동건을 NV 분쟁 처리결과와 연계 계속 입장을 유보해온 EC의무성의한 협상 태도에 강력 항의함에 따라, EC가 수락에 동의함으로써 합의(여타국 은오래전에 동의의사 표명)

　　다. 부패성 물질관련 문안추가(10.3항 및 15.5항)

　　- 토의없이 별첨 1 문안대로 합의

　　2. 주요 토의 사항

　　가. 패널 보고서 채택(14.4항등 관련 인도제안)

　　- 인도가 10.30-31 동 문제 논의시 표출된 각국의 의견(GVW-2234 참조)을 참작,

통상국　　2차보　　경기원　　재무부　　농수부　　상공부

91.11.23　　09:11 WH

외신 1과 통제관

0184

14.2, 12.4, 15.4,15.5, 15.12 항 관련 별첨 3수정안을 제출(단,분쟁당다국은 동의함에도 붙구하고 제3국 이의제기 또는 반대하는 패널보고서 처리 문제는 갓트25조에 따라 처리되는 방안도 고려 가능하나, 일단상기 제안에는 포함치 않았음을 설명)

- 인도는 15.4항 'OR PARTICIPATE' 이하삭제이유(아국), 제3국의 상소기구에 대한 서면진술 제출권 인정 여부(일본), 제3국의범위(카나다)등에 관한 질문에 아래와 같이 답변

0 상소기구 심의과정에 제3국도 당사국과 같이 참여할수 있는 가능성 제공

0 특정 법률적 측면 검토가 주임무이므로 서면 진술제출은 패널의 경우와는 달리인정 붙필요

0 무역 이해가 있는 경우도 한정되는 패널의 제3국과는 다른 개념이므로 현실적무역 이해가 없는 국가도 포함.

- 상기 제의에 대해 EC 는 이제까지 논의방향에 급격한 변경을 가져오는 제안이라고 평가 가장 강경한 반대 의사를 표명하였고, 기타선진국도 패널이 선례형성 효과는 갖지않음에도 붙구하고 제3국 권리를 지나치게 확대하는점(미국,카나다, EC, 북구, 홍콩,일본),이사회에 의한 60일간의 의무적 심의가 불필요한 지연 초래 가능성(미국,카 나다), 사법부적 성격의상소기구의 입법기관에 해당된다고 볼수 있는 이사회로 부터 법해석과 관련 지침을 받는 것과같은 효과 발생(미국)등의 문제점을 지적,대체적으로 부정적 반응을 보임에 따라 인도가 관심 표명 국과 협의후 계론키로 함.

- 한편, 동 인도수정안 심의 과정에서 미국은 제소국이 패소할 경우 동일 사항에 이해관계를 갖고 있는 제 3국이 다시 제도하는 경우 피소국에게는 지나치게 부담(형법상의 일사부재리 원칙과 반함)이 되는 현 제도상의 문제점을 지적하고, 이문제도언젠가는 GATT내에서 해결해야 할 사항이라는 의견을 제시, 아국포함 다수국이 공감을 표시함

나. NV 분쟁

1) 23조 1항 C 케이스

- 제소국이 제소당시부터 GATT 23조 1항 A,B,C중 택일하고, 이를 패널이 변경치못하도록 해야한다는 미국, EC, 일본의 의견에 따라, 카나다 홍콩은 별첨 4 신 수정안을 제시

PAGE 2

0185

- 동 수정안에 대해 미국, EC, 스위스는 마지막문장이 상기 취지에 비추어 문제점이 있음을 다시 지적

2) 23조 1항 B 케이스

- EC 가 B CASE 전체에 관한 별첨 5 TEXT를 제시, 이를 중심으로 토의

- 24.1항 관련 뉴질랜드가 상기 C CASE 의 홍콩,카나다 초안과 문안봉일 필요성을 지적, 특히 EC안에 'THE ATTAINMENT OF ANY OBJECTIVE IS BEINGIMPEDED'가 누락된문제점을 지적하고, 미국, 홍콩이 동조한바, EC는 과거에 이를 이유로 제소된 케이스가 전무하였으며 이를 명문화하는데는 어려움이 있다고(이유는 제시치 않음)하고검토해 보겠다는 반응을 보임

- 동항 ' TO THE EXTENT'와 관련 미국, 카나다는 상기 C 케이스에서와 마찬가지로 GATT 23조1항에 제소국이 A,B,C 중 명백히 선택하도록(EITHER OR)되어 있고, NV분쟁으로 제소시 패널이 위반 분쟁으로 판정할 가능성이 희박하다는 문제점을 지적

- 반대로 아국은 제소국은 위반 분쟁으로 제소하였으나 패널이 NV 으로 판정할 경우 일반절차에 따른 것인지의 여부를 문의한 바, 홍콩은 이경우 패널절차는 종료되고 제소국이 희망하면 NV 분쟁으로 다시 제소 가능한 것으로 보아야 할것이라는 의견 피력

- 24.3항 관련 뉴질랜드는 17.1항에 괄호 처리된 두번째 문장을 24.3항에 통합하거나, 23.3항의 두번째 문장 삭제중 택일 또는 CONAISTENCY유지 필요성을 언급하였고, EC 는 NV분쟁에 관한 특별 절차를 도입하려는 주요 이유중의 하나가 중재 기능을강화 하려는 것이므로 17.1항 두번째 문장의 삭제를 주장(반면, 뉴질랜드는 17.1항 3번째 문장이 NV 분쟁일반 분쟁이 양자 모두에게 적용된다는 입장)

- 24.4항 관련 미국은 중재자의 피해수준 판정과 관련 20.4항에 반영된 등가개념이 누락되어 있음을 지적

- 24.5항에 대해서는 호주, 뉴질랜드가 보상이 상호만족 스러운 조정의 일부가 될 수 있다는 문안에 대해 보상만을 특정적으로 지적한데 대한 문제점을 제기한바, EC는 위반 분쟁경우와는 달리 NV의 경우에는 보상이 일시적성격만을 갖지 않는다고 보기 때문이라고 답변

3. 기타 사항

가. 패, 상소기구의 권고(17.1항, 알젠틴 제안)

- 알젠틴 제안 자체에 대해서는 토의없이 현TEXT 상의 17.1항을 두고 EC와

PAGE 3

0186

뉴질랜드간 상기 2항 '나'와 같은 의견 대립이 반복됨.(뉴질랜드는 3번째 문장이 NV 분쟁,일반분쟁에 모두 적용된다고 주장 EC 는 일반분쟁에만 적용된다는 입장 및 2번째 문장 이삭제 주장)

나. 분쟁해결 절차의 최대시한(19.4항)

- 미국, 카나다가 첫째 괄호 내용을 양보할수 없다 하면서 둘째 괄호 내용을 뉴측제안내용으로 대체하자고 하였으나 아국, EC,일본등이 반대

- 아국은 이제까지 합의된 절차에 따르면 최대시한이 18개월이 아니라 19개월이되어야 함을 지적한바, 사무국이 정확한 소요기간을 확인키로함

다. 각주 2 삭제 또는 표현 완화 문제(1.1항)

- 제안국 미국이 OPTION 2(표현 완화 방안)을철회하고 OPTION 1을 기초로 이에 반대하는 칠레와 양자협의를 계속키로 함.

라. 신속한 분쟁해결의 중요성 인정(1.2항추가문안)

- EC 를 제외하고는 반대 국가가 없었음

마. 분쟁에서의 입증 책임등(1.7항)

- 제안국 미국은 4번째 문장 삭제 주장을 철회하고 갓트 2조 내용의 반복에 불과한 3번째문장의 삭제만을 요구

- EC 만이 NV 분쟁에 연계 현단계에서 동의불가 입장 표명

사. 합리적 이행기간의 지침(19.3 BIS항)

- 역시 EC만이 반대입장을 표명

- 이에대해 미국은 EC 가 NV 분쟁 문제에 관한 자국 입장 관철을 위해 상기 '라', '마' 항및 동 문제와 같이 기술적인 문제에 대한 합의를 BLOCK 하고 있는 협상 태도를 강력히 항의하고 EC 가 연계를 주장하고 있음을 명기(HIGHLIGHT) 하자고 주장

아. 중장정부의 책임(2.1항 BIS 및 20.7항 BIS)

- 제안국 카나다는 EC 가 주장하는 각주(FOOTNOTE) 추가에 동의의사를 밝혔으나미국은 '갓트하에서 체결하는 여타 협정등에 따른 의무' 문단이 통합 분쟁해결 절차관련 문제가 있을 수 있다는 이유로 당분간 유보 입장 표명

자. 66년 절차(1.10항)

- 구체 토의없이 통합문안에 OPTION 1과 2를동시에 추가키로 잠정 합의

카. 동일 사한 처리(8.4항), 분쟁해결 절차와 GATT25조와의 관계(1.8항), 보복의사전승인(20.7항)등에 대해서는 토의 생략

PAGE 4

타. 여타 협상 분야 분쟁해결 절차와의 조화문제관련 LINDER 고문은 LACARTE 의장이 농산물, 섬유, 규범 제정 3개분야 의장앞으로 조화 필요성을 언급한 서한(GVW-2075)을 바롱하였으며, 서비스, TRIPS 분야에 대해서는 의견이 엇갈리고 있음을 DUNKEL의장에게 보고하고 동 처리를 DUNKEL 의장에게 일임하였다고 함.

첨부: 1. 91.11.14 OUTSTANDING PROPOSAL LIST

2. 4.1항 각주 관련 미국 수정안

3. 14.4항 관련 인도 수정안

4. NV 분쟁관련 홍콩, 카나다 수정안

5. NV 분쟁관련 EC 수정안

(GVW(F)-0527).끝

(대사 박수길-국장)

PAGE 5

0188

14.11.91   Dispute Settlement

Outstanding proposals concerning the Consolidated Text are listed
hereunder. The relevant texts are annexed.

0189

- 2 -

(US proposal)

I. General Provisions

Paragraph 1.1

Footnote 2

Option 1: Delete Footnote 2

Option 2: Move the supernumeral to after the first sentence in paragraph 1.2, and revise footnote 2 to read as follows:

"It is noted that Article XXV also affords an appropriate avenue for clarifying the existing provisions of the General Agreement."

****

(New Zealand proposal)

II. General Provisions

Paragraph 1.2 : Add new third sentence

Contracting parties recognise that the prompt settlement of situations in which a contracting party considers that any benefits accruing to it directly or indirectly under the General Agreement are being impaired by measures taken by another contracting party, is essential to the effective functioning of the General Agreement and the maintenance of a proper balance between the rights and obligations of contracting parties.

****

(US proposal)

III. General Provisions

Paragraph 1.7

Delete the **third** sentence.   Articles XXIII:1(b) and XXIII:1(c) speak for themselves; it is unnecessary to paraphrase them in this text.

~~Delete the last sentence. This sentence is repeated in para. 24.2.~~

****

(US proposal)

IV. General Provisions

Paragraph 1.8

The second sentence should be **deleted.** Alternatively, it should be **bracketed or otherwise highlighted** in the same way as other parts of the text for which decisions are related, including paras. 4.1, 14.4, 15.13, and 20.3.

0190

V. 1966 Procedures

LDC
Developing Country

Option 1   (~~Mexico proposal~~)
Delete Attachment BISD 14S/18 and replace paragraph 1.10 with the following two paragraphs:

1.10 This Understanding shall be applied only with respect to new requests under Article XXII:1 and XXIII:1 made on or after the date of entry into force of this Understanding. With respect to disputes for which the request under Article XXII:1 or XXIII:1 was made before the date of entry into force of this Understanding, GATT dispute settlement rules and procedures in effect immediately prior to the date of entry into force of this Understanding shall continue to apply.

1.11 Notwithstanding paragraph 1.10 above, if a complaint is brought by a developing contracting party, that contracting party may choose to apply, as an alternative to this Understanding, the provisions of the Decision of the CONTRACTING PARTIES of 5 April 1966 (BISD 14S/18), instead of the provisions of this Understanding. In that event, the same procedures shall apply that would have applied to cases brought pursuant to the 1966 Decision immediately prior to the date of entry into force of this Understanding, including the procedures contained in the Decision of the Council of 12 April 1989 (BISD 36S/21).

Option 2   (US proposal)
Delete Attachment BISD 14S/18 and replace paragraph 1.10 with the following:

1.10 This Understanding shall be applied with respect to all new requests under Article XXII:1 and XXIII:1 made on or after the date of entry into force of this Understanding. With respect to disputes for which the request under Article XXII:1 or XXIII:1 was made before the date of entry into force of this Understanding, GATT dispute settlement rules and procedures in effect immediately prior to the date of entry into force of this Understanding shall continue to apply.

****

(Canada proposal)

VI. Provisions Governing All Regional and Local Levels of Government

Paragraph 2.1bis

2.1 bis Each contracting party undertakes to accord sympathetic consideration to and afford adequate opportunity for consultation regarding any representations made by another contracting party concerning measures affecting the operation of the General Agreement taken within the territory of the former.

---

(1) Inclusion of paragraphs 20.7bis and 2.1bis herein are conditioned on inclusion of identical paragraphs in "The Understanding on the Interpretation of Article XXIV of the General Agreement on Tariffs and Trade". Should that Understanding be amended, the question of inclusion of the paragraphs herein shall be reconsidered.

0191

- 4 -

(EC proposal)

VIbis Provisions Governing all Regional and Local Levels of Government

At the end of the <u>footnote</u> reproduced in Proposal VI insert the following:

Inclusion of paragraphs 20.7bis and 2.1bis is <u>without prejudice to any obligations resulting from any other agreement or understanding concluded under the auspices of GATT</u> concerning measures adopted by regional or local governments or authorities within the territory of a contracting party.

****

(US Proposal)

VII. Establishment of a Panel

Proposed footnote to <u>paragraph 4.1</u>:

If the complaining party so requests, a meeting of the Council shall be convened for this purpose upon ten days advance notice, in accordance with past practice.

****

(Venezuela proposal)

VIII.   Measures Previously Examined by a Panel

Modify <u>paragraph 8.4</u> to read:

"If a third party considers a measure already the subject of a panel nullifies or impairs benefits accruing to it under the General Agreement, and if that party's complaint is limited to the same specific measure identified in the request for the previous panel, that party may have recourse to GATT dispute settlement procedures on an expedited basis. Such a dispute shall be referred to the original panel wherever possible. Where the panel determines that such a situation is involved, it may shorten the timetable for the panel process originally set pursuant to paragraph 10.4."

****

(Collective proposal)

IX. Panel Procedures

Paragraph 10.3 line 4

After the word "process" insert the following: ",taking into account the provisions of paragraph 2.8, if relevant."

0192

- 5 -

(India proposal)

X.   Adoption of Panel Reports

Proposal for substituting paragraph 14.4

Within sixty days of the issuance of a panel report to the contracting parties, the report shall be adopted by the Council by the traditional practice of consensus, unless one of the parties formally notifies the Council of its decision to appeal and/or there are differences of opinion in the Council on the legal interpretations developed by the panel. In the latter event, the Council shall refer the report to the Appellate Body with a view to seeking a confirmation of the legal interpretations developed by the panel.

Paragraph 15.4   Add a new sentence

However, the GATT Council may also refer a panel report to the Appellate Body for seeking a confirmation of the legal interpretations developed by the panel in accordance with paragraph 14.4.

Paragraph 15.6

The Appellate Body shall consider only those issues of law covered in the panel report and legal interpretations developed by the panel.

****

(collective proposal)

XI. Standing Appellate Body

Paragraph 15.5 line 3

Insert a new second sentence which reads as follows: "In fixing its timetable the appellate body shall take into account the provisions of paragraph 2.8, if relevant."

****

(Argentina proposal)

XII.   Panel and Appellate Body Recommendations

Paragraph 17.1

Option 1: In the fifth line after the words "shall recommend" insert the following "either the withdrawal or modification of the measure or that the contracting party concerned make a mutually satisfactory adjustment".

Option 2: "the solution it considers appropriate to restore the balance of rights and obligations under the General Agreement, including the withdrawal or modification of the measure".

0193

UR(우루과이라운드).제도분야 협상 그룹 회의, 1991   199

(US proposal)

XIII. Reasonable Period Guidelines

Add a new paragraph 19.3bis and renumber the following paragraphs accordingly:

Paragraph 19.3bis:

In arbitration pursuant to paragraph 19.3(c), a guideline for the arbitrator should be that the reasonable period of time to implement panel or appellate body recommendations should not exceed <u>fifteen months</u> from the adoption of a panel or appellate body report. However, that time may be shorter or longer, depending upon the particular circumstances.

****

(New Zealand proposal)

XIV. Surveillance of Implementation of Recommendations and Rulings

Paragraph 19.4:

Revise the last clause of 19.4 to read: "provided that, <u>unless the parties agree that</u> there are exceptional circumstances, the total time shall not exceed eighteen months."

****

XV. Level of suspension

Paragraph 20.7

[7. The <u>level</u> [amount] of suspension shall, if requested <u>sixty days or less before the end of the reasonable period of time</u> by one of the parties, be determined before expiry of the reasonable period of time, in accordance with the relevant procedures under paragraphs 20.3, <u>20.4 and 20.5</u> above, and on the understanding that such suspension shall not come into effect before the Council has granted the authorization provided for in paragraph 20.3]

0194 -

XVI.   Provisions Governing All Regional and Local Levels of Government

Place after Paragraph 20.7

20.7bis The dispute settlement provisions of the General Agreement may be invoked in respect of measures affecting its observance taken by regional or local governments or authorities within the territory of a contracting party. When the CONTRACTING PARTIES have ruled that a provision of the General Agreement has not been observed, the responsible contracting party shall take such reasonable measures as may be available to it to ensure its observance. The provisions relating to compensation and suspension of concessions or other obligations apply in cases where it has not been possible to secure such observance.[1]

---

[1] Inclusion of paragraphs 20.7bis and 2.1bis herein are conditioned on inclusion of identical paragraphs in "The Understanding on the Interpretation of Article XXIV of the General Agreement on Tariffs and Trade". Should that Understanding be amended, the question of inclusion of the paragraphs herein shall be reconsidered.

****

(EC proposal)

Proposal XVIbis:

At the end of the footnote reproduced in Proposal XVI insert the following:

Inclusion of paragraphs 20.7bis and 2.1bis is without prejudice to any obligations resulting from any other agreement or understanding concluded under the auspices of GATT concerning measures adopted by regional or local governments or authorities within the territory of a contracting party.

****

XVII. Arbitration   (Switzerland proposal)

Modify paragraph 23.4 to read:

23.4 Sections 19 and 20 of this Understanding shall apply mutatis mutandis to arbitration awards.

****

(EC proposal)

XVIII.   Section 24. Non-Violation

Paragraph 24.1

24.1.   The procedures in this Understanding shall apply, subject to the provisions of paragraphs 24.2 through 24.5 below, if and to the extent that the complaining party alleges, and the panel or the appellate body determines, that the case concerns nullification or impairment of benefits under the General Agreement without violation thereof within the meaning of Article XXIII:1(b).

0195

- 8 -

(Integration proposal)

XVIIIbis Non-violation

Insert the following new paragraph 10.6bis:

10.6bis If the complaint concerns nullification or impairment of benefits under the General Agreement without violation thereof, within the meaning of Article XXIII:1(b), the complaining contracting/ party shall include a detailed justification in support of such complaint in its written submission.

Revise para 19.3 to read:

2.   At a Council meeting held within thirty days of the adoption of the panel or appellate body report, the contracting party concerned shall inform the Council of its intentions in respect of implementation of the recommendations and rulings under Article XXIII:2.

(a) If the panel or appellate body has found that a measure is inconsistent with the General Agreement, and if it is impracticable to comply immediately with the recommendations and rulings, the contracting party concerned shall have a reasonable period of time in which to do so. The reasonable period of time shall be:

     (i) the period of time proposed by the contracting party concerned, provided that such period is approved by the Council; or, in the absence of such approval:

     (ii) a period of time mutually agreed by the parties to the dispute within forty-five days following adoption of the recommendations and rulings; or, in the absence of such agreement:

     (iii) a period of time determined through binding arbitration within ninety days following adoption of the recommendations and rulings.

(b) If and to the extent that the panel or appellate body has determined that the case brought before it concerns nullification or impairment of benefits under the General Agreement without violation thereof, within the meaning of Article XXIII:1(b), and if the parties do not agree, within forty-five days following adoption, that the implementation proposed by the party concerned will result in a mutually satisfactory adjustment, the reasonable period of time for implementation and the level of benefits which have been nullified or impaired shall be determined through binding arbitration within 90 days following adoption.

Revise paragraph 17.1 to read:

Where a panel or the appellate body concludes that a measure is inconsistent with the General Agreement, it shall recommend that the contracting party concerned bring the measure into conformity with the General Agreement. Where a measure has been found to constitute a case of nullification or impairment of benefits under the General Agreement without violation thereof, there is no obligation to withdraw [or modify] the

0196

measure. However, in such cases, the panel or the appellate body shall recommend that the contracting party concerned make a mutually satisfactory adjustment. In addition to its recommendations, the panel or appellate body may suggest ways in which the contracting party concerned could implement the recommendations.

━━

Add the following footnote to para 20.3:

[1] In cases concerning nullification or impairment of benefits under the General Agreement without violation thereof, the arbitrator's decision provided for in paragraph 19.3 with respect to the level of benefits shall be in lieu of the arbitration provided for in paragraph 20.3.

****
(Argentina proposal)

XVIIIter   Section 24 Non-Violation Complaints

Paragraph 24.1:

After the words "General Agreement" in the fifth line add the following sentence "nullify or impair any benefit accruing to it directly or indirectly or impedes the attainment of any objective under the General Agreement".

Paragraph 24.3:

"Where a measure has been found to constitute a case of nullification or impairment of benefits under the General Agreement the panel or the appellate body shall recommend that the measure be withdrawn or modified or that the contracting party concerned make a mutually satisfactory adjustment."

Paragraph 24.4:

In the second line from the bottom replace "but" for the word "and".
In the last line delete the word "not".

Paragraph 24.5:

Maintain only: "The provisions of Section 20 shall apply".

Paragraph 24.6:

Delete both options.

0197

4ㅋ 19. ハ.1ㅣ

첨부2

REVISED FOOTNOTE TO PARA. 4.1

If the complaining party so requests, a meeting of the Council shall be convened for this purpose within fifteen days of the request, provided that at least ten days' advance notice is given, in accordance with past practice.

0198

- 10 -

(EC proposal)

XIX.   Article XXIII:1(c) Complaints

Paragraph 24.6

1.   The Council shall refer any complaint brought under Article XXIII:1(c) to a special working party. This working party will examine the facts of the matter in the light of the relevant provisions of the General Agreement; it will signal any general problems affecting the General Agreement as a whole; it will address recommendations for a mutually satisfactory adjustment to the parties and/or issue general recommendations to the CONTRACTING PARTIES. The report of the special working party will be issued within twelve months.

2.   On the basis of the report, the Council may take appropriate action by consensus.

****

(Hong Kong and Canada proposal)

XIXbis   Article XXIII:1(c)

Paragraph 24.6

Notwithstanding the provisions of this Understanding, where a party has recourse to dispute settlement based upon Article XXIII:1(c), or a panel determines, that any matter falls under the provisions of Article XXIII:1(c), the GATT dispute settlement rules and procedures contained in the Decision of the Council of 12 April 1989 (BISD 36S/61) shall apply from the point at which the panel report has been issued to the contracting parties for consideration for adoption instead of the rules and procedures of this Understanding. In the event that a panel finds that other provisions of Article XXIII:1 are also applicable in the same case, the panel shall issue separate panel reports addressing only the Article XXIII:1(c) issue for purposes of this different procedure.

0199

INDIA

Adoption of Panel Reports

14.2 Contracting parties having objections to panel reports shall give written reasons to explain their objections, for circulation during the sixty-day period during which the panel report is under consideration by the Council as provided in paragraph 14.4.

14.4   Within sixty days of the issuance of a panel report to the contracting parties, the report shall be adopted by the Council unless one of the parties to the dispute formally notifies the Council of its decision to appeal or the Council decides [otherwise] [by consensus] [not to adopt the report]. This adoption procedure is without prejudice to the right of contracting parties to express their views on a panel report.

Paragraph 15.4

Only parties to the dispute, not third parties, may appeal a panel decision.

Paragraph 15.5

60+60

As a genral rule, the proceedings shall not exceed sixty days from the expiry of the sixty day period during which the panel report is under consideration of the Council to the date the appellate body issues its decision. When the appellate body considers that ....

Paragraph 15.12

The appellate body shall address each of the issues raised by the parties to the dispute and the issues raised in the written communications, as provided for under paragraph 14.2.

0200

対策 4.

19.11.91

Hong Kong and Canada Proposal

PROCEDURES FOR ARTICLE XXIII:1(c) DISPUTES

~~Option 1~~

A panel may <u>only make</u> rulings and recommendations under Article XXIII:1(c) <u>where a party considers</u> that any benefit accruing to it directly or indirectly under the GATT is being nullified or impaired or the attainment of any objective is being impeded as the result of the existence of any other situation. / <u>Where and to the extent</u> that a party has alleged a matter falls under Article XXIII:1(c) and a panel determines that the matter falls under Article XXIII:1(c), the procedures of this Understanding shall apply up to and including the point in the proceedings that the panel report has been issued to the contracting parties. / The GATT dispute settlement rules and procedures contained in the Decision of the Council of 12 April 1989 (BISD 36S/61) shall apply for consideration for adoption, and thereafter. /

In the event that a panel finds that other provisions of Article XXIII:1 are also applicable in the same case, the panel shall issue a panel report addressing any matters falling under Article XXIII:1(a) and (b) and a separate report on matters falling under Article XXIII:1(c).

0201

Non-violation

EC

Section 24 - Non-violation

24.1   The procedures in this Understanding shall apply, subject to
       the provisions of paragraphs 24.2 through 24.5 below, If and to
       the extent that the complaining party considers, and the panel
       or the appellate body determines, that the case concerns
       nullification or impairment of benefits under the General
       Agreement without violation thereof within the meaning of
       Article XXIII:1(b).

24.2   The complaining party shall present a detailed justification in
       support of any complaint made pursuant to paragraph 24.1 above.

24.3   Where a measure has been found to constitute a case of
       nullification or impairment of benefits under the General
       Agreement without violation thereof, there is no obligation to
       withdraw [or modify] the measure. However, in such cases, the
       panel or the appellate body shall recommend that the
       contracting party concerned make a mutually satisfactory
       adjustment.

24.4   In accordance with paragraph 19.3, the contracting party
       concerned shall inform the Council of its intentions in respect
     - of implementation of the recommendations and rulings under
       Article XXIII:2. If the parties do not agree, within forty-five
       days following adoption, that such implementation will result
       in a mutually satisfactory adjustment, the reasonable period of
       time for implementation and the level of benefits which have
       been nullified or impaired shall be determined through binding
       arbitration within ninety days following adoption, pursuant to
       paragraph 19.3. Upon request by either party, the arbitrator
       may also suggest ways and means of reaching a mutually
       satisfactory adjustment, but such suggestions shall not be
       binding upon the parties.

24.5   The provisions of Section 20, [with the exception of paragraph
       20.7] shall apply, provided that compensation may be part of a
       mutually satisfactory adjustment and provided that the
       arbitration foreseen in paragraph 24.4 above shall replace,
       with respect to the determination of the level of benefits
       having been nullified or impaired, the arbitration foreseen in
       paragrah 20.3.

1.7   Omit third and fourth sentences

17.1   Omit sentence in square brackets

0202

외 무 부

종 별 :

번 호 : GVW-2486   일 시 : 91 1128 1900

수 신 : 장 관(통기, 경기운, 재무부, 농수부, 상공부)

발 신 : 주 제네바대사

제 목 : UR/제도분야(분쟁해결)비공식 협의

연: GVW-2418

1. 11.27 표제 비공식 협의(LINDEN고문주재)에서는 연호 11.14 현재 OUTSTANDINGPROPOSAL 목록중 남은 잇슈, 타협사운야에서 적용할 분쟁해결 관련 통일(UNIFORM)문안 에 관한 카나다 제안, 일방조치 억제 공약관련 조항(21항)에 대한 토의가 있었음(이 성주참사관 참석). 사무국은 연호 11.18-20 간 회의시 합의내용을 포함시킨 11.27자 통합문안 및 OUTSTANDING PROPOSAL 목록(별첨 1)을 배포함.

2. 회의 벽두 LINDEN 고문은 11.29(금) 17:00 개최예정인 TNC 회의에 맞추어 그이전까지 합의되는 사항은 합의된 내용으로, 합의를 못하는 사항은 괄호등으로 처리된 상태로 단일TEXT에 포함시킨다는 전제하에 트의에 임해줄것을 요청함.

3. 토의 결과 OUTSTANDING LIST 상의 ITEM II (1.2항), III (1.7 항)및 상기 UNIFORM 문안관련 카나다 제안에 대해서는 문안 자체에 대한 합의가, 여타 IV (1.8 항), VI (2.1 항 BIS), XIII (19.3 항) BIS), VXV (20.7항), XVI(20.7 항BIS)에 관해서는단 일 TEXT 에의 포함방식(괄호 또는 OPTION 형식등)에 대한 합의가 이루어졌으며, ITEM X (14.4 항등 관련 인도제안)등 여타 4개 ITEM 과 일방조치 억제관련 조항(2.1항)에 대해서는 결론을 내리지 못하거나 계속 검토키로 되었음. NON-VIOLATION분쟁관련 제안 (ITEM XII 포함)은 시간부족으로 토의치 못함에 따라 11.28 오전 토의를계속 키로 함.

4. 한편 사무국이 상기 11.27 자 통합문안 19.4항(분쟁해결 절차의 최대시한)에 11.18-20 회의시아국, EC, 일본의 주장에 따라 뉴질랜드 절충안을 제 3의 괄호로 설정한 것과 관련, 미국이 기존의 2개 괄호대신 뉴측제안으로 합의할것을 주장했으나 EC 가 선두에 나서 정치적 잇슈임을 내세워 반대(아국 및 일본도 새통합 문안대로 3개의 괄호 유지를 지지)한 바, 이에 대해 미국은 사사건건 정치적 잇슈임을 내세워

통상국   2차보   경기원   재무부   농수부   상공부

PAGE 1   91.11.29   08:09 WH

외신 1과 통제관

0203

협상진전을 방해하는 EC 의 태도를 비난하면서 EC만이 관심을 가지고 있는 NON-VIOLATION 관련조항을 봉합문안에서 삭제할 것을 요구하는등 강한 불쾌감을 표시함.

5. 토의 내용의 상세는 아래와 같음.

가. 문안 합의 내용

(1) ITEM II (신속한 분쟁해결의 중요성, 1.2항)

- 상기 4항 미구의 강한 불만 표시에 따라 유일한 유보입장 표명국인 EC 가 더이상 반대치 않으므로써 합의

- 단, 동 문안 추가시 현문안 2번째 및 3번째문장의 논리적 흐름을 저해하는 점을 감안 1.2 항BIS를 신설키로 함.

(2) ITEM III(1.7 항)- 역시 유일한 유보입장 표명국인 EC 가 더이상 반대치 않으므로써 3번째 문장을 삭제키로 합의하고, EC 의 요청으로 4번째 문장은 괄호처리

(3) 타협상 분야 분쟁해결에 적용될 통일(UNIFORM) 문안 (카나다제안)

- 카나다가 제안한 별첨 2 문안에 대해 1 번째 및 2번째 괄호를 ' INSTRUMENT' 로 대체하고, 3번째 괄호도 구태여 괄호 처리할 필요성이 없다는 점이 지적되어 괄호없는 문안에 합의

- 동문안의 향후 처리 방안에 관한 아국등의 문의에 대해 사무국은 LACARTE 의장이 3개 협상그룹 의장에게 다시 송부토록 하겠다 하였으며, 미국은 SVC, TRIPS 협상분야에 대해서도 연호3항 '다' 와 같이 DUNKEL 총장에게 일임해야 할것임을 주장

나. 단일 TEXT 에의 포함방식에 합의한 사항

(1) ITEM IV(분쟁해결 절차와 GATT 25 조의관계, 1.8항)

- 미국의 1.8항 제 2문장 괄호처리 요구에 대해 멕시코가 그렇다면 제 1문장도 함께 괄호 처리해야 한다고 반대입장 표명, (미국은 이제까지의 협상결과가 무엇에 대한 CONSENSUS 인가에 대한 변경을 가져온 것일뿐 컨센서스 자체에 대한 관행을 바꾼것은 아니기 때문에 'TRADITIONAL'이라는 표현은 정확한 표현이 아님을 언급)

- 홍콩, 뉴질랜드, 아국등은 CONSENSUS 의 정확한 개념, 관행에 대한 사무국의 연구를 요청하고, 당분간은 현 TEXT 를 그대로 유지할것을 주장.

- LINDEN 고문이 제시한 절충안(멕시코, EC등도 이를 수락)에 따라 괄호 처리 대신 4.1 항등 관련 항의 처리결과를 보고 결정한다는 내용의 각주를 신설키로 함.

(2) ITEM VI 및 XVI (중앙정부 책임, 2.1 항BIS 및 20.7 항 BIS)

PAGE 2

0204

- 유일한 반대국인 EC 가 양보, 본문은 단일 TEXT 에 괄호 처리된 상태로 포함키로 하고, 각주는 여타 각주와 구분키 위해 ASTERIK 로 하기로 합의

(3) ITEM XIII (합리적 이행기간, 19.3 항 BIS)

- 역시 EC만이 반대해온 사항으로 괄호 상태로단일 TEXT 에 포함키로 합의

(4) ITEM XV(보복의 사전 승인, 20.7항)

- LINDEN 고문의 제외와 절충안 제안국인카나다, 뉴질랜드의 희망에 따라 OPTION2 로단일 TEXT 에 포함키로 합의

(이에 따라 사실상 3개의 OPTION 있게 되는결과가 됨)

(1) ITEM X (패널 보고서 채택, 14.4 항등 관련인도제안)

- 제안국 인도는 연호 11.18-20 토의시와 같이 동제안의 목적이 PANEL 결정이 제3국을 구속하거나 선례를 형성치 않는다는 GATT 의 관행과 상소기구는 법적 해석 문제만 다룬다는 이제까지의 합의 결과에 본질적인 변경을 가하자는 것이 아니라, 이사회의 정치적 역할과 패널의 결정이 상기 갓트 관행에도 불구 사실상 제 3국 이해에영향을 미칠수 있다는 현실을 감안할 제안임을 설명하고, 15.12항을 'ISSUES OFLEGAL INTERPRETATION RAISED BY THE PARTIES TO THE DISPUTEAND IN THE WRITTEN COMMUNICATIONS ,,,,,'로 수정하겠다는 의사 표명(이문제는 당초 패널보고서 채택에 한해서는 기존의 방식에 따르겠다는 목적의 제안이었으나, 참가국들의 소극적인 반응에 접한 인도가 방향을 수정, 이사회 권능 및 제3국 권리 강화(특히 후자)측면을 부각시킴으로써 본래 의 제안 취지는 퇴색한 결과 초래)

- 인도는 특히 미관세법 337 조 분쟁을 예로 들면서 직접적인 무역 이해가 없는제3국도 GATT체제 전반에 중대한 영향을 미칠가능성이 있는 패널 보고서에 대해서는 문제를 제기할 수 있어야 할 것임을 강조

- EC 및 아국은 인도 수정제의 15.4 항 관련상기와 같은 중대한 문제가 있음에도불구 분쟁당사국이 상소치 않으면 제 3국으로서는 독자적인 상소권한이 없다는 문제점에 대한 인도의 해명을 요구하였으며

- 미국은 본문제가 GATT 25조에 따른 공동행동과의 관계를 언급하고, 홍콩 및 EC도 여사한 중대문제는 GATT 25 조에 따르는 것이 바람직하다는 의견 개진

- 놀웨이는 동건 관련 현 TEXT 의 15.12 항의'EACH OF THE ISSUES RAISED BY THEPARTIES TO THE DISPUTEDURING THE APPELLATE PROCEEDING ' 과 법률 문제로 국한한 15.6 항간의 상호 불일치 문제를 지적하고, 이런점에서 인도 수정안 15.12

항이 확실한 문안이 될수도 있다는 입장 및 14.4항의 2번째 문장을 삭제하면 인도의 15.5항주정제의와 동일한 효과를 낼수 있다는 의견을 제시

 - 상기 인도제안의 단일 TEXT 에의 수용문제와 관련, 브라질만이 인도안에 지지입장을 표명하였을뿐, EC, 미국, 카나다, 호주등은 분쟁 당사국이 제기하는 문제이상으로 상고 기구의 권한 확대 곤란 및 절차지연 가능성등을 이유로 반대의견을, 일본, 홍콩, 스위스, 멕시코는 14.4항의 2번째 문장 삭제, 이사회에서 60일간의 토의 가능성을 열어줌으로써 이사회의 역할을 강화한다는 중도적 입장을 표명했으나, 결론을내리지 못함.

 (2) 일방조치 억제 공약(21항)

 - 동건은 OUTSTANDING PROPOSAL 에 포함된 사항은 아니나, 미국이 동 조항을 절차 자동화 관련 조항과 연계시킨 현 각주의 기본 취지는 개념(CONCEPT)을 연계시킨 것일뿐 현문안(WORDING)을 연계시킨것은 아니라 하고, 오해소지를 없애기 위해 21.1항 전체에 대한 괄호 처리를 요구한바, 아국, 일본, 홍콩, 브라질, 카나다등 다수국이반대

 - 특히 EC는 NV 분쟁관련 미국의 대 EC비난을 언급하면서 미국의 협상 태도야 말로 극히 불성실한 자세라고 공박

 - 21.1항 문안에 대한 구체적 대안 유무 및 동문안 제시 가능시기에 관한 사무국의 문의에 대해 미국은 11.29 TNC에서 타분야 협상의 윤곽이 나타나기 전에는 이에관해 언질할 입장에 있지 않다고 답변

 (3) 기타 ITEM I(각주 2 삭제문제)는 미국, 칠레간 양자 협의중 VII (도일 사안처리, 8.4항)은 베네주엘라가 관심 표명국과 협의 계속, XII(패널 및 상소기구의 권고, 17.1항)은 VN분쟁과 함께 토의할 사항이브로 토의 생략

 첨부: 1. 91.11.27 OUTSTANDING PROPOSAL 목록

 2. 타협상분야 분쟁해결 절차에 적용될 통일문안 관련 카나다 제안. 끝

 GVW(F)-554)

 (대사 박수길-국장)

GVW(гห)-0554   11/28 1/00

"GVW-2486첨부"

27.11.91   Dispute Settlement

With regard to the text dated 14 November 1991 the following action has
been agreed: (i) proposals VII (Establishment of a Panel), IX (Panel
Procedures), XI (Standing Appellate Body) and XVII (Arbitration) have been
agreed and have been incorporated in the Consolidated Text; (ii) proposal
V (Decision of 5 April 1966) has been incorporated in the Consolidated
Text and the Attachment has been deleted; (iii) proposal VIbis has been
incorporated in VI (Regional and Local levels of Government); (iv)
proposal XVIbis has been incorporated in proposal XVI (Regional and Local
Levels of Government); (v) proposal XIV (Surveillance of Implementation of
Recommendations and Rulings) has been incorporated in the Consolidated Text
as a third option in square brackets; (vi) proposal XVIIIbis
(Non-Violation) has been withdrawn.

Outstanding proposals concerning the Consolidated Text are listed
hereunder. The relevant texts are annexed.

554-P-1

0207

- 2 -

I. General Provisions

Paragraph 1.1

Footnote 2

Delete Footnote 2

****

II. General Provisions

Paragraph 1.2 : Add new third sentence

Contracting parties recognise that the prompt settlement of situations in which a contracting party considers that any benefits accruing to it directly or indirectly under the General Agreement are being impaired by measures taken by another contracting party, is essential to the effective functioning of the General Agreement and the maintenance of a proper balance between the rights and obligations of contracting parties.

****

III. General Provisions

Paragraph 1.7

Delete the third sentence. Articles XXIII:1(b) and XXIII:1(c) speak for themselves; it is unnecessary to paraphrase them in this text.

****

IV. General Provisions

Paragraph 1.8

The second sentence should be deleted. Alternatively, it should be bracketed or otherwise highlighted in the same way as other parts of the text for which decisions are related, including paras. 4.1, 14.4, 15.14, and 20.3.

****

0208

H4- P-2

- 3 -

VI. Provisions Governing All Regional and Local Levels of Government

Paragraph 2.1bis

2.1 bis   Each   contracting   party undertakes   to   accord   sympathetic
consideration to and afford adequate opportunity for consultation regarding
any representations made by another contracting party concerning measures
affecting the operation of the General Agreement taken within the territory
of the former.[1]

___

[1] Inclusion of paragraphs 20.7bis and 2.1bis herein are conditioned on
inclusion of identical paragraphs in "The Understanding on the
Interpretation of Article XXIV of the General Agreement on Tariffs and
Trade". Should that Understanding be amended, the question of inclusion of
the paragraphs herein shall be reconsidered. Inclusion of paragraphs
20.7bis and 2.1bis is without prejudice to any obligations resulting from
any other agreement or understanding concluded under the auspices of GATT
concerning measures adopted by regional or local governments or authorities
within the territory of a contracting party.

****

VIII.   Measures Previously Examined by a Panel

Modify paragraph 8.4 to read:

"If a third party considers a measure already the subject of a panel
nullifies or impairs benefits accruing to it under the General
Agreement, and if that party's complaint is limited to the same
specific measure identified in the request for the previous panel,
that party may have recourse to GATT dispute settlement procedures on
an expedited basis. Such a dispute shall be referred to the original
panel wherever possible. Where the panel determines that such a
situation is involved, it may shorten the timetable for the panel
process originally set pursuant to paragraph 10.3."

****

X.   Adoption of Panel Reports

Paragraph 14.2

Contracting parties having objections to panel reports shall give
written reasons to explain their objections, for circulation during
the sixty-day period during which the panel report is under
consideration by the Council as provided in paragraph 14.4.

Paragraph 14.4

Within sixty days of the issuance of a panel report to the contracting
parties, the report shall be adopted by the Council unless one of the
parties to the dispute formally notifies the Council of its decision
to appeal or the Council decides [otherwise] [by consensus] [not to
adopt the report]. This adoption procedure is without prejudice to
the right of contracting parties to express their views on a panel
report.

0209

(54-P-3)

- 4 -

Paragraph 15.4

Only parties to the dispute, not third parties, may appeal a panel
decision.

Paragraph 15.5

As a general rule, the proceedings shall not exceed sixty days from
the expiry of the sixty·day period during which the panel report is
under consideration of the Council to the date the appellate body
issues its decision. When the appellate body considers that ....

Paragraph 15.12

The appellate body shall address each of the issues raised by the
parties to the dispute and the issues raised in the written
communications, as provided for under paragraph 14.2.

****

XII.   Panel and Appellate Body Recommendations

Paragraph 17.1

Option 1: In the fifth line after the words "shall recommend" insert
the following "either the withdrawal or modification of the measure or
that the contracting party concerned make a mutually satisfactory
adjustment".

Option 2: "the solution it considers appropriate to restore the
balance of rights and obligations under the General Agreement,
including the withdrawal or modification of the measure".

****

XIII.   Reasonable Period Guidelines

At the end of paragraph 19.3(c) add the following sentence:

In such arbitration, a guideline for the arbitrator should be that the
reasonable period of time to implement panel or appellate body
recommendations should not exceed fifteen months from the adoption of
a panel or appellate body report. However, that time may be shorter
or longer, depending upon the particular circumstances.

****

0210

- 5 -

XV. Level of suspension

Paragraph 20.7

[7. The level [amount] of suspension shall, if requested sixty days
or less before the end of the reasonable period of time by one of the
parties, be determined before expiry of the reasonable period of time,
in accordance with the relevant procedures under paragraphs 20.3, 20.4
and 20.5 above, and on the understanding that such suspension shall
not come into effect before the Council has granted the authorization
provided for in paragraph 20.3]

****

XVI. Provisions Governing All Regional and Local Levels of Government

Place after Paragraph 20.7

20.7bis The dispute settlement provisions of the General Agreement
may be invoked in respect of measures affecting its observance taken
by regional or local governments or authorities within the territory
of a contracting party. When the CONTRACTING PARTIES have ruled that
a provision of the General Agreement has not been observed, the
responsible contracting party shall take such reasonable measures as
may be available to it to ensure its observance. The provisions
relating to compensation and suspension of concessions or other
obligations apply in cases where it has not been possible to secure
such observance.

---

[1]Inclusion of paragraphs 20.7bis and 2.1bis herein are conditioned on
inclusion of identical paragraphs in "The Understanding on the
Interpretation of Article XXIV of the General Agreement on Tariffs and
Trade". Should that Understanding be amended, the question of inclusion of
the paragraphs herein shall be reconsidered. Inclusion of paragraphs
20.7bis and 2.1bis is without prejudice to any obligations resulting from
any other agreement or understanding concluded under the auspices of GATT
concerning measures adopted by regional or local governments or authorities
within the territory of a contracting party.

****

XVIII.   Section 24. Non-Violation

Paragraph 24.1

The procedures in this Understanding shall apply, subject to the
provisions of paragraphs 24.2 through 24.5 below, if and to the extent
that the complaining party considers, and the panel or the appellate
body determines, that the case concerns nullification or impairment of
benefits under the General Agreement without violation thereof within
the meaning of Article XXIII:1(b).
Paragraph 24.2

The complaining party shall present a detailed justification in
support of any complaint made pursuant to paragraph 24.1 above.

0211

- 6 -

Paragraph 24.3

Where a measure has been found to constitute a case of nullification or impairment of benefits under the General agreement without violation thereof, there is no obligation to withdraw [or modify] the measure. However, in such cases, the panel or the appellate body shall recommend that the contracting party concerned make a mutually satisfactory adjustment.

Paragraph 24.4

In accordance with paragraph 19.3, the contracting party concerned shall inform the Council of its intentions in respect of implementation of the recommendations and rulings under Article XXIII:2. If the parties do not agree, within forty-five days following adoption, that such implementation will result in a mutually satisfactory adjustment, the reasonable period of time for implementation and the level of benefits which have been nullified or impaired shall be determined through binding arbitration within ninety days following adoption, pursuant to paragraph 19.3. Upon request by either party, the arbitrator may also suggest ways and means of reaching a mutually satisfactory adjustment, but such suggestions shall not be binding upon the parties.

Paragraph 24.5

The provisions of Section 20, [with the exception of paragraph 20.7] shall apply, provided that compensation may be part of a mutually satisfactory adjustment and provided that the arbitration foreseen in paragraph 24.4 above shall replace, with respect to the determination of the level of benefits having been nullified or impaired, the arbitration foreseen in paragraph 20.3.

Paragraph 1.7

Omit third and fourth sentences.

Paragraph 17.1

Omit sentence in square brackets.

****

XVIIIter   Section 24 Non-Violation Complaints

Paragraph 24.1:

The procedures in this Understanding shall apply, subject to the provisions of paragraphs 24.2 through 24.5 below, where a party resorts to dispute settlement based upon Article XXIII: 1(b) alleging that the introduction or intensification of a measure not in conflict with the General Agreement nullify or impair any benefit accruing to it directly or indirectly or impedes the attainment of any objective under the General Agreement.

0212

554-P-6

- 7 -

Paragraph 24.2:

The complaining contracting party shall present a detailed
justification in support of any complaint made pursuant to paragraph
24.1 above.

Paragraph 24.3:

Where a measure has been found to constitute a case of nullification
or impairment of benefits under the General Agreement the panel or the
appellate body may recommend that the measure be withdrawn or modified
or that the contracting party concerned make a mutually satisfactory
adjustment.

Paragraph 24.4:

In accordance with paragraph 19.3 the contracting party concerned
shall inform the Council of its intentions in respect of
implementation of the recommendations and rulings under
Article XXIII 2.

Paragraph 24.5:

If the party concerned fails to implement the panel or the appellate
body recommendations and rulings the provisions of Section 20 shall
apply.

****

XIX. Article XXIII:1(c) Complaints

Paragraph 24.6

1.   The Council shall refer any complaint brought under Article
XXIII:1(c) to a special working party. This working party will
examine the facts of the matter in the light of the relevant
provisions of the General Agreement; it will signal any general
problems affecting the General Agreement as a whole; it will address
recommendations for a mutually satisfactory adjustment to the parties
and/or issue general recommendations to the CONTRACTING PARTIES. The
report of the special working party will be issued within twelve
months.

2.   On the basis of the report, the Council may take appropriate
action by consensus.

****

XIXbis   Article XXIII:1(c)

Paragraph 24.6

A panel may only make rulings and recommendations under
Article XXIII:1(c) where a party considers that any benefit accruing
to it directly or indirectly under the GATT is being nullified or
impaired or the attainment of any objective is being impeded as the
result of the existence of any other situation. Where and to the
extent that a party has alleged a matter falls under Article
XXIII:1(c) and a panel determines that the matter falls under Article

0213

ᄃ54-ᄼ-ᄀ

- 8 -

XXIII:1(c), the procedures of this Understanding shall apply up to and including the point in the proceedings that the panel report has been issued to the contracting parties. The GATT dispute settlement rules and procedures contained in the Decision of the Council of 12 April 1989 (BISD 36S/61) shall apply for consideration for adoption, and thereafter.

In the event that a panel finds that other provisions of Article XXIII:1 are also applicable in the same case, the panel shall issue a panel report addressing any matters falling under Article XXIII:1(a) and (b) and a separate report on matters falling under Article XXIII:1(c).

0214

654-9-8

CANADA

20 November 1991

The provisions of Articles XXII and XXIII of the General Agreement,
and the Understanding on Rules and Procedures Governing the Settlement of
Disputes under Articles XXII and XXIII of the General Agreement on Tariffs
and Trade as adopted by the CONTRACTING PARTIES shall apply to
consultations and the settlement of disputes under this [Agreement]
[Understanding], [except as otherwise specifically provided herein].

0215

외 무 부

종 별 :

번 호 : GVW-2495   일 시 : 91 1129 1100

수 신 : 장 관(통기,경기원,재무부,농림수산부,상공부)

발 신 : 주 제네바 대사

제 목 : UR/제도분야 비공식 협의(분쟁해결)

연: GVW-2418

1. 11.28 표제회의에서는 NON-VIOLATION 분쟁만이 논의된바 동 결과 아래 보고함.
(이성주 참사관 참석)

가. 23조 1항 B 케이스 분쟁

- EC 가 별첨 1 수정안을 제시한바, 동 수정안은연호 11.18-20 토의시 수개국이지적한 '갓트 목표달성 저해'를 24.1 항에 추가하고, 24.4 항 및 24.5항을 보다 단순화한 외에 24.5 항의 하단부를 삭제함으로써 NV 분쟁의 경우에도 필요시 2차례의 중재(19.3 항 중재 및 20.3항 중재)를 거칠수 있도록 한 내용임.

- 호주, 뉴질랜드는 철회, 수정의 의무가 없고(24.3항) 보상이 최종 해결책이 될수 있다고(24.5항)명시적으로 규정할 경우, 보상 제공 이외의 여타해결책(철회, 수정등) 모색 노력에 DISINCENTIVE가 됨으로써 장래 NV 분쟁의 급증이 우려된다고 지적하 고, 24.3항의 'OR MODIFY'를 삭제하거나 (호주), 첫번째 문장 전체를 삭제(뉴질랜드)할 것과 24.5 항 보상이 상호만족스러운 해결책의 일부가 될수 있다는 문안의 삭제를 주장(홍콩, 브라질 동조)

- 반면 인도는 EC 수정안이 보다 명확한방향으로 개선되어 받아들일 용의가 있다고 평가하고 24.5 항 보상 및 24.3항 OR MODIFY를 유지하고자 하는 EC 입장을 지지

- 놀웨이도 EC 수정안을 유용한 제안으로 평가하고 24.5항 및 24.3항 관련 상기인도와 동일의견(단, 24.4항 마지막 문장의 중재자가 제시하는구체적 해결 방안의 구속력 불부여에 대해서는 반대입장 피력)

- 스위스는 24.3항에 대해서는 호주, 뉴질랜드입장을, 24.5항에 관해서는 EC, 인도 입장 지지

- 미국, 카나다는 24.3항에 '갓트 목표달성 저해'가 누락된점을 지적한 외에는 특

통상국	구주국	외정실	분석관	청와대	안기부	경기원	재무부	농수부
상공부								

       91.11.30   01:00 FL

외신 1과 통제관

0216

별한 의견 표명없었음.

- EC 는 상기 의견에 대해 24.3항 관련 미국,카나다의 지적은 기술적 사항으로 수용 용의가 있으나 호주, 뉴측 제기문제는 VN 분쟁과 일반분쟁의 차이점을 없애는 것이나 마찬가지이므로 받아들이기 어려우며, EC 가 그간 계속양보해온점을 상기시키면서 더이상의 양보는 곤란하다고 언급

- 문안을 다시 개선하여 제시하겠다는 EC의 제의에 미국이 EC 의 독자적인 DRAFT에 맡기기 보다 소규모 초안 작성 그룹 구성을 제의 수개관심국이 오후에 초안 작성 작업을 진행키로 함.

- 한편 11.29 TNC 이전까지 마련키로 한 단일초안에 NV 분쟁관련 초안 수용 문제에 관해서 EC 는 자국안 및 알젠틴안등을 OPTION 형식으로 하여 더이상 의미가 없는브랏셀초안을 대체할 것을 주장한 반면, 미국이 유보입장을 표명 상기 초안 작성 작업 결과를 보고 11.29 오전 중 수용 방법을 추가 검토키로 함.

나. 23조 1항 C 케이스 분쟁

- 카나다, 홍콩의 별첨 2 수정문안에 대해 미국,EC 가 마지막 문장관련 연호 문제점을 다시 지적한데 대해, 카나다는 CASE SHIFTING은 안되지만 단일 케이스 이긴 하나 일반 및 불위반조치가 섞여 있는 혼합 케이스에 대비할 필요가 있다고 설명

2. 한편, 11.29 17:00 비공식 TNC 관련 WORKINGDOCUMENT 로서 분쟁해결 분야의 경우 새로운 통합문안이 준비되는 것과 관련 미국은 통합분쟁해결 절차와 교차 보복문제가 아직도 남아있음을 상기시키면서 동 통합문안이 동문제토의를 배제하는 것은 아님을 분명히 할필요가 있음을 강조함.첨부: 1. 23조 1항 B 분쟁관련 EC 수정안

2. 23조 1항 C 분쟁관련 카나다, 홍콩 수정안.끝

(GVW(F)-556)

(대사 박수길-국장)

24.1   A panel may only make rulings and recommendations under Article
        XXIII:1 (b) where a party considers that any benefit accruing
        to it directly or indirectly under the GATT is being nullified
        or impaired or the attainment of any objective of the Agreement
        is being impeded as the result of the application by a
        contracting party of any measure, whether or not it conflicts
        with the provisions of the General Agreement. Where and to the
        extent that a party considers and a panel or the appellate body
        determines that a case brought under Article XXIII:1 (b)
        concerns a measure which does not conflict with the General
        Agreement, the procedures in this Understanding shall apply,
        subject to the provisions under paragraphs 24.2 through 24.5
        below.

24.2   The complaining party shall present a detailed justification in
        support of any complaint relating to a measure which does not
        conflict with the General Agreement.

24.3   Where a measure has been found to constitute a case of
        nullification or impairment of benefits under the General
        Agreement without violation thereof, there is no obligation to
        withdraw [or modify] the measure. However, in such cases, the
        panel or the appellate body shall recommend that the
        contracting party concerned make a mutually satisfactory
        adjustment.

24.4   The provisions of Section 19 shall apply, it being understood
        that the arbitration provided for in paragraph 19.3, upon
        request by either party, may include a determination of the
        level of benefits which have been nullified or impaired and may
        also suggest ways and means of reaching a mutually satisfactory
        adjustment; such suggestions shall [not] be binding upon the
        parties.

24.5   The provisions of Section 20 [except paragraph 20.7] shall
        apply, provided that compensation may be part of a mutually
        satisfactory adjustment as final settlement of the dispute.

$1\cdot 45 \cdot 2$.

PROCEDURES FOR ARTICLE XXIII:1(C) DISPUTES

Such   *considers*

A panel may only make rulings and recommendations under
Article XXIII:1(c) where a party considers that any benefit
accruing to it directly or indirectly under the GATT is being
nullified or impaired or the attainment of any objective is being
impeded as the result of the existence of any situation other than
those under Articles XXIII:1(a) and (b). Where and to the extent
that (a) party ~~has alleged a matter falls under Article XXIII:1(c)~~
and a panel determines that the matter falls under Article
XXIII:1(c), the procedures of this Understanding shall apply up to
and including the point in the proceedings that the panel report
has been issued to the contracting parties. The GATT dispute
settlement rules and procedures contained in the Decision of the
Council of 12 April, 1989 (BISD 36S/61) shall apply for
consideration for adoption, and surveillance and implementation of
recommendations and rulings.

In the event that a panel finds that other provisions of
Article XXIII:1 are also applicable in the same case, the panel
shall issue a panel report addressing any matters falling under
Article XXIII:1(a) and (b) and a separate report on matters falling
under Article XXIII:1(c).

$558-2-2$ 0219

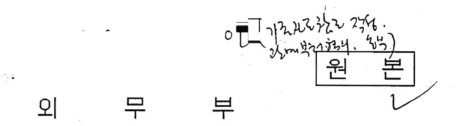

외 무 부

종 별 :

번 호 : GVW-2487   일 시 : 91 1129 0930

수 신 : 장관(통기,경기원,재무부,농림수산부,상공부)

발 신 : 주제네바대사

제 목 : UR/분쟁해결(교차보복)

연: GVW-2338

1. UR 협상 마무리 단계에서 EC, 카나다가 제안하고 있는 MTO 체제하의 INTEGRATED DISPUTE SETTLEMENT SYSTEM 또는 미국의 경우와 같이 분쟁해결 자체차원에서의 INTERATED DISPUTE SETTLEMENT SYSTME 문제가 제기됨으로써, 이와 관련한 교차보복이 인정 여부 및 인정시 동 MODALITIES 를 여하히 설정할 것인가의 문제가 본격 거론될가능성이있으며, 써비스 협상에서도 동 교차보복 문제가 논의되고 있음.

2. 분쟁해결 그룹 차원에서는 연호 11.14. 최초로 기본적인 원칙 논의만 있었을뿐아직 구체적 제안이 제시된 단계는 아니나, 교차보복제도에관한 미국의 의지가 강하고 여타 대부분의 선진국도 현실적 제약 요인을 감안 일정 조건및 규율하의 교차보복을 희망하나 동 제도도입 자체에는 미국과 입장을 같이 함으로서, 개도국의 반대에도불구하고 협상 최종단계 또는 후속협상 단계에서 동 문제 논의가 구체화될 가능성에대비, 아래사항 포함 이문제에 관한 아국의 대처 입장을 예상되는 UR 협상의 최종결과 및 공세적 측면과 수세적 측면등을 종합적으로 검토, 회시 바람.

    0 교차보복 인정여부에 관한 아국의 기본입장

    - 인정 반대시 가능한 대응 논리 포함

    0 아국이 수락 가능한 대안(FALLBACK POSITION)으로서 교차보복의 인정범위

(대사 박수길-국장)

통상국	장관	차관	2차보	경기원	재무부	농수부	상공부

91.11.29   18:58 DW

외신 1과 통제관

0220

외 무 부

종 별 :

번 호 : GVW-2518

일 시 : 91 1129 2030

수 신 : 장관(통기, 경기원, 재무부, 농림수산부, 상공부)

발 신 : 주 제네바 대사

제 목 : 최종의정서(MTO)

연: GVW-2405

대: WGV-1648

1. 11.29 오전 LINDEN 보좌관 주재 MTO 에 대한 비공식 회의가 개최되었는바, 동 회의에서 EC 및 카나다가 공동으로 작성한 별첨 MTO설립 협정 초안을 제시하였음. (오참사관 참석)

2. 금일 회의에서는 구체적인 협의를 하지 않고 EC 및 카나다측이 그동안 비공식 협의에서 논의된 사항을 종합, 동 초안을 작성하였다는점, 동 초안은 WORKING PAPER 의 성격에 지나지 않으며, 앞으로 더 검토보완이 필요하다는 취지 성명을 하였음.

3. 동 초안은 MTO 의 설립 취지, MTO 의 관장협정범위, 회원국, 가입, MTO 의 기능, 조직사무국, 예산, MTO의 지위, 타기구와의 관계,부표, 개정, 청취, 발효, 부적용, 최종조항으로 구성되어 있으며, 부록 1A 는 상품 분야, 1B는 서비스, C 는 낙농제품 협정등 4개 동경라운드 협정을 염두에 두고 있음.

4. 동 협상 초안에 대한 다음 협의는 12.5(목) 로 예정되고 있는바, 동 초안에 대한 본부의 검토의견을 차기 회의 이전에 당관에 회보 바람.

첨부: MTO 설립 협정 초안. 끝

(GVW(F)-565)

(대사 박수길-국장)

통상국 2차보 경기원 재무부 농수부 상공부

91.11.30   09:43 DQ

외신 1과 통제관

0221

GNW(3)-585 1112ρ1ρ30
GNW-2578 전신 November 29, 1991

AGREEMENT ESTABLISHING THE MULTILATERAL TRADE ORGANIZATION

The MEMBERS,

Recognizing that their relations in the field of trade and economic endeavour should be conducted with a view to raising standards of living, ensuring full employment and a large and steadily growing volume of real income and effective demand, developing the full use of the resources of the world at sustainable levels, and expanding the production and exchange of goods and services,

Being desirous of contributing to these objectives by entering into reciprocal and mutually advantageous arrangements directed to the substantial reduction of tariffs and other barriers to trade and to the elimination of discriminatory treatment in international trade relations,

Determined therefore, to preserve the basic principles and to further the objectives of the General Agreement on Tariffs and Trade and to develop an integrated, more viable and durable multilateral trading system encompassing the GATT as modified, all Agreements and Arrangements concluded under its auspices and the complete results of the Uruguay Round multilateral trade negotiations,

Agree as follows:

Article I

Establishment of the Organization

The Multilateral Trade Organization (herein after referred to as "the MTO") is hereby established in order to implement the substantive results of the Uruguay Round negotiations and to undertake other functions as set out in this Agreement.

Article II

Scope of the MTO

1.   The Multilateral Trade Organization (MTO) shall provide the common institutional framework for the conduct of trade relations between the members of the MTO in matters related to the General Agreement on Tariffs and Trade (as amended by the Uruguay Round Agreements and on a definitive basis), the Tokyo Round Arrangements and Agreements, and the Uruguay Round Agreements, Decisions and Understandings.   The list of

585-ρ-1

Agreements and legal instruments covered by this agreement is set out in Annex 1, as may be amended (herein after referred to as the Multilateral Trade Agreements). Agreements listed in Annexes 1A and 1B shall have all members as parties. Agreements listed in Annex 1C may have limited membership.

2. The General Agreement on Tariffs and Trade, as amended by the Uruguay Round Agreements, referred to above is legally distinct from the Agreement known as the General Agreement on Tariffs and Trade dated 30 October 1947.

3. The MTO shall provide the forum for further negotiations among its members concerning their multilateral trade relations as may be decided by the Ministerial Conference or the General Council.

Article III

Membership

Membership in the MTO shall be open to all GATT contracting parties and the European Communities, subject to the provisions of Article XIV. By accepting the MTO Agreement, members accept all Agreements and legal instruments listed in Annexes 1A and 1B.

Article IV

Accession

1. Any government which has not become a member pursuant to Article III, or is not a contracting party to the GATT at the time of the entry into force of this Agreement, including a government acting on behalf of a separate customs territory possessing full autonomy in the conduct of its external commercial relations and of other matters provided for in this Agreement, may accede on terms to be agreed between such government and the General Council of the MTO.

2. Decisions on accession of new Members shall be taken by the General Council and shall be approved by a two-thirds majority of votes cast and that such majority shall comprise more than half the MTO members.

Article V

Functions of the MTO

1. The MTO shall have authority to take appropriate actions to ensure the effective implementation, facilitate the operation and further the objectives of the Multilateral Trade Agreements set out in the Annexes to this Agreement, subject to limitations specified in these Agreements.

2. The MTO shall administer an Integrated Dispute Settlement System as set out in Annex 2, as may be amended. These rules and procedures shall apply to all Multilateral Trade Agreements set out in Annex 1A and 1B. The procedures shall also apply to the Multilateral Trade Agreements listed in Annex 1C to the extent that the parties to a dispute are members of these Agreements.

3. The MTO shall administer a Trade Policy Review Mechanism as set out in Annex 3, as may be amended.

4. The MTO shall cooperate with the IMF, the IBRD and affiliated agencies with a view to achieving greater coherence in global policy making.

Article VI

Structure of the MTO

1. There shall be a Ministerial Conference, consisting of Ministers responsible for international trade, which shall meet at least once every two years. The task of the Ministerial Conference shall be to review and supervise the operation of, and determine actions necessary to carry out the functions of, the MTO and the Multilateral Trade Agreements, to launch further negotiations as appropriate, and to decide on the implementation of results that may have been negotiated among and adopted by members of the MTO.

2.1 There shall be a General Council consisting of representatives of all the members, which shall meet at least twice each year. The task of the General Council shall be to supervise the operation of the MTO and the Multilateral Trade Agreements, in the time between Ministerial Conferences, and decide on all issues conferred on it by this agreement and by the Ministers.

2.2 The General Council shall carry out the functions of the MTO and may, to this effect, establish a Dispute Settlement Body, a Trade Policy Review Mechanism Body, and subsidiary bodies, including a Goods Council, a Services Council, a Committee on Budget and Administration, a Committee on Trade and

/585-P-3

Development, and a Balance of Payments Committee. The General
Council shall establish its own rules of procedure and shall
adopt the rules of procedure of the Councils for Goods and
Services and its other bodies.

3.1   There shall be a Council for Goods and a Council for Services,
consisting of representatives of all members responsible
respectively for trade in Goods and for trade in Services,
which shall meet at least eight times per year.

3.2   The Goods Council shall oversee the functioning of the
Agreements on Trade in Goods as set out in Annex 1A, as well
as any other functions assigned to it by the General Council,
except that the functions of dispute settlement shall be
exercised by the Dispute Settlement Body. The Goods Council
shall, as required, establish Committees to oversee the
operation of the Agreements set out in Annexes 1A, or other
subsidiary bodies, and shall approve their rules of procedure.

3.3   The Services Council shall oversee the functioning of
Agreements on Trade in Services as set out in Annex 1B, as
well as any other functions assigned to it by the General
Council, except that the functions of dispute settlement shall
be exercised by the Dispute Settlement Body. The Services
Council shall, as required, establish Committees to oversee
the operation of the Agreements set out in Annexes 1B, or
other subsidiary bodies, and shall approve their rules of
procedure.

Article VII

The Secretariat

1.   The General Council shall appoint a Director-General as head
of the Secretariat of the MTO. The powers, duties, conditions
of service and terms of office of the Director-General shall
conform to regulations approved by the General Council.

2.   The Director-General shall appoint members of the staff, and
shall fix their duties and conditions of service in accordance
with regulations approved by the General Council.

3.   The responsibilities of the Director-General and of the
members of the staff shall be exclusively international in
character. In the discharge of their duties, they shall not
seek or receive instructions from any government or from any
other authority external to the Organization. They shall
refrain from any action which might reflect on their positions
as international officials. The Members shall respect the
international character of the responsibilities of these
persons and shall not seek to influence them in the discharge
of their duties.

4. At the time of entry into force of the MTO, as far as practicable, the GATT Director-General and the ICITO/GATT Secretariat shall become the Director-General and Secretariat of the MTO.

Article VIII

Budget and Contributions

1. The Director-General shall present to the General Council the annual budget estimates and financial statement of the MTO. The General Council shall approve the accounts and the budget.

2. The General Council shall apportion the expenditures of the Organization among the Members, in accordance with a scale of contributions to be fixed by the General Council, and each Member shall individually contribute promptly to the Organization its share of these expenditures.

3. The General Council shall decide on administrative measures to be taken with regard to Members in arrears of their contributions.

4. The Budget Committee shall elaborate the provisions on the MTO budget and MTO contributions for adoption by the General Council. The provisions shall be based, as far as practicable, on the provisions and practices for the GATT budget.

Article IX

Status

1. The MTO shall have legal personality.

2. The MTO shall enjoy in the territory of each of the Members such legal capacity, privileges and immunities as may be necessary for the exercise of its functions.

3. The representatives of the Members and the officials of the MTO shall enjoy such privileges and immunities as are necessary for the independent exercise of their functions in connection with the MTO.

4. The privileges and immunities to be accorded by a Member to the MTO, to its officials and to the representatives of its Members shall be similar to those accorded by that member to specialized agencies of the United Nations, to their officials and to the representatives of their members, under the Convention on the Privileges and Immunities of the Specialized Agencies, or under similar arrangements.

Article X

Relations with other Organizations

1. The General Council of the MTO shall make arrangements with intergovernmental bodies and agencies which have related responsibilities to provide for effective cooperation and the avoidance of unnecessary duplication of activities.

2. The General Council of the MTO may make suitable arrangements for consultation and cooperation with non-governmental organizations concerned with matters within the scope of the MTO.

Article XI

Joint Action

1. At meetings of the General Council, each Member of the MTO shall be entitled to one vote, and, except as otherwise provided for in this Agreement, decisions of the General Council shall be taken by a majority of votes cast.

2. In exceptional circumstances not elsewhere provided for in this Agreement and the Multilateral Trade Agreements under Annexes 1A and 1B, the General Council may waive an obligation imposed on a member by this Agreement or a Multilateral Trade Agreement under Annex 1A or 1B; _Provided_ that any such decision shall be approved by a two-thirds majority of votes cast and that such majority shall comprise more than half the MTO members.

Article XII

Amendments

1. Amendments to this Agreement, or to any of Multilateral Trade Agreements listed in Annex 1A or B, shall be adopted by the Ministerial Conference on the basis of consensus of all members. Such amendments shall become effective upon acceptance by two-thirds of the members.

2. Any member accepting an amendment to this Agreement or any of the Multilateral Trade Agreements listed in Annex 1A or 1B shall deposit an instrument of acceptance with the Director-General of the MTO within such period as the Ministerial Conference may specify. The Ministerial Conference may decide that any amendment made effective under this Article is of such a nature that any member which has not accepted it within a period specified by the Ministerial Conference shall be free to withdraw from this Agreement, or to remain a member with

the consent of the Ministerial Conference or the General Council.

3. Amendments to the Agreements in Annex 1C shall follow the amending procedures in those agreements.

4. Amendments to the rules and procedures set out in Annexes 2 and 3 shall be taken by consensus in the General Council.

Article XIII

Withdrawal

Any Member of the MTO may withdraw from this Agreement. Any member, upon withdrawal from this agreement, shall cease to be a party to the Multilateral Trade Agreements in Annexes 1A and 1B. The withdrawal shall take effect upon the expiration of six months from the date on which written notice of withdrawal is received by the Director-General of the MTO.

Article XIV

Entry into Force

1. This Agreement shall be open for acceptance, by signature or otherwise, as from [1 November 1992] [a date set by the implementing conference] to all governments that qualify under Article III. This Agreement shall enter into force on [1 January 1993], the same date as the other Uruguay Round results become effective.

2. This Agreement shall remain open for acceptance by governments that qualify under Article III until [1 January, 1995] [a date determined by the General Council of the MTO]. For these governments, it shall enter into force on the thirtieth day following the deposit of the instrument of ratification or acceptance.

3. After [1 January, 1995], any other Uruguay Round participant may apply for membership under the accession provisions set out in Article IV.

Article XV

Non-application of the Agreement between
particular Members

1. This Agreement and all Multilateral Trade Agreements listed in Annexes 1A and 1B of this Agreement shall not apply as between any member and any other member if either of the members, at the time either becomes a member, does not consent to such application.

2. The General Council may review the operation of this Article in particular cases at the request of any member and make appropriate recommendations.

Article XVI

Final Provisions

1. The MTO shall respect the rules, decisions and customary practice of the General Agreement on Tariffs and Trade and the Tokyo Round Agreements in carrying out its functions and tasks.

2. No reservations may be entered in respect of any provision in the Multilateral Trade Agreements in Annex 1A and 1B. Reservations entered in respect of the Agreements in Annex 1C can only be made in accordance with the relevant provisions of those Agreements.

3. Prior to entry into force of this Agreement, the text of this Agreement shall be deposited with the Director-General to the CONTRACTING PARTIES of the General Agreement on Tariffs and Trade, in his capacity as depositary of the Uruguay Round results. He shall promptly furnish a certified true copy thereof and a notification of each acceptance thereof to each signatory of the Agreement on the MTO. The Agreement shall, upon its entry in to force, be deposited with the Director-General of the MTO, as well as any amendments thereto.

4. This Agreement shall be registered in accordance with the provisions of Article 102 of the Charter of the United Nations.

Done at --- this -- day of --- one thousand nine hundred and ninety---, in a single copy, in the English, French and Spanish languages, each text being authentic.

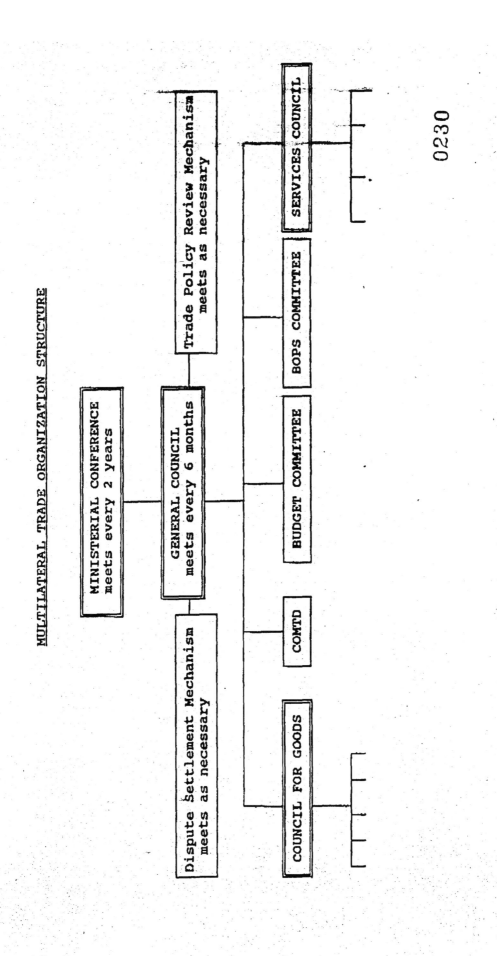

MULTILATERAL TRADE ORGANIZATION STRUCTURE

발 신 전 보

WGV-1648   911120 1834 BE   종별: 지급

번 호 :

수 신 : 주 제네바 대사. 총영사

발 신 : 장 관 (통 기)

제 목 : UR/제도분야(MTO)

대 : GVW-2327

1. MTO 설립의 근본 목적중의 하나가 UR 협상 결과의 이행이므로 균형된 UR 협상 package 도출이 MTO 설립 문제에 관한 구체적인 논의의 전제 조건이며, 동 전제하에 MTO를 설립한다는 원칙에 반대치 않는다는 것이 아국의 기본입장임.

2. MTO 설립 협정에서 가장 문제가 되는 것은 회원 자격(membership) 규정으로서 UR 협상 결과 일괄 수락 체약국과 비~~일괄~~ 또는 수락지연 체약국의 수락 체약국의 가입 조건을 달리함으로써 기존 갓트 체약국의 지위에 중대한 변화를 초래할 소지가 있는바, MTO 설립 문제는 UR 협상 package의 윤곽이 드러나는 싯점에서 참가국간 정치적 타결에 의해 결정~~되고,~~ 이에따른 ~~사안이며~~ 세부사항~~을~~은 검토하여 검토, 타결하는 과정에서 논의될수 있을 협약안을 ~~마무리하는데 상당 기간이 소요될~~것으로 하고있음 예상함.

3. 따라서 대호 이씨●카나다 제안과 관련 상기 기본입장에 의거 대처바라며, 동 제안의 문제점은 하기와 같은바 동건 논의시 참고바람.

0231

가. 회원자격(3조)

　　o 2년의 가입 준비기간을 거쳐 95.1.1까지 UR 협상 결과를 일괄 수락치 않는
　　　체약국은 신규 가입 절차를 밟도록 하고 있으나 신규 가입시 새로운 권리,
　　　의무 관계를 교섭토록 하는 경우 가입절차가 지연되어, 다자간 무역체제
　　　강화(참가국 확대)에 역행하는 결과를 초래할 우려가 있음.

나. MTO의 구조(5조)

　　o 상품관련 특별이사회와 서비스 관련 특별이사회를 별도로 구성하는 것은
　　　분쟁해결 체제를 이원화하는 결과를 초래할 우려가 있으며 이는 MTO의
　　　주요 기능중의 하나인 통합 분쟁해결 절차의 시행(4조)과 모순될 것임.

다. 부　표(6조)

　　o 일반이사회의 결정을 2/3 과반수로 한것과 관련, 기타기구(각료회의 및
　　　특별이사회)의 의사 결정방법 및 의결정족수에 대해 언급이 없는바
　　　이에 대한 검토가 필요함.

　　o 기존의 갓트 관행인 컨센서스 방식 유지 여부가 불분명한 것도 문제점임.

라. 기타 검토를 요하는 사항

　　o 경과 규정(갓트체제와 MTO 체제 공존 기간중 양자간의 관계)

　　o 통합분쟁 해결 절차 시행과 관련 부문간 교차 보복 가능성의 명문화 여부

　　o MTO 설립 협약으로서 전문과 6개 조항만으로 구성하는 것은 불충분하며,
　　　세부사항 검토 필요(MTO 산하기구 및 사무국의 구성 및 권한, 재정 관련
　　　사항, MTO의 특권과 면제 및 타국제기구와의 관계, 탈퇴 절차등).

　　　　　　　　　　끝.　　　　　　　　　(통상국장 대리 최　혁)

0232

발 신 전 보

WGV-1750   911203 1840 DW

번 호 :   종별 : 지급

수 신 : 주   제네바   대사. 총영사

발 신 : 장 관 (통 기)

제 목 : UR/최종의정서 (MTO)

대 : GVW-2518

연 : WGV-1648

한반문서로 재분류(1991.12.31.)

1. MTO 설립에 원칙적으로 반대치 않는다는 아국 기본입장에 변화가 없으나, 균형된
    UR 협상 package 도출이 불투명한 현재 상황에서 MTO 설립 관련 구체사항에 대한
    본격적인 논의를 개시하는 데는 유보적인 입장임.

2. 대호 MTO 설립 협정 수정안의 특징

    가. 동 협정안이 전문과 16개 조항으로 구성되어 설립 협정의 형태를 갖추고
        있는 점에서 MTO 설립에 대한 구체적인 논의를 유도하려는 선진국측의
        의도를 반영

    나. 회원자격

        1) 핵심쟁점인 회원자격 규정과 관련, 금번 수정안 2조 2항에 "47년도 갓트
           협정과 UR 협상 결과 개정된 갓트협정이 법적으로 상이하다"는 법적 의제
           (legal fiction)를 도입한 것은 UR 이전의 갓트협정과 MTO와의 연결
           고리를 단절하여 일정시한(95.1.1)까지 UR 협상 결과를 일괄 수락하여
           MTO에 가입치 않는 갓트체약국의 기득권을 박탈할 수 있는 법적 근거로
           삼으려는 의도로 분석됨.

0233

2) 2조 2항은 또한 "MTO가 갓트협정의 원칙, 결정 및 관행을 존중한다"고

규정한 16조 1항과도 기술적인 모순 내포

다. single undertaking

○ 3조(MTO 가입시 모든 UR 협상 결과 수락) 및 16조 2항(UR 협상 결과의
2조1항,

일부에 대한 유보 불가)을 통해 의무적 일괄 수락의 명문화를 시도

라. 분쟁해결

○ MTO가 통합 분쟁해결 절차를 시행하고(5조 2항) 이를 전담할 분쟁해결

기구를 일반이사회 산하에 신설(6조 2.1, 3.2, 3.3)토록 규정하고 있는바,

이는 1)기존의 갓트이사회가 전담하던 분쟁해결 기능을 신설되는 분쟁해결

기구에 이관토록 함으로써 기존의 갓트 관행에 대한 중대한 변화를 초래하고

2) 교차보복을 제도적으로 가능케 하는 길을 열어 놓는다는 문제점 내포

3. 12.5 회의 대책

가. 일반사항 (general comment)

○ 현재 UR 협상의 결과를 예단할 수 없기 때문에 일괄 수락 문제에 대한
통합 분쟁해결 절차 시행
컨센서스가 형성될 수 없으며,(교차보복) 문제도 UR 제도분야에서뿐 아니라

TRIPs 및 SVC 협상그룹에서 깊이있게 다루어져야할 문제임. 금번 수정안은

이러한 극히 민감한 쟁점들을 MTO 설립을 기정 사실화하는 입장에서 접근

함으로써 시기 상조의 문제점뿐 아니라 균형된 협상 결과의 도출 노력에

영향을 미칠 우려가 있음. *이임우*

나. 조문별 입장 (상기 1항 기본입장을 전제로 필요시 세부 토의에 참여)

1) II조 2항 (MTO의 범위)

- 갓트 협정은 47.10.30 성립이래 다자간 무역협상등을 통해 일관성을

유지하면서 발전해 왔으며, UR 협상으로 인해 갓트협정의 법적인 지위에

변화가 초래된 것으로 볼 수 없음 (예컨대 TRIPs와 SVC 협정도 갓트협정의 *상*

기본원칙에 근거하여 성립)

- 또한 MTO는 umbrella 성격의 협정으로서 47.10.30 성립하여 지금까지

발전(evolve)해온 갓트협정에 법적인 연원이 있으므로 2조 2항의

구별(differentiation)은 적절치 않음.

- 또한 XVI조 1항과도 기술적으로 모순임.

0234

Ⅱ조1항,

2) Ⅲ조 및 XⅥ조 2항 (single undertaking)

- 일괄 수락 문제는 무엇보다도 균형된 UR 협상 package의 도출이
  전제되어야 하는바, 동 문제는 UR 협상 결과의 윤곽이 드러난 후에
  검토해야 함.

3) Ⅲ조, Ⅳ조 1항 및 XⅣ조 2항 및 3항 (회원자격)

- 전체적인 UR 협상 결과를 국내적 절차 상의 문제로 인해 95.1.1까지 수락치
  못하는 갓트체약국들이 다자간 무역체제로부터 배제되는 결과를 초래할
  우려가 있으므로 신중하게 검토해야 할 사항임.

4) Ⅴ조 2항 및 Ⅵ조 2.2, 3.2, 3.3항 (통합 분쟁해결)

- 이사회의 가장 중요한 기능중의 하나가 분쟁해결이므로 분쟁해결 기구를
  신설하는 경우 이사회가 유명무실 해질 우려가 있는등 기존의 갓트내의
  관행에 중대한 변화를 초래할 우려가 있음. ~~현재 진행중인 분쟁해결 협정과~~
  ~~상충된다는 점이 고려되야 함~~.

5) Ⅷ (예산 및 분담금)

- MTO의 과도한 기구 확장으로 인해 체약국의 추가 부담이 과중해져서는
  안됨. ~~며, 합리적인 분담금 비율 재조정이 필요함~~.   끝.

(통상국장   김 용 규)

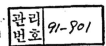

발 신 전 보

WGV-1784   911207 1149 DU

	분류번호	보존기간

번   호 :   종별 :

수   신 : 주 제네바 대사. 총영사

발   신 : 장   관 (통기)

제   목 : UR/분쟁해결 (교차보복)

대 : GVW-2487

1. 교차보복 문제는 UR 협상의 타결, UR 협상 결과의 일괄 수락 및 MTO 설립과 연관되어
    있으며, 아울러 일방조치 억제 공약 수락 여부 및 신분야에서의 협상 결과가 주요
    변수로 작용할 것이므로 현재로서는 그 결과를 예단하기 어려움.

2. 현재 UR 협상의 전망이 불투명한 점을 감안, 하기와 같이 원칙적으로 교차보복 반대
    입장을 견지하되, 교차보복 허용이 대세로 굳혀질 경우에 대비, 2차적 입장에 따라
    탄력적으로 대처바람.

    가. 기본입장 : 교차보복 반대

    ㅇ 교차보복을 허용하는 경우 신분야에서 상대적으로 열세인 아국에게 불리하게
       작용할 소지가 있는바, 교차보복 반대의 기존 입장을 고수하며, 논거로서
       하기 사항 제시

    1) 원칙적인 측면

       - TRIPs 협정 및 SVC 협정이 UR 협상의 결과로서 새롭게 정립되는
         규범이므로, 상품분야와 TRIPs, SVC 분야는 법적으로 상이한 체계를
         이루고 있음.

			기안자성명		과장		국장		차관	장관	보안통제	
앙고재	91년 12월 7일	통상과	안명수		심의관		진영					외신과통제

0236

2) 현실적인 측면 (계량화 상의 문제점)

  - 상품분야 내에서도 미, 이씨, 멕시코간 Super Fund 패널 케이스에서
    볼 수 있듯이 보복의 수준을 결정하는 것은 이에 대한 구체적인
    기준이 정립되어 있지 않기 때문에 기술적으로 상당히 어려움.

  - 하물며 신분야의 경우 이제 처음으로 협정이 설립되는 단계에 있으며,
    UR 협상 타결후 상당기간 동 협정의 실제 운용을 통하여 신분야에서의
    무역에 대한 경험을 축적시켜 나가야 하는바, 통계등 관련자료가
    구비되지 않은 현재의 상황에서 신분야에서의 무역 수준을 계량화하여
    상품분야와 수량적인 비교를 하는 것은 불가능할 것임.

  - 현재 UR/제도분야 협상그룹에서 논의되고 있는 분쟁해결 관련
    Understanding에 따르면 "패널 권고사항 불이행시 허용되는 보복의
    수준에 대해 문제가 발생하는 경우 동건이 원 패널 또는 사무총장이
    지명하는자의 중재에 회부되며, 보복의 대상이 되는 무역의 양은
    상황에 비추어 적절한 수준이 되어야 한다 (L.3 및 4)고 규정되어
    있는바, 동 규정은 보복의 대상을 동일 분야에서 찾아야 한다는
    뜻으로 해석되어야 하며, 타분야에서 보복 대상을 찾을 경우 보복의
    수준 산정과 관련 복잡한 문제가 발생할 것임.

3) 자의성 개입 우려

  - 교차보복 허용시, 보복 대상 및 보복의 수준 결정시 자의성이 개입할
    여지가 생기며, 이로 인하여 무역의 안정성 및 예측 가능성을 저해할
    우려가 있음.

4) 교차보복의 무기화

  - 보복 능력을 갖춘 주요 선진국들은 교차 보복 허용시 이를 강력한
    leverage로 활용할 수 있게 될 것인바, 중소 체약국들은 일방적으로
    불리한 입장에 처하게 된다는 문제점이 있음.

나. 2차적 입장 (Fall-back position)

ㅇ 교차 보복 허용이 대세로 형성되는 경우, TRIPs와 SVC 분야에서 이미
상당부분 시장을 개방한 아국으로서는 수용 가능할 것으로 보이며, 다만
이경우 무조건적인 교차보복의 허용이 아닌 엄격한 기준과 규율하에
제한적으로 허용하는 하기 방안 제시
(이경우 미국이외의 일부 선진국들도 이에 동조할 것으로 예상)

가) 보복 대상 조치를 동일 분야, 동일 카테고리에서 찾는것을 기본원칙으로 함.

나) 동일분야 동일 카테고리에서 보복대상 조치를 찾는것이 불가능할 경우
동일분야내 여타 카테고리에서 허용

다) 동일분야 내에서 보복 대상조치를 찾는것이 현실적으로 어려울 경우 여타
분야에서의 보복을 허용하되 작업반을 설치하고, 보복 요청국에 의해
동일분야 내에서 유효한 보복이 이루어질 수 없음이 입증될 경우 보복
대상 및 수준을 확정.   끝.   (통상국장   김 용 규)

0238

외 무 부

110-760 서울 종로구 세종로 77번지   / (02)720-2188   / (02)725-1737

문서번호 통기 20644-　**45398**

시행일자 1991.12. 9.(　　)

취급		장　　관	
보존		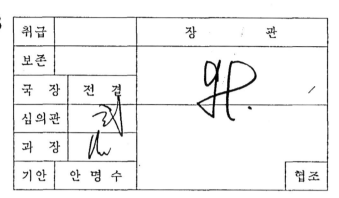	
국장	전 결		
심의관			
과장			
기안	안 명 수		협조

수신 주 제네바 대사

참조

제목 UR/제도분야 ~~교차보복 문제~~

　　　연 : WGV-1784

　　　표제건과 관련하여 당부가 12.6 경기원 주재로 개최된 UR 대책 실무회의에
상정한✔자료를 별첨과 같이 송부합니다.

첨 부 : 동 자료 1부.　　　　　　　　　끝.

외　무　부　장　관

0239

UR/제도분야 : 교차보복(Cross retaliation) 문제

1991. 12. 5.

외   무   부

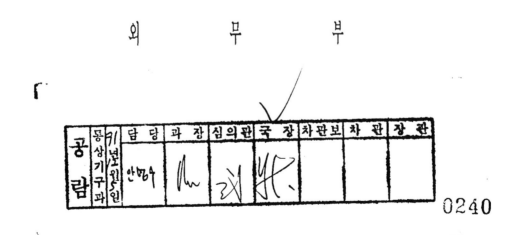

공람	통상기구과	기년원일	담당	과 장	심의관	국 장	차관보	차 관	장 관
			안명수						

0240

0241

1. 쟁 점

가. 내 용

o UR 협상 결과 새로이 규범이 성립되는 부문(sector), 즉 개정된 GATT(전통적인 상품분야), 지적소유권 분야 및 서비스 분야 상호간에 교차 보복을 인정할 것인지 여부

o 특히 신분야인 지적소유권 및 서비스 분야와 상품분야간의 교차 보복이 문제가 됨. 예컨대 서비스 분야인 telecommunications와 관련된 분쟁시 패널 권고사항의 불이행으로 인하여 보복을 승인하게 되는 경우 승소국이 패소국이 수출하는 텔레콤 장비(상품분야)의 수입을 제한할 수 있도록 할 것인지의 여부임.

나. 논의현황

교차보복 문제는 분쟁해결 협상그룹 내에서 타협상 분야의 분쟁해결 절차와의 조정 문제와 관련하여 거론된바 있으며, 최근에는 이씨, 카나다가 11.29 MTO 설립 협정안에서 통합 분쟁해결 절차(integrated dispute settlement system)의 시행을 MTO의 주요 기능으로 명시 함으로써 동 문제가 본격 거론될 가능성이 있음.

1) 분쟁해결 협상그룹 내에서의 논의 현황
   o 갓트 22조 및 23조에 근거한 정규 분쟁해결 절차와 동경라운드 MTN Code에 근거한 분쟁해결 절차가 병존 함으로인해 forum shopping 등의 문제점이 발생함에 따라 분쟁해결 협상그룹에서 논의되고 있는 새로운 분쟁해결 절차와 UR 협상 결과로서 나오게 되는 여타 협정상의 분쟁해결 절차를 상호 조화시키는 것이 바람직하다는 논의가 대두

1

0242

o 이를 위하여 여타 협상그룹 의장들에게 소관 협상그룹 내에서
  논의되고 있는 협정(예컨대 반덤핑 협정, 원산지 협정, 세이프가드
  협정, 섬유 협정등)중 분쟁해결 관련 조항에 하기 text(안)가
  포함되어야 한다는 뜻을 전달하기로 의견이 접근

  "Except as otherwise provided for in this agreement,
  consultations and the settlement of disputes with respect
  to any matter affecting the operation of this agreement
  shall be subject to the rules and procedures of Articles
  XXII and XXIII of the General Agreement and the Dispute
  Settlement rules and procedures as adopted by the CONTRACTING
  PARTIES."

o 이와 관련 개도국들은 교차보복의 가능성을 이유로 분쟁해결
  절차의 조정 원칙이 신분야에도 적용되는데에는 반대 입장을 표명

o 이에따라 Lacarte 제도분야 협상그룹 의장이 10월 하순경 상품
  분야의 3개 협상그룹(농산물, 섬유, 규범제정) 의장에게 제도분야
  (분쟁해결) 협상그룹에서 타결되는 분쟁해결 절차와 타협상
  그룹에서 논의되고 있는 분쟁해결 절차간의 조화가 필요하므로
  소관 협정중 분쟁해결 관련 조항에 상기 text를 포함하여 줄것을
  제의하는 취지의 서한을 발송 하였으나, SVC와 TRIPs 협상그룹
  의장에게는 브라질등 개도국들의 반대로 서한 발송을 보류함.

2) MTO 설립 문제와의 관련성

o 이씨, 카나다는 11.29 MTO 설립 협정안을 제출한바, 동 협정안에
  따르면 MTO의 주요 기능으로서 통합 분쟁절차를 시행하고("The MTO
  shall administer an Integrated Dispute Settlement System.."),
  이를 전담할 분쟁해결 기구(Dispute Settlement Body)를 신설토록
  하는 내용이 포함되어 있음.

2

○ 상기 이씨, 카나다의 제안은 교차보복을 제도적으로 가능캐
하는 길을 열어 놓으려는 시도로 분석되며, MTO 설립 문제와
관련하여 교차보복 문제에 대한 논의가 본격화될 가능성이 있음.

2. 각국 입장

가. 미 국

○ UR 협상이 전 분야에서 참가국들의 권리.의무가 균형을 이루는
package를 추구하고 있는 만큼, 권리 침해시 해당분야뿐 아니라
타분야에서의 보복도 허용함으로써 전체적인 권리.의무 관계의
재균형의 도모를 용이하게 해야함.

나. 이씨, 카나다, 스위스, 북구

○ 동일분야에서의 보복에 우선을 두되 불가능할 경우 충분한 정당성
입증 조건하에 부문간 교차 보복 허용

○ 특정분야를 교차 보복 대상에서 제외하는 방안도 고려 가능

다. 인도, 이집트, 브라질, 홍콩, 아세안등 개도국

○ 하기 논거를 근거로 교차보복 허용 반대
  - 상품, SVC, TRIPs가 서로 다른 별개의 법체계를 이루고 있으므로
    분야별로 자체적, 내부적인 권리.의무상의 균형도모에 국한되어야 함.
  - 신분야의 경우 피해 수준의 정확한 계량화 및 상품분야와의 등가적
    산정이 불가능함.
  - SVC 분야에 대한 보복 효과는 상품분야에서보다 훨씬 장기적이고
    광범위함.

3

0244

- 보복력이 제한된 개도국에 대한 선진국의 일방적 무기화 가능성이 우려됨.
- 예외 설정시 협상력이 큰 선진국에게 불리한 분야가 우선 제외될 경우, 개도국에게 더욱 불리함.
- SVC, TRIPs, TRIMs는 새로운 분야이므로 일정기간 시행해 본후 검토하는 것이 타당함.

3. 전망 및 대책

가. 전 망

O 현재 교차보복 허용 문제에 관하여 선진국들은 신분야에서 개도국들이 시장을 개방하도록 압력을 가하기 위한 수단으로서 허용을 주장하고 있으며, 이에 대해 개도국들이 강하게 반발하고 있는 상황임.

O 또한 동 문제는 UR 협상의 성공적 타결, 의무적 single undertaking 수락 및 MTO 설립과 연관이 있으며, 아울러 미국이 일방조치 억제 공약을 수락할 것인지의 여부, TRIPs 및 SVC 협상그룹 내에서의 협상 결과 등이 주요변수로 작용할 것인바, 현재로서는 결과를 예단하기 어려움.

나. 대 책

> 현재 UR 협상의 전망이 불투명한 점을 감안, 원칙적으로 기본입장 (교차보복 반대)에 따라 대처하되, 교차보복 허용이 대세로 굳어질 경우에 대비, 2차 입장(Fall-back position)을 수립하여 탄력적으로 대처

1) 기본입장 (교차보복 반대)

O 교차보복을 허용하는 경우 신분야에서 상대적으로 열세인 아국에게 불리하게 작용할 소지가 있으므로 교차보복 반대의 아국 기존 입장을 고수하며 이에 반대하는 논거로서 하기 사항 제시

4

0245

가) 원칙적인 측면

- TRIPs 협정 및 SVC 협정이 UR 협상의 결과로서 새롭게
  정립되는 규범이므로, 상품분야와 TRIPs, SVC 분야는
  법적으로 상이한 체계를 이루고 있음.

나) 현실적인 측면 (계량화 상의 문제점)

- 상품분야 내에서도 미, 이씨, 멕시코간 Super Fund 패널
  케이스에서 볼 수 있듯이 보복의 수준(level of
  retaliation)을 결정하는 것은 이에 대한 구체적인 기준이
  정립되어 있지 않기 때문에 기술적으로 상당히 어려움.

- 하물며 신분야의 경우 이제 처음으로 협정이 설립되는
  단계에 있으며, UR 협상 타결후 상당기간 동 협정의 실제
  운용을 통하여 신분야에서의 무역에 대한 경험을 축적시켜
  나가야 하는바, 통계등 관련자료가 구비되지 않은 현재의
  상황에서 신분야에서의 무역 수준을 계량화하여 상품분야와
  수량적인 비교를 하는 것은 불가능할 것이며, 또한
  자의적인 요소가 개입될 소지가 큼.

- 현재 UR/제도분야 협상그룹에서 논의되고 있는 분쟁해결
  관련 Understanding에 따르면 "패널 권고사항 불이행시
  허용되는 보복의 수준에 대해 문제가 발생하는 경우
  동건이 원 패널 또는 사무총장이 지명하는자의 중재에
  회부되며, 보복의 대상이 되는 무역의 양은 상황에 비추어
  적절한 수준이 되어야 한다" (L.3 및 4)고 규정되어 있는바,
  동 규정은 보복의 대상을 동일 분야에서 찾아야 한다는
  뜻으로 해석되어야 하며, 타분야에서 보복 대상을 찾을
  경우 보복의 수준 산정과 관련 복잡한 문제가 발생할 것임.

5

0246

- 교차 보복을 허용함으로써 자의성이 개입할 여지가 생기는
  경우 무역의 안정성 및 예측 가능성이 저해될 우려가
  있으며, 일부 능력을 갖춘 주요 선진국들은 교차 보복
  허용시 이를 강력한 무기로 활용할 수 있게 될 것인바,
  이경우 중소 체약국들은 일방적으로 불리한 입장에
  처하게 된다는 문제점이 있음.

2) 2차적 입장 (Fall-back position)

ㅇ 교차 보복 허용이 대세로 형성되는 경우, TRIPs와 SVC 분야에서
  이미 상당부분 시장을 개방한 아국으로서는 수용 가능할 것으로
  보이며, 다만 이경우 무조건적인 교차보복의 허용이 아닌 엄격한
  기준과 규율하에 제한적으로 허용하는 방안 제시토록 함.
  (이경우 미국이외의 일부 선진국들도 이에 동조할 것으로 예상)

ㅇ 교차보복 허용 관련 기준으로서 하기 사항 제시
  가) 보복 대상 조치를 동일 분야, 동일 카테고리에서 찾는것을
     기본원칙으로 함.
  나) 동일분야 동일 카테고리에서 보복대상 조치를 찾는것이
     불가능할 경우 동일분야내 여타 카테고리에서 허용
  다) 동일분야 내에서 보복 대상조치를 찾는것이 현실적으로
     어려울 경우 여타분야에서의 보복을 허용하되 작업반을
     설치하고, 보복 요청국에 의해 동일분야 내에서 유효한
     보복이 이루어질 수 없음이 입증될 경우 보복 대상 및
     수준을 확정.   끝.

6

0247

외 무 부

종 별 : 지 급

번 호 : GVW-2593 일 시 : 91 1210 1930

수 신 : 장 관(통기, 경기원, 재무부, 농수부, 상공부)

발 신 : 주 제네바 대사

제 목 : UR/제도 분야 (분쟁해결) 비공식 협의

1. 표제 협의가 12.10 LACARTE 의장 주재로 개최되어 교차보복, 자동화문제 및 일방조치 억제 문제를 논의함. (이성주 참사관 참석)

2. 회의 벽두 LACARTE 의장은 12.20 DEADLINE 을 맞추기 위해 향후 약 1주간 집중 협상을 통해 분쟁해결에 관한 UNBRACKETED TEXT 를 작성할 예정이며, (최종의정서및 MTO 문제는 당분간보류), 이를 위해 필요하다면 일련의 양자 협의를 갖는것도 고려중인바 이에는 협상 전권을 가진대표가 참석해야 할 것이라 하였음.

(동의장에 의하면 12.10 저녁 개최예정인 DUNKEL총장 주재 협상 그룹의장단 회의에서 각 GROUP별 TEXT 작성 관련 의장의 기여 방안등 향후행동 계획을 논의 예정이라함.)

3. 금일 논의된 3개 의제중 표차 보복문제에 관해서는 11.14 논의(GVW-2338) 시와 같이선.개도국이 엇갈린 입장을 반복하는 가운데 EC가 절충안이라는 이름으로 별첨(1) NON-PAPER 를 제시하였으며, 일방주의 억제문제 관련해서는 의장의 종용으로 미국으로부터 21항에 대한 별첨(2)수정문안 제시가 있었는바, 차기 회의가 12.11오후로예정되어 있음을 감안 특히 동 미국수정안 관련 본부 검토의견 지급 회시 바람.

4. 의제별 세부 토의 내용은 아래와 같음(토의순서별)

가. 교차 보복

- 의장이 GATT 내에서 보복은 극히 예외적(RARE)인 현상이라고 언급하고, 교차보복문제에 관해 각국이 어느정도 신축성을 갖고있는지 밝혀 달라고 토의를 유도

- 미국은 11.14 토의시와 같이, UR 협상 결과의 전체적(GLOBAL) 균형측면을 재강조하면서 동균형 파괴시의 회복(REBALANCING)과 위반국에대한 준수 촉구 INCENTIVE로 서 교차 보복 도입이중요함을 강조

통상국	2차보	구주국	정와대	안기부	경기원	재무부	농수부	상공부

91.12.11 06:36 FN

외신 1과 통제관

0248

- 미국에 이어 홍콩, 브라질, 아국, 인도, MALAYSIA등이 1차적으로 11.14 논의시의 논거를 반복하면서 개념적(CONCEPTUAL), 기술적(TECHNICAL) 및실재적(PRACTICAL) 측면에서 교차 보복 도입에 반대한다는 입장을 표명하고, 필요하다면 4년후 재검토단계에 가서 고려하는 것이 바람직 하다고 언급. (기타 콜롬비아, 베네주엘라, 이집트, 알 젠틴등도 반대)

. 아국은 개도국의 보복능력 결여 현실및 선진국의 일방적 무기화 가능성과 현단계에서는 강화된 분쟁해결 절차의 효과적 시행확보가 최우선 과제라는 점을 중점 강조

. 홍콩은 서비스 협정의 경우 범위가 광범하므로 내부에서의 REBALANCING 이 가능 할 것이라는 점 언급 (인도도 동일 내용 언급)

. 인도, 브라질 은 TRIPS 분야에 여하히 보복이 가능한지의 의문을 집중 제기

. 브라질은 GLOBAL BALANCE 와 LINKAGE 는 별개임을 주장

- 뉴질랜드, 카나다, 호주, 스위스등은 교차 보복 도입 필요성을 지지함. (호주는 중소규모 국가에 대한 영향을 고려 무제한 (UNFETTERED)의 교차 보복보다는 이사회에 의한 정당성 심의등 적절한CHECKS AND BALANCES 가 구비된 제도 도입이 필요하다는 의견제시)

- 일본은 적극적으로 나서지는 않았으나 전반적으로 선진국의 입장에 동조하는 태도였으며, 태국은 OPEN-MINDED 한 자세에서 검토용의 표명

- EC 는 동의제 논의 마지막 단계에 상기 2항 NON-PAPER 를 제시하면서, 각국의검토를 요청

나. 분쟁해결 절차의 자동화 문제

- 카나다, 미국이 CLEAN TEXT (SHALL 및 'UNLESS ,.,.NOTTO' FORMULA)를 지지하고 홍콩, 뉴질랜드가 동조

- 미국은 봉합문안 1.8 항 첫째문장의 'TRADITIONAL CONSENSUS' 관련 11.27 논의시 표명한입장(GVW-2486 5항 '나' 참조)를 되풀이 하면서 동경라운드 낙농협정 7조 2 항(D) 와 동일한 내용의 주석을 설정할 것을 주장

- 상기에 대해 아국, 일본, 브라질, EC 가일방조치 억제 공약을 조건부로 자동화문제를 받아들일 용의가 있음을 표명

- 인도는 모든 문제는 CONSENSUS 방식을 변경한데서 야기되고 있다고 하면서, CONSENSUS MINUSTWO 원칙하에 전통적 CONSENSUS 방식으로 되돌아 가는 것이

바람직하지않겠는가 하는 의견을 제시하고, 태국이 이에 동조

　다. 일방조치 억제문제

　- 의장의 정치적 성격외에도 현 21항 문안상에도 기술적인 문제점이 많다고 지적해온 미국의 주장을 상기시키면서 미국에 대해 문제점의 구체적 지적 및 대안 제시를 요 구

　- 미국은 현 문안은 정치적 의도가 강하게 내포되어있다는 문제 뿐만 아니라 (I)항의 경우 UR협상 전부가 아니고 GATT 분쟁해결 절차에대한 준수의무만 언급한점, (동 공약은 분쟁해결 차원의 문제가 아니라는 입장), (II)항의 패널 권고 준수의무와 관련 동 권고를 이행치 않고도 보상 제공이 가능하며 보복등의대응 수단도 마련되어 있는점, (III) 항은 2개국간 협의에 의한 GATT 불일치 조치등은 포함치 않고 있는점(역시 분쟁해결 차원의문제가 아니라는 입장) (IV) 은 각국이 분쟁해결 절차의 준수의무 를 지는 것과 국내법자체를 개정하는 것은 전혀 별개의 문제라는점에서 현문안에 문제점이 많다고 설명한후,위반 행위에 대한 구제 조치 강구 권한이 국제법상일반원칙 상 인정되고 있음을 감안하고, 다수국이 일방조치 억제 공약에 중요성을 부여하는 취지가 분쟁을 GATT 절차를 통해서만 해결하자는 의도에서 출발한다고 이해되므로, 우선 GATT 를 통한 구제조치를 완료를 의무화하는 내용으로 문안을 수정할필요성이 있다고 언급

　- EC 가 구체적 문안제시 전에는 논의키 어렵다고 주장함에 따라, 미국은 현재 문제되고 있는 다수문제점과 연계조건을 명시한 상기 3항의 수정문안을 제시 (동 구체 토의는 없었음)

　라. 기타

　- 사무국은 12.10 자 통합문안을 작성, 배포함.

　첨부: 1. 교차 보복에 관한 EC 의 NON-PAPER

　2. 일방조치 억제 공약관련 미국제안. 끝

　(GVW(F)-953)

　(대사 박수길-국장)

PAGE 3

0250

(별첨 1)

Cross-retaliation

Members [of the Dispute Settlement Board] shall apply the following procedures in seeking to suspend concessions or other obligations:

A. <u>Under the GATS</u>

a) The general principle is that members should first seek authorization to suspend concessions or other obligations in the same services sector as that under which the Panel has made a determination of inconsistency or nullification or impairment.

b) If the party concerned considers that it is not practically possible to suspend concessions or other obligations in the same sector, it shall state the reasons therefor and it may seek to suspend concessions or other obligations in other service sectors under that Agreement. The GATS Council or the sectoral body concerned, as the case may be, shall be informed of such request and may give its opinion to the Dispute Settlement Board within ...... days.

c) If the party concerned considers that it is not possible to suspend concessions or other obligations in other service sectors under the GATS, it shall state the reasons therefor and it may seek authorization to suspend concessions or other obligations under the GATT. The GATT Council shall be informed of such request and may give its opinion to the Dispute Settlement Board within ..... days.

B. <u>Under the GATT</u>

a) The general principle is that members should first seek authorisation to suspend concessions or other obligations under the GATT(*)

b) If the party concerned considers that it is not practically possible to suspend concessions or other obligations under the GATT, it shall state the reasons therefor and it may seek authorization to suspend concessions or other obligations under the GATS. The GATS Council or the sectoral body concerned, as the case may be, shall be informed of such request and may give its opinion to the Dispute Settlement Board within ..... days.

(*) It is understood for the moment that "GATT" will include other agreement on goods and the TRIPs agreement

0251

21. Strengthening the Multilateral System

21.1 Provided that the maximum time limits set forth in
paragraph 19.4 above are not exceeded, the complaining party
[should/shall] not determine that any provision of the General
Agreement has been violated except through recourse to dispute
settlement in accordance with these procedures; and
[should/shall] take into account the results of such dispute
settlement in exercising its rights under Article XXIII:2 to
suspend concessions or other obligations.

NOTE: This proposal is linked to and conditioned upon acceptance
of the following formulations in other parts of the text (most of
which are currently bracketed):

Para. 1.8   Delete "the traditional practice of" from the
                   first sentence, and replace second sentence in
                   current text, so that para. 1.8 reads as follows:

                   "Where these GATT rules and procedures provide for
                   the Council to take a decision, it shall do so by
                   the practice of consensus."1 The procedures
                   foreseen in GATT dispute settlement are without
                   prejudice to the possibility that the contracting
                   parties may take joint action under Article XXV to
                   adopt authoritative interpretations of the General
                   Agreement."

                   Add the following footnote:

                   1 "The Council shall be deemed to have decided by
                   consensus if no member of the Council formally
                   objects to the decision."

Para. 4.1:   "...unless at that meeting the Council decides by
                   consensus not to establish a panel."

                   Footnote: "If the complaining party so requests,
                   a meeting of the Council shall be convened for
                   this purpose within 15 days of the request,
                   provided that, in accordance with past practice,
                   at least ten days' advance notice is given.

Para. 14.4:   "...or the Council decides by consensus not to
                   adopt the report."

Para. 15.5:   "In no case shall the proceedings exceed ninety
                   days."

Para. 15.14:   "...unless the Council decides by consensus not to
                   adopt the appellate report."

0252

Para. 19.3(c): "In such arbitration, a guideline for the
                 arbitrator should be that the reasonable period of
                 time to implement panel or appellate body
                 recommendations should not exceed fifteen months
                 from the adoption of a panel or appellate body
                 report. However, that time may be shorter or
                 longer, depending on the particular
                 circumstances."

Para. 19.4:   "...in no event shall the total amount of time
                 exceed eighteen months."
                              OR
                 "...unless the parties agree that there are
                 exceptional circumstances, the total time shall
                 not exceed eighteen months."

Para. 20.3:   "...unless the Council decides by consensus to
                 reject the request."

0253

이 (여강제보) 이

원 <u>L본</u>

외 무 부

종   별 :

번   호 : GVW-2605   일   시 : 91 1211 2050

수   신 : 장 관(봉기, 경기원, 재무부, 농수산부, 상공부)

발   신 : 주 제네바 대사

제   목 : UR/제도분야(분쟁해결) 비공식 협의

    연: GVW-2593

    1. 12.11. 비공식 TNC 회의 직후 LACARTE 의장주재로 개최된 표제 비공식 협의에서는 일방조치 억제 공약문제와 NON-VIOLATION분쟁문제가 논의되었음.

    (이성주 참사관 참석)

    2. 일방조치 억제에 관해서는 EC가 미국안에 대응하는 자신의 문안을 제시, 각국이 양문안에 대한 COMMENT 형식으로 진행된바, 아국 포함거의 대부분의 국가가 미국안의 제반 문제점을 지적하면서, <u>EC 문안 선호 또는 기존 문안 선호입장을 밝혔음.</u>

    3. NON-VIOLATION 분쟁에 관해서는 OPTION 1 (EC안) 및 OPTION 2 (뉴, 호주 절충안)을 두고 EC와 호주, 뉴질랜드가 상반된 견해가 대립한바, 대부분 이미 수차례 표명된 입장의 반복에 불과했고, 특히 EC는 OPTION 1 이내부정치 사정을 고려한 최대한의 양보선임을 거듭 강조하였을뿐 특별한 진전이 없었음. 한편 알젠틴은 그동안 거의 완전히 등한시되어온 자국제안 (OPTION 3)관련 대사가 직접참석, 자국입장 (NV 분쟁에 관한 별도 절차가 불필요하다고 보나 이를 설정한다면 반드시 PANEL 이적절한 해결책을 권고 할수 있어야 함)에 변함이 없음을 강조함.

    4. 기타 사무국이 교차보복에 관한 NON-PAPER (별첨2)를 배포하였으며, TANZANIA 의 ZAMAL대사가 출석 22항 (최빈개도국 우대)의 내용이 미흡하다는 불만을 토론함.

    5. 의제별 세부토의 내용은 아래와 같음.

    가. 일방조치 억제 공약

    - 미국은 토의 벽두 NV 분쟁 불포함, 후반부와 통합문안 20항과의 문제, 피소국의 의무 (기존TEXT SUB-ITEM I 및 II) 불언급등 자국제안에 보완 여지가 많음을 시인하고, 개선문안을 제안하겠다고 언급

    - 이에대해 EC가 일방조치 억제에 관한 확고한 공약이 UR 협상 성공에 필수적임을

통상국   2차보   경기원   재무부   농수부   상공부

PAGE 1   91.12.12   09:30 WG

                                           외신 1과 통제관
                                              0254

강조하고 기존 TEXT 는 미국을 제외한 모든 국가가 동의한 문안임을 상기시키면서 미국이 모호하고 기대에 미흡한 (AMBIGUOUS AND WEAK) 문안을 제시하였으므로 EC 로서는 대안을 제시할 수밖에 없다하면서 별첨 문안을 제시

- 이어 브라질, 놀웨이, 아국, 일본, 카나다, 오지리, 스위스, 홍콩, 인도, 태국등이미국 안에 대한 실망 및 문제점을 지적

0 아국은 다자체제 강화에 필수적인 기존안 SUB-ITEM IV가 누락된점 및 SUB-ITEM III 에 대해서도 일시적 자제 공약에 불과한점, 모호한문안 (TAKING INTO CONSIDER,TION) 으로 통합문안 20항에 관계없이 일방적 보복 시행 가능성을 열어두고 있는 점등 미국안의 문제점을 지적하고, EC안의 대다수 국가의 관심 사항을 적절히 반영하고 있다는 점에서 좋은 협상의 기초가 될수있을 것이라는 의견 피력

0 기타 특기할 언급사항으로는 인도가 미국문안의'EXERCISING ITS RIGHTS UNDER ART XXIII.2' 관련 동권한은 이사회의 보복 승인을 요청할 권한일뿐 보복 시행권이 아님을, 카나다는 갓트위반행위에 대한 제제 필요성이 동 제제수단의 갓트 위반을 정당화 할수 없다는 점을, 일본은 최대시한 (18개월)을 넘겼을 경우 일방조치가 가능한 것으로 해석될 수 있다는점, 뉴질랜드는 패소국의 준수 의무규정도 중요한 문제임등을 지적함.

- 호주, 뉴질랜드는 미국안에 대한 실망 및 비판분위기에는 동조하면서도 새로운 개선안을 내겠다는 미국의 언급내용을 환영한다고하는등 미국에 대해 다소 부드러운 입장을 취함.

나. NV 분쟁

- OPTION 1과 2간의 2가지 차이점 (철회 또는 수정의무 없음을 명시할 것인지의 여부 및 보상제공이 상호 만족스러운 해결의 일부가 될수있다는 문안 존치여부)을 두고 뉴질랜드, 호주와 EC간의 기존대립 입장 반복

- 미국으로부터 19.3 항상의 중재를 통해 합리적 이행기간 및 보상규모가 동시에 결정될 수도있도록 규정한 양 OPTION(C)항의 내용 관련합리적 이행기간이 장기간으로 결정될 경우 보상의 기준 시점문제가 불분명한점, 일본으로부터는 호주, 뉴질랜드 양국이 분쟁해결절차의 자동화문제에 관해서는 CLEARER TEXT 를 주장하면서 NV 분쟁과 관련해서는 의도적 모호성을 선호하는 이유에 관 질문과 EC 및 뉴,호주 양국간 적절히 절충안을 모색하는 것이 바람직하다는 카나다의 의견개진이 있었을뿐 구체적 진전이 없었음.

첨부: 1 일방조치 억제 공약관련 EC 제안

2. 교차보복에 관한 사무국 NON-PAPER

(GVW(F)-0600).끝

(대사 박수길-국장)

주 제 네 바 대 표 부

번 호 : GVW(F) - 0600   년월일 : 11211   시간 : 2050

수 신 : 장   판 (통기, 경기원, 재무부, 농수산부, 상공부)

발 신 : 주 제네바대사

제 복 : GUW-2605

총 3 매(표지포함)

보 안 봉 재	

외신과 봉 재	

600-3-1

0257

91.12.11
준다본은

"The contracting parties :

- shall not make unilateral determination to the effect that their
rights under the GATT have been violated or benefits accruing to
them under the GATT have been nullified or impaired as long as the
Council has not adopted a panel or appellate report to this effect;

- shall not make any unilateral determination of the reasonable
period of time or of the level of the suspension of concessions or
other obligations under the GATT and shall not unilaterally impose
any suspension of concessions or other obligations under the GATT
as long as the Council has not given its authorization for such
suspension in conformity with this Understanding";

- shall adapt their trade legislation so as to make the above-
mentioned unilateral measures impossible."

600-3-2

0258

11.12.91

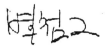

CROSS RETALIATION

Non-Paper by the Secretariat

1.   The GATT provision on retaliation in Article XXIII:2 stipulates that
the CONTRACTING PARTIES may authorize a contracting party "to suspend the
application to any other contracting party or parties of such concessions
or other obligations under this Agreement as they determine to be
appropriate in the circumstances".

2.   A decision on cross-retaliation could extend the scope of retaliation
to cover "concessions or other obligations" in any agreement to be included
in the cross-retaliation system. (The expression "concessions" would be
interpreted as covering, _inter alia_, commitments in the Services and TRIPs
areas.) From a legal point of view, such a construction would not cause a
problem.

3.   From a practical point of view, there are likely to be difficulties in
calculating the appropriate level of cross-retaliation, for example when
the retaliation would consist in tariff increases when a government has not
fulfilled its commitments in the maritime transport area. It has proved
difficult to establish the level of appropriate retaliation inside the
goods area. A secretariat note on methodological questions raised by
various possible calculations (Spec(88)48) was prepared in connection with
requests for authority to retaliate in the Superfund dispute.

4.   An issue which has not so far come up when retaliation has been
envisaged in the goods area, but which is now being discussed in the
Services and TRIPs areas, without any conclusions having yet been reached
is the so-called "acquired rights". The question is whether from a legal
point of view, retaliatory measures can be taken which infringe on
pre-existing rights of private parties, _inter alia_ property rights.   This
issue is closely linked to domestic legislation in countries concerned.

6 ου - 3- 3   0259

발 신 전 보

분류번호 | 보존기간

번 호 : WGV-1807 911211 1849 DW 종별 : 긴급

수 신 : 주 제네바 대사. 총영사//

발 신 : 장 관 (통 기)

제 목 : UR/제도분야 : 일방조치

대 : GVW-2593

대호 관련 본부 입장 하기 통보함.

1. 미측 수정안의 문제점

   가. 일방조치 관련 미측 수정안의 의도는 분쟁해결 관련 UR 협상 결과와 무관하게
        일방조치 발동권을 유지하는데 있음.

   나. 통합 Text 21항의 취지가 모든 체약국이 일방조치의 발동 억제를 공약하고
        관련 국내 무역법령을 갓트 분쟁해결 절차에 일치시킴으로써 다자간 무역체제를
        강화하는데 있음에 반해 미측 수정안은 일방조치 발동 억제의 범위를 갓트
        분쟁해결 절차에 소요되는 최대 시한이내로 국한시킴으로써 일시적인 억제에
        촛점이 맞춰져 있음. 또한 국내 무역관련 법령을 갓트 분쟁해결 절차에
        일치시키는 의무를 명시치 않을 경우, 미국이 UR 협상 결과 이행시 동 의무를
        이행치 않을 우려가 있음. 미국의 국내법 우고상

   다. 또한 23조 2항에 의거한 권리행사(보복)시 분쟁해결 결과를 "고려"하도록
        함으로써 분쟁해결 관련 절차 규정등을 위배하면서 패소국에 대해 일방적인
        보복조치를 발동할 수 있는 여지를 남기고 있는것 또한 문제점으로 분석됨.

보안통제

양고재 | 기안자성명 | 과장 | 국장 | 차관 | 장관 | 외신과통제

0260

라. UR 협상 외적 요소로서, 미측 수정안에 의할 경우 ~~미국은~~, 갓트의 규율 대상을 벗어나 있는 분야(예 : 조선, 철강)에서 일방조치 발동권을 계속 유지하게 된다는 문제점이 있으며, 또한 향후 미국이 노동권과 무역과의 관계를 빌미로 일방조치를 발동할 가능성도 배제할 수 없음.

2. 아측 입장 : 하기 논거를 통해 통합 Text 원안 고수

　　가. 통합 21.1

　　　　- UR 분쟁해결 협상 목표의 근본 취지가 다자간 무역체제의 강화에 있으므로 일방조치 억제 공약이 선행되어야 하며, 이를 위한 보장 장치로서 국내 무역 법령이 갓트 분쟁해결 절차와 일치시켜야 함.

　　　　- 갓트내에서의 분쟁해결 절차가 자동화되며, SG 협상 결과 회색조치가 철폐될 것임을 감안, 체약국간의 무역관련 모든 분쟁이 갓트 분쟁해결 절차를 통해 신속하게 해결하는 제도적 장치가 마련되므로 이를 위한 보완 조치로 통합 Text 21항이 필수적임.

　　나. 통합 Text 1.8

　　　　- 지금까지 갓트 결정이 consensus에 의해 이루어져 왔으므로 traditional 이라는 표현을 포함하는 것이 바람직함.

　　　　- 갓트조문에 대한 권위있는 해석과 관련, 이는 근본적인 문제로서 갓트조문의 해석은 체약국의 권리.의무 관계에 직결된 문제이므로 모든 체약국이 납득할 수 있어야 하므로 이를 25조에 의해 가능토록 하는 것은 바람직 하지 않음.

　　다. 기타 조항 (4.1, 14.4, 15.5, 15.14, 19.3(C), 19.4, 20.3)

　　　　- 동 조항들은 분쟁해결 절차의 엄격화 및 지연방지에 관한 것으로 아국은 by consensus를 포함시키지 않는 것을 선호하나 통합 Text 21항 채택을 전제로 미측 제의에 반대치 않음.　끝.　(통상국장　김 용 규)

0261

원 본

외 무 부

종 별 :

번 호 : GVW-2633　　　　　　　　　　일 시 : 91 1213 1100

수 신 : 장관(봉기, 경기원, 재무부, 농림수산부, 상공부)

발 신 : 주 제네바 대사

제 목 : UR 제도분야(분쟁해결) 비공식 협의

연: GVW-2605

1. 12.12 속개된 표제회의에서는 일방조치 관련 미국 및 EC 가 연호 12.11 협의시 표출된 의견의 일부를 반영 다시 제시한 문안(별첨 1 및 2) 및 교차 보복관련 EC 가 교차 보복 지지국과의 협의를 거쳐 보완(교차 보복의 기준 및 교차보복 승인에 자동화된 절차 적용등 추가), 제시한 문안(별첨 3)을 기초로 상기양 문제가 주로 논의되었음.

2. 또한 카나다로부터 통합 분쟁해결 절차 관련 PAPER (별첨 4)의 제시 및 이에 대한 간단한 설명이 있었으나, 시간 부족으로 이에 대한 토의는 12.13 오전계속키로 함.

3. 기타 EC 가 NON-VIOLATION 분쟁관련 21.1(D) 항 수정문안(별첨 5) 및 TANZANIA 가 22 항(최빈개도국 우대) 수정안(별첨 6)을 제시하였으나 시간 부족으로 논의되지 못함.

4. 의제별 세부 토의 내용은 아래와 같음.

　가. 일방조치 억제

- 미국은 12.11 제시된 의견을 새로운 문안에 최대한 반영하였으나, 행정부에 재량의 여지가 없는 (MANDATORY) 국내법의 경우와는 달리 재량권이 있는 (DISCRETIONARY) 국내법은 국제법과 상충한다 하더라도 여사한 국내법의 존재 자체가 위반을 구성한다고 볼수 없으므로 (미.태국 분쟁관련 PANEL 보고서를 예시), GATT 불일치 국내법의 개정 공약만은 절대로 받아들일수 없다고 주장

- 반면 EC 는 자국의 새로운 문안 2 항 4 번째 PARA 는 전체 조항중 가장 핵심적 사항으로 동 조항이 받아들여지지 않을 경우 새로운 분쟁해결 TEXT 전체를 수락할수 없다고 대응.

통상국 안기부	장관 경기원	차관 재무부	1차보 농수부	2차보 상공부	경제국	외정실	분석관	청와대

91.12.14　07:13
외신 2과 통제관 CA

0262

- 인도, 브라질, 아국, 태국, 일본등이 미국의 논리는 일응 수긍 가능하나 여사한 국내법의 존재가 다자체제에 위협이 되어온 현실적 문제점이 있음을 들어상기 미국 주장에 반론을 제기하고, 기타 미국안이 TIME-LIMIT 만을 특히 강조한 점 (아국, 브라질), 최대시한 초과시 일방 조치 가능성(일본, 아국, 인도, 카나다), 미국안 21. 2(II) 의 필요성 여부(패널등의 결정으로 충분하다는 입장)등 미국제안의 문제점 제기

- 놀웨이는 갓트 불일치 국내법의 개정이 어렵다면 동 법을 적용치 않겠다는 (SHALL NOT APPLY) 공약으로 대체하는 방안도 있을 것이라고 언급한바, 이에 대해 의장은 진지하게 고려해 볼만한 제안이라고 평가

- EC 제안에 대해서는 대부분의 국가가 DRATTING 의 개선 필요성만을 언급하고 전반적으로 큰 문제가 없다는 의견이었으나, 다만 인도가 GATT 밖의 문제틀의이유로한 일방 조치 문제도 아울러 포함되어야 한다는 입장을 표명했고 이에 대해 일본 및 아국이 동조하였으나, 미국은 갓트밖의 문제는 갓트 분쟁해결 절차에 관한 TEXT 에서 다루어질 사항이 아니라는 반대의견을 밝혔고 EC 도 소극적인반응을 보임.

- 한편 뉴질랜드는 패소국의 패널 결정 준수 공약(봉합 문안의 SUB-ITEM II) 반영이 양국안에 모두 미흡함을, 카나다는 23 조 1 항 (C) 해당 NON-VIOLATION 분쟁이 취급되지 않은 문제점을 지적

- 의장은 미.EC 양측에 추가 개선 용의를 문의하면서, 동 용의가 없을 경우에는 제 3 자 (자신을 암시하는 것으로 이해됨)가 문안을 작성할수 밖에 없다고 언급한바, 미.EC 는 본질적 내용 변경을 어렵다고 반응

나. 교차 보복

- 교차 보복의 기준 및 교차 보복 승인시 자동화된 절차 적용을 추가한 EC 의 새로운 제안에 대해 인도, 브라질, 아국, 유고만이 교차 보복 개념 자체에 반대한다는 입장을 표명했을 뿐, 대부분의 선진국(일본도 포함) 들은 개선된 안으로서 평가 하면서 도의의 기초가 될수 있다고 대체적인 지지 입장 표명

- 홍콩은 GATT 와 GATS 간의 교차 보복 인정에 반대하는 기본 입장은 불변 이라고 하면서도 EC 가 제시한 기준의 유용성은 인정

- 인도는 GATT 내에서도 GATS 와 같이 동일 부분 우선 원칙을 적용할 필요성도 있지 않겠느냐는 문제 제기

다. 봉합 분쟁해결 절차(카나다 PAPER)

- 카나다는 자국의 PAPER 가 MTO 설립 협정의 ANNEX 로 첨부되거나, 통합 문안(CONSOLIDATED TEXT)의 적절한 부분에 삽입되는 두가지 가능성을 모두 염두에 두고 작성되었다고 전제한후 동 PAPER 의 내용을 설명

,, 이하 5 항부터 GVW-2643 으로 계속됨. 합본 처리 바람.

PAGE 3

0264

관리번호 91-9‍‍‍‍‍‍‍‍‍‍‍‍‍‍‍‍‍‍‍‍‍‍40

외　무　부

종　별 :

번　호 : GVW-‍‍1643　　　　　　　　　　일　시 : 91 1213 1100

수　신 : 장관(통기, 경기원, 재무부, 농림수산부, 상공부)

발　신 : 주 제네바 대사

제　목 : GVW-2633 호의 계속

5. 평가및 대책

가. 평가

- 카나다가 제기한 상기 통합 분쟁 해결 절차(IDS)는 교차 보복 문제와 밀접히 연관된 사항임.

- 상기 양문제는 EC 와 카나다가 각각 표면상 전면에 나섰을뿐 선진국 상호간에는 긴밀한 협의하에 일치된 자세로 협상에 임하고 있는 것으로 감지됨.

0 특히 카나다가 MTO 합의 실패를 대비 자국 PAPER 를 통합 TEXT 에 삽입 (GRAFTED IN)할 가능성도 아울러 언급한 것은 MTO 설립에 대한 선진국 내부 의견대립에 관계없이 IDS 는 관철하겠다는 의도로 분석

- 또한 12.10 교차 보복 논의 서두에 LACARTE 의장이 교차 보복은 GATT 내에서 극히 예외적으로 적용되어 왔을뿐이라고 언급한후 각국의 FLEXIBILITY 여부를 문의한 것도 교차 보복에 관한 선진국의 희망을 전혀 도외시 할수 없다고 판단하여 개도국의 신축성을 타진하기 위한 의도였던 것으로 분석됨.

- 또한 원칙문제에 대한 합의가 이루어질 경우 이를 TEXT 에 수용하는 문제는 최종단계 협상 및 추후 협상 과정에서 충분히 처리될수 있는 비교적 단순한 기술적 사항에 불과함.

- 따라서 협상 시한이 촉박함에도 불구하고 이들 양문제에 대한 선진국의 의도가 상당부분 반영된 가능성이 없지 않음.

나. 대책

- 아국은 교차 보복에 관한 3 차례 논의시 계속 반대입장을 표명해 왔으나 IDS 문제는 교차 보복문제와의 연관성만 배제된다면 아국으로서도 구태여 반대할 만한 실익과 명분이 없는 것으로 사료됨.

통상국 안기부	장관 경기원	차관 재무부	1차보 농수부	2차보 상공부	경제국	외정실	분석관	청와대

PAGE 1

91.12.14　08:53

외신 2과　통제관 BW

0265

- 따라서 아국에게 다소 불리하게 작용할 소지가 있는 교차 보복 문제에 대해서는 당분간 반대 입장을 견지하되, IDS 문제에 관해서는 적극적 반대 입장을 개진치 않음으로써 아국이 갓트 분쟁해결 절차의 강화에 지나치게 소극적이라는 인상을 심어주지 않는 것이 바람직할 것으로 판단되는바, 이에 대한 본부입장 지급 회시 바람.

첨부: 1. 일방조치 관련 미국문안

2. 일방조치 관련 EC 문안

3. 교차 보복관련 EC 문안

4. 통합분쟁해결 절차 관련 카나다 PAPER

5. NV 분쟁관련 EC 의 21.1(D) 수정문안

6. 최빈 개도국 우대 관련 탄자니아 수정안. 끝

(GVW(F)-609)

(대사 박수길-국장)

예고 91.12.31. 까지

주 제 네 바 대 표 부

번 호 : GVW(F) - *60P*   년월일 : *11213*   시간 : *1200*

수 신 : 장   판 (통기, 301원, 24무부, 농법식상부, 상상복)

발 신 : 주 제네바대사

제 목 : " *한위* "

총 (6 매(표지포합)

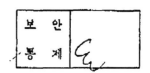

보 안	G
봉 제	

외신과	
봉 제	

0267

60P-16-1

별첨1

R E V I S E D

21. Strengthening the Multilateral System

21.1 All participants in the dispute settlement process shall abide by these rules and procedures, including the time limits set forth in this Understanding.

21.2 ~~Provided that the maximum time limits set forth~~ in ~~this~~ Understanding are not exceeded, the complaining party (i) [should/shall] not determine that any provision of the General Agreement has been violated, or that any benefit accruing to it under the General Agreement has been nullified or impaired within the meaning of Article XXIII:1(b), except through recourse to dispute settlement in accordance with these procedures; (ii) [should/shall] use the panel or appellate body report as the basis for determining whether there has been a violation, or nullification or impairment within the meaning of Article XXIII:1(b); and (iii) if it wishes to suspend concessions or other obligations pursuant to Article XXIII:2 in such case, it [should/shall] do so in accordance with the procedures set forth in this Understanding.

NOTE: This proposal is linked to and conditioned upon acceptance of the following formulations in other parts of the text (most of which are currently bracketed):

Para. 1.8 Delete "the traditional practice of" from the first sentence, and replace second sentence in current text, so that para. 1.8 reads as follows:

"Where these GATT rules and procedures provide for the Council to take a decision, it shall do so by the practice of consensus."1 The procedures foreseen in GATT dispute settlement are without prejudice to the possibility that the contracting parties may take joint action under Article XXV to adopt authoritative interpretations of the General Agreement."

Add the following footnote: "The Council shall be deemed to have decided by consensus if no member of the Council formally objects to the decision."

Para. 4.1: "...unless at that meeting the Council decides by consensus not to establish a panel."

0268

Footnote: "If the complaining party so
requests, a meeting of the Council shall
be convened for this purpose within 15
days of the request, provided that, in
accordance with past practice, at least
ten days' advance notice is given.

Para. 14.4:   "...or the Council decides by consensus
not to adopt the report."

Para. 15.5:   "In no case shall the proceedings exceed
ninety days."

Para. 15.14:   "...unless the Council decides by
consensus not to adopt the appellate
report."

Para. 19.3(c): "In such arbitration, a guideline for the
arbitrator should be that the reasonable
period of time to implement panel or
appellate body recommendations should not
exceed fifteen months from the adoption of
a panel or appellate body report.
However, that time may be shorter or
longer, depending on the particular
circumstances."

Para. 19.4:   "...in no event shall the total amount of
time exceed eighteen months."
                     OR
"...unless the parties agree that there
are exceptional circumstances, the total
time shall not exceed eighteen months."

Para. 20.3:   "...unless the Council decides by
consensus to reject the request."

Sec. 24   If it is agreed that there should be a
separate section on non-violation cases,
there must be acceptable provisions in
that section.

0269

んp P- 16- 3

별첨 2

1. For the settlement of their disputes under the GATT, contracting parties shall have recourse exclusively to the rules and procedures of the present Understanding.

2. The contracting parties :

   - shall not make *any* unilateral determination to the effect that their rights under the GATT have been violated or benefits accruing to them under the GATT have been nullified or impaired unless the Council has adopted a panel or appellate report to this effect;

   - shall not make any unilateral determination of the reasonable period of time or of the level of the suspension of concessions or other obligations under the GATT during the dispute settlement procedure;

   - shall not unilaterally impose any suspension of concessions or other obligations under the GATT unless the Council has given its authorization for such suspension in conformity with this Understanding;

   - shall adapt their trade legislation so as to make the above-mentioned unilateral measures impossible.

Key element

0270

별첨 3

CROSS-RETALIATION

Members, seeking authorization to suspend concessions or other obligations under the covered agreements, and the Dispute Settlement Board, in deliberating about such requests for authorization, shall apply the following procedures and observe the following criteria.

A. Under the GATS(*)

a) The general principle is that members should first seek authorization to suspend concessions or other obligations in the same services sector as that under which the Panel has made a determination of inconsistency or nullification or impairment.

b) If the member concerned considers that it is not practically possible to suspend concessions or other obligations in the same sector, it may seek to suspend concessions or other obligations in other sectors under the GATS. It shall state the reasons therefor and address the criteria listed under C below.

   The Council on Services or the sectoral body, as the case may be, shall be informed of such request and may give its views to the Dispute Settlement Board at a meeting of the Board held for that purpose.

c) If the member concerned considers that it is not practically possible to suspend concessions or other obligations in other sectors under the GATS, it may seek authorization to suspend concessions or other obligations under the GATT. It shall state the reasons therefor and address the criteria listed under C below. The Council on Goods shall be informed of such request and may give its views to the Dispute Settlement Board at a meeting of the Board held for that purpose.

B. Under the GATT(*)

a) The general principle is that members should first seek authorization to suspend concessions or other obligations under the GATT.

b) If the member concerned considers that it is not practically possible to suspend concessions or other obligations under the GATT, it may seek authorization to suspend concessions or other obligations under the GATS. It shall state the reasons therefor and address the criteria listed under C below. The Council on Services or the sectoral body, as the case may be, shall be informed of such request and may give its views to the Dispute Settlement Board at a meeting of the Board held for that purpose.

(*) These headings and other references to GATS and GATT need to be adapted later to the MTO Treaty annexes, *or to the annexed to be attached to the instrument for integrated dispute*

0271

- 2 -

C. <u>Criteria</u>

In making its request under A (b), A (c), or B (b) above, the member concerned shall address the following criteria :

a) the quantity of the trade available in the sector or under the agreement under which the Panel has made a determination of inconsistency or nullification and impairment and the importance of it to the member making the request;

b) the broader economic elements involved both in the damage suffered as a consequence of the inconsistency, or the nullification or impairment and in the consequences of the suspension of concessions or other obligation for which authorization is sought;

c) the principal objective of seeking authorization to suspend concessions or other obligations outside the sector or the agreement under which the Panel has made a determination of inconsistency or nullification or impairment.

D. <u>Deliberation of the Dispute Settlement Board</u>

The Dispute Settlement Board shall deliberate on the requests for authorization under A (b), A (c) and B)b) above and may express its views on them, before authorizing the suspension of concessions or other obligations pursuant to (section 20.3 of the Consolidated Texts).

0272

$60P - 16 - 6$

12 December 1991

ELEMENTS OF AN INTEGRATED DISPUTE SETTLEMENT SYSTEM
Dispute Settlement Body[1]

1.   The PARTIES to this Understanding agree that the rules and procedures in this Understanding shall apply to disputes brought under the Agreements listed in Annex 1 to this Understanding ("the covered Agreements"), subject to any special or additional provisions on dispute settlement contained in the covered Agreements.

2.   Parties hereby establish a Dispute Settlement Body to implement the procedures set out in this Understanding for disputes arising under the covered Agreements. It shall have authority to establish panels, adopt panel and Appellate Body reports, maintain surveillance of implementation of rulings and recommendations, and authorize suspension of concessions and other obligations under any of the covered Agreements.

3.   Membership in the Body shall be open to [members of the MTO] [representatives of Parties to or Signatories of all of the covered Agreements set out in Annexes 1A and 1B, provided that they are also a contracting party to the GATT].[2] Councils and Committees charged with the administration of the covered Agreements shall be fully informed of developments in disputes involving obligations under the Agreements that they administer.

4.   Where the rules and procedures of this Understanding provide for the Dispute Settlement Body to take a decision, it shall do so by consensus.[3]

5.   The Dispute Settlement Body shall follow the procedures outlined in this Understanding, except where special or additional procedures exist in

---

[1] The name of this Body may be changed.

[2] This presupposes a single undertaking.

[3] This provision could be changed depending on changes to paragraph 1.8 of the Consolidated Text.

0273

- ⅞ -

a particular covered Agreement. Such special or additional procedures are
set out in Annex 2 to this Understanding. To the extent that there is a
difference between the procedures of this Understanding and the provisions
of the covered Agreement, the provisions of the covered Agreement shall
prevail. In disputes involving provisions under more than one covered
Agreement under review, and where the parties to the dispute cannot agree
on procedures, the Director-General, in consultation with the parties to
the dispute and the Chairman of the Dispute Settlement Body shall determine
the procedures to be followed. The Director-General shall be guided by the
principle that special or additional procedures should be used where
possible and the procedures set out in this Understanding should be used to
the extent necessary to avoid conflict.[6]

---

[6]This provision should be re-examined in the light of the results of
the Round.

6oP-16-8   0274

- 3 -

Establishment of panel

1   The Dispute Settlement Body shall meet as necessary to carry out its functions within the time-frames provided in this Understanding.[1] If the complaining party so requests, a panel shall be established at the latest at the Dispute Settlement Body meeting following that at which the request first appears as an item on the Dispute Settlement Body's regular agenda, unless at that meeting the Dispute Settlement Body decides [otherwise] [by consensus] [not to establish a panel].

---

[1]A meeting of the Body shall be convened for this purpose within fifteen days of the request, provided that at · least ten days' advance notice is given.

6 of —16 —P   0275

- 4 -

Composition of Panels

1. Panels shall be composed of well-qualified governmental and/or
non-governmental individuals, including persons who have served on or
presented a case to a panel, served as a representative to the GATT or
other Committee or Council or in the secretariat, taught or published on
international trade law or policy, or served as a senior trade policy
official of a party.

2.   To assist in the selection of panelists, the secretariat shall
maintain an indicative list of governmental and non-governmental
individuals possessing the qualifications outlined in paragraph 1 above,
from which panelists may be drawn as appropriate. That list shall replace
the roster of non-governmental panelists that was established by the GATT
CONTRACTING PARTIES on 30 December 1984, and other rosters and indicative
lists established under any of the covered Agreements, but shall include
the names of persons on those rosters and indicative lists at the time of
entry into force of this Understanding. PARTIES may periodically suggest
names of governmental and non-governmental individuals for inclusion on the
indicative list, providing relevant information on their knowledge of
international trade and of the covered agreements, and those names shall be
added to the list upon approval by the Dispute Settlement Body. For each
panelists on the list, the list shall indicate specific areas of experience
or expertise of the individuals in the sectors or matters under the covered
agreements.

3.   If there is no agreement on the members within twenty days from the
establishment of a panel, at the request of either party, the Chairman of
the Dispute Settlement Body, in agreement with the Chairman of the relevant
Committee or Council shall form the panel by appointing the panelists whom
he considers most appropriate in accordance with any relevant special or
additional procedure of the covered Agreement, after consulting with the
parties to the dispute. The Chairman of the Dispute Settlement Body shall
inform the parties of the composition of the panel thus formed no later
than ten days from the date he receives such a request.

0276

- 5 -

Forum/Norm Shopping

Terms of Reference of Panels

1.   Panels shall have the following terms of reference unless the parties
to the dispute agree otherwise within twenty days from the establishment of
the panel:

> "To examine, in the light of the relevant provisions of all covered
> Agreements cited by the parties to the dispute, the matter referred to
> the Dispute Settlement Body by [name of party] in document DS/... and
> to make such findings as will assist the Dispute Settlement Body in
> making recommendations or in giving rulings.

2.   Panels shall address the relevant provisions of any covered agreement
cited by the parties to the dispute.

0277

/of - 16 - 11

- b -

Conflict of Substantive Provisions

1.   Where a panel or the Appellate Body determines that the substantive provisions of any covered Agreement conflict with the substantive provisions of any other covered Agreement, the panel or Appellate Body shall not attempt in its findings to resolve the conflict, but shall issue a report containing a description of the facts of the matter, a summary of the arguments of the parties and an identification of the provisions the panel or Appellate Body considers to be in conflict. A panel or Appellate Body report which does not contain recommendations due to a conflict between substantive provisions shall be referred to the parties for appropriate action.

2.   In the event that a panel determines that some aspects of the complaint are not affected by the conflict of substantive provisions, the panel shall issue a panel report, separate from the report issued pursuant to paragraph 1 above, addressing those aspects of the complaint. Such a report shall be subject to the normal procedures set out in this Understanding.

0278

- 7 -

Compensation and the Suspension of Concessions[1]

1. The Dispute Settlement Body shall be the body that authorizes the suspension of concessions or other obligations of any covered Agreement in accordance with the provisions of those Agreements.

2. The Dispute Settlement Body may not authorize suspension of concessions or other obligations where it has been determined in a covered Agreement that those concessions or other obligations may not be suspended.

3. The arbitrator shall not examine the nature of the suspended concessions or other obligations but shall determine whether the level is appropriate in the circumstances. The arbitration may also determine if the proposed suspension of concessions or other obligations proposed for suspension is allowed under the covered Agreement. The parties shall accept the arbitrator's determination as final.

---

[1]Any procedures and criteria on cross-retaliation shall go in this section.

- 8 -

Non-Violation Complaints

1. Where particular Agreements contain provisions related   to
non-violation disputes, the following procedures shall apply.[1]

---

[1]This provision should be reviewed in the light of the results in
other Groups.

0280

ٮٯ-16-1٪

백첨5　91.12.12
조 양변인

24.1 (d)　The provisions of Section 20 [with the exception of para. 20.7] shall apply; they shall not constitute an obstacle to whatever may be the contents of a mutually satisfactory adjustment as a final settlement of the dispute.

0281

(op-16-15)

별첨 6.

Special Provisions involving Least-Developed Countries

In case of the Least Developed Countries,

(i) Article XXII shall not apply.

(ii) Article XXIII shall apply to the extent a Least
     Developed Contracting party considers itself to
     be an aggrieved party. In such a circumstance
     the Director General shall, upon request by a least-
     developed contracting party, offer his good offices,
     conciliation and mediation with a view to assisting
     the parties to settle the dispute, before a request
     for a panel is made. The Director-General, in
     providing the above assistance, may consult any
     source which he deems appropriate.

Explanatory Observation

If the Declaration of the Punta del Este is to be meaningful so
far as the Least Developed Countries are concerned, they need a very
special protection. They are in no position to take any action against a
strong Contracting party which has many avenues of placing pressure
on the Least Developed. With such a thin (almost skin-deep) and
extremely narrow range of its commodity dominated export trade profile,
it is not possible for a country earning less than 75 U.S. cents per
head per day to inflict injury on stronger economies.

However, a stronger Contracting party may, for a variety of
reasons, not always of a trade nature but disguised as such, may
decide to take take punitive measures directly or indirectly against a
Least Developed Country. In such an event the particular Least
Developed country has no other recourse to defending its interests save
the rather imperfect Art. XXIII, as modified in our proposal.

0282

외 무 부

원 본

종   별 :

번   호 : GVW-2642   일   시 : 91 1213 1800

수   신 : 장 관(통기,경기원,재무부,농림수산부,상공부)

발   신 : 주 제네바 대사

제   목 : UR/제도분야(분쟁해결) 비공식 협의

1. 12.13.개최된 표제협의 (LACARTE 의장 주재)에서는 12.10 배포된 새로운 통합문안 (CONSOLIDATED TEXT: 파편 송부)을 기초로 남아있는 문제를 하나하나 점검해 나가는 방식으로 토의를 진행한바 다소 경미한 하기사항에 대해서만 합의를 보았을뿐 자동화 문제를 비롯한 주요쟁점에 대해서 문제점을 TAKE NOTE하였을뿐임

   - 미.칠레간 양자협의 결과를 받아들여 각주 1삭제

   - EC 의 양보도 합리적 이행기간의 지침관련조항 (19.3항 C) 괄호 제거

   - 21.4항과의 일관성 유지 차원에서 17.1항의 INNER BRACKET 삭제

   - 15.5항 부패성 물질의 경우 패널 일정 단축가능성 부여 문안의 괄호 제거

   - 패널의 WORKING PROCEDURE (ANNEX) 12항(K)을 2-3주로 단축

2. 미국, 칠레간 양자협의 결과 자동화가 받아들여질 경우 1.8항 제2문장을 삭제키로 합의가 이루어짐에 따라 양국은 별첨 1 PAPER 를 제시한바, 이에대해 인도가 자동화 문제와 25조 공동행동의 직접적인 연관성에 의문을 표시하고, 당사국은 제외가 제3국에 대해 25조행동의 가능성을 열어준다면 고려 가능하다는 의견을 피력하였고, 미국은 자국의 일방조치관련 문안상에 열거된 부수조건중 1.8항 관련부분을 상기시키면서 일방조치 관련 자국 문안을 인도가 수락한다면 인도의 의견을 받아들일용의가 있다고 언급함.

3. 한편 미국은 17.2항 다음에 별첨 2문안을 17.3항으로 추가할 것을 새로이 제안한바, EC가자국의 기존입장 (MTN/GNG/NG 13/W 12) 를 상기시키면서 지지 의견을 표명하였으나 의장, 인도,일본, 카나다, 뉴질랜드는 소극적 반응을 보임.특히 인도는 절차의 자동화 등으로 이사회의 정치적 역할이 대폭 축소된 상황에서 다시 이사회의 해석기능 (INTERPRETATIONAL ROLE) 까지 제약을 가하는 결과가 될것임을 우려하고 패널 결정은 당사국만 구속한다는 규정을 설정하는 방식으로 절충할 수는 있다는

통상국   2차보   경기원   재무부   농수부   상공부

91.12.14   10:09 WG

외신 1과   통제관

0283

입장을 표명하였으며, 의장 또한 명시적 규정이 없는 경우로 한정한다면 고려가능하나 협상결과 미 결사항 전체로 확대하여 패널의 결정권을 제약하는 것은 지나친 요구라는 반응을 보였음.

이에 대해 미국은 현 17.2항 문안은 PANEL이명시적 규정이 없는 부분에 대해 새로운 RULE을 만들어 낼수 있는 것으로 잘못해석될 가능성도 있다는 우려에서 동 제안을 하게 되었다하고 의장의 제시한 방향에 따라 재검토하겠다고 언급함.

4. 금일 협의시 미국 및 EC 는 일방조치 관련각각 다시 새문안을 제시함

(별첨 3 및 4)

첨부: 1. 1.8항 관련 미국,칠레 공동제안

2. 17.3항 관련 미국제안

3. 일방조치 관련 미국제안

4. 일방조치 관련 EC 제안

(GVW(F)-0613).끝

(대사 박수길-국장)

주 제 네 바 대 표 부

번 호 : GVW(F) - 0613   년월일 : 11213   시간 : 1800

수 신 : 장   판 (동기 · 경기원 · 재무 · 농수산 · 상공부).

발 신 : 주 제네바대사

제 목 : GVW-2642 첨부

총 6 매 (표지포함)

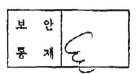

보 안 동 재	
외신과 동 재	

613-1-

0285

(별도첨부)

13.12.91
12.05

Chile

Keep the second sentence of paragraph 1.8, and in a footnote read:

^cThis sentence will be deleted if the criteria of automaticity in the text of GATT Dispute Settlement is approved by the CONTRACTING PARTIES.

0286

613-1-2

13.12.91

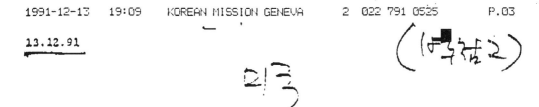

Insert a new paragraph 17.3

"A panel or the Appellate Body shall not give rulings and recommendations
on matters of substance or procedure on which negotiations have failed to
result in express rules."

in the absence of express rules

0287

613-6-3

백법3   一 ' ＂ ⊇:   91.12.13

R E V I S E D

21. Strengthening the Multilateral System

21.1 All participants in the dispute settlement process
shall abide by these rules and procedures, including the
time limits set forth in this Understanding, and parties
concerned shall not delay implementation of
recommendations or rulings within the reasonable period
of time determined under paragraph 19.3.

21.2 Provided that the maximum time limits set forth in
this Understanding are not exceeded, the complaining
party (i) [should/shall] not determine that any
provision of the General Agreement has been violated, or
that any benefit accruing to it under the General
Agreement has been nullified or impaired within the
meaning of Article XXIII:1, except through recourse to
dispute settlement in accordance with these procedures;
(ii) in determining whether there has been a violation,
or nullification or impairment within the meaning of
Article XXIII:1, [should/shall] do so consistent with the
adopted panel or appellate body report; and (iii) if it
wishes to suspend concessions or other obligations
pursuant to Article XXIII:2 in such case, it
[should/shall] do so by following the procedures set
forth in this Understanding.

NOTE: This proposal is linked to and conditioned upon
acceptance of the following formulations in other parts
of the text (most of which are currently bracketed):

Para. 1.8   Delete "the traditional practice of" from
                   the first sentence, and replace second
                   sentence in current text, so that para.
                   1.8 reads as follows:

                   "Where these GATT rules and procedures
                   provide for the Council to take a
                   decision, it shall do so by the practice
                   of consensus."1 The procedures foreseen
                   in GATT dispute settlement are without
                   prejudice to the possibility that the
                   contracting parties may take joint action
                   under Article XXV to adopt authoritative
                   interpretations of the General Agreement."

                   Add the following footnote: "The Council
                   shall be deemed to have decided by
                   consensus if no member of the Council
                   formally objects to the decision."

0288

6/3-6-4

Para. 4.1:   "...unless at that meeting the Council
                  decides by consensus not to establish a
                  panel."

                  Footnote: "If the complaining party so
                  requests, a meeting of the Council shall
                  be convened for this purpose within 15
                  days of the request, provided that, in
                  accordance with past practice, at least
                  ten days' advance notice is given.

Para. 14.4:   "...or the Council decides by consensus
                  not to adopt the report."

Para. 15.5:   "In no case shall the proceedings exceed
                  ninety days."

Para. 15.14:   "...unless the Council decides by
                  consensus not to adopt the appellate
                  report."

Para. 19.3(c):   "In such arbitration, a guideline for the
                  arbitrator should be that the reasonable
                  period of time to implement panel or
                  appellate body recommendations should not
                  exceed fifteen months from the adoption of
                  a panel or appellate body report.
                  However, that time may be shorter or
                  longer, depending on the particular
                  circumstances."

Para. 19.4:   "...in no event shall the total amount of
                  time exceed eighteen months."
                             OR
                  "...unless the parties agree that there
                  are exceptional circumstances, the total
                  time shall not exceed eighteen months."

Para. 20.3:   "...unless the Council decides by
                  consensus to reject the request."

Sec. 24   If it is agreed that there should be a
                  separate section on non-violation cases,
                  there must be acceptable provisions in
                  that section.

0289

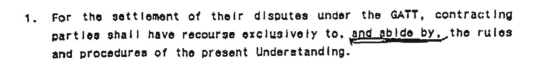

13.12.91

1. For the settlement of their disputes under the GATT, contracting parties shall have recourse exclusively to, and abide by, the rules and procedures of the present Understanding.

2. The contracting parties :

   – shall not make any unilateral determination to the effect that their rights under the GATT have been violated, benefits accruing to them under the GATT have been nullified or impaired or the attainment of any objective of the GATT is being impeded unless the Council has adopted a panel or appellate report to this effect;

   – shall not make any unilateral determination of the reasonable period of time or of the level of the suspension of concessions or other obligations under the GATT during the dispute settlement procedure;

   – shall not unilaterally impose any suspension of concessions or other obligations under the GATT unless the Council has given its authorization for such suspension in accordance with this Understanding;

   – shall adapt their trade legislation so as to make the above-mentioned unilateral measures impossible.

613-6-6

0290

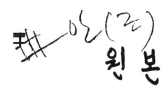

외 무 부

종   별 :

번   호 : GVW-2624   일   시 : 91 1214 1200

수   신 : 장 관(봉기, 경기원, 재무부, 농수부, 상공부, 특허청)

발   신 : 주 제네바 대사

제   목 : UR / 최종의정서

　　12.13(금) 14:30-17:00 간 LACARTE 의장 주재로 91.3.25자 사무국이 작성한 최종의정서 초안에 대한비공식 협의가 개최된바, 요지 아래보고함.(오참사관 참석)

　　1. 모든 참가국들은 최종의정서는 기본적으로 UR협상결과를 확인하고 동 결과를각국의비준절차에 회부키로 하는 <u>정치적인 문서</u>이며,각국에 법률적인 의무를 부과하는 것이아니라는데 의견을 같이함.

　　2. 초안 1항의 부속서 처리문제와 관련, 당초초안대로 <u>3개의 부속서</u>로 할 것을 주장하는 인도,브라질과 <u>하나의 부속서</u>로 하자는 선진국이대립하였으나, 푼타 선언 및중간 평가협의사항을 언급하고 <u>한나의 부속서로 하기로합의함.</u>(푼타 선언에서 상품분야와 서비스 분야를구분하였고 이행문제는 각료급 회의가 결정키로한점, 중간 평가회의에서 TRIPS 협정이행문제도 각료급 회의가 결정키로 한점을 감안)

　　3. 초안 2항 관련, 최종의정서를 채택함으로써각국은 <u>각기 비준절차에</u> <u>회부키로합의(AGREE)</u>키로 하는데 의견이 모아짐.

　　4. 초안 3항 관련 UR 협상 결과의 잠정적용에 관한 문구를 삭제키로 합의함.

　　5. 초안 8항 관련, ⃝인도가 모든 협상분야의 결과를보기전까지는 SINGLE UNDERTAKING 에 동의할수없다는 강한 유보 의사를 표명하였으며,선진국들은 SINGLE UNDERTAKING 을 주장하였음.

　　6. 12.14(토) 오후 최종의정서에 관한 협의를계속키로 하였으며, MTO 문제도 협의예정임.끝

　　(대사 박수길-국장)

통상국	2차보	외정실	안기부	경기원	재무부	농수부	상공부	특허청

PAGE 1   91.12.15   01:02 FO

　　　　　　　　　　　　　　　　　　　　　　　　　　　　　　외신 1과 통제관

　　　　　　　　　　　　　　　　　　　　　　　　　　　　　　0291

분류번호	보존기간

발 신 전 보

WGV-1834   911216 0939 DQ

번 호 : _____   종별 : **지급**

수 신 : 주   제네바   대사. 총영사 //

발 신 : 장 관 (통 기)

제 목 : UR/분쟁해결 : 통합 분쟁해결 절차

대 : GVW-2643

대호 관련 귀관 건의대로 대처바람.   끝.   (통상국장 김 용 규)

일반문서로 재분류(1981. 12. 31.)

보 안
통 제

앙고재	81년1월16일	기안자성명		과 장	국 장	차 관	장 관	

외신과통제

0292

외 무 부

원 본

종 별 :

번 호 : GVW-2653   일 시 : 91 1215 1430

수 신 : 장 관(봉기, 경기원, 재무부, 농림수산부, 상공부, 특허청)

발 신 : 주 제네바 대사

제 목 : UR / 최종의정서

　　　연: GVW-2624

　　　12.14(토) 14:30-18:00간 LACARTE 의장 주재로 UR최종의정서 및 MTO
설립문제에관한비공식협의가 개최된바 결과 아래보고함. (오참사관 참석)

　　　1. 최종의정서(91.3.25자 사무국 초안을 기초로 협의)

　　　가. 3항

　　　- 미국은 UR 협상 결과 이행문제에 관한각료회의 결과가 없이는 UR PACKAGE 를
의회에제출키 어렵다는 점을 지적하고, 개최시기, 회의개최에 대한 GUIDELINE등이
필요함을지적함

　　　- EC 는 최종의정서 채택시 MTO 설립협정을 일괄 채택함으로써 UR 협상이행문제를
동시에 해결할 것을 희망하였으나, 그시점까지 MTO 설립에 관한 완전한 합의가이루어
질수 있느냐의 여부에 따라 최종의정서의일부로 채택하든지 아니면 별도
각료회의를개최하되, 가능한한 UR 협상 결과채택회의에 이어서 개최하는 방향으로
의견이접근됨.

　　　나. 5항 및 6항

　　　- 5항에 MTO 설립이 바람직하다는 점을 언급하고, MTO 협정안을 최종의정서에
첨부하는 대신6항을 삭제키로 함.

　　　- 첨부된 MTO 협정안 추가 협상을 요한다는취지의 COVER NOTE 를 붙이기로 함.

　　　다. 7항

　　　- 최종의정서는 정치적 문서이며, 각료회의에서 UR협상결과 이행에 관한
결정을하게되면이때부터는 의미가 없는 서류가 된다는점에서최빈 개도국에 대한
유예기간부여 문제는최종의정서에서는 삭제하고 별도 PROTOCOL형태로 작성키로
함. (북구 및최빈개국 대표가구체내용을 협의 의장과 추후 협의키로 함)

통상국　　2차보　　청와대　　경기원　　재무부　　농수부　　상공부　　특허청

PAGE 1   91.12.16   06:09 FO

　　　　　　　　　　　　　　　　　　　　외신 1과 통제관

0293

라. 8항

- SINGLE UNDERTAKING 문제는 8항 문안상 ACCEPTS AWHOLE 의 표현은 사용하되 구속력 없는 정치적성격임을 암시하는 표현을 첨부하는 선에서의장이 적절히 처리키로함.

2. MTO

- EC,카나다 공동제안 MTO 설립 협정안에 대한1차적인 의견 교환을 하였으며, 금일 협의내용을 기초로 공동제안국이 12.15(일)까지 새로운TEXT 를 준비, 재협의키로함.

- 인도는 TRIPS 협정이 상품에 관한 협정과더불어 ANNEX 1A 에 포함되는데 반대의사를표명하고, 통합분쟁 해결절차에 유보의사를 밝힘

- 미국, 스위스등은 서비스와 상품에 관한 이사회를하나로 통합할 것을 제의함

- 아국은 UR협상 결과로 현 GATT 협정과 MTO체제하의 GATT 의 법적 형태가 변동된다는가정의 부당성, 2조 2항 및 16조 1항의 규정의모순을 지적함

- 미국은 NON-APPLICATION 규정과 관련,각협정에서 가능하도록 규정한 경우 협정별로NON-APPLICATION 을 원용할 수 있어야 함을지적하고, FINAL PROVISION 관련 개별 협정에대한 유보가 가능해야 함을 주장함.끝

(대사 박수길-국장)

PAGE 2

0294

외 무 부

종 별 :

번 호 : GVW-2654   일 시 : 91 1215 1700

수 신 : 장 관(봉기,경기원,재무부,농림수산부,상공부)

발 신 : 주 제네바 대사

제 목 : UR/제도분야(분쟁해결)비공식 협의

　　12.14(토) 오전,오후에 걸쳐 계속된 표제협의에서는 일방조치, NON-VIOLATION 분쟁, 14.4항등과관련된 인도제안 및 최빈개국 우대문제(탄자니아제기)를 토의한 결과, 마지막 2가지문제에 대해서는 합의에 이르렀으나, 일방조치, NV 분쟁에 대해서는 뚜렷한진전이없었으므로 명일 오후(시간 미정) 토의를 계속키로한바, 동 결과 아래 보고함.

　　1. 일방조치

　O 미국은 12.13자 자국 문안이 아래 4가지 사항을개선했다고 설명

　　- 21.1항에 뉴질랜드 관심 반영

　　- GATT 23.1항 C해당 NV 분쟁포함

　　- 21.2(II)의 문안 강화(DO SO CONSISTENT WITH)

　　- 21.2(III)의 문안 강화(DO SO BY FOLLOWING)

　O 상기에 대해 인도,일본,아국, 브라질,태국,카나다등이 미.EC 양문안을 비교하면서 EC 문안선호 입장을 표명하고 12.12. 협의시 언급된 미국문안상의 문제점(TIME-LIMIT 부각, PROVIDED THAT이하 문단의 문제점)을 계속 지적

　O 특히 일본은 EC 문안 1항 모든 분쟁을 갓트분행해결 절차에만 의거하여 해결토록 규정한점을 지지하면서 미국안은 이와 달리 GATT 23조1항 3개 CATEGORY 의 어느하나에도 속하지 않은사항의 경우 일방 조치가 가능할 수 있다는문제점을 지적하였으나, 미국은 동 문제는 갓트분쟁해결 절차 차원의 문제가 아니라는 반론을강하게 되풀이 하고 EC 문안은 정치성을 강하게내포하고 있어서 수락할 수 없다는 입장 개진

　O 의장은 상기 일본의 주장관련 UR 협상 결과강화된 갓트 체제내에서는 일본이 우려하는사태를 상정키 어렵다는 견해를 표명, 미국의입장에 동조하는 태도를 보임

통상국　2차보　정와대　경기원　재무부　농수부　상공부

PAGE 1

91.12.16　06:08 FO

외신 1과 통제관

0295

O 일본은 또한 EC 문안이 갓트에서 인정하고있는 일방조치(19조 SAFEGUARDS, 21조 안보상의예외등) 마저 금지된다고 해석될수 있으므로EC문안 2항 3문단 UNLESS 다음에 'IT CONFORMSTO RELEVENT GATT PROVISION' 틀 추가할 것을 제의

2. NV 분쟁

O 24.1(D)에 관한 EC 의 연호 양보안에 대해뉴질랜드는 TAUTOLOGY 불과하다고 말하면서 수락불가 입장 개진

O 아직도 의견이 대립하고 있는 문제로서 NV분쟁에 20.7항의 적용문제와 <u>NV 분쟁의경우 PANEL 대신 중재자(ARBITRATOR)만이 상호만족할만한 해결책에 이르는 수단 및방법(WAYS AND MEANS)</u>을 제시할 수 있다는EC의 요구 수락 여부라고 하면서, EC와 NZ의의견개진을 요청한바, 양국은 상반된 입장을되풀이(EC 는 동 문제를 PANEL 아니고중재에맡기자는 것이 EC 제안의 핵심적 취지라는입자, 뉴질랜드는 17.1항과 상충되므로일반분쟁과의 여사한 구분을 받아들일수 없다는입장)

O 상기에 대해 미국이 패널 구성원과 중재자가동일한 사람이 될 경우 문제가 상당부분해소될수도 있을 것이라고 하면서 19.3항에도20.3항과 동일한 규정(중재는 가능한 당초패널에 맡김)을 추가할 것을 제의한바, EC 는유보입장 표명(미국은 19.3항에도 여사한 언급이있었으며, 이는 사무국의 착오로 누락되었다고하면서 사무국의 확인을 요청)

3. 14.4항등 관련 인도제안

- 의장의 권유에 따른 미,EC,인도간 개별절충을 통해 별첨(1)과 같은 합의(인도의 제안취지가 제3국 권한 및 이사회의 역할 차원에있었음을 감안 갓트 규정의 해석관련 25조공동행동의 가능성을 열어주는 문안을 1.8 BIS로 신설하는 대신 인도는 대부분의 제안철회)에 이르고 이에 북별히 반대한 국가가없었으므로 동 절충 내용대로 합의 도달

4. 최빈개도국 우대

- 연호 탄자니아 문안에 대해 미국,카나다등선진국이 반대 입장을 표명하였으나,인도가제시한 절충안을 일부 수정하여 별첨 2 문안에합의

첨부: 1. 14.4항 관련 합의문안

2. 최빈개도국 우대관련 합의문안

(GVW(F)-0623).끝

(대사 박수길-국장)

PAGE 2

0296

14 December 1991

Add new 1.8ter or 1.8 bis

> The provisions of this Understanding are without prejudice to the rights of contracting parties to seek authoritative interpretation of provisions of the General Agreement through joint action under Article XXV.

14.2 Delete bracketed language

14.4 Delete second set of square brackets (language is retained)

15.4 Delete bracketed language and add the following second sentence:

> "Third parties which have notified the Council of a *substantial* ~~substantive~~ interest in the matter pursuant to paragraph 8.2 may make written submissions to, and may be given an opportunity to be heard by, the Appellate Body.

15.5 Delete bracketed text beginning with word "expiry" in second line and ending with word "decision" in fourth line.

15.12 The Appellate Body shall address each of the issues raised in accordance with paragraph 15.6 during the appellate proceeding.

623-2-1

0297

14.12.91

15.35

(대책첨 2)

최빈개도국 난권 하늘다 보얀

22.1 In this regard, contracting parties shall exercise due restraint in raising matters under Article XXIII involving a least developed contracting party. If nullification or impairment is found to result from a measure taken by a least developed contracting party, complaining parties shall exercise due restraint in asking for compensation or seeking authorization to suspend the application of concessions or other obligations pursuant to Article XXIII:2.

2-2

623- 2-2

0298

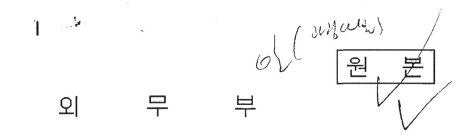

외 무 부

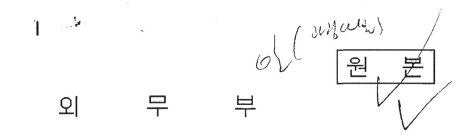

종 별 :

번 호 : GVW-2664   일   시 : 91 1216 1200

수 신 : 장 관(통기,경기원,재무부,농림수산부,상공부,특허청)

발 신 : 주 제네바 대사

제 목 : UR/제도 분야 협의

12.15(일) 오전, 오후 LINDEN 보좌관 주재제조분야에 대한 협의가 개최된바, 결과 아래보고함.(오참사관 참석)

1. 통화.금융.무역정책간의 일관성(COHERENCE)문제

0 브랏셀 각료 회의에 제출된 문서(35/REV.1)를 기초로 협의하였으나 환율 안정을 세계교역확대, 기타 경제문제 해결과 직접적으로 연계시키고져 하는 이씨측 입장과이에 반대하는 미국입장의 대립으로 전혀 진전을 보지못함.

- 금일 회의시 미국은 UR 협상 종료후에 경우에따라 일방조치를 취할수 있도록 하는 것을 암시하는 별첨(1) 제안을 하였는바, 일본, EC를 비롯 많은 국가가 동제안은COHERENCE문제와 관련이 없으며, 미국의 제안의도가 UR협상결과를 무의미하게 하는것이라고 반대함에따라 이를 철회하였으나 미국은 다른 기회에 이문제를 제기하겠다는 점을 밝힘.

2. MTO 설립

- 12.14(토) 협의 결과를 반영, 공동제안국(멕시코추가)이 MTO 설치 협정 2차 초안(별첨 2)을 제시,이를 기초로 협의하였으며, 계속 추가 협의키로 함.

- 1조 관련, 스웨덴은 기구의 명칭 변경가능성(예 GAT) 을 검토할것을 제의

- 2조 관련, 인도는 비롯한 개도국들은 ANNEX 1A(상품협정)에 TRIPS 포함을 반대. 미국,일본은 상품분야와 서비스 분야의 별개 이사회설치에 반대

- 3조 관련, 개도국들은 통합분쟁해결에 반대

- 11조 관련, 미국은 각국이 MTO 에 가입시PPA(잠정 적용의정서)에서 규정한 조건을그대로 유지한다는 제안(별첨 3)을 함으로써 조부조항 원용 근거를 확보코저 하였음. 이에대해 EC, 호주, 뉴질랜드등이 강한 반대의사를 밝힘.

- 13조 관련, 미국은 별도 협정별 부적용 필요성을 제의하였고, 인도, 브라질등은

통상국 특허청	2차보	구주국	청와대	안기부	경기원	재무부	농수부	상공부

PAGE 1   91.12.17   00:26 FN

외신 1과 통제관

0299

SECTOR 별(예:상품분야, 서비스 분야) 부적용을 제의하였으며, 일부 국가는 동 조항 전체의 삭제를, 일부 국가는 이조항으로 인해 UR 협상결과가 제대로 이행될수 없다는 점을 지적, 신중처리 할 것을주장

  - 14 조 관련, 각국의 비준 지연에 따른 문제점 해결을 위한 경과 규정 필요성이 제기됨.

  - O 16조 관련, 미국은 상품분야 협정에 유보를할수 없다는데 반대.

  첨부: 1. COHERENCE 관련 미국제안 1부

  2. MTO 설립 2차 초안 1부

  3. MTO 회원국에 대한 미국제안 1부. 끝

  (GVW(F)-626)

  (대사 박수길-국장)

주 제 네 바 대 표 부

번 호 : GVW(F) - *626*   년월일 : *1216*   시간 : *1200*

수 신 : 장   관 (공기, 경기천, 재무부, 농림수산부, 상공부, 동력외)

발 신 : 주 제네바대사

제 목 : *GVW - 2664 회부*

총 *12* 매(표지포함)

보 안	
봉 제	

외신과	
봉 제	

0301

-XII-91

US

All contracting parties should be able to find a balance of
benefits in the multilateral system of the post-Uruguay Round
period. Where underlying problems giving rise to this
consideration have not found any effective and operational
answer in the negotiations, particularly as concerns the lack
of trade policy concessions and removal of structural barriers
by countries in surplus, individual contracting parties will
need to assess the balance of benefits.

0302

December 15, 1991

AGREEMENT ESTABLISHING THE MULTILATERAL TRADE ORGANIZATION

The MEMBERS,

Recognizing that their relations in the field of trade and economic endeavour should be conducted with a view to raising standards of living, ensuring full employment and a large and steadily growing volume of real income and effective demand, developing the full use of the resources of the world at sustainable levels, and expanding the production and trade in goods and services,

Being desirous of contributing to these objectives by entering into reciprocal and mutually advantageous arrangements directed to the substantial reduction of tariffs and other barriers to trade and to the elimination of discriminatory treatment in international trade relations,

Determined therefore, to preserve the basic principles and to further the objectives of the General Agreement on Tariffs and Trade and to develop an integrated, more viable and durable multilateral trading system encompassing the GATT as modified, all Agreements and Arrangements concluded under its auspices and the complete results of the Uruguay Round multilateral trade negotiations,

Agree as follows:

Article I

Establishment of the Organization

The Multilateral Trade Organization (herein after referred to as "the MTO") is hereby established.

Article II

Scope of the MTO

1.   The Multilateral Trade Organization (MTO) shall provide the common institutional framework for the conduct of trade relations between the members of the MTO in matters related to the General Agreement on Tariffs and Trade (as it results from the Final Act of the Uruguay Round on a definitive basis), the Tokyo Round Arrangements and Agreements, and the Uruguay Round Agreements, Decisions and Understandings.   The list of Agreements and legal instruments covered by this Agreement is set out in Annexes 1 and 2, (herein after referred to as the

626-12-3

0303

Multilateral Trade Agreements), and the instruments in Annexes 3 and 4. Agreements listed in Annexes 1, 3 and 4 shall have all members as parties. Agreements listed in Annex 2 may have limited membership.

2. The General Agreement on Tariffs and Trade, as it results from the Final Act of the Uruguay Round, referred to above is legally distinct from the Agreement known as the General Agreement on Tariffs and Trade dated 30 October 1947.

3. The MTO shall provide the framework for the implementation of the agreements annexed hereto, and any further agreements that may be negotiated and accepted under the auspices of this Agreement.

Article III (old V)

Functions of the MTO

1. The MTO shall have authority to take appropriate actions to ensure the effective implementation, facilitate the operation and further the objectives of this Agreement and the agreements annexed hereto, subject to limitations specified in these agreements.

2. The MTO shall provide the forum for further negotiations among its members concerning their multilateral trade relations as may be decided by the Ministerial Conference.

3. The MTO shall administer an Integrated Dispute Settlement System as set out in Annex 3. These rules and procedures shall apply to all Multilateral Trade Agreements set out in Annex 1. The procedures shall also apply to the Multilateral Trade Agreements listed in Annex 2 to the extent that the parties to a dispute are members of these agreements.

4. The MTO shall administer a Trade Policy Review Mechanism as set out in Annex 4.

5. The MTO shall cooperate, as appropriate, with the International Monetary Fund, the International Bank for Reconstruction and Development and affiliated agencies with a view to achieving greater coherence in global policy making.

Article IV (old X)

Relations with other Organizations

1. The General Council of the MTO shall make arrangements with intergovernmental bodies and agencies which have related responsibilities to provide for effective cooperation and the avoidance of unnecessary duplication of activities.

0304

2. The General Council of the MTO may make suitable arrangements for consultation and cooperation with non-governmental organizations concerned with matters within the scope of the MTO.

Article V (old VI)

Structure of the MTO

1. There shall be a Ministerial Conference which shall meet at least once every two years. The task of the Ministerial Conference shall be to review and supervise the operation of, and determine actions necessary to carry out the functions of, this Agreement and the agreements annexed hereto, to launch further mutilateral trade negotiations as appropriate, and to decide on the implementation of results that may have been negotiated among and adopted by members of the MTO.

2.1 There shall be a General Council open to representatives of all the members, which shall meet at least twice each year. The task of the General Council shall be to carry out the functions of the MTO, including the supervision of the operation of this Agreement and the agreements annexed hereto, in the time between Ministerial Conferences, and decide on all issues conferred on it by this Agreement and by the Ministers.

2.2 The General Council shall establish a Dispute Settlement Body, a Trade Policy Review Mechanism, and subsidiary bodies, such as a Goods Council, a Services Council, a Committee on Budget and Administration, a Committee on Trade and Development, and a Balance of Payments Committee. The General Council shall establish its own rules of procedure and shall approve the rules of procedure of its subsidiary bodies.

3.1 There shall be a Council for Goods and a Council for Services, open to representatives of all members, which shall meet at least eight times per year.

3.2 The Goods Council shall oversee the functioning of the Agreements on Trade in Goods as set out in Annex 1A, as well as any other functions assigned to it by the General Council, except that the functions of dispute settlement shall be exercised by the Dispute Settlement Body. The Goods Council shall, as required, establish Committees to oversee the operation of the Agreements set out in Annexes 1A, or other subsidiary bodies, and shall approve their rules of procedure.

3.3 The Services Council shall oversee the functioning of Agreements on Trade in Services as set out in Annex 1B, as well as any other functions assigned to it by the General Council, except that the functions of dispute settlement shall be exercised by the Dispute Settlement Body. The Services Council shall, as required, establish Committees to oversee

0305

6-26-12-5

the operation of the Agreements set out in Annexes 1B, or other subsidiary bodies, and shall approve their rules of procedure.

Article VI (old VII)

The Secretariat

1. The General Council shall appoint a Director-General as head of the Secretariat of the MTO. The powers, duties, conditions of service and terms of office of the Director-General shall conform to regulations approved by the General Council.

2. The Director-General shall appoint members of the staff, and shall fix their duties and conditions of service in accordance with regulations approved by the General Council.

3. The responsibilities of the Director-General and of the members of the staff shall be exclusively international in character. In the discharge of their duties, they shall not seek or receive instructions from any government or from any other authority external to the Organization. They shall refrain from any action which might reflect on their positions as international officials. The Members shall respect the international character of the responsibilities of these persons and shall not seek to influence them in the discharge of their duties.

4. At the time of entry into force of the MTO, and until such time as the General Council shall have acted pursuant to paragraph 1, as far as practicable, the GATT Director-General and the ICITO/GATT Secretariat shall become the Director-General and Secretariat of the MTO.

Article VII (old VIII)

Budget and Contributions

1. The Director-General shall present to the General Council the annual budget estimates and financial statement of the MTO. The General Council shall approve the accounts and the budget.

2. The General Council shall apportion the expenditures of the Organization among the Members, in accordance with a scale of contributions to be fixed by the General Council, and each Member shall individually contribute promptly to the Organization its share of these expenditures.

3. The General Council shall decide on measures to be taken with regard to Members in arrears of their contributions.

626-12-6

0306

4. The Budget Committee shall elaborate the provisions on the MTO
    budget and MTO contributions for adoption by the General
    Council. The provisions shall be based, as far as practicable,
    on the provisions and practices for the GATT budget.

Article VIII (old IX)

Status

1. The MTO shall have legal personality.

2. The MTO shall enjoy in the territory of each of the Members
    such legal capacity, privileges and immunities as may be
    necessary for the exercise of its functions.

3. The representatives of the Members and the officials of the
    MTO shall enjoy such privileges and immunities as are
    necessary for the independent exercise of their functions in
    connection with the MTO.

4. The privileges and immunities to be accorded by a Member to
    the MTO, to its officials and to the representatives of its
    Members shall be similar to those accorded by that member to
    specialized agencies of the United Nations, to their officials
    and to the representatives of their members, under the
    Convention on the Privileges and Immunities of the Specialized
    Agencies, or under similar arrangements.

5. The MTO may conclude a headquarters agreement, as appropriate.

Article IX (old XI)

Joint Action

1. At meetings of the General Council, each Member of the MTO
    shall be entitled to one vote, and, except as otherwise
    provided for in this Agreement, decisions of the General
    Council shall be taken by a majority of votes cast.

2. In exceptional circumstances not elsewhere provided for in
    this Agreement and the Multilateral Trade Agreements under
    Annex 1, the General Council may waive an obligation imposed
    on a member by this Agreement or a Multilateral Trade
    Agreement under Annex 1; Provided that any such decision shall
    be approved by a two-thirds majority of votes cast and that
    such majority shall comprise more than half the MTO members.

626-12-7

0307

Article X (old XII)

Amendments and Modifications

1. Negotiations for amendments to this Agreement, or to any of Multilateral Trade Agreements in Annex 1, shall be concluded by the Ministerial Conference on the basis of consensus.

2. Any member accepting an amendment to this Agreement or any of the Multilateral Trade Agreements in Annex 1 shall deposit an instrument of acceptance with the Director-General of the MTO within such period as the Ministerial Conference may specify. Such amendments shall become effective upon acceptance by two-thirds of the members.

3. The Ministerial Conference may decide that any amendment made effective under this Article is of such a nature that any member which has not accepted it within a period specified by the Ministerial Conference shall be free to withdraw from this Agreement, or to remain a member with the consent of the Minsterial Conference.

4. Amendments to the agreements in Annex 2 shall be made in accordance with the amending procedures in those agreements.

5. Modifications to the instruments set out in Annexes 3 and 4 shall be taken by consensus in the General Council.

Article XI (old III)

Original Membership

Membership in the MTO shall consist of all GATT contracting parties and the European Communities which accept this Agreement and all Multilateral Trade Agreements in Annex 1, and the instruments in Annexes 3 and 4.

Article XII (old IV)

Accession

1. Any state or separate customs territory possessing full autonomy in the conduct of its external commercial relations and of other matters provided for in this Agreement, which accepts this Agreement and all Multilateral Trade Agreements in Annex 1, and the instruments in Annexes 3 and 4 may accede on terms to be agreed between it and the General Council.

2. Decisions on accession of new Members shall be taken by the General Council and shall be approved by a two-thirds majority of votes cast and that such majority shall comprise more than half the MTO members.

626 - 12 - 8

0308

Article XIII (old XV)

Non-application of the Agreement between particular Members

1. This Agreement and all Multilateral Trade Agreements listed in Annex 1 shall not apply as between any member and any other member if either of the members, at the time either becomes a member, does not consent to such application.

2. The General Council may review the operation of this Article in particular cases at the request of any member and make appropriate recommendations.

Article XIV

Entry into Force and Deposit

1. This Agreement shall be open for acceptance, by signature or otherwise, as from [1 November 1992] [a date set by the implementing conference] to Uruguay Round participants that qualify under Article XI. This Agreement shall enter into force on [1 January 1993], the same date as the other Uruguay Round results become effective.

2. This Agreement shall remain open for acceptance by Uruguay Round participants that qualify under Article XI until [1 January, 1995] [a date determined by the General Council of the MTO]. For these participants, it shall enter into force on the thirtieth day following the deposit of the instrument of ratification or acceptance.

3. After [1 January, 1995], any other Uruguay Round participant may apply for membership under the accession provisions set out in Article XII.

4. Prior to entry into force of this Agreement, the text of this Agreement shall be deposited with the Director-General to the CONTRACTING PARTIES of the General Agreement on Tariffs and Trade, in his capacity as depositary of the Uruguay Round results. He shall promptly furnish a certified true copy thereof and a notification of each acceptance thereof to each signatory of the Agreement on the MTO. The Agreement shall, upon its entry in to force, be deposited with the Director-General of the MTO, as well as any amendments thereto.

5. This Agreement shall be registered in accordance with the provisions of Article 102 of the Charter of the United Nations.

0309

Article XV (old XIII)

Withdrawal

1. Any Member of the MTO may withdraw from this Agreement. Any member, upon withdrawal from this Agreement, shall cease to be a party to the Multilateral Trade Agreements in Annex 1 and the instruments in Annexes 3 and 4. Such withdrawal shall take effect upon the expiration of six months from the date on which written notice of withdrawal is received by the Director-General.

2. Withdrawal from the agreements in Annex 2 shall be governed by the provisions of those agreements.

Article XVI

Final Provisions

1. The MTO shall respect the rules, decisions and customary practice of the General Agreement on Tariffs and Trade and the Tokyo Round Agreements in carrying out its functions and tasks.

2. No reservations may be entered in respect of any provision in the Multilateral Trade Agreements in Annex 1. Reservations entered in respect of the Agreements in Annex 2 can only be made in accordance with the relevant provisions of those Agreements.

3. In the event of a conflict between the provisions of this Agreement and the provisions of any of the Multilateral Trade Agreements Annex 1, the provisions of this Agreement shall prevail.

Done at --- this -- day of --- one thousand nine hundred and ninety---, in a single copy, in the English, French and Spanish languages, each text being authentic.

0310

Annex 1

Annex 1 A covers:

- the General Agreement on Tariffs and Trade, as it results from the Final Act of the Uruguay Round, and its associated legal instruments, except the PPA;

- the Tokyo Round Codes as they result from the Final Act of the Uruguay Round and their associated legal instruments, except those Codes and Arrangements found in Annex 2; and

- the TRIPs Agreement.

Annex 1B covers:

- the General Agreement on Trade in Services.

Annex 2

Annex 2 covers:

- the Civil Aircraft Agreement;

- the Government Procurement Code;

- the Dairy Arrangement; and

- the Bovine Meat Arrangement.

Annex 3

Annex 3 covers:

- the Integrated Dispute Settlement Understanding.

Annex 4

Annex 4 covers:

- the Trade Policy Review Mechanism.

0311

첨부3.

Re-draft of Article XI

Relates to Annex...

Membership in the MTO shall be open to all GATT contracting parties and the European Communities. By accepting this MTO Agreement, members accept all Multilateral Trade Agreements in Annex 1, including acceptance on a definitive basis of the General Agreement on Tariffs and Trade, subject to the conditions set out in the PPA and the Protocols of Accession, as well as the instruments in Annexes 3 and 4.

0312

626-12-12

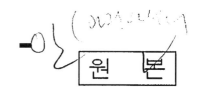

외 무 부

종 별 :

번 호 : GVW-2682
일 시 : 91 1216 2130

수 신 : 장 관(통기,경기원,재무부,농수산부)

발 신 : 주 제네바대사

제 목 : UR/제도분야 비공식협의(분쟁해결)

12.16. 오전 표제협의(LINDEN 국장 주재)에서는 통합분쟁해결 절차(IDS)관련 카나다가 12.12 제출한 PAPER(GVW-2633)을 토의한바, 동 결과 아래 보고함.

(이성주 참사관 참석)

1. 전반적 의견

- 아국, 브라질,홍콩, 이집트등은 분쟁해결 절차의 FRAGMENTATION 현상 및 FORUMSHOPPING 방지를 위해 절차적 측면에서 촛점을 맞추어 IDS를 마련하는 데에는 이견이 없으나, IDS가 교차보복의 도입을 위한 목적이라면 반대한다는 의견을 개진

- 인도는 사법화된 분쟁해결 절차를 TRIPS 및 서비스분야에 적용할 수 없다는 기본입장을 천명하였으나, 토의 자체를 거부하지는 않았음

- 아국과 인도는 ANNEX 2로 첨부될 SPECIAL ANDADDITIONAL PROCEDURES(SAP) 의내용이 중요함을 언급하고, 인도는 동 내용을 알기전에 자국입장을 결정할 수 없다는 입장을 , 아국은 12.20이전에는 각 그룹이 협상 결과를 알수 없다는 현실적 문제점을 지적

- 카나다는 상기 문제점이 있음을 인정하면서도 SAP 내용 결정을 기술적 사항이될수있다는 의견과 함께 12.20 의장 문안에 IDS 관련사항이 반영되기를 바란다고 언급

- 호주, 뉴질랜드는 가급적 SAP 의 범위는 최소한으로 축소되어야 한다는 의견을, 미국은 위생검역등을 예시하면서 필요한 특수성은 충분히 반영되어야 할것이라는의견을 제시

2. 조항별 검토

가. 일반규정(1-3 페이지)

- 미국은 2항 관련 DISPUTE SETTLEMENT BODY(SB)가 유일한 옵션이 아니며 동 역할

통상국   2차보   경기원   재무부   농수부

PAGE 1
91.12.17   09:31 WH

외신 1과 통제관
0313

을 이사회가수행(COUNCIL IN DISPUTE SETTLEMENT MODE) 할수도 있음을 언급

- 인도가 교차보복 반대입장에서 2항 말미의 'ANY OFTHE COVERED AGREEMENTS'의문제점을 제기하고, 이집트, 아국, 브라질도 교차 보복 반대입장 재피력 ✓

- 미국은 ANNEX 1의 내용이 시급히 확정되어야 한다고 하고 스위스가 SINGLE ANNEX 선호 입장을 밝힌 반면, 인도, 브라질, 베네주엘라는 TRIPS관련 반대의견 개진

- 아국은 협정간 절차가 상이할 경우 사무총장이 적용절차를 결정할 수 있도록 한 문안(5항)관련 , DSB 가 창설된다면 동 DSB의장이 결정하는 것이 타당할 것이라는의견피력

나. 패널의 설치

- 카나다가 DSB 는 AD HOC BASIS 에서 필요시 수시 개최될것임을 재확인

다. 패널의 구성

- 3항 패널 리스트 선정이 DSB 의장으로 바뀐것과 관련 VENEZUELLA 가 해명을 요구한데 대해 미국, 카나다는 사무총장 보다는 DSB의장이 적임자 선정에 보다 정통할수 있기때문이라고 설명

라. FORUM SHOPPING

- 아국이 TOR 내용과 중복되는 2항의 필요성에 의문을 제시하고, 일본, 인도가 동조하였으나 EC는 중복되어도 특별히 문제될것이 없다하면서 특별한 이유제시 없이 삭제에 반대입장 표명.

- 인도는 TOR 상의 'ALL OF THE COVEREDAGREEMENTS'관련 피소국의 입장에서는 가급적 다수의 협정을 CITE 하는 경향이 예상되며 이경우 다수분야 전문성 확보 차원에서 패널리스트 구성도 어려워 질 뿐아니라 패널에도 과중한 부담이될 것이라는 이유로 이의를 제기한데 대해 미국, EC는 반대의견(패널의 단순화 가능) 개진

- 아국은 TOR 문안이 CONTRACTING PARTIES 에서DSB 를 바뀐것과 관련 충분한 검토가 필요하다는 의견 개진

마. 실질 규정의 상충(7페이지)

- 놀웨이가 실질 규정의 상충문제야말로 절차상의 상충문제보다 훨씬 중요한 사항 이라고 언급하고 동 사항이야말로 ANNEX 로 포함시켜야 되지 않겠느냐는 의견을 제시

- 미국은 많지는 않을 것으로 보나 사무국이 다수 협정 상호간에 실질규정의 상충여부에 대한 조사를 해줄수 있는지 문의하고, 상충시 패널이 해당사항에 대한 결정을 내리지 않고 이사회(CP)에 회부한다는 현문안(1항 말미)이 적절한

PAGE 2

0314

접근방식인지 의문이라는 의견 개진

   - 인도와 브라질은 인도가 TOR 언급시 지적한 문제점(상기 '라'항)을 다시 언급.끝

   (대사 박수길-국장)

외 무 부

종 별 :

번 호 : GVW-2683 　　　　　　　　　　 일 시 : 91 1216 2250

수 신 : 장 관(통기, 경기원, 재무부, 농림수산부, 상공부, 특허청)

발 신 : 주 제네바대사

제 목 : UR/제도분야(최종의정서, MTO)

　　연: GVW-2664

　　12.16(월) 오전, 오후 LINDEN 보좌관 주재 최종의정서 및 MTO 에 관한 비공식협의 결과 아래 보고함. (오참사관 참석)

　　1. 최종의정서

　　- 금일회의에서는 UR 협상 결과의 국제적 이행을 위한 제도적 장치를 마련키 위해 MTO를 설립키로 하고, 푼타선언에 따라 각료겹 특별총회에서 UR 협상 결과 이행문제를 결정키로 하며(시기 괄호), 각국의 비준상황을 보아 92.12말 이전 협정의 발효시기를 결정키 위한 각료회의를 개최키로 하는 문안에 대체적인 합의를 봄

　　2. MTO

　　- EC, 카나다가 12.15(일) 합의한 내용을 기초로 한 3차초안을 제시하고, 이를 기초로 협의를 계속할 것을 제안하였으나, 각국이 12.15 문제 제기한 내용들이 3차 초안에 제대로 반영되지 않을 점이 지적되면서(괄호 형태로도 반영되지 않음) 대다수국가가 이러한 형태의 MTO 협의는 더이상 계속할 수 없다는 강경한 입장을 개진함.

　　- 이에 따라 회의 대세가 12.20 TNC 회의에 의장이 금번 3차 초안을 제시할 경우(의장이주석을 통해 후속 협상이 필요하다는 점을 지적하더라도) 이는 결코 GROUP TEXT 가 될수 없다는데 대체적인 합의가 이루어졌으며, 사무국이 일단 2차 초안에 대한 각 조항별 수정안, 또는 각국의 의견개진 사항을 정리하여 12.20 TNC회의에서 제출할 초안 성격 여부를 1.17(화)회의에서 결정키로 함. 끝

　　(대사 박수길-국장)

통상국　　2차보　　경기원　　재무부　　농수부　　상공부　　특허청

PAGE 1 　　　　　　　　　　　　　　　　　　　　　 91.12.17　　09:41　WH

　　　　　　　　　　　　　　　　　　　　　　　　　 외신 1과　통제관

　　　　　　　　　　　　　　　　　　　　　　　　　　　　0316

발 신 전 보

분류번호	보존기간

번   호 : WJA-5662   911217 1425 DU   종별 : _____

WEC -0822

수   신 : 주   일본, EC   대사. 총영사///

발   신 : 장 관 (통 기)

제   목 : UR 협상

UR 협상 타결시 ~~동 협상 결과의 국내적 이행과 관련 참고코자 하니~~, 귀주재국이

UR 협상 결과를 이행하는데 필요한 국내법 절차의 내용 및 소요기간등 관련사항을 파악

보고바람.   끝.   (통상국장   김 용 규)

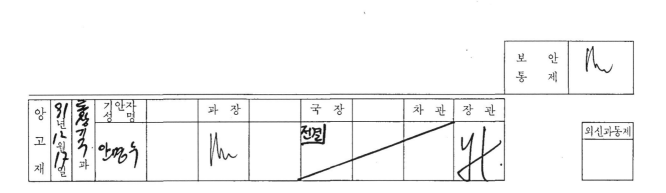

0317

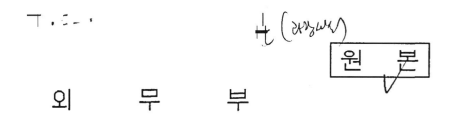

외 무 부

종 별 :

번 호 : GVW-2690 　　　　　　　　　일 시 : 91 1217 1920

수 신 : 장관(통기, 경기원, 재무부, 농수산부, 상공부, 특허청)

발 신 : 주 제네바 대사

제 목 : UR/제도 분야

　　12.17(화) 오전, 최종의정서 및 COHERENCE 문제에관한 비공식협의 결과 아래 보고함(오참사관참석)

　　1. 최종의정서(LINDEN 보좌관 주재)

　　- 12.17 자 별첨 사무국 NON-PAPER(별첨 1) 를 중심으로 협의

　　가. 1항 UR 협상결과 및 MTO 협정안을 4개의 별개의 ANNEX 로 하는 방안(인도, 브라질등개도국)과 하나의 ANNEX 로 하고 주석을 붙이는 방안(선진국)에 대해 합의를이루지 못함.

　　나. 3항의 '협정의 바람직한 발효시기와 관련, 일본은 93.7월, 스위스는 94.1월을제의하였음, 또한 미국은 각료회의 개최시기에 대해 협상종료후 가능한한 빠른 시점으 로 할것(주석에언급)을 제의하였음.

　　다. 최빈개도국에 대한 문제는 문안에 합의치못하고 추후 재협의키로 함.

　　라. 6항 협상결과의 SINGLE UNDERTAKING 문제와관련 인도, 브라질은 AS A WHOLE의 괄호를없애는 대신 DESIRABILITY 를 추가할 것을 주장, 합의를 이루지 못하였는바, 미국은 인도, 브라질이계속 반대할 경우에는 괄호를 그대로 놓아두는것이 방안이라고 함.

　　2. 통화, 금융, 무역정책간의일관성(COHERENCE)(LACARTE 대사 주재)

　　- 브랏셀회의 제출문서(35/REV 1) 의 10항을별첨 절충안과 같이 합의하하가고, 12항의 괄호를제거함으로써 COHERENCE 문제에 관해서는 합의TEXT 를 마련함.

　　첨부: 1. FINAL ACT 에 관한 12.17자 사무국NON--PAPER 1부

　　　　　2. COHERENCE 관련 합의문 1부(GVW(F)-0638).끝

　　(대사 박수길-국장)

통상국 상공부	2차보 특허청	외정실	분석관	청와대	안기부	경기원	재무부	농수부

PAGE 1 　　　　　　　　　　　　　　　　　　　　91.12.18　　08:56 BX

　　　　　　　　　　　　　　　　　　　　　　　외신 1과 통제관

　　　　　　　　　　　　　　　　　　　　　　　　　　0318

<u>Secretariat Non-Paper</u>
15 December 1991

DRAFT FINAL ACT EMBODYING THE RESULTS OF THE
URUGUAY ROUND OF MULTILATERAL TRADE NEGOTIATIONS

1.   Having met .... from ... to ... . 19.. at
.... in order to conclude the Uruguay Round of Multilateral Trade
Negotiations, the representatives of the Governments and of the European
Communities, members of the Trade Negotiations Committee (hereinafter
referred to as "participants"), agree that the Agreements, Decisions and
Understandings on trade in goods, as set out in Annex I, and the General
Agreement on Trade in Services, as set out in Annex II, [the Agreement on
Trade-Related Aspects of Intellectual Property Rights, including Trade in
Counterfeit Goods, as set out in Annex III[1]], and the Agreement
Establishing the Multilateral Trade Organization, as set out in Annex IV,
embody the results of their negotiations and form an integral part of this
Final Act. They acknowledge that these texts may be subject to
rectifications of a formal character that do not affect the substance or
meaning of the texts.

2.   By adopting the present Final Act, participants agree to submit, as
appropriate, the legal texts and instruments included in the Annexes for
the consideration of their respective competent authorities with a view to
seeking approval of these legal texts and instruments in accordance with
appropriate procedures of the participant concerned.

3.   Participants agree on the desirability of acceptance of the Uruguay
Round Agreements by all participants with a view to their entry into force
as early as possible and not later than [1 January 1993]. As foreseen in
the final paragraph of the Punta del Este Declaration, Ministers meeting
on the occasion of a Special Session of the CONTRACTING PARTIES, to be held
prior to the end of [1992], will decide on the implementation of the
Agreements, Decisions and Understandings attached hereto, and will
determine a date for the entry into force of such instruments.

4.   Participants agree on the desirability of the application by the
contracting parties, as from the date of entry into force of the Uruguay
Round results, of the General Agreement on Tariffs and Trade on a
definitive rather than on a provisional basis.

---

[1]Ministers agreed at the Mid-Term Review that the negotiations on
Trade-Related Aspects of Intellectual Property Rights are without prejudice
to the views of participants concerning the institutional aspects of the
international implementation of the results of the negotiations in this
area which is to be decided pursuant to the final paragraph of the Punta
del Este Declaration, i.e. by Ministers meeting at a Special Session of the
CONTRACTING PARTIES.

3-1.
638-4-2

0319

- 2 -

5.   Participants further agree, in order to provide the administrative infrastructure for the international implementation of the Uruguay Round results, to establish a new organizational structure [a new Multilateral Trade Organization] which shall service the General Agreement on Tariffs and Trade and the Uruguay Round Agreements, and shall provide the forum for negotiations of agreements in related areas.   Pursuant to the final paragraph of the Punta del Este Declaration, Ministers will meet in a Special Session of the CONTRACTING PARTIES to decide on the international implementation of the results not later than ......   Subsequently, and taking into account the status of national ratification efforts, they shall meet to decide the timing of the Agreements' entry into force.

6.   Without prejudice to the measures on special and more favourable treatment in favour of developing participants which appear in the Annexes, the participants agree that least-developed participants [shall] [should] be granted a grace period of [x] years as from the date of entry into force of the relevant legal instruments, during which they will not be required to apply$_2$ the new commitments negotiated in the course of the Uruguay Round.$_3$,

7.   Participants agree that [all] the Uruguay Round Agreements, enumerated in Annexes [I, II and IV] [I to IV] shall be open for acceptance [as a whole] [without exception], by signature or otherwise, by all participants in the Uruguay Round of Multilateral Trade Negotiations.^{4} This is without prejudice to the requirement that such participants who are not contracting parties to the GATT must negotiate their terms of accession to the [GATT].

8.   This Final Act and the texts set out in the Annexes shall be deposited with the Director-General to the CONTRACTING PARTIES to the General Agreement on Tariffs and Trade who shall promptly furnish to each participant in the Uruguay Round of Multilateral Trade Negotiations a certified copy thereof.

---

*This provision may be deleted to the extent substantive issues are addressed in the final text on the MTO.

^{2}The final form and place of the provisions contained in this paragraph are to be considered in connection with the decision on the implementation of the results of the Uruguay Round, as set out in paragraph 3 above.

^{3}The provisions of Part I of the Punta del Este Declaration are relevant.

^{4}The question of the acceptance by participants in the Uruguay Round who have not accepted Tokyo Round Agreements and Arrangements, of texts resulting from the renegotiation of such Agreements or Arrangements remains to be considered.

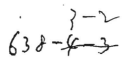

0320

- 3 -

DONE at ...., this .... day of .... one thousand nine hundred and ninety-........ in a single copy, in the English, French and Spanish languages, each text being authentic.

3-3

0321

외 무 부

종 별 :

번 호 : GVW-2701   일 시 : 91 1218 1230

수 신 : 장 관(봉기, 경기원, 상공부, 재무부, 농림수산부)

발 신 : 주 제네바대사

제 목 : UR/제도분야 비공식 협의(분쟁해결)

1. 12.17(화) 표제협의 분쟁해결 관련 논의사항을 아래 보고함,

    가. 일방조치

    - 일본이 별첨(1) 문안을 제시하고, 인도, 브라질, 이집트, 아국, 홍콩, 태국, 파키스탄 등이 일본안의 기본 내용에 지지 입장 표명

    - 미국은 동 문안 역시 EC 문안과 같이 정치성이 강하고 분쟁해결 절차에 관한 TEXT 에 포함될 사항이 아니며(미국으로서는 분쟁해결 TEXT안에서는 자국제안 이상의 내용은 들어갈수 없다는 입장) 행정부로서는 의회의 입법권을 제약하는 내용의 공약을 할수 없으며, 특정국가의 특정법률을 집중적인 공격 목표로 하는 토의 방식은 비생산적이라고 확고한 반대입장 표명

    - 카나다는 미.카 FTA 분쟁해결 절차를 예로들면서 일본문안 1항(GATT 분쟁해결절차에만 의존) 이 지나치게 광범위하다는 의견을 제시

    나. 교차보복

    - 의장 미, EC, 카나다등의 협의 제출한 별첨(2)문안을 중심으로 토의

    - 인도가 선두에 나서 'SECTOR'의 명확한 정의 필요성, 교차보복 승인절차에는 전통적 컨센서스방식을 적용하는등 안전장치 설정의 필요성을 주장

    - 아국, 홍콩, 파키스탄, 이집트, 브라질, 말레이시아, 베네주엘라등이 보복승인절차관련 상기 인도주장에 동조

    - 호주, 놀웨이, 스위스등은 교차보복 승인 타당성심사를 ARBITRATION 에 맡길것을 제의(아국은 작업단도 고려 가능함을 언급)하였으나 미국, 인도가 각각 상반된 입장에서 수락 불가입장표명(미국은 주관성 개입 가능성, 입증 책임의전가 가능성을 언급),- 카나다가 전체 TIME-LIMIT안에서 현 TEXT 23.4항에 규정된 중재 절차에 회부하고 입증책임을 피보복 대상국에 지도록하는 방안에 대한 검토 필요성을

통상국   2차보   경기원   재무부   농수부   상공부

91.12.19   08:04 WH

                                        외신 1과 통제관

                                        0322

제의하고, 홍콩이 이에 대해 구체 문안 제시를 요구

　- 뉴질랜드, 호주는 규정단순화를 이유로 협정간 교차보복에 대해서만 특별 규정을 두고 협정내보복에 대해서는 언급치 말것을 주장(농산물을 염두에 둔 것으로 분석됨)한바, EC가 반대하고 LINDEN 국장도 써비스 협상 그룹내서 SECTOR 간보복 문제가 논의되고 있음을 상기 시킴

　다. 기타

　- 사무국이 12.17자로 UPDATE된 봉합문안을 배포

　- 동 봉합문안 1.8항 후단 괄호처리 부분을 완전 삭제키로 합의

　- 상소기구 위원임명(15.2항) 관련 별첨(3)수정문안에 합의

　- 미국이 17.3항 관련 12.13.자국제안을 별첨(4)와 같이 수정제의하였으나, EC 제외한 다수국 반대로 합의 실패

　2. LACARTE 의장은 명 12.18.18:00 에 협상을 마감하여 12.20 TNC 문안은 UNBRACKETED TEXT 가 될것이라고 회의 벽두 언급함.

　첨부: 1. 일방조치 관련 일본 문안

　2. 교차보복 관련 수정 문안

　3. 15.2항 수정 합의 문안

　4. 17.3항 관련 미국의 수정문안.

(GVW(F)-645)

(대사 박수길-국장)

PAGE 2

0323

주 제 네 바 대 표 부

번 호 : GVW(F) - *645*   년월일 : *112·18*   시간 : *1800*

수 신 : 장   관 (*통기, 경기원, 상공부, 재무부, 농건수산부*)

발 신 : 주 제네바대사

제 목 : *GVW-2701 회부*

총 *6* 매 (표지포함)

보 안 봉 재	

외신과 등 재	

645-6-1

0324

(별첨 1.)
(7-12-'91)

Dispute Settlement (Unilateralism)

JAPAN

Reaffirming that each contracting party shall maintain its concessions and abide by its obligations under the GATT, as provided for in the GATT.

1. The contracting parties, in respect of the settlement of disputes involving rights and obligations under the GATT, in relation to other contracting parties, shall not have recourse, to any procedure other than the procedures envisaged in this Understanding.

3 2. For the purposes of para 1 above, the contracting parties shall ensure that their trade legislations are consistent with and implemented in accordance with the provisions of the GATT and this Understanding.

2 2. The contracting parties:

- shall not make any unilateral determination to the effect that their rights under the GATT have been violated, benefits accruing to them under the GATT have been nullified or impaired or the attainment of any objective of the GATT is being impeded unless the Council has adopted a panel or appellate report to this effect;

0325

- shall not make any unilateral determination of the reasonable period of time or of the level of the suspension of concessions or other obligations under the GATT during the dispute settlement procedure;

- shall not unilaterally impose any suspension of concessions or other obligations under the GATT pursuant to Article 23:2 unless the Council has given its authorization for such suspension in accordance with this Understanding.

0326

(북첨2)
17-12-91.

17.12.91

Insert at end of 20.2 of Integrated Text

1.   In considering what concessions or other obligations to suspend, the complaining party shall apply the following principles and procedures:

(a) the general principle is that the complaining party should first seek to suspend concessions or other obligations in the same sector (s) as that in which the Panel or Appellate Body has found a violation or other nullification or impairment.

(b) if that party considers that it is not practicable or effective to suspend concessions or other obligations in the same sector, it may seek to suspend concessions or other obligations in other sectors under the same agreement.

(c) if that party considers that it is not practicable or effective to suspend concessions or other obligations in other sectors under the same agreement, and that the circumstances are serious enough, it may seek to suspend concessions or other obligations under another agreement.

(d) in applying the above principles, that party shall take into account:

    (i) the quantity of the trade available in the sector or under the agreement under which the Panel or Appellate Body has found a violation or other nullification or impairment, and the importance of such trade to that party;

    (ii) the broader economic elements related to the nullification or impairment and the broader economic consequences of the suspension of concessions or other obligations for which authorization is sought.

(e) if that party decides to request authorization to suspend concessions or other obligations pursuant to (b) or (c) above, it shall state the reasons therefor in its request. At the same time as the request is forwarded to the Dispute Settlement Board, it also shall be forwarded to the relevant Councils or in the case of a request pursuant to (b), the relevant sectoral bodies.

2.   The Dispute Settlement Board shall consider the reasons given by the complaining party in its request pursuant to (b) or (c) above, and in authorizing the suspension of concessions or other obligations pursuant to paragraph [20.3], may express any views on the matter.

0327

(별첨3)
17-12-91

Revise 15.2 to read as follows:

15.2 Members of the Appellate Body shall be appointed by the
CONTRACTING PARTIES to serve for a four year term, and may be
reappointed. However, the terms of three of the seven members
appointed immediately after the entry into force of this
Understanding shall expire at the end of two years. Vacancies
shall be filled as they arise. A member appointed to replace a
member whose term of office has not expired shall hold office for
the remainder of his or her predecessor's term.

0328

17-12-1911
ㅇ국첨4

Insert a new paragraph 17.3

While a panel or the Appellate Body may interpret or apply the relevant provisions examined, it shall not give rulings and recommendations on matters of substance or procedure on which there are no express rules.

explicit —
agreed —
specific —

NORWAY
CANADA — ...
Singapore .
Arg.
Australia
Korea
Thailand.
N.Z.

Community. — replace

US — not withdrawing

6 cos. — 6 — 6   *0329*

외 무 부

종 별 :

번 호 : GVW-2741 　　　　　　　　　　 일 시 : 91 1219 1830

수 신 : 장 관(봉기,아이,정총,경기원,재무부,농림수산부,상공부,특허청)

발 신 : 주 제네바 대사

제 목 : UR/제도분야(MTO)

　　연: GVW-2690

　　표제 비공식 회의가 12.18(수) LACARTE 의장주재로 개최되어 MTO 협정안과 관련 12.17 자배포된 문서(별첨 팩스 송부)에 대한 논의를 종결하였는바, 주요 내용 아래보고함.(신서기관참석)

　　O MTO 의 범위(제 2조) 관련, MTO 협약안 ANNEX 2에 규정된 협약(동경라운드 일부 협약)을 일정 기간까지 가입키로 하는 1조 BIS두번째 문장에 대해 홍콩, 호주, 말련 등이 반대함.

　　O MTO 의 기능(제 3조 5항)중 타 국제기구와의 협력문제와 관련 EC 는 무역, 금융 정책간 일관성 제고를 위해 IMF, IBRD 를 명시적으로 규정하자고 하였으며, 페루,브라질, 파키스탄은 '유엔기관 및 전문기구'로 포괄적으로 명시하자고 제안함.

　　O 비정부간 기구와의 협력(제 4조 2항)과 관련,말련, 인니, 파키스탄의 요청에 따라 일반 이사회의 사전 승인 요건을 명시하기로 함.

　　O MTO 일반 이사회의 산하기관(제 5조 3항)조항과 관련, 미국은 상품, 서비스 외TRIPS 이사회 별개 설립을 반대하고 동 조항에서 산하기관을 명시하지 않고 추후 각료 이사회에서 결정하도록 하자고 제안함.(스위스 동조) 이에 대해 브라질, 인도등개도국은 동건 토의를 각료회의로 연기하는 것이 해결책이 될수 없다고 반박하면서 3개 이사회 구성을 지지하였으며, EC 도 3개 이사회구성을 지지할 용의가 있다고 언급함.

　　O MTO 창설 회원(제 11조)과 관련, 갓트 가입시PPA (잠정 적용의정서)에 규정한조건을 유지한다는 12.15 자 미국 제안에 대해 규범제정그룹에서의 동건 협상 결과에 따른다는 내용의 별첨 각주를 첨부하기로 합의함.

　　O 신규가입 요건(제 12조)과 관련, 중국은 조약법에 관한 비엔나 협약에

통상국	2차보	아주국	구주국	외정실	청와대	안기부	경기원	재무부
농수부	상공부	과기처						

91.12.20　　06:12 FN

외신 1과 통제관

0330

의하면국가만이 국제협약의 주체가 될수 있다고 규정되어 있으며,또한 유엔 직속 및 전문기구 에는 국가만이 가입할수 있도록 되어 있다고 하면서, 관세영역은 독자적으로 MTO에 가입할수 없다록 규정한 별첨 수정안을 제출함. (파키스탄 지지)

이에 대해 미국은 MTO 의 가입 주체에 관세영역을 포함한 것은 정치적인 주권개념과관계가 없으며 상업적 편리성을 도모하기 위한것이며, MTO 는 UN 전문기구의 하나로 상정하고있지 않다고 하면서 현행 규정 유지를 주장함.(EC, 스위스 지지)

0 특정 회원국 사이의 협약 부적용(제 13조)과 관련 미국은 부적용 요건을 제한한 1항 BIS삭제를 요청였으며, EC, 스위스는 SINGLEUNDERTAKING 원칙에 위배하며, 강대국의 무기가 될수 있다는 점을 지적하면서 반대함.(인도,브라질 동조)

0 MTO 협약 발효(제 14조)와 관련, UR 협상결과 이행을 위한 각료회의에서 MTO 협약에대한 각국의 가입 개시 시점과 협약 발효 시점을 결정토록 하고 UR 협상 참가국의 MTO 협약에대한 수락 허용 기간은 각료회의에서 달리 정하지 않는한 95. 1 까지로 하기로함.

0 일방 조치 억제문제에 관한 내용을 제 16조(최종 조항)의 일부로 포함키로 함.(별전 보고)

첨부: 1. 12.17 자 MTO 협약안

2. MTO 협약안 2조, 11조, 16조 각주3. MTO 협약안 12조 간련 중국 수정안. 끝

(GVW(F)-661)

(대사 박수길-국장)

〈별첨 I 〉

17 December 1991

AGREEMENT ESTABLISHING THE MULTILATERAL TRADE ORGANIZATION

The MEMBERS,

Recognizing that their relations in the field of trade and economic endeavour should be conducted with a view to raising standards of living, ensuring full employment and a large and steadily growing volume of real income and effective demand, developing the [full] [optional] use of the resources of the world at sustainable levels, and expanding the production and trade [in goods and services],

[Recognizing further that the attainment of these objectives is particularly urgent for developing countries,]

Being desirous of contributing to these objectives by entering into reciprocal and mutually advantageous arrangements directed to the substantial reduction of tariffs and other barriers to trade and to the elimination of discriminatory treatment in international trade relations,

Determined therefore, to preserve the basic principles and to further the objectives of the General Agreement on Tariffs and Trade and to develop an integrated, more viable and durable multilateral trading system encompassing the GATT as modified [with all rights and obligations of its contracting parties], all Agreements and Arrangements concluded under its auspices and the complete results of the Uruguay Round multilateral trade negotiations,

Agree as follows:

Article I

Establishment of the Organization

The Multilateral Trade Organization (hereinafter referred to as "the MTO")¹[the General Agreement on Trade Organization (hereinafter referred to as "the GAT"¹)] is hereby established.

---

¹The appropriate initials will have to be inserted in all places in this text where "MTO" appears.

661 - 12 - 1

0332

- 2 -

Article II

Scope [and Functions] of the MTO

1.   The Multilateral Trade Organization (MTO) shall provide a common institutional framework for the conduct of trade relations between the members of the MTO in matters related to the General Agreement on Tariffs and Trade (as it results from the Final Act of the Uruguay Round on a definitive basis), the Tokyo Round Agreements and Arrangements, and the Uruguay Round Agreements, Decisions and Understandings. The list of Agreements and legal instruments covered by this Agreement is set out in [the] Annexes [.] 1 and 2, (hereinafter referred to as the Multilateral Trade Agreements), and the instruments in Annexes 3 and 4. Agreements listed in Annexes 1, 3 and 4 shall have all members as parties. [Agreements listed in Annex 2 may have limited membership.]

[1bis Agreements and legal instruments (hereinafter referred to as the Plurilateral Trade Agreement) listed in Annex 2 may have for the present limited membership. MTO members which are not presently signatories to these Agreements and legal instruments will adhere to them until the date of [x].]

2.   The General Agreement on Tariffs and Trade [with all rights and obligations of its contracting parties, as annexed], as it results from the Final Act of the Uruguay Round referred to above, is legally distinct from the Agreement known as the General Agreement on Tariffs and Trade dated 30 October 1947.

[3.   The MTO shall provide the framework for the implementation of the agreements annexed hereto, and any further agreements that may be negotiated and accepted under the auspices of this Agreement.]

[Article III

Functions of the MTO]

[1.   The MTO shall [have authority to] take appropriate action to ensure the effective implementation, facilitate [the administration and] the operation, and further the objectives of this Agreement and the agreements annexed hereto, subject to limitations specified in these agreements.]

[1.   The MTO shall provide the framework for the implementation of the Agreements annexed hereto, and any further Agreements that may be negotiated and accepted under the auspices of this Agreement.]

2.   The MTO shall provide the forum for further negotiations among its members concerning their multilateral trade relations as may be decided by the Ministerial Conference.

[3.   The MTO shall administer an Integrated Dispute Settlement System as set out in Annex 3. These rules and procedures shall apply to all Multilateral Trade Agreements set out in Annex 1. The procedures shall

0333

also apply to the Multilateral Trade Agreements listed in Annex 2 to the
extent that the parties to a dispute are members of these Agreements.]

4.   The MTO shall administer a Trade Policy Review Mechanism as set out
in Annex 4.

[5. The MTO shall cooperate, as appropriate, [inter alia,] with the
International Monetary Fund, the International Bank for Reconstruction
and Development and affiliated agencies, with a view to achieving
greater coherence in global policy-making.]
                         economic

Article IV

Relations with other Organizations

1.   The MTO shall [establish relations with other organizations
relevant to the Multilateral Trade Agreements annexed hereto,] make
arrangements [for consultation and cooperation] with intergovernmental
bodies and agencies [concerned with matters within the scope of the
MTO.] which have related responsibilities, to provide for effective
cooperation [and the avoidance of unnecessary duplication of
activities].

2.   The MTO may make suitable arrangements for consultation and
cooperation with non-governmental organizations concerned with matters
within the scope of the MTO.

Article V

Structure of the MTO

1.   There shall be a Ministerial Conference [open to representatives of
all the members,] which shall meet at least once every two years. The
task of the Ministerial Conference shall be to review and supervise the
operation of, and determine actions necessary to carry out the functions
of, this Agreement and the agreements annexed hereto, to launch further
mutilateral trade negotiations as appropriate, and to decide on the
implementation of results that may have been negotiated among and
adopted by members of the MTO.

2.   There shall be a General Council open to representatives of all the
members, which shall meet [at least twice each year [once each month])
The task of the General Council shall be to carry out the functions of
the MTO, including the supervision of the operation of this Agreement
and the agreements annexed hereto, in the time between Ministerial
Conferences, and decide on all issues conferred on it by this Agreement
and by the Ministers.

3.   The General Council shall establish [a Dispute Settlement Body, a
Trade Policy Review Mechanism, and] subsidiary bodies, [as appropriate.]
[such as a Goods Council, a Services Council, [a TRIPs Council,] a
Committee on Budget [,Finance] and Administration, a Committee on Trade

661-12-3

0334

 - 4 -

and Development, and a Balance of Payments Committee.] The General
Council shall establish its own rules of procedure (and shall approve the
rules of procedure of its subsidiary bodies.)

[4. There shall be a Council for Goods ("Goods Council") and a Council
for Services ("Services Council"), [and a Council for TRIPs ("TRIPs
Council").] open to representatives of all members, which shall meet at
least eight times per year.]

[5. The Goods Council shall oversee the functioning of the Agreements
on Trade in Goods as set out in Annex 1A, as well as any other functions
assigned to it by the General Council, except that the functions of
dispute settlement shall be exercised by the Dispute Settlement Body.
The Goods Council shall, as required, establish Committees to oversee
the operation of the Agreements set out in Annexes 1A, or other
subsidiary bodies, and shall approve their rules of procedure.]

[6. The Services Council shall oversee the functioning of Agreements on
Trade in Services as set out in Annex 1B, as well as any other functions
assigned to it by the General Council, except that the functions of
dispute settlement shall be exercised by the Dispute Settlement Body.
The Services Council shall, as required, establish Committees to oversee
the operation of the Agreements set out in Annexes 1B, or other
subsidiary bodies, and shall approve their rules of procedure.]

[7. The TRIPs Council shall oversee the functioning of the Agreement on
Trade-Related Intellectual Property Rights, including Trade in
Counterfeit Goods, as set out in Annex 1 C, as well as any other
functions assigned to it by the General Council, except that the
functions of dispute settlement shall be exercised by the Dispute
Settlement Body. The TRIPs Council shall, as required, establish
Committees to oversee the operation of the Agreements set out in Annex 1
C, or other subsidiary bodies, and shall approve their rules of
procedure.]

Article VI

The Secretariat

1. The General Council shall appoint a Director-General as head of the
Secretariat of the MTO. The powers, duties, conditions of service and
terms of office of the Director-General shall conform to regulations
approved by the General Council.

2. The Director-General shall appoint members of the staff, and shall
fix their duties and conditions of service in accordance with
regulations approved by the General Council.

3. The responsibilities of the Director-General and of the members of
the staff shall be exclusively international in character. In the
discharge of their duties, they shall not seek or receive instructions
from any government or from any other authority external to the
Organization. They shall refrain from any action which might reflect on

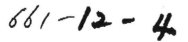

0335

their positions as international officials. The Members shall respect the international character of the responsibilities of these persons and shall not seek to influence them in the discharge of their duties.

4.   At the time of entry into force of the MTO, and until such time as the General Council shall have acted pursuant to paragraph 1, as far as practicable, the GATT Director-General and the ICITO/GATT Secretariat shall become the Director-General and Secretariat of the MTO.

Article VII

Budget and Contributions

1.   The Director-General shall present to the General Council the annual budget estimates and financial statement of the MTO. The General Council shall approve the accounts and the budget.

2.   The General Council shall apportion the expenditures of the Organization among the Members, in accordance with a scale of contributions to be fixed by the General Council, and each Member shall individually contribute promptly to the Organization its share of these expenditures.[2]

3.   The General Council shall decide on measures to be taken with regard to Members in arrears of their contributions.

4.   The Budget Committee shall elaborate the provisions on the MTO budget and MTO contributions for adoption by the General Council. The provisions shall be based, as far as practicable, on the provisions and practices for the GATT budget.

Article VIII

Status

1.   The MTO shall have legal personality.

2.   The MTO shall enjoy in the territory of each of the Members such legal capacity, privileges and immunities as may be necessary for the exercise of its functions.

3.   The representatives of the Members and the officials of the MTO shall enjoy such privileges and immunities as are necessary for the independent exercise of their functions in connection with the MTO.

---

[2] [The establishment of the MTO should not increase the financial obligations of the members.]

661-12-5

0336

- 6 -

4.   The privileges and immunities to be accorded by a Member to the
MTO, to its officials and to the representatives of its Members shall be
similar to those accorded by that member to specialized agencies of the
United Nations, to their officials and to the representatives of their
members, under the Convention on the Privileges and Immunities of the
Specialized Agencies, or under similar arrangements.

5.   The MTO may conclude a headquarters agreement, as appropriate.

Article IX

Joint Action

1.   At meetings of the General Council, each Member of the MTO shall be
entitled to one vote, and, except as otherwise provided for in this
Agreement, decisions of the General Council shall be taken by a majority
of votes cast.

[1bis The General Council shall have the authority to interpret the
provisions of the Agreements annexed hereto.]

2.   In exceptional circumstances not elsewhere provided for in this
Agreement and the Multilateral Trade Agreements under Annex 1, the
General Council may waive an obligation imposed on a member by this
Agreement or a Multilateral Trade Agreement under Annex 1; Provided
that any such decision shall be approved by a two-thirds majority of
votes cast and that such majority shall comprise more than half the MTO
members.

Article X

Amendments and Modifications

1.   Negotiations for amendments to this Agreement, or to any of
Multilateral Trade Agreements in Annex 1, shall be concluded by the
Ministerial Conference on the basis of consensus.

2.   Any member accepting an amendment to this Agreement or any of the
Multilateral Trade Agreements in Annex 1 shall deposit an instrument of
acceptance with the Director-General of the MTO within such period as
the Ministerial Conference may specify. Such amendments shall become
effective upon acceptance by two-thirds of the members.

3.   The Ministerial Conference may decide that any amendment made
effective under this Article is of such a nature that any member which
has not accepted it within a period specified by the Ministerial
Conference shall be free to withdraw from this Agreement, or to remain a
member with the consent of the Minsterial Conference.

4.   Amendments to the agreements in Annex 2 shall be made in accordance
with the amending procedures in those agreements. *Such amendments*
shall be notified to General Council.

- 7 -

5.   Modifications to the instruments set out in Annexes 3 and 4 shall be taken by consensus in the General Council.

M C ~~~~ or

Article XI

Original Membership

[Membership in the MTO shall [be open to] consist of all] GATT contracting parties and the European Communities which accept this Agreement and all Multilateral Trade Agreements in Annex 1, [including acceptance on a definitive basis of the General Agreement on Tariffs and Trade, subject to the conditions set out in the Protocol of Provisional Application and the Protocols of Accession] [and the instruments in Annexes 3 and 4.] [, shall become original members of the MTO.]

Article XII

para. 1 b of

Accession

1.   Any state or separate customs territory possessing full autonomy in the conduct of its external commercial relations and of other matters provided for in this Agreement, which accepts this Agreement and all Multilateral Trade Agreements in Annex 1, and the instruments in Annexes 3 and 4 may accede on terms to be agreed between it and the General Council.

2.   Decisions on accession of new Members shall be taken by the General Council and shall be approved by a two-thirds majority of votes cast and that such majority shall comprise more than half the MTO members.

[Article XIII

Non-application of the Agreement between particular Members

1.   This Agreement and all Multilateral Trade Agreements listed in Annex 1 [The Multilateral Trade Agreements listed in Annex 1 A, or the Multilateral Trade Agreements listed in Annex 1 B] [, or the Multilateral Trade Agreements listed in Annex 1 C] shall not apply as between any member and any other member if either of the members, at the time either becomes a member, does not consent to such application. [Such intention shall be notified to the General Council in advance of a decision being taken on membership.]

[1bis Paragraph 1 shall apply to the Multilateral Trade Agreements listed in Annex 1 only to the extent that non-application rights have been invoked under those Agreements.)]

2.   The General Council may review the operation of this Article in particular cases at the request of any member and make appropriate recommendations.]

861-12-7

0338

Article XIV

Entry into Force and Deposit

1.   This Agreement shall be open for acceptance, by signature or otherwise, as from [1 November 1992] [a date set by the Implementing Conference] to Uruguay Round participants that qualify under Article XI. This Agreement shall enter into force on [1 January 1993], the same date as the other Uruguay Round results become effective. | *a date set by m ZC*

2.   This Agreement shall remain open for acceptance by Uruguay Round participants that qualify under Article XI until [1 January, 1995] [a date determined by the General Council of the MTO] [a date set by the Implementing Conference]. For these participants, it shall enter into force on the thirtieth day following the deposit of the instrument of ratification or acceptance. [Participants accepting the MTO Agreement pursuant to this provision shall implement the concessions established in the Multilateral Trade Agreements annexed hereto as if they had entered into force on the date of entry into force of the MTO.] *not providers but Z-C decide otherwise*

3.   After [1 January, 1995], any other Uruguay Round participant, may apply for membership under the accession provisions set out in Article XII.

4.   Prior to entry into force of this Agreement, the text of this Agreement shall be deposited with the Director-General to the CONTRACTING PARTIES of the General Agreement on Tariffs and Trade, in his capacity as depositary of the Uruguay Round results. He shall promptly furnish a certified true copy thereof and a notification of each acceptance thereof to each signatory of the Agreement on the MTO. The Agreement shall, upon its entry in to force, be deposited with the Director-General of the MTO, as well as any amendments thereto.

Article XV

Withdrawal

1.   Any Member of the MTO may withdraw from this Agreement. Any member, upon withdrawal from this Agreement, shall cease to be a party to the Multilateral Trade Agreements in Annex 1 and the instruments in Annexes 3 and 4. Such withdrawal shall take effect upon the expiration of six months from the date on which written notice of withdrawal is received by the Director-General.

2.   Withdrawal from the agreements in Annex 2 shall be governed by the provisions of those agreements.

661 - 12 - 8

- 9 -

Article XVI

Final Provisions

1.   The MTO shall respect the rules, decisions and customary practice of the General Agreement on Tariffs and Trade and [its associated legal instruments, including] the Tokyo Round Agreements [and Arrangements] in carrying out its functions and tasks.

2.   No reservations may be entered in respect of any provision in the Multilateral Trade Agreements in Annex 1. Reservations entered in respect of the Agreements in Annex 2 can only be made in accordance with the relevant provisions of those Agreements.

3.   In the event of a conflict between the provisions of this Agreement and the provisions of any of the Multilateral Trade Agreements in Annex 1, the provisions of this Agreement shall prevail.

4.   This Agreement shall be registered in accordance with the provisions of Article 102 of the Charter of the United Nations.

Done at --- this -- day of --- one thousand nine hundred and ninety---, in a single copy, in the English, French and Spanish languages, each text being authentic.

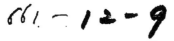

0340

- 10 -

[ANNEXES]

Annex 1

[Annex 1 A covers:]

- the General Agreement on Tariffs and Trade, as it results from the Final Act of the Uruguay Round, and its associated legal instruments, except the Protocol of Provisional Application;

- the Tokyo Round Agreements and Arrangements as they result fromthe Final Act of the Uruguay Round and their associated legal instruments, except those Agreements and Arrangements found in Annex 2; and

[Annex 1 C covers:]

- the Agreement on Trade-Related Intellectual Property Rights, including Trade in Counterfeit Goods (TRIPs);

[Annex 1 B covers:]

- the General Agreement on Trade in Services.

Annex 2

Annex 2 covers:

- the Agreement on Trade in Civil Aircraft;

- the Agreement on Government Procurement;

- the International Dairy Arrangement; and

- the Arrangement Regarding Bovine Meat.

[- the Agreement on Implementation of Article VII]

Annex 3

Annex 3 covers:

- the Integrated Dispute Settlement Understanding.

Annex 4

Annex 4 covers:

- the Trade Policy Review Mechanism.

161 - 12-10

0341

〈별첨 2〉

Footnote to Articles II, XI and XVI(2):

The provisions of the MTO Agreement are without prejudice to the substantive results of the Uruguay Round as it affects the existing rights of contracting parties under paragraph 1(b) of the Protocol of Provisional Application and under equivalent provisions of the Protocols of Accession.

61-12-11

0342

〈별첨37〉

China

Article XII
Membership

1. Any state not member of the MTO, which accepts this Agreement and all Multilateral Trade Agreements in Annex 1, and the instruments in Annexes 3 and 4 may accede to the MTO on terms to be agreed between it and the General Council.

2. If a government acting on behalf of a separate customs territory possesses or acquires full autonomy in the conduct of its external commercial relations and of the other matters provided for in this Agreement, such territory shall, on terms to be agreed between it and the General Council, be deemed to be a member of the MTO, provided that the above-mentioned fact of the territory is established by a responsible state and the territory accepts this Agreement all Multilateral Trade Agreements in Annex 1, and the instruments in Annexes 3 and 4.

3. Decisions on paragraph 1 and 2 shall be taken by the General Council and shall be approved by a two-thirds majority of votes cast and that such majority shall comprise more than half the MTO members.

661-12-12

0343

외 무 부

종 별 :

번 호 : GVW-2735

일 시 : 91 1219 1630

수 신 : 장관(봉기, 경기원, 상공부, 재무부, 농림수산부)

발 신 : 주제네바대사

제 목 : UR/제도분야 비공식 협의(분쟁해결)

1. 표제협의의 분쟁해결 관련 사항 토의는 12.19.오전 및 동일 야간(12.19.04:00까지 계속)의 2차례에 걸쳐 진행, 미결쟁점 대부분에 대해 합의 또는 합의 직전 단계에 이름으로써 12.20제출될 의장문안의 윤곽이 드러나게됨.

(이성주 참사관 참석)

2. 최대 관심사항인 일방조치문제는 12.17 야간이후 계속된 미.EC간 막후 절충을통해 브랏셀 TEXT SUB-ITEM IV에 해당하는 갓트 불일치 국내법의 수정문제는 분쟁해결 TEXT 에서 언급하는 대신 '수정이 필요한 경우, 이를 위하여모든 조치를 취한다'는 별첨(1) 문안을 MTO협정안의 16조(FINAL PROVISION) 4항으로 하고 여타3개 SUB-ITEM 에 대해서는 미국 문안과 EC문안의 중간선에서 합의한 별첨(2) 문안을 분쟁해결통합문(CONSOLIDATED TEXT)에 두기로 합의한 바를 전체 참가국이 아무런 이의 없이동의함.(이에 따라 패널 설치등 절차자유화문제는 FULL AUTOMATICITY FORMULA 로 합의)

3. 최종일 협의 과정에서 최대 난제는 오히려 교차보복문제였었는바, 의장이 미국,EC,인도와 협의하여 제시한 별첨(3) 문안에 대해 장시간 논란끝에 아래와 같이 거의 합의됨.(의장이 명백한 RULING은 하지 않았으나 대부분 합의된 것으로 양해하는 분위기)

가. 우선 뉴질랜드, 호주가 써비스 협상에서 SECTOR간 교차보복이 논의되는 것과는 관계없이 본그룹에서는 협정간 교차보복(CROSS-AGREEMENTRETALIATION) 문제만 다루어야 한다는 입장을 반복한데 대해, EC가 반대함으로써 대립하였으나, 카나다가 'SECTOR' 및'AGREEMENT'에 대한 명확한 정의 규정을 추가함으로써 GATT 내에서는 'SECTOR'간 구분을 없애고자 하는 호.뉴 양국의 입장을 반영시켜주자는 절충안을 제시하고 EC가 이에 동의함으로써 별첨(4) 문안을 추가키로 합의

통상국 2차보 외정실 분석관 청와대 안기부 경기원 재무부 농수부
상공부

91.12.20 08:37 BX

외신 1과 통제관

0344

나. 이어서 놀웨이, 스위스,카나다, 호주, 뉴질랜드등 선진국이 의장안에 지지입장을 표명한데 반해,알젠틴을 선두로 파키스탄, 이집트,베네주엘라,중국,모로코등 일부 개도국이 기존입장을 되풀이 반대 또는 수락불가 입장을표명함에 따라 협상임 교착상태에 빠졌고, 이에미국 대표가 동 문제는 일방주의에 대한 자국의양보, MTO,IDS(봉합분쟁해결절차)등의 잇슈와 상호 밀접히 연계된 사항(PACKAGE)으로 교차보복이수락되지 않으면 일방조치 관련 양보안의 철회및 89.4.중간평가 합의에로 되돌아 갈수 밖에없다는 강한 입장을 표명한후 퇴장, 일시적으로 정회하는 등 협상 분위기가악화됨

다. 속개된 회의에는 미국의 LAVOREL 대사가 직접 참석, 상기 미국의 강경 입장을 되풀이하고,의장 및 사무국도 각국의 신중한 판단 및 협조를 촉구한바, 이에 선진국들이 찬성입장을 반복하고,사전 미.EC간 타협내용을 파악, 의도적 침묵을 지키던 아국,홍콩,싱가폴,태국,멕시코,브라질,일본중에 일부가 찬성 또는 불반대의 뜻을 표명(일본, 태국은 찬성, 홍콩,멕시코는 불반대)함으로써 반대입장을 주도해온 알젠틴이의장의 판단에 일임하겠다는 선으로 양보함(파키스탄,이집트,모로코는 반대입장 고수)

라. 인도는 TRIPS, 반덤핑 분야에서의 반대급부를 조건으로 쎄이프가드 및 분쟁해결 분야에서 선진국측으로 입장을 선회, 정회기간중에도 교차보복을 포함한 미.EC PACKAGE 수락 불가피성을여타 개도국 대표에게 설득하는 노력을 보임.

4. NV 분쟁에 관해서도 최종순간까지 상당한논란이 계속되어 결국 문안자체에는합의에이르지는 못하고 의장 판단에 맡기기로 합의함(23조1항 C해당 NV 분쟁은 논란없이 OPTION 2로 합의)

- 미,EC간 사전 의견 조정을 거쳐 의장이 OPTION1(EC안)채택을 종용하였으나

- 호주, 뉴질랜드가 연호입장(OR MODIFY 삭제 및보상을 최종 해결의 일부로 간주함에 반대)을되풀이 하고, 알젠틴이 이에 동조함으로써 논란이확대됨

O EC, 미국, 일본,아국은 OR MODIFY 포함한OPTION 1의 문안지지

O 카나다, 놀웨이, 스위스,태국,싱가폴은 OPTION 1은 지지하되, OR MODIFY 삭제희망

O 호주, 뉴질랜드,(D)항 문안 수정 및 OR MODIFY삭제(알젠틴, 브라질동조)-EC가별첨(5) 양보 문안을 제시하였으나 합의도출 실패

5. 기타 봉합문안(CONSOLIDATED TEXT)상의 여타문제도 특별한 문제없이 모두

합의에이르렀음(별첨 6 TEXT 에 표시된 합의사항참조)

6. 한편 통합 분쟁해결절차(IDS)문 제는 12.18오전 회의를 통해 대체적 합의에 도달한바 동결과는 별전 보고함

7. 따라서 12.20 제출될 의장 TEXT 중 분쟁해결관련 부분은 아래 3가지 TEXT로 구성될 것으로 전망됨.

가. 봉합문안(CONSOLIDATED TEXT)

- 별첨 (6) 참조

단, NV 분쟁조항에서 OR MODIFY 삭제여부는 불투명하나 (D) 항 관련 EC 양보안은반영될 것으로 판단됨. 나. 봉합분쟁해결 TEXT(IDS)

- 별첨(7) 참조

- 단, 추가 작업을 요한다는 취지의 ANNOTATION 을부기

다. 교차보복관련 별도 TEXT

- 별첨 (3),(4) 참조

- 의장의 명백한 의사표시는 없었으나 현단계에서는 GATT 분쟁해결절차만을대상으로 한 봉합문안에 포함시킬 수 없으므로별도 TEXT가 될것으로 판단(향후 INTEGRATD TEXT에의 포함 용도)

첨부: 1. 일방주의 관련 MTO 문안

2. 일방주의 관련 CONSOLIDATED TEXT 포함 문안

3. 교차보복관련 문안

4. 교차보복관련 추가문안(정의관련)

5. NV 분쟁관련 EC 양보문안

6. 봉합문안(CONSOLIDATED TEXT)

7. IDS 문안.

(GVW(F)-0659).끝

(대사 박수길-국장)

0346

외 무 부

종 별 :

번 호 : GVW-2747   일 시 : 91 1219 2030

수 신 : 장관(통기, 경기원, 재무부, 농림수산부, 상공부, 특허청)

발 신 : 주 제네바 대사

제 목 : 최종 의정서

연: GVW-2690

1. 연호 12.17(화) 비공식 협의 결과에 따라 갓트사무국은 12.18(수) 자로 최종의정서에 관한 PAPER를 별첨과 같이 작성하였는바, LACARTE의장이 분쟁해결 절차, MTO문제, 최빈개도국 문제등을 12.19 새벽까지 협의한관계로 동 최종의정서 문안을 더 협의할 시간적여유가 없음.

2. 갓트 사무국측에 의하면 LACARTE 의장은 동최종의정서 문안에 대해 추가 협의를 할 필요가 없다는 생각을 갖고 있다하며, 그간의 협의결과를 기초로 자신이 최종문안을 작성예정이라함.

3. 1항에서 언급하고 있는 첨부 INSTRUMENTS 에는 MTO 설립협정(안)도 포함되는것이며, 3항의 IMPLEMENTATION CONFERENCE 는 92년말 전으로 괄호로 표기하고 있으나 동회의는 FINAL ACT채택회의에 이어서 개최할 가능성을 염두에두고 있는 것임을 참고 바람.

첨부: 12.18 자 FINAL ACT 사무국 PAPER

(GVW(F)-663) 1매끝.

(대사 박수길-국장)

통상국 특허청	장관		2차보	구주국	경기원	재무부	농수부	상공부

PAGE 1   91.12.20   21:05 FL

외신 1과 통제관

0347

062

주 제 네 바 대 표 부

번 호 : GVW(F) - 0663   년월일 :11/21   시간 :2030

수 신 : 장   관 (통기, 경기원, 재무부, 농림수산부, 상공부, 특허청)

발 신 : 주 제네바대사

제 목 : GVW-2747 첨부

총 5 매(표지포함)

보 안 통 재	

외신과 통 재	

663-5-1   0348

18 December 1991

DRAFT FINAL ACT EMBODYING THE RESULTS OF THE
URUGUAY ROUND OF MULTILATERAL TRADE NEGOTIATIONS

1.   Having met [................... from ... to ... . 19.. at
.... in order to conclude the Uruguay Round of Multilateral Trade
Negotiations, the representatives of the Governments and of the European
Communities, members of the Trade Negotiations Committee (hereinafter
referred to as "participants"), agree that the Agreements, Decisions and
Understandings, as set out in the annexes attached hereto[1] (hereinafter
referred to as "instruments"), embody the results of their negotiations and
form an integral part of this Final Act.

2.   By adopting the present Final Act, participants agree to submit, as
appropriate, the annexed instruments for the consideration of their
respective competent authorities with a view to seeking approval of these
instruments in accordance with appropriate procedures of the participant
concerned.

3.   Participants agree on the desirability of acceptance of the
instruments by all participants with a view to their entry into force as
early as possible and not later than [1 January 1993]. Participants
further agree, in order to provide the administrative infrastructure for
the international implementation of the Uruguay Round results, to establish
a Multilateral Trade Organization. Pursuant to the final paragraph of the
Punta del Este Declaration, Ministers will meet in a Special Session of the
CONTRACTING PARTIES to decide on the international implementation of the
results not later than not later than the end of [1992]. Subsequently, and
taking into account the status of domestic ratification efforts, they shall
meet prior to the end of [1992] to decide the timing of the instruments'
entry into force.

4.   Participants agree on the desirability of the application by the
contracting parties, as from the date of entry into force of the Uruguay
Round results, of the General Agreement on Tariffs and Trade on a
definitive rather than on a provisional basis.

5.   Participants agree that the instruments shall be open for acceptance
[as a whole], by signature or otherwise, by all participants in the Uruguay
Round of Multilateral Trade Negotiations. This is without prejudice to the
requirement that such participants who are not contracting parties to the
GATT must negotiate their terms of accession to the GATT.

---

[1]Ministers agreed at the Mid-Term Review that the negotiations on
Trade-Related Aspects of Intellectual Property Rights are without prejudice
to the views of participants concerning the institutional aspects of the
international implementation of the results of the negotiations in this
area which is to be decided pursuant to the final paragraph of the Punta
del Este Declaration, i.e. by Ministers meeting at a Special Session of the
CONTRACTING PARTIES.

663-5-2   0349

- 2 -

6.   This Final Act and the texts of the instruments set out in the Annexes shall be deposited with the Director-General to the CONTRACTING PARTIES to the General Agreement on Tariffs and Trade who shall promptly furnish to each participant in the Uruguay Round of Multilateral Trade Negotiations a certified copy thereof.

     DONE at ...., this .... day of .... one thousand nine hundred and ninety-........ in a single copy, in the English, French and Spanish languages, each text being authentic.

663-5-3

0350

18 December 1991

DRAFT FINAL ACT EMBODYING THE RESULTS OF THE
URUGUAY ROUND OF MULTILATERAL TRADE NEGOTIATIONS

1.   Having met [................... from ... to ... . 19.. at
.... in order to conclude the Uruguay Round of Multilateral Trade
Negotiations, the representatives of the Governments and of the European
Communities, members of the Trade Negotiations Committee (hereinafter
referred to as "participants"), agree that the Agreements, Decisions and
Understandings, as set out in the annexes attached hereto[1] (hereinafter
referred to as "instruments"), embody the results of their negotiations and
form an integral part of this Final Act.

2.   By adopting the present Final Act, participants agree to submit, as
appropriate, the annexed instruments for the consideration of their
respective competent authorities with a view to seeking approval of these
instruments in accordance with appropriate procedures of the participant
concerned.

3.   Participants agree on the desirability of acceptance of the
instruments by all participants with a view to their entry into force as
early as possible and not later than [1 January 1993]. Participants
further agree, in order to provide the administrative infrastructure for
the international implementation of the Uruguay Round results, to establish
a Multilateral Trade Organization. Pursuant to the final paragraph of the
Punta del Este Declaration, Ministers will meet in a Special Session of the
CONTRACTING PARTIES to decide on the international implementation of the
results not later than ~~not later than~~ the end of [1992]. Subsequently, and
taking into account the status of domestic ratification efforts, they shall
meet prior to the end of [1992] to decide the timing of the instruments'
entry into force.

4.   Participants agree on the desirability of the application by the
contracting parties, as from the date of entry into force of the Uruguay
Round results, of the General Agreement on Tariffs and Trade on a
definitive rather than on a provisional basis.

5.   Participants agree that the instruments shall be open for acceptance
[as a whole], by signature or otherwise, by all participants in the Uruguay
Round of Multilateral Trade Negotiations. This is without prejudice to the
requirement that such participants who are not contracting parties to the
GATT must negotiate their terms of accession to the GATT.

----

[1]Ministers agreed at the Mid-Term Review that the negotiations on
Trade-Related Aspects of Intellectual Property Rights are without prejudice
to the views of participants concerning the institutional aspects of the
international implementation of the results of the negotiations in this
area which is to be decided pursuant to the final paragraph of the Punta
del Este Declaration, i.e. by Ministers meeting at a Special Session of the
CONTRACTING PARTIES.

663-5-4   0351

- 2 -

6.   This Final Act and the texts of the instruments set out in the Annexes shall be deposited with the Director-General to the CONTRACTING PARTIES to the General Agreement on Tariffs and Trade who shall promptly furnish to each participant in the Uruguay Round of Multilateral Trade Negotiations a certified copy thereof.

     DONE at ...., this .... day of .... one thousand nine hundred and ninety-........ in a single copy, in the English, French and Spanish languages, each text being authentic.

663-5-5   0352

정 리 보 존 문 서 목 록

기록물종류	일반공문서철	등록번호	2019100005	등록일자	2019-10-01
분류번호	764.51	국가코드		보존기간	영구
명 칭	UR(우루과이라운드) / 보조금.상계관세 회의, 1991				
생 산 과	통상기구과	생산년도	1991~1991	담당그룹	다자통상
내용목차					

0001

재   무   부

관협 22710-   3기   (503-9296)   1991. 7. 16.
수신 외무부장관
참조 통상국장
제목 UR 보조금·상계관세협상

    '91.7.22-26간 스위스 제네바에서 개최예정인 표제협상에
당부 대표로 엄낙용 주제네바 대표부 재무관 및 김동진 재무관보를
현지 참석케 하오니 별첨 세부 쟁점별 아국입장의 전달 및 필요
조치를 취하여 주시기 바랍니다.

첨부 세부 쟁점별 아국입장 1부.

재   무   부   장

0002

세부 쟁점별 아국입장

1. 미결 쟁점 및 아국입장

쟁점 1) 농산물 보조금 포함여부

- 의장안 내용
  - o 언급없음

- 주요국 입장
  - o〈브라질등 개도국 및 미국,호주 등 농산물수출국〉: 동 협정안은 농산물
    보조금에도 적용됨
  - o〈일본, EC, 한국, 북구〉: 농산물보조금은 농산물 그룹에서 별도로 다룰
    것을 주장

- 아국입장
  - o 농산물협상그룹은 농산물교역과 관련된 모든 측면에 대하여 일차적인
    책임을 지고 있으며 지금까지 본협상과 별도로 논의를 진행시켜 왔으므로,
    농산물 보조금에 대한 논의도 농산물협상그룹에 일임하도록 함.

  - o 보조금협상그룹은 농산물협상그룹이 합의한 결과를 수용함으로써, 농산물
    보조금에 대해서도 규율할 수 있음.

- 아국의 입장 및 우선순위
  - o 농산물보조금은 별도의 농산물협상그룹의 결과를 수용
  - o 우선순위 : 적극 반영

0003

- 의장안 내용

o 개도국에게는 금지보조금인 수출보조금을 줄 수 있도록 함.

· 최빈개도국(Annex7 에 열거된 29개국)은 수출보조금을 지급할 수 있음.

· 기타 개도국(Annex 8에 열거)은 단계적으로 수출보조금을 감축하도록 하고, 조치가능보조금의 구제절차를 적용함 (국가별로 4구분하여 감축 기간을 다르게 하여, 한국등 선발개도국은 수출보조금을 줄수 없도록 함)

o 기타 우대내용

· 심각한 손상 추정(제6.1조)의 적용을 배제

· 아래의 경우에는 상계조치를 하지 못하도록 함.

(a) 소액보조금 (보조비율 미정)

(b) 수입국의 시장점유율이 일정수준 이하인 품목에 대한 보조금, 단 이러한 품목들이 복수의 국가들로부터 수입될때는 총수입액이 시장 점유율의 일정비율을 초과하지 않아야 함.

- 주요국 입장

o 〈선발 개도국을 제외한 모든 국가〉

· 개도국은 경제발전 정도에 따라 국제사회에서의 의무를 분담해야 하며, 따라서 개도국별 차별대우를 규정한 의장안에 찬성

o 〈미국, 북구, 스위스등 선진국〉

· 선진국과 경쟁관계에 있는 한국등 선발개도국은 선진국과 동일한 의무를 부담해야 함

o 〈한국, 싱가폴, 말레이지아〉

· 개도국 분류는 각료선언에서 본협상에 위임된 사항이 아님.

0004

- 아국입장

    o 개도국 분류는 본 협상에의 위임사항이 아니며, 이는 보다 전문적인
      기관에 의한 전반적, 객관적 판단을 필요로 하며

    o 또한, 본 협상에서의 개도국 분류는 중요한 선례로서 일반적인 국제
      관계에 영향을 미치기 때문에 임의적인 개도국 분류에 반대함.

    o 서면으로 대안 제시
        . 최저개도국을 제외한 개도국은 일률적으로 일정기간내 수출보조금 폐지를
          약속
        . 다만 동기간 만료시점에 가서 경제개발의 낙후등으로 이를 이행 수 없는
          국가의 대해서는 기간 연장 허용

    o 그러나, 개도국 분류를 통해 혜택이 박탈되는 국가는 한국·싱가폴·말련 등
      극소수 국가이고, 따라서 이같은 아국등의 입장은 선진국이나 후진국 어느쪽
      으로 부터도 지지를 받기가 힘들 것으로 예상

- 아국 입장 및 우선순위

    o (제1안) : 상기 아국이 서면으로 제출한 대안
    o (제2안) : 의장안을 수용하고 Annex 8 개도국 List에 아국포함

0005

쟁점 3) 심각한 손상(Serious prejudice) 추정(제6.1조)

- 의장안 내용

o 아래 보조금은 조치가능보조금으로 하되, 이들은 무조건 심각한 손상을 초래하는 것으로 간주함.

o 따라서, 위의 보조금을 지급하는 국가는 이들 보조금이 심각한 손상을 입히지 않았음을 입증해야하는 부담을 지게되며(6.2조), 이러한 입증이 없을 경우 구제절차에 의해 대응조치가 가능함.

  · 물품의 보조금액 비율이 [5]%를 초과하는 보조금
  · 특정산업에서 발생하는 영업손실을 보전하기 위한 보조금
  · 어떤 기업의 영업손실을 보전하기 위한 보조금
  · 직접적인 채무감면

- 동 조항의 배경
  o 의장안은 국내보조금의 금지화를 주장하는 미국입장과 이에 반대하는 EC 등의 주장을 절충한 것임.

- 주요국의 입장

o 〈미국〉 : 아래의 국내 보조금은 금지보조금으로 분류주장.
  · 영업손실을 보전하기 위한 무상지원
  · 채무의 직접 감면
  · 조달 및 관리비용 이하의 금리에 의한 정부 대출
  · 손실이 예상되는 부문에 대한 지분 투자
  · 적정비용보다 낮은 보증료에 의한 대출 보증
  · 생산 성과부 보조금

0006

o 〈EC·일본·개도국〉: 국내보조금의 금지화에 반대

· E C : 보조금 규율은 무역에 미치는 부정적 효과에 따라 대처하는
          방식이어야 함.
· 일 본 : 보조금 규율강화와 함께 대응조치 남용방지대책도 필요
· 헝가리 : 국내보조금의 금지 완화 주장

- 아국입장

o 아국은 해당보조금 지급국가에게 과도한 입증책임을 지게하고, 분쟁의 소지를
  제공한다는 이유에서 적극적으로 이에 반대해 왔음.

o 그러나, 심각한 손상추정은 개도국 우대조항(제27 제4항)에 의해 개도국에는
  적용되지 않으므로,

o 아국이 추후 개도국 List (Annex8)에 포함될 경우 동 규정은 아국에 대해
  적용되지 않음.

- 아국 입장 및 우선순위

o (1안) : 제6.1조 삭제지지(적극적 반대입장 유보)
o (2안) : Annex 8의 개도국 List에 포함될때, 의장안 수용

0007

쟁점 4) 수량기준 채택여부 (제6.1조 (a))

- 의장안 내용

  o 보조금액 비율이 [5]%를 초과할 경우 심각한 손상이 있는 것으로 추정함

- 주요국 입장

  o <미국, 북구, 캐나다, 호주, 뉴질랜드, 스위스등> : 찬성국가

  - 미국 : 보조금 규율강화를 위해서는 반드시 채택필요

  - 북구 : 수량기준이 문제를 갖고 있으나, 보조금 규율강화를 위한 별도의 대안이 없음

  o <EC, 일본, 한국, 싱가풀, 개도국등> : 반대국가

  - E C : 다른 수단을 통한 보조금 규율강화 주장, 도입하더라도 기존 보조금에 대해서는 관용필요

  - 일본 : 원칙적으로 반대. 도입하더라도 천재지변등의 경우에 지급되는 보조금은 제외되어야 함

- 아국입장

  o 적극적으로 반대하여 왔음.

  o 보조금은 무역효과에 따라서 규제되어야 하는데, 수량기준은 이러한 보조금과 무역효과간의 상관관계를 무시하는 것이며, 시행상 수출기업에게 심각한 손상을 끼치지 않았음을 증명해야 하는등 과도한 업무부담을 초래함.

0008

o 그러나 보조금 규율강화를 주장하는 미국 등의 입장이 강경하고, 이를
  반대하던 EC·일본도 수량기준의 채택가능성을 암시하고 있으므로
  아국이 강경입장을 견지하더라도 관철될 가능성이 크지 않을 것으로 예상됨

o 또한 개도국 우대조항(제27조제4항)에 의하면 수량기준에 의한 심각한
  손상추정은 개도국에게는 적용되지 않으므로, 수량기준이 채택되더라도
  아국이 개도국 분류에 포함될 경우 동 조항은 적용되지 않음.

- 아국 입장 및 우선순위

  o (1안) : 제6.2조(a) 삭제지지(적극적 반대입장 유보)

  o (2안) : 수량기준의 상향조정 여부가 논의될 경우, 상향조정 지지

쟁점 5) 허용보조금의 요건(제8조)

- 의장안 내용

  o 특정성있는 다음 보조금은 제한된 조건, 특히 수치상한을 두어 허용

    · 연구개발보조금 : 기본적인 산업연구는 소요비용의 [20]% 초과금지
                     응용연구개발은 소요비용의 [10]% 초과금지
    · 구조조정보조금 : 생산시설의 감축, 폐기위한 비용의 [X]% 초과금지
    · 환경보호보조금 : 소요비용의 [20]% 초과금지
    · 지역개발보조금 : 전국평균보다 [15]%이상 낙후지역의 개발만 허용

- 주요국 입장

  o 〈미 국〉: 허용보조금의 범위가 지나치게 확대되었음

  o 〈개도국〉: 허용보조금의 요건이 지나치게 엄격함

0009

- 아국입장

  o 아국의 경우 <u>연구개발, 구조조정, 지역개발, 환경보호등은 필수적인 것으로 향후</u>
    <u>이들 지원사례가 증가할 것을 예상되므로, 가능한 한 허용보조금의 요건을</u>
    <u>완화하는 것이 바람직함</u>.

- 아국입장 및 우선순위

  o <u>허용보조금의 요건완화 여부가 논의될 경우 요건완화 입장 지지</u>
    · (1안) : <u>수치한도 삭제 지지</u>
    · (2안) : <u>수치한도 상향조정 지지</u>

쟁점 6) 복수의 허용보조금 수혜(제8.5조)

- 의장안 내용

  o 특정기업이 복수의 허용보조금을 수혜할 경우, 단지 한가지 보조금만을
    허용보조금으로 봄

- 주요국 입장

  o〈미 국〉: 복수의 허용보조금 수혜금지

  o〈EC,일본,한국등〉: 복수의 허용보조금 수혜가능

- 아국입장

  o <u>각 허용보조금은 상당히 제한적인 요건을 충족하는 경우에만 허용되므로,</u>
    <u>한가지 보조금만 허용하는 것은 지나친 제한임</u>

  o 허용보조금은 보조금 자체의 성질에 따라 허용되는 것이므로, 중복지급
    된다 하더라도 허용보조금의 성질이 변하는 것이 아니므로 허용되어야 함

- 아국입장 및 우선순위

  o <u>동 조항 (8.5조) 삭제</u>

0010

쟁점 7) 보조금액 산정기준(제14조)

- 의장안 내용

o 보조금액 계산방법은 각국 법령에 규정하되 명료하고(transparent), 적정
하여야(adquately)하며, 다음 지침에 부합하여야 함

  (a) 정부의 투자는 민간투자가들의 통상적인 투자관행과 비교

  (b) 정부의 대출은 당해 대출금리와 시장금리를 비교

  (c) 정부의 대출보증은 당해 대출이자율과 동 보증이 없었을 경우의 이자율을
      비교

  (d) 정부에 의한 재화, 용역의 공급 또는 구매의 경우는 시장가격과 비교
      결정

  (e) 시장가격이 존재하지 않을 경우(정부가 유일한 공급자 또는 수요자인
      경우) 차별여부에 의해 구분

  → 상기 의장안은 원칙적으로 수혜자 수익기준(시장가격과 비교)을 채택
    하고 있음

- 주요국 입장

  o〈미 국〉

    · 의장안이 수혜자 수익개념에 충실치 못함

    · 보조금은 일반 민간투자자의 합리적 투자 및 대출원칙 등을 기준으로
      산정되어야 함(수익기준 강화)

  o〈북구, EC, 카나다, 일본〉

    · 북 구 : 보조금 산정기준의 명확화 주장, 정부비용개념 지지

    · EC, 카나다, 일본 : 의장안이 수익기준에 근거하고 있어 기술적으로
                        보조금액 산정을 더욱 어렵게 하므로, 동 기준은
                        정부 비용개념을 채택하여야 함

0011

- 아국입장

o 수익기준의 불합리성

(i) 복잡한 실제 시장에서 적절한 비교대상 시장가격을 안다는 것이
불가능한 경우가 많고

(ii) 시장가격에는 기업의 정상이윤이 포함되고 있으므로 이를 기준으로 할
경우 이윤부분도 보조금으로 간주될 가능성이 있음.

o 정부비용기준의 장점

(i) 비용파악이 비교적 용이하고,

(ii) 보조금 부분이 축소되는 효과가 있음

- 아국입장 및 우선순위
· (1안): 정부비용기준 채택 주장
· (2안): 수익기준 채택 수용

0012

쟁점 8) 지방정부보조금에 대한 규율(제2.1.d조)

- 의장안 내용
  - o 특정지역내에 있는 기업에게 주는 보조금은 지급기관에 관계없이 특정적인 것으로 봄. 단, 허용대상 지역개발보조금에는 본규정 적용 배제

- 주요국 입장
  - o 〈카나다, 호주〉
    - · 지방정부도 중앙정부와 같은 수준의 의무를 부담하는 것이므로,
    - · 지방정부가 관할내에 있는 모든 기업에게 지급하는 보조금은 특정성이 없음.
  - o 아직까지 협상에서 본격적으로 쟁점화 되지는 않고 있음.

- 아국입장
  - o 아국의 경우 장기적 측면에서 지방자치제의 정착이후, 지방정부의 보조금 활용 가능성도 고려할 필요가 있으나,
  - o 아국과 같이 지방의 재정자립도가 낮고, 중앙집권적인 국가에서는 사실상 지방정부가 독자적으로 재원을 확보해서 지원하는 순수한 지방정부보조금은 많지 않을 것으로 생각됨
  - o 반면, 지방정부의 재정자립도가 비교적 높은 수준에 있는 연방국가의 경우 지방정부 보조금을 규제밖에 둘 경우 보조금 규제의 실효성이 약화됨.
  - o 따라서 의장안 제2.1조d 규정상 특정지역이 특정지방정부를 포함하는 것으로 해석된다면, 아국입장과 일치됨

- 아국입장 및 우선순위
  - o (1안) : 의장안 2.1(d) 존속 지지 (적극적 주장은 유보)
  - o (2안) : 반대입장 수용가능

0013

2. 아직까지 논의안된 쟁점 및 아국입장

1) 경미한 보조금에 대한 조사 중단요건 (제11.7조)

- **의장안 내용**

  o 조사당국이 보조금지급 및 피해사실에 관한 충분한 증거가 없다고 판단할 경우에는 즉시 조사신청을 기각하고 조사중단

  o 보조금액, 피보조수입량 및 보조금 지급으로 인한 피해가 경미한 경우에도 즉시 조사중단

  · 보조금액이 경미한 경우 : 보조비율이 [×]% 이하

  · 피보조수입량이 경미한 경우 : 수입국내 유사물품 시장에서의 동 수입 비중이 [Y]% 이하로서, 이들 국가들로부터의 전체수입비중이 동 국내 시장의 [Z]% 이상이 아닌 경우

- **아국입장**

  o 이에 대해서 <u>아직까지 전혀 논의된 바가 없으므로</u> 어느 정도의 수준으로 이들 비율이 결정될 것인지 예측이 곤란하나, 제6.1조 수량기준에 의한 심각한 피해 추정 보조비율이 [5%]에 불과하므로, 이는 매우 낮은 수준이 될 것으로 예상됨

  o 다만, <u>MTN 반덤핑협상에서는 덤핑율이 경미할 경우 조사중단이 논의되고 있는 바, 아국은 4%를 주장</u>하였으나, 미국, EC 등은 동 비율이 지나치게 높음을 이유로 반대하고 있음.

- **아국입장 및 우선순위**

  o <u>경미한 보조 비율</u>

  · (1안): 4%(5) 주장 (MTN 반덤핑협상의 아국입장)

  · (2안): 4%(5) 미만 수용

  o <u>수입비중 기준</u> : 가능한한 높은 수준 지지

  · (1안): 2% 주장

  · (2안): 2% 미만 주장

  o <u>국내시장 점유비중</u> : 가능한한 높은 수준 지지

0014

2) 보호대상 국내산업의 최저생산비율(제16조)

- 의장안 내용

  o 본 협정의 목적상 "국내산업"이라 함은 유사물품의 국내 생산자 전부 또는
  이들 물품의 국내 총생산의 상당부분(major proportion)을 생산하는 생산자
  집단을 의미함

  o 단, 생산자가 피보조물품, 유사물품의 수출자 또는 수입자와 특수관계에
  있거나, 그 자신이 수입자인 경우는 국내산업에서 제외

  o "상당부분"이라 함은 유사물품의 국내총생산의 가액대비, 적어도 [X]%
  이상을 의미함

- MTN 반덤핑협상의 논의

  o 종전 반덤핑 Code에는 major proportion의 정의가 없었으나,
  신협정에서는 수량화된 기준을 채택하기로 하였으며, 아국과 개도국은
  50%를 주장하는데 반해, 미국, EC 등은 이의 하향조정을 주장

- 아국입장

  o 제소권자의 범위를 국내산업의 50%이상인 자로 한정시켜 무분별한 상계관세
  의 제소를 방지함.

  . 세부적인 수치가 논의될 경우 50% 주장

0015

3) 우회수출 판정기준(제21.1조)

- 의장안 내용

    o 본 협정에 의한 상계관계가 부과된 이후

    (ⅰ) 상계관세 대상국으로부터 상계 대상물품을 가공, 조립하기 위한
        부품이 수입되고, 동부품 가액이 조립, 완성된 물품 가액과 동일
        하거나 [×]%를 초과하는 경우 또는

    (ⅱ) 상계관세 대상국으로부터 상계 대상물품을 가공, 조립하기 위한
        부품이 제3국으로 수출되고, 그 제3국이 조립, 완성된 물품을
        다시 수출할 때 부품가액이 조립, 완성된 물품가액과 동일하거나
        [×]%를 초과하는 경우에는

    o 체약국은 본조 제2항과 제3항에 규정된 조건에 따라 제4항과 제5항에
      정해진 조치를 적용할 수 있음

- MTN 반덤핑협상 내용

    o 대상부품이 조립, 완성된 물품가액의 주요비율(predominant
      proportion) [전체부품가액의 (75)%이상]을 차지하고, 이들 부품이 당해
      완성물품을 위한 핵심부품일 것. 단, 조립공정으로 인한 부가가치가
      수입국내에 조립, 완성되는 유사물품의 공장도가격(ex-factory cost)의
      [20]% 이상인 경우에는 조치대상이 아님(제12.1조(v))

    o 아국은 MTN 반덤핑협상에서 90% 주장함.

    o 보조금·상계관세 협상과 반덤핑협상의 규정형태가 상이함을 이유로 상기
      비율 축소를 주장할 경우

        · 보조금협상안은 전체물품가액 기준 당해부품가액 비율

        · 반덤핑협상안은 전체부품가액 기준 당해부품가액 비율

        → 이 경우 낮은 수준으로 절충가능

- 아국입장 및 우선순위

    o (1안): 90% 주장 (MTN 반덤핑협상의 아국입장)
    o (2안): 하향조정 가능

0016

외 무 부

원 본

종 별 :

번 호 : GVW-1410 　　　　　일 시 : 91 0725 1800

수 신 : 장관(통기,재무부,농림수산부,상공부)

발 신 : 주 제네바 대사

제 목 : UR/ 보조금.상계관세 협상

　　　7.24 당지에서 개최된 표제협상 토의 내용 아래 보고함.(엄재무관, 김재무관보,상공부 김사무관참석)

　　　1. 비공식 회의

　　　- 의장은 각국이 관심을 가지고 있거나 우선적으로 다루어져야 할 사항에 대해각국의 의견 개진을 요망하고 동 의견을 기초로 향후 협상을 진행시켜나갈 계획임을 언급함.

　　　- 대부분의 참가국은 브랏셀 회의에 제출된 의장 초안이 향후 협상의 기초가 될수 있다는데 의견을 같이 하였으나 각국별 주요 사안에 대한 의견은 다음과 같음.

　　　0 미국: 허용 보조금 인정은 각국이 보조금 지급경쟁 유발, 제 6조의 수량 기준도입 불가피

　　　0 EC, 일본: 허용 보조금 범위의 제한성, 제6조의 부당성, 개도국 문제, C.V.D 절차등의 추가작업 필요

　　　0 카나다,호주, 뉴질랜드: 보조금 규율과 C.V.D규정과의 긍넝, 제 6조, 제 8조와의 균형

　　　0 스위스, 북구: 허용 보조금과 규제 대상보조금과의 균형, 지방정부 보조금 포함.

　　　0 아국, 싱가폴, 홍콩: 개도국 분류 방식부당(졸업개념 도입반대), 보조금 규율과 C.V.D규정과의 균형 유지, 제 6조의 수량 기준 도입반대, 지방정부 보조금 포함.

　　　0 개도국(인도, 브라질, 이집트 등): 개도국 분류방식 재검토, C.V.D 절차 강화

　　　0 항가리, 폴랜드: 시장경제로의 전환기에 있는 국가에게도 개도국 우대 원칙 적용

　　　- 의장은 칠레등이 지적한 적용범위(COVERAGE)와 관련 동 협정과 농산물등에서의 측정협정은 일반법과 특별법과의 관계와 유사하여 농산물 협상 결과 아무런 협정이 체결되지 아니할 경우에는 동 협정이 모든 물품에 대한 보조금을 규율하며 농산물

통상국　　2차보　　재무부　　농수부　　상공부

PAGE 1 　　　　　　　　　　　　　　　　　91.07.26　07:50 DF
외신 1과 통제관
0017

협정이 체결되어 농산물 보조금에 대한 별도 규정이 있을 경우에는 농산물 보조금은 그 규정에 의한다고 분명히 언급하였으나, EC, 일본은 특정 분야의 협상결과가 불부명한 상황에서 이를 논의하는 것은 적절하지 못함을 주장함.

- 또한 의장은 각국 의견 개진을 기초로하여 9.23주간에 비교적 논란이 적은 부문부터 비공식 협상을 진행할 계획임을 설명함.

2. 공식회의

- 금일 오후 속개된 공식회의에서 의장은 비공식 회의에서 논의된 사항을 간략히보고하면서 9.23 주간에 회의를 속개할 예정임을 언급하고 금번 회의 종료함.
끝

(대사 박수길-국장)

재　　무　　부

관협 22710-4122　　　　　(503-9296)　　　　　1991. 9. 25.

수신　외무부장관

참조　통상국장

제목　UR 보조금·상계관세협상

　　　'91.9.30 - 10.4 간 스위스 제네바에서 개최예정인 표제협상에
당부 대표로 엄낙용 주제네바 대표부 재무관 및 김동진 재무관보를 현지
참석케 하오니 별첨 세부 쟁점별 아국입장의 전달 및 필요조치를 취하여
주시기 바랍니다.

첨부　세부 쟁점별 아국입장 1부. 끝.

재　　무　　부　　장

I. 주요 쟁점사항과 아국입장

1. 미결 쟁점 및 아국입장

쟁점 1) 동 협정의 농산물 보조금 포함여부

- 의장안 내용
  o 언급없음

- 주요국 입장
  o 〈브라질, 미국, 호주, 카나다〉: 동 협정안은 농산물보조금에도 적용됨

  o 〈일본, EC, 북구〉: 농산물보조금 포함 반대 → 농산물 협상그룹에서
     별도로 다룰 것을 주장

- 아국입장 : 농산물 보조금의 포함 반대

  o 농산물협상그룹은 농산물교역과 관련된 모든 측면에 대하여 일차적인
     책임을 지고 있으며 지금까지 본협상과 별도로 논의를 진행시켜 왔으므로,
     농산물 보조금에 대한 논의도 농산물협상그룹에 일임하도록 함.

  o 보조금협상그룹은 농산물협상그룹이 합의한 결과를 수용함으로써, 농산물
     보조금에 대해서도 규율할 수 있음.

0019

쟁점 2) 개도국 우대조치 (제27조)

- 의장안 내용

> o 개도국에게는 금지보조금인 수출보조금을 줄 수 있도록 하되,
>   개도국별로 차별적인 우대
>   · 최빈개도국(Annex7) →   수출보조금 지급허용
>   · 기타개도국(Annex8) →   단계적으로 수출보조금 감축
>   · 한국등 선발개도국 →   수출보조금 지급 금지
>
> o 기타 우대내용 (개도국별 구분없이 일률적인 우대)
>   · 심각한 손상 추정(제6.1조)의 적용을 배제
>   · 아래의 경우 상계조치 불가
>   (a) 소액보조금
>   (b) 수입국의 시장점유율이 일정수준 이하인 품목에 대한 보조금

※ 동조항의 배경

   o 의장안은 선발개도국의 개도국 우대적용 폐지(졸업)를 주장하는 미국입장과
     이에 반대하는 한국등 선발개도국의 주장을 절충한 것임.

- 주요국 입장

   o 〈선발 개도국을 제외한 모든 국가〉: 의장안 찬성
     · 개도국은 경제발전 정도에 따라 국제사회에서의 의무를 분담해야 하며,
       따라서 개도국별 차별대우를 규정한 의장안에 찬성

   o 〈한국, 싱가폴, 말레이지아〉: 의장안 반대
     · 개도국 분류는 각료선언에서 본협상에 위임된 사항이 아님.

0020

- 아국입장

　　< 1안 > : 개도국 분류 반대 → 서면대안 (기제출)

　　　o 개도국 분류는 본 협상에 위임된 사항이 아니며, 이는 보다 전문적인
　　　　기관에 의한 전반적, 객관적 판단을 필요로 함.

　　　o 서면 대안
　　　　. 최저개도국을 제외한 개도국은 일률적으로 일정기간내 수출보조금 폐지
　　　　　약속
　　　　. 다만 동기간 만료시점에 가서 경제개발의 낙후등으로 이를 이행 수 없는
　　　　　국가에 대해서는 기간 연장 허용

　　< 2안 > : 의장안 수용 및 기타개도국 List (Annex 8) 에 아국 포함

　　　o 개도국 분류를 통해 수출보조금 지급 혜택이 박탈되는 국가는 한국·싱가폴·
　　　　말련 등 극소수이므로 개도국 분류반대의 아국등 입장은 선진국이나 후진국
　　　　어느쪽으로 부터도 지지를 받기 힘듬.

　　　o 기타 우대내용의 혜택이라도 적용받는 것이 아국에 실익이 됨.

0021

쟁점 3) 금지보조금의 범위(제3.1조)

- 의장안 내용

---

o 법률상 또는 사실상 수출성과에 따른 보조금 (부속서I의 수출보조금
  목록 포함) 및

o 수입물품 대신 국산물품 사용에 따른 보조금의 지급금지

- 주요국의 입장

  o 〈미국, 일본, 호주, 카나다〉 : 의장안 찬성

    . 미국 : 수입대체 국내보조금 및 일정한 국내보조금도 금지보조금화 주장

  o 〈북유럽, 인도〉 : 의장안 반대 → 국내보조금의 금지화 반대

- 아국입장

  〈 1 안 〉 : 의장안 반대 → 수출보조금만 금지보조금으로 분류

    o 금지보조금은 체약국에 직접 지급금지의무를 부과하므로 수출증대를 통한
      무역왜곡효과가 명백한 보조금에 한정하여야 하며, 따라서 부속서I의 수출
      보조금 목록에 한정하여 금지보조금으로 분류하여야 함.

    o 국내보조금은 국내사회, 경제적 목표달성을 위한 것이며, 이러한 국내보조금
      은 어느정도 수입대체효과를 가질 수 있음.

    o 그러나 이는 국내보조금의 부수적 효과이므로 조치가능보조금으로 분류하여
      타국산업에 불리한 영향시 상계관세부과등 규제하는 것아 타당함

  〈 2 안 〉 : 의장안 수용

0022

쟁점 4) 심각한 손상(Serious prejudice) 추정(제6.1조)

- 의장안 내용

o 다음의 조치가능 보조금은 그 지급만으로 무조건 심각한 손상을 초래
  하는 것으로 간주하여 보조금 지급국이 심각한 손상을 일으키지
  않았음을 입증하지 않는 경우 구제절차에 따라 대응조치함.

  · 물품의 보조금액 비율이 [5]%를 초과하는 보조금
  · 특정산업에서 발생하는 영업손실을 보전하기 위한 보조금
  · 기업의 영업손실을 보전하기 위한 보조금
  · 직접적인 채무감면

※ 동 조항의 배경
  o 의장안은 국내보조금의 금지화를 주장하는 미국입장과 이에 반대하는 EC 등의
    주장을 절충한 것임.

- 주요국의 입장
  o 〈미국〉: 위의 국내 보조금은 금지보조금으로 분류주장.
  o 〈EC · 일본 · 개도국〉: 동 조항은 너무 엄격한 규제임.

- 아국입장

  〈 1 안 〉: 의장안 반대 → 동 조항 삭제
    o 아국은 해당보조금 지급국가에게 과도한 입증책임을 지게하고, 분쟁의 소지를
      제공한다는 이유에서 적극적으로 이에 반대해 왔음.

  〈 2 안 〉: 개도국 List 에 포함시 의장안 수용
    o 심각한 손상추정은 개도국 우대조항에 의해 개도국에는 적용되지 않으므로,
    o 아국이 개도국 List (Annex8)에 포함될 경우 동 규정은 아국에 대해
      적용되지 않음.

0023

쟁점 5) 수량기준 채택여부 (제6.1조 (a))

- 의장안 내용

o 보조금액 비율이 [5]%를 초과할 경우 심각한 손상이 있는 것으로 추정함

- 주요국 입장

  o〈미국, 북구등〉: 보조금 규율강화를 위해서는 채택 필요

  o〈EC, 일본〉: 다른 수단을 통한 보조금 규율강화 주장

- 아국입장

  〈 1 안 〉: 의장안 반대

    o 보조금은 무역효과에 따라서 규제되어야 하는데, 수량기준은 이러한 보조금과
      무역효과간의 상관관계를 무시하는 것이며, 시행상 수출기업에게 심각한
      손상을 끼치지 않았음을 증명해야 하는등 과도한 업무부담을 초래함.

  〈 2 안 〉: 수량기준의 상향조정(20-30%)하여 의장안 수용

    o 개도국 우대조항에 의해 수량기준에 의한 심각한 손상추정은 개도국에게는
      적용되지 않으므로,

    o 수량기준이 채택되더라도 아국이 개도국 분류에 포함될 경우 동 조항은
      적용되지 않음.

0024

- 의장안 내용

o 특정성있는 다음 보조금은 제한된 조건, 특히 수치상한을 두어 허용

· 연구개발보조금 : 기본적인 연구는 소요비용의 [20]% 초과금지

   응용연구개발은 소요비용의 [10]% 초과금지

· 구조조정보조금 : 생산시설의 감축, 폐기위한 비용의 [X]% 초과금지

· 환경보호보조금 : 소요비용의 [20]% 초과금지

· 지역개발보조금 : 전국평균보다 [15]%이상 낙후지역의 개발만 허용

- 주요국 입장

o 〈미 국〉 : 허용보조금의 범위가 지나치게 확대되었음

o 〈개도국〉 : 허용보조금의 요건이 지나치게 엄격함

- 아국입장

〈 1 안 〉 : 수치상한 삭제

o 아국의 경우 연구개발, 구조조정, 지역개발, 환경보호등은 필수적인 것으로 향후

이들 지원사례가 증가할 것을 예상되므로, 가능한 한 허용보조금의 요건을

완화하는 것이 바람직함.

〈 2 안 〉 : 수치상한 상향조정

0025

쟁점 7) 복수의 허용보조금 수혜(제8.5조)

- 의장안 내용

> o 특정기업이 복수의 허용보조금을 수혜할 경우, 단지 한가지 보조금만을
>   허용보조금으로 봄

- 주요국 입장

    o <미   국> : 의장안 찬성

    o <EC,일본> : 의장안 반대 → 독소조항이라 주장

- 아국입장 : 의장안 반대

    o 각 허용보조금은 상당히 제한적인 요건을 충족하는 경우에만 허용되므로,
      한가지 보조금만 허용하는 것은 지나친 제한임

    o 허용보조금은 그 성격상 무역왜곡효과가 없어 허용되는 것이므로,
      중복지급 된다 하더라도 허용보조금의 성질이 변하는 것이 아님

0026

- 의장안 내용

> o 구체적인 계산방법은 각국의 법령에서 정하되 다음 지침에 부합할 것
>
> o 정부의 대출은 당해 대출금리와 상업금리 비교
>
> o 정부의 대출보증은 보증시 대출금리와 보증이 없을시 금리 비교
>
> o 정부에 의한 재화, 용역의 공급 또는 구매의 경우는 시장가격과 비교
> 결정
>
> → 상기 의장안은 수혜자 수익기준(시장가격과 비교)을 채택하고 있음.

※ 수혜자 수익기준 : 기업등이 정부로부터 자금을 조달받는 비용과 공개시장
에서 조달하는 비용간 차이

정부비용기준 : 정부가 부담하게 되는 비용 (예 : 정부의 자금조달이자율 -
대출이자율)

- 주요국 입장

  o 〈미　국〉 : 의장안 원칙적 찬성 → 수혜자 수익기준보다 강화

  o 〈북구, EC, 카나다, 일본〉 : 의장안 반대 → 정부비용 기준

- 아국입장 : 의장안 반대 지지

  〈 1 안 〉 : 정부비용 기준

    o 수익기준은 실제 적용상 적절한 비교대상 시장가격의 파악이 어려움.

    o 반면 정부비용기준은 비용파악이 비교적 용이함.

  〈 2 안 〉 : 의장안 수용

0027

쟁점 9) 지방정부보조금에 대한 규율(제2.1.d조)

- 의장안 내용

o 특정지역내에 있는 기업에게 주는 보조금은 지급기관에 관계없이 특정적인
  것으로 봄.

- 주요국 입장

  o 〈카나다, 호주〉 : 의장안 반대

    · 지방정부가 관할내에 있는 모든 기업에게 지급하는 보조금은 특정성 없음.

  o 〈스위스, 북구〉 : 의장안 찬성 → 지방정부 보조금도 규제

- 아국입장

  〈 1 안 〉 : 의장안 찬성

    o 아국과 같이 지방의 재정자립도가 낮고, 중앙집권적인 국가에서는 사실상
      지방정부가 독자적으로 재원을 확보해서 지원하는 순수한 지방정부보조금은
      많지 않을 것으로 생각됨

    o 지방정부의 재정자립도가 비교적 높은 수준에 있는 연방국가의 경우 지방정부
      보조금을 규제밖에 둘 경우 보조금 규제의 실효성이 약화됨.

  〈 2 안 〉 : 반대입장 수용 가능

    o 아국의 경우 장기적 측면에서 지방자치제의 정착이후, 지방정부의 보조금 활용
      가능성도 고려

0028

2. 아직까지 논의안된 쟁점

- 상계조치와 관련된 절차 및 규정을 명확히 하기 위한 세부적인
  수치를 정하는 사항들

  o 상계조치와 반덤핑조치의 절차 및 규정이 매우 유사한 관계로 현재
    반덤핑협상그룹에서 논의되고 있으며, 그 결과가 도출되는 대로
    보조금·상계관세 협정에 수용될 전망임.

- 기타

1) 상계조치 제소권자인 국내산업 제한(제16조)

- 의장안 내용

  o 상계조치의 제소는 유사물품의 국내총생산액의 [X]% 이상 생산하는

    생산자 집단이 할 수 있음.

- 반덤핑 협상의 논의

  o 아국등 개도국   :   [X]% ⇒ 50% 주장

  o 미국·EC 등   :   50% 하향조정 주장

- 아국입장 : 논의시 반덤핑 협상에서의 아국입장

2) 경미한 보조금등에 대한 조사중단(제11.7조)

- 의장안 내용

  o 다음의 경우 상계조치의 조사 중단

    . 경미한 보조금액   :   보조비율 [X]% 이하

    . 경미한 수입량   :   수입국 시장점유율 [Y]% 이하

- 반덤핑 협상의 논의

  o 아국등 개도국   :   경미한 덤핑율 [X]% ⇒ 5% 주장,
                          시장점유율 [Y]% ⇒ 3% 주장

  o 미국·EC 등   :   하향조정 주장

- 아국입장 : 논의시 반덤핑 협상에서의 아국입장

0029

3) 우회수출 판정기준 (제21.1조)

- 의장안 내용

    o 수입물품에 대해 상계관세가 부과된 이후, 상계관세를 회피하기 위해
       다음과 같은 우회수출시, 우회수출된 부품액이 완성물품액의 [X]%
       이상일 때 규제

        . 수입국내에 부품 반입하여 조립, 가공하여 수출

        . 제3국에서의 조립, 가공을 통한 우회수출

- 반덤핑 협상의 논의

    o 아국등 개도국 : [X]% ⇒ 75% 이상

    o 미국·EC 등   : [X]% ⇒ 40~50%

- 아국입장 : 논의시 반덤핑 협상에서의 아국입장

4) 특정산업 지원제도 (Targeting)

- 미국안으로 의장안에는 포함되어 있지 않음.

  o 보조금이 지급되고

  o 유사품목에 대해 정부의 조정·계획에 의한 아래 관행이 두개이상 시행될 경우

    targeting 존재

    i) 국내시장 보호
    ii) 카르텔 장려 또는 묵인
    iii) 차별적 또는 특혜적인 정부구매관행
    iv) 정부 또는 민간의 투자유도
    v) 수출제한
    vi) 제품 개발 및 상품화에 따른 위험감소를 위한 시장 조작
    vii) 보조금 혜택을 촉진시키기 위한 기타 관행 및 계획

  o 동 targeting 이 5조에 의한 불리한 영향 야기시 상계조치 대상

- 아국 입장

  o 개념이 지나치게 광범위하고, 객관적인 식별방법이 결여되어 있음.

  o 상계조치 남용 초래 가능성 있음

0030

5) 경과조치

- 의장안 내용

  o '90.11.1 이전 시행보조금으로 본 협정에 위배되는 것은

    i) 91.1.1 또는 가능한 한 가장 조속히 위원회에 통보

    ii) 본 협정의 자국 발효일로부터 [5]년 이내에 본 협정에 일치하도록 수정

  o 어떤 체약국도 이들 보조금의 범위확대 또는 199 .1.1 이전 만료후 갱신 불가

- 아국입장

  o 가능한 한 기존보조금 허용기간 [5]년을 확대 연장

0031

Ⅱ. 한·미 양자협의 대책

1. 미결 쟁점에 대한 기존의 양국입장

구 분	의 장 안	미 국	한 국
조치가능 보조금	o 일정 국내보조금의 심각한 손상 추정	o 의장안 찬성	o 의장안 반대
	o 수량기준 채택	o 의장안 찬성	o 의장안 반대
허용보조금	o 일정한 제한하에 4가지 보조금의 지급허용	o 의장안보다 엄격 한 제한 주장	o 의장안 제한조건 완화 주장
	o 복수의 허용보조금 수혜 금지	o 의장안 찬성	o 의장안 반대
개도국 우대조치	o 개도국의 구분 및 차별	o 의장안 찬성	o 의장안 반대
보조금액 산정기준	o 원칙적으로 수혜자 수익기준(시장가격과 비교) 채택	o 시장가격에 의한 수익기준 강화 주장	o 정부 비용개념 기준 채택
국내산업의 정 의	o 유사물품의 국내 총생산 액의 [X]%이상 생산하는 생산자 집단	o 50% 이하의 하향 조정	o [X]%가 50% 주장
농산물 보조금 포함여부	언급 없음.	o 동 협정안은 농산물 보조금에 도 적용 주장	o 농산물 보조금은 농산물 협상그룹 에서 별도 규정 주장

2. 쟁점별 아국의 협상대책

가. 기본입장

- 보조금 상계협상이 재개되는 초기단계이므로 아국의 수정입장 제시는 시기
  적으로 적절치 않음 → 기존입장 고수
- 그러나 세부쟁점에 대한 논의가 구체화될 경우, 동 협상타결에 적극적으로
  노력하고 있다는 인식을 줄수 있도록 수정입장 제시
  - o 아국의 심대한 경제적 이해가 걸린 분야는 관철
  - o 아국입장 관철 불가능한 분야 및 아국에의 영향이 적은 분야는 타 쟁점과
    trade-off 하여 수용

0032

나. 쟁점별 아국의 협상대책

(1) 양보할 수 없는 쟁점

쟁 점	기존입장	향후입장	고수이유

o 농산물보조금의
  동협정 적용
	반 대
	
	⇒ 농산물보조금은
	  농산물 협상그룹
	  결과 수용
		기존입장 고수	o 농산물보조금
			  적용시 아국농업
			  정책이 극도로
			  제한됨.

o 허용보조금의
  중복지급 금지
	반 대	기존입장 고수	o 향후 보조금 활용
			  가능성 높음

o 국내산업의 정의	50% 주장	기존입장 고수	o 자의적인 상계관
			  세 제소에 따른
			  수출업계의 손해
			  방지

(2) bargaining 할 수 있는 쟁점

쟁 점	기존입장	향후입장	수정이유

o 허용보조금의
  제한조건
	제한조건 완화
	
	⇒ 수치한도내용
	  삭제
		제한조건 완화
		
		⇒ 수치한도 상향
		  조정
			o 아국입장 관철
			  불가능

o 심각한 손상의
  추정
	반 대
	
	⇒ 동조항(6.1) 삭제
		수 용	o 개도국 우대규정
			  에 의해 아국에
			  대해서는 적용안됨

o 수량기준채택문제	반 대
	
	⇒ 동조항(6.1.a)
	  삭제
		기준 상향조정하여
		수용
		(5%→20~30%)
			o 개도국 우대규정
			  에 따라 아국에
			  대해서는 적용
			  안됨.

o 선발개도국 차별
  취급
	반 대	부속서 8에 아국
		포함
			o 아국입장 관철
			  불가능

o 보조금액 산정기준	수익기준 채택반대
	⇒ 정부비용 기준
	  채택 주장
		수익기준 수용	o 아국입장 관철
			  불가능

0033

발 신 전 보

번 호 : WGV-1292 910926 1757 FO 종별 :

수 신 : 주 제네바 대사. 총영사)

발 신 : 장 관 (통 기)

제 목 : UR/보조금.상계관세

1. 9.30-10.4간 귀지에서 개최되는 규범제정 분야 협상 관련, 보조금.상계관세 분야 협상에는 관계부처 사정상 본부대표 파견이 어려우니 귀관 관계관이 참석토록 조치바람.

2. 보조금.상계관세 분야 쟁점별 세부입장 자료는 규범제정 분야 협상에 참가할 상공부 직원이 지참하니 동 자료에 따라 적의 대처바람.   끝.

(통상국장 대리 최 혁)

앙 고 재	기안자 성명	과 장	국 장	차 관	장 관	보 안 통 제
						외신과통제

외 무 부

종 별 :

번 호 : GVW-1933　　　　　　　　　일 시 : 91 1007 1800

수 신 : 장 관(통기,경기원,재무부,상공부)

발 신 : 주 제네바 대사

제 목 : UR/보조금 상계관세 비공식 협의

　　　당지서 10.2-10.3 에 걸쳐 MACIEL 협상 그룹 의장의 사회로 개최된 표제 요지 아래 보고함(엄재무관,재무부 최사무관 참석)

　　　가. 협상 초안 28조 경과기간에 대하여 호주는 5년을 제의하였고 대부분 국가가동의하였으나 미국과 EC 는 지나치게 장기간이라는 이유로 유보 견해를 표명함.

　　　나. 29조 시장경제 전환국에 대한 특별조치와 관련하여 항가리가 별첨 서면제안을 제출하였는바 많은 개도국들은 동 사항이 개도국 우대 문제와 연계하여 검토하여야 함을 주장하였음.

　　　다. 1 A조 NEW PRACITICES 에 관하여 미국은 TARGETING 보조금과 같은 효과가 있으므로 규제되어야 한다고 주장한데 대하여 일본은 구체성이 없으므로 논의가 어렵다고 반박하였고 미국은 조속히 문안을 작성 제출하겠다고하였음.

　　　라. 2.1조 본문 및 14조(D), (E)항 관련 영토적 적용문제에 대하여 멕시코는 동 조항이 자국의자원을 다른나라에 개방하게끔 강제하는 부작용을 가질 수 있다고 주장한 데 대하여 브라질, 인도등이 동의하였으며 미국은 동 조항들이 정부당국에 의한 특혜적 구매 또는 공급으로 제 3국 수출자에 불이익을 초래하는 것을 방지하는 취지라고 답변 함.

　　　마. 3. 1조 A항 각주 1의 사실상수출 보조금과 관련하여 호주, 싱가폴은 동 개념이 너무 광범위하게 적용되어 국내 보조금도 같은 제약을 받을 우려가 잇사고 주장 하였으며 미국, EC등은 우회적 조치에 대한 우려때문에 법적보조금에 국한 시킬 수 없다고 반대하였음.

　　　바. 3.1조 B항 수입대체 보조금과 관련하여 호주,브라질, 이집트등은 삭제를 주장하였으며 미국, 일본, 카나다는 동 보조금이 갓트 3조 위반이므로 동 조항을 유지하여야 한다고 주장하였음.

통상국　　2차보　　경기원　　재무부　　상공부

사. ANNEX 1 의 H항 및 I 항 관련 인도는 자본재 및 서비스 수입등도 포함될 수있도록 하여야 한다고 주장하였는 바 미국, EC 는 현행 규정의 유지가 바람직하다고 반대 하였음. K 항의 OECD수출 금유 규정과 관련하여 인도는 이를 별도취급할 수없다고 주장하였으며 미국, EC 는 그예의 취급이 필요하다고 반대함. 동 제도의 갓트 봉보와 관련하여 미국은 조속히 이를 갓트에 공식 봉보하겠다고 발언하였음.

아. ANNEX 8 의 운영방법을 위한 별도 협의가 갓트사무국 MS ENDERS 의 사회로 이루어 졌는바 사무국측은 별첨안의 기술적 논의사항을 배포하였음.

- 싱가폴은 이와 관련한 필요 정보의 취득, 계산방법 보조금의 정량화등의 기술적 어려움을 언급하였으며 EC 는 보조금의 통지 의무가 있기때문에 본 협정이 성립되면 기술적 방법도 함께 결정할 수 있다고 하였음.

- 아국은 사무국안중 수출보조금 비율산정을 위한 대안으로 제시된 평균치 산정방식 (대안 1,2)는 협정초안 27.2조 B 항에 개별 품목에 대하여 보조금 비율을 규율토록 되어있는 규정과 위배되므로 대안이 될 수 없다고 주장하였는바 EC 는 대안 3은 너무 복잡하여 운영이 곤란하므로 해석에 신축성을 두어 평균개념을 도입할 수 있도록 하는 것이 필요하다고 발언함.

- 아국은 싱가폴, 말레이지아등과 동 사항과 관련동 회의이후 별도로 모임을 갖고 개도국 졸업개념의 도입이 정치적인 이유뿐 아니라 기술적인 이유로도 시행이 불가함을 설득하기 위한 논리의 개발 및 대안제시의 검토등이 필요하다는점에 합의하고 10.7. 이를 위하여 다시 협의를 갖기로 하였음.

첨부: 1. 제 29조 항가리 제안 1매

2. ANNEX 8 사무국 기술적 토의 자료 2매

(GVW(F)-0392). 끝

(대사 박수길-국장)

$GVW(Ħ)-03/2$ //007 /800

" $GVW-$ /P33 첨부"

Hungary
3.10.91

Part IX: Transitional arrangements

Article 29

Signatories in the process of transformation into a market,
free enterprise economy may apply measures inconsistent with
other provisions of this Agreement but necessary for such a
transformation. Such measures and programmes are included into
their respective Annexes.[1]

Footnote to Article 29

1/ An actionable programme or measure included in the Annex
becomes non-actionable for the period defined in the Annex.

Explanatory comments

Such Annexes will be agreed upon with other signatories and
enclosed to the agreement before its entering into force. The
measures and programmes included in the Annexes may be applied
during a transitory period of (X) years.

The necessary transparency will be ensured by detailed annual
notifications to the Committee by signatories invoking Article
29 on their respective measures and programmes.

0037

Annex VIII-Technical issues

Determination of the initial export subsidy rate or [x]

The replacement of the [x] with a precise figure for each country listed in Annex VIII first requires a definition of export subsidy rate. Options include:

(i) "the quantum of all export subsidies granted on a country's exports, divided by the value of those exports";

(ii) "the average of export subsidy rates granted to individual products weighted by their trade shares in exports";

(iii) "a schedule of export subsidy rates granted to individual products".

The second issue concerns the manner in which the [x] is determined for each country. Options include:

(i) the actual rate of export subsidization by a country;

(ii) the average of actual rates of export subsidization by countries apart from/including Note 1 countries;

(iii) a uniform rate agreed by the signatories.

The option of the actual rate of export subsidization applied by a country raises a number of technical issues, including:

(i) Base year;

(ii) Notification procedures;

(iii) A method for assessing the value of different types of export subsidy programs (such as those listed in Annex I);

(iv) Technical assistance;

(v) Verification or counternotification procedures;

(vi) A role for the Committee in deciding differences between notifications and counternotifications.

./.   0038

1

The option of an average rate based on actual rates requires that the exercise described above be completed in order to proceed to a computation of the average. A uniform rate requires no notification exercise.

Export competitiveness in a product (Note 2)

The first issue concerns the criterion for export competitiveness in a product. The text currently reads:

"Export competitiveness in a product consists of a country's exports of that product having reached a share of at least [4] per cent in world exports of that product."

and the issue is whether the [4] should be replaced with another figure.

The second issue concerns the definition of product, bearing in mind the availability of data. The text currently reads:

"For the purpose of Annex VIII, a product is defined as a Section heading of the Harmonized System nomenclature".

In the Harmonized System, there are four levels of aggregation to choose from:

(i) Section (21 product categories);

(ii) Chapter or 2-digit (97 product categories);

(iii) Heading or 4-digit (1241 product categories);

(iv) Sub-heading or 6-digit (5019 product categories).

Data at the Section, Chapter and Heading levels will be available beginning in calendar year 1992. Data at the Sub-heading level will be available beginning in calendar year 1993 as the implementation of the Harmonized System is completed.

0033

외 무 부

종 별 :

번 호 : GVW-1936   일 시 : 91 1008 1200

수 신 : 장 관(통기, 경기원, 재무부, 상공부, 농수부)

발 신 : 주 제네바 대사

제 목 : UR/보조금.상계관세 개도국 우대 관련 대아세안 업무협의

연: GVW-1933

연호 제 아 항과 관련, 당관 엄 재무관은 싱가폴 대표부에서 싱가폴, 말레이지아, 태국등 아세안 국가들과 상호 협조 방안을 논의하고 아래사항에 대하여 잠정적으로협의하였는바, 본부의견 회시 바람.

가. 차기 협상 그룹의 ANNEX 8 관련 기술적협의를 위한 회의(10.10 예정)에서는아국이 사무국 초안(GVW(F)-0392)에 대하여 평균 개념의 도입이 불가한 법률적 논리를 설명하고 싱가폴이 개별 품목의 보조금 비율 산정이 사실상 기술적으로 불가능하다는 것을 주장하기로 하였음.

나. 위와 같은 주장을 통하여 개도국 재분류가 사실상 시행 불가능한 방안임을 설득하고 이에 대한 대안을 말레이지아가 아래와 같은 내용으로 준비하여 비공식 문서로 제출키로 함.

- 개도국별 구분없이 일정기간(예: 8년) 경과후부터 수출 보조금의 상한선을 설정하여 일율 적용함.

- 협정 초안 ANNEX 중 NOTE 2 의 세계수출 시장 점유율에 의한 특별 대우 적용배제는 이를 긍정적으로 반영함.

- 현행 협정 14조 5항의 개도국 약속 노력 조항을 개도국 의무로 포함시키는 것을 검토함.

다. 위와 같은 입장의 관철이 어려운 때에는수시로 협의하여 대처방안을 모색함.끝

(대사 박수길-국장)

통상국   2차보   경기원   재무부   농수부   상공부

PAGE 1   91.10.08   23:39 FO

川

제

관협 22710-446   (503-9296)   1991. 10. 10.

제목   개도국 관세적 양허시의 수수관련 품목에 관한 대처

보조금.상계관세 분야의 '91.10.10 정을 전 최종안 작성을 위하여
6 개고과의 공동보고를 취하여 개도국 분류의 양태를 추선하고자 하는
 내 사안가 개요부안의 별성과 같이 완성하오니 후 저녁 귀부적의 검토의
 그에 대하을 통보하여 주시기 바랍니다.

첨부   개도국 분야의 양허시의 수계안 및 가부의 검토자료 1부. 끝.

재   무   부   상   관

관세국장

개도국 분류에 있어서의 아세안국가와의 공동대처

목 적

o '91.10.10(목) UR 보조금·상계관세협상(기술적 협의회의)에서의 공동대처

- 기술적 협의대상 내용(10.2 보조금·상계관세협상에서 배포 및 토의)

　o Annex8(기타 개도국)의 Initial Export Subsidy 계산방법에 대한 3가지
　　Option중 선택문제

　　① [x]% = $\dfrac{\text{수출보조금 총액}}{\text{수출총액}}$ (평균 수출보조율)

　　② [x]% = 평균 수출보조율(시장점유율을 고려한 개별품목의 가증평균)

　　③ 개별품목별 수출보조율

　⇒ 아국은 10.2 회의에서 Option ①, ②의 평균수출보조율은 협정안 27.2조
　　B항에서 개별품목에 대해 보조금 비율을 규율하는 규정과 위배되므로 대안이
　　될 수 없다고 주장
　　EC는 Option ②은 너무 복잡하여 운영이 곤란하므로 해석에 신축성을 두어
　　평균개념을 도입할 수 있도록 하자고 주장

- 주제네바대표부의 본부의견 회신요청 내용

　┌──────────────────────────────────────┐
　│ o 아세안 6개국과 공동보조를 취하여 개도국 분류 반대 │
　└──────────────────────────────────────┘

대처방계

　o 아국은 직전회의에서와 같이 수출보조금 계산방법에서 평균개념도입 불가능
　　주장(Option ①, ② 반대)

　o 상기품은 개별품목의 보조금비율 선정이 사실상 불가능함 주장(Option ③
　　채택 기술상 불가)

0042

ㅇ 2단계

o 이와 같은 주장을 통하여 개도국 분류가 사실상 시행불가능한 방안임을 설득

o 말레이지아가 비공식 문서로 서면대안 제출

> 개도국별 구분없이 일정기간(예:3년) 경과후부터 수출보조금의 상한선
> 설정하여 적용

ㅇ 기타

o Annex8의 Note 2의 세계수출 시장점유율이 [4]%이상인 물품에 대해서는

   개도국우대 내용(수출보조금의 지급허용)이 적용되지 않도록 하는 규정에는

   양보가능한 것으로 입장 정립

o 기존 보조금·상계관세협정의 개도국 조항중 14조 5항의 개도국 약속노력

   조항을 개도국 의무로 조정하여 협정안에 포함시키는 것을 검토키로 함.

   ※ 14조 5항 규정

      개발도상 서명국은 수출보조금의 지급이 경쟁과 개발 필요성에 상응

      하지 않을때는 동 수출보조금을 감축하거나 제거한다는 약속을 제시

      하도록 노력하여야 한다.

o 위와 같은 입장관철이 어려울시에는 수시로 협의하여 공동대처 방안을

   모색함.

검토의견

o 개도국 분류에 대해 아세안국가와 공동대처하여 반대한다는 것은 아국의

   협상력 제고를 위해 바람직함.

o 개도국 분류반대에 따른 서면대안 내용도 아국이 기제출한 서면대안과

   유사하므로 제네바대표부안에 찬성함.

   ※ 기존의 아국 서면대안

      · 최저개도국을 제외한 개도국은 일률적으로 일정기간내 수출보조금
        폐지를 약속

      · 다만 동기간 만료시점에 가서 경제개발의 낙후 등으로 이를 이행할
        수 없는 국가에 대해서는 기간연장 허용.

0043

발 신 전 보

분류번호	보존기간

번   호 : WGV-1355   911010 1351 FO   종별 : 지급

수   신 : 주   주 제네바 대사. 총영사

발   신 : 장 관 (통 기)

제   목 : UR/보조금.상계관세 협상

대 : GVW-1936,1933

개도국 분류에 대해 아세안 국가와 공동 대처하여 반대하는 것은 아국의 협상력 제고에 도움이 되며, 대호 아세안 국가와의 협의 내용도 아국이 기제출한 서면 대안과 유사하므로 대호로 추진바람.   끝.   (통상국장 김 용 규)

보 안 통 제	

앙고재	91년 10월 18일	통기과	기안자 성명 송봉헌	과 장		국 장	차 관	장 관	외신과통제

외 무 부

종 별 :

번 호 : GVW-1975   일   시 : 91 1011 1900

수 신 : 장관(봉기,경기원,재무부,상공부,농림수산부)

발 신 : 주제네바대사

제 목 : UR/보조금,상계관세 협상 개도국 분류문제

　　　협의연: GVW-1933(GVW(F)-0392)

　　가. 당관 엄재무관은 10.10 갓트 ENDERS담당관과 만난 연호에 첨부된 사무국
토의자료에 관하여 논의하였음. 아측은 수출보조금의 정의와 관련하여 대안 1 및 대안
2에 제시된 방법이 동 협정초안 27.2(B) 항과 상치됨을 설명하였는바 동 담당관은
이를 납득하고 동토의 자료를 다시 작성키로 하였음. 기술적 사항으로 토의될 대상은
(X), 즉 최초기준 수출 보조비율 산출방식에 국한토록하고 개도국의 의무 이행여부를
검토할 수출 보조비율은 27.2(B)항에 따라 각 개별 수출 품목별로 계산되어야 하는
것을 명백히 하기로 함. 새로 작성될 자료에 의한 기술적 토의는 10.14.개최될예정임.

　　나. 아측은 동 협의후 싱가폴 대표와 별도로 협의를갖고 이러한 토의 자료의
수정이 개도국 재분류제안의 기술적 문제점을 부각시키는데 도움이 될 것이라는데
의견을 같이하였음.싱가폴측은 10.14.회의에서 동 제안이 사실상 시행하기 어렵다는
점을최대한 주장하겠다고 함.

　　다. 아측은 10.11. 브라질 대표부에서 개최된 개도국간의 보조금 상계관세
협상평가협회에 참석하여 위의 개도국 재분류 문제에 관하여 모든 개도국들이 보다
봉일되고 강력한 의견을 주장할것을 촉구하였음. 동 회의에는 인도, 이집트,멕시코,
콜롬비아, 아르헨티나,태국, 말레이지아등이 참석하여 협정초안에 대한 자국관심
사항등의 의견을 교환하였는바 종래 회의에서 주장되어 오던 개도국들의 입장이 반복
표명되었음.끝

　　(대사 박수길-국장)

통상국　　2차보　　경기원　　재무부　　농수부　　상공부

PAGE 1   91.10.12   07:04 FN

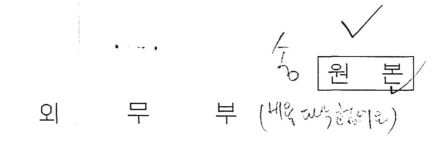

외　무　부 （비밀　때까지해야오）

종　별 :

번　호 : GVW-2004　　　　　　　　　　일　시 : 91 1015 1800

수　신 : 장 관(봉기, 경기원, 재무부, 상공부, 농림수산부)

발　신 : 주 제네바 대사

제　목 : UR/보조금, 상계관세 협상 개도국 분류문제협의

　　연: GVW-1975

　　10.14(월) 갓트 사무국 ENDERS 담당관 주재로개최된 표제 문제 비공식 협의 내용아래보고함. (엄재무관, 김재무관보 참석)

　　가. 사무국은 수정 토의자료(별첨)를 배포하고설명함.

　　나. 아국, 싱가폴, 말레이지아는 새 토의자료가 ANNEXVIII 에 게기될 최초 보조금 비율을 산출하는OPTION 을 열거하고 있으나 이는 협정 초안 27.2조에 따른 개별 품목별 보조금 비율 산출 및의무이행 여부 확인이 기술적으로 가능한가와 연계하여 검토되어야 하며, OPTION 2 에 따른 최초보조금 산출에 있어서도 실제로 계산함에있어서 는 기간, 단위당 가격 계산을 위한 수출수량 및 수출 단위, 각종 다양한 보조제도의 수량화 문제등 많은 기술적인 어려운 문제가 있으며, 이러한 계산을 하기 위해 각 서 명국이 모든정보를 위원회에 통보하여야 하고 위원회가 시의적절하게 개별 품목별로 보조비율을 계산해야 하는바, 이러한 작업이 실제로 가능할 지에 강한의문을표시하였음.

　　다. 이씨는 상기 논지는 TEXT 규정중 수량화를 전제로하는 모든 조문(예 6.1 조등)에 해당하는것이며 이러한 논지로 수량화가 불가능하다면 협정의 설립이 불가능하며, 결국 협정의 설립 시행이 불가능하다는 주장은 기술적 토의 사항이 아닌 정책적 결정사항이라 언급한바, 아국, 싱가폴은 본협의는 27.2 조(B) 및 ANNEX VIII 의 기술적문제 점을 검토하는 것인바, 동 개도국 분류제도의 기술적 시행 가능성을 살펴보지도 않고형식 논리적인 규정을 제정하는 것은 매우 우려할일이라고 지적함.

　　라. 이집트, 파키스탄은 OPTION 2(A) 가 선택 가능한안이라 주장하고 인도는 OPTION 중 OPTION 2(A) 가 비교적 좋은 안이나 이도 여러가지 기술적인 문제가 있음을 언급하였는바, 아측은 사무국 토의 자료에의한 각 OPTION 은 개도국 수출 보조금

통상국　2차보　2차보　구주국　청와대　안기부　경기원　재무부　농수부
상공부

PAGE 1　　　　　　　　　　　　　　　　　　91.10.16　　05:00 FN

　　　　　　　　　　　　　　　　　　　　　외신 1과 통제관
　　　　　　　　　　　　　　　　　　　　　　　　　　0046

비율의 상한 수준을 정하는 정책적 사안이며, 단순한기술적 사항이 아님을 환기시킴.

　마. 의장은 상기 논의 사항을 규범제정 협상그룹에 보고 예정이라 하고 토의를 종결함.

　첨부: 사무국 OPTION PAPER 1부. 끝

　(GVW(F)-415)

　(대사 박수길-국장)

$Guw.31 - 415$ $11015 1800$
$Guw - 2004$ 전반

Agenda 14 October 1991

1. Determination of the initial export subsidy rate or [x]

<u>Option 1</u>

A uniform or ceiling rate agreed by signatories.

<u>Option 2</u>

The actual rate of export subsidization by a country.

<u>Option 3</u>

The average of actual rates of export subsidization by countries.

2. Calculation of initial rate of export subsidization for Options 2 and 3

For Option 2, the actual rate of export subsidization may be interpreted as either (a) the overall rate of export subsidization, in which case the [x] would be replaced with a single figure; or (b) the rate of export subsidization of individual products, in which case the [x] would be replaced by figures corresponding to products.

In (a), a method for the calculation of the initial export subsidy is:

"the quantum of all export subsidies granted on exports of a country, divided by the total value of exports".

In (b), a calculation of the rate of export subsidization on a product could be obtained as:

"the quantum of all export subsidies granted on exports of a product, divided by the value of exports of that product".

For Option 3, the rates of export subsidization applied by countries on an overall basis ((a) above), are added up and divided by the number of countries. Therefore, only a method to calculate the initial export subsidy rate on an overall basis is required, namely:

"the quantum of all export subsidies granted on exports of a country, divided by the total value of exports".

1

2-1

0048

3. **Notification procedures for Options 2 and 3**

    (i) Base year;

    (ii) Method for assessing the value of different export subsidy
programmes (such as those listed in Annex I);

    (iii) Technical assistance.

4. **Other business**

2

0049

외 무 부

종 별 :

번 호 : GVW-2068　　　　　　　　　일 시 : 91 1021 1130

수 신 : 장관(통기,경기원,재무부,농림수산부,상공부)

발 신 : 주제네바대사

제 목 : UR/보조금.상계관세 개도국 협의

연: GVW-2004

　　가. 당관 엄재무관은 동 협상분야 싱가폴 협상담당자와 함께 10.17.갓트사무국 WOZNOWSKI 갓트규범국장 및 ENDERS 담당관을 접촉하였는바 이들 사무국 관계자들은현협 정초안 ANNEX VIII에 의한 개도국 분류 대우가 기술적으로 많은 어려움이있다는 점에 개인적인 공감을 표시하고 이에대한 가능한 대안을 문의하였음. 아울러 여타 개도국들과의 공감대를 넓혀가는 것이 바람직하다는 의견이 있었음.

　　나. 또한 아측과 싱가폴은 10.18 브라질 대표부에서 개최된 보조금 협상분야 개도국간 협의에참석하여 아측이 준비한 협상초안 27.2조 및 ANNEXVIII 에 대한(별첨)을 배포하고 여타 개도국들의공동보조 필요성을 설득하였음.

　　이에대해 브라질, 말레이지아, 태국 ,파키스탄,알젠등은 공감을 표시하였으나 인도는 소극적 입장이었음. 동 회의에서는 본건 이외에 2조,3.1조, 14조, ANNEX I 등이 함께 논의되었는바 당일 협의 참가국간의 공동제안등은 시기적으로 불가능하지만 금명간 작성될 의장 TEXT 에 가능한 개도국 의견을 반영하기 위하여 노력하기로 함. 이의 일환으로 내주중 브라질측이 MACIEL 의장과 관심 개도국 협상 담당자간의협의를 주선하기로 하였음.

　　첨부: 27.2 조 및 ANNEX VII, VIII 에 대한대안(아국 배포)

　　(GVW(F)-0431) 끝

　　(대사 박수길-국장)

통상국　　2차보　　경기원　　재무부　　농수부　　상공부

91.10.22　　07:48 DU

외신 1과 통제관

0050

27.2 Accordingly, this Agreement shall not prevent developing country signatories from adopting measures and policies to assist their industries, including those in the export sector. In particular, the commitment of Article 3 shall not apply to developing country signatories referred to in Annex VII. The commitment of Article 3 shall not apply to other developing country signatories for 10 years from the date of entry into force of this Agreement. If subsidies are still deemed necessary beyond this period of time, the developing country in question shall enter into consultation with the Committee, which will determine whether an extension is justified after examining indicators of the country including per capita GNP, economic growth rates and balance of payments position. If the developing country obtains an extension, it will hold periodic consultations with the Committee every 3 years to determine the necessity of maintaining the subsidies. If the Committee determines that the subsidies are no longer warranted, the developing country should bring these subsidies which are inconsistent with Article 3 into conformity with the provision within 3 years of the date of the decision of the Committee.

Annex VII, as developing country signatories to whom the commitment of Article 3 shall not be applied, countries whose GNP per capita has not reached $1,000 per annum are to be listed in addition to the least-developed country signatories.

Annex VIII, to be deleted.

0051

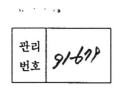

외　무　부

종　별 :

번　호 : GVW-2086　　　　　　　　　　　일　시 : 91 1022 1730

수　신 : 장관(봉기, 경기원, 재무부, 농림수산부, 상공부)

발　신 : 주 제네바대사

제　목 : UR 분야별 협상대책(규범제정그룹-보조금,상계관세 분야)

　　연: GVW-2083

　　1. 주요쟁점

　　가. 허용보조금의 범위와 국내 보조금 규제 강화

　　- 미국은 현 협상 초안중 허용 보조금의 범위가 너무 광범위하다고 주장

　　- EC 는 허용보조금의 범위는 수량기준의 도입등을 통한 국내보조금 규제 강화와 균형을 이루고 있는 것이므로 양자를 연계하여 검토할 것을 주장

　　나. 협상 COVERAGE

　　- 케언즈그룹 등은 동 협정이 농산물에도 적용되는 일반협정임을 주장

　　- EC, 일본, 아국등은 농산물 보조금은 농산물 협상에서 다룰 것을 주장

　　다. 개도국 재분류 문제

　　- 수출 보조금 허용과 관련하여 개도국을 소득수준등 기준으로 5 등급으로 재분류

　　- EC 등 선진국 및 여타 개도국 지지, 아국, 싱가폴등은 개도국 재분류에 반대

　　2. 협상 진전 상황

　　가. 허용보조금과 국내 보조금 규제를 둘러싼 미국과 EC 간의 대립이 심각하여 동 분야 협상 타결이 관건이 되고 있으나 양국간의 가시적인 협상 진전이 이루어 지지 않고 있음

　　나. 그동안 MACIEL 의장 주재회의에서는 이러한 핵심분야를 제외하고 기술적 사항의 토의만 이루어졌으며 미국, EC 간의 조속한 입장 타결을 기다리고 있는 분위기임

　　다. 개도국 재분류 문제에 대하여는 수차례 기술적 토의가 있었는바 아국, 싱가폴 등의 꾸준한 설득으로 그 기술적 문제점에 대한 갓트 사무국 및 일부 개도국들의 공감을 얻어가고 있으나, EC, 일본, 인도, 이집트등이 아국등의 견해에 계속 반대하고

통상국	장관	차관	1차보	2차보	구주국	경제국	외정실	분석관
청와대	안기부	경기원	재무부	농수부	상공부			

PAGE 1

있음

3. 전망 및 대책

가. 미국과 EC 의 입장 대립으로 동 분야도 협상타결이 어려운 하나로 인식되고 있으나 양국의 입장은 농산물 협상에서의 진전상황과 매우 밀접한 연관을 갖고 있다고 보여짐. 그러나 양국간의 절충이 허용보조금등에 대한 현 협상 초안을 크게 변경하게 되지는 않을 것이라는 것이 일반적 관측임. 또한 상계관세 분야의 많은 부분은 반덤핑 협상의 결과가 반영되어질 것임

나. 현 협정 초안에 대하여 유보적인 견해를 갖고 있는 다수 개도국 및 호주등은 자국 의견 반영을 위한 협정안 수정을 주장하고 있으나 11 월중 DUNKEL 의장의 REV 2 에 포함될 동 협정초안은 미국, EC 간의 명확한 합의가 없는한 현 골격을 대부분 그대로 유지하게 될 것이라는 지배적 견해임

다. 아국은 허용 보조금 중복 지급, 심각한 피해의 추정, 보조금액 산정 기준등의 쟁점과 관련하여 여타 개도국 등과 공동 보조로 현 협정초안의 개선을 도모하는 동시에 개도국 재분류 문제에 대하여는 그 정치적 의미 특히 농산물 협상에의 파급 우려등을 감안하여 이를 삭제할 수 있도록 최대한의 협상력을 집중토록 할것임. 끝

(대사 박수길-국장)

예고:91.12.31. 까지

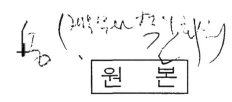

외 무 부

원 본

종   별 : 지   급

번   호 : GVW-2096

일   시 : 91 1022 2000

수   신 : 장관(봉기,경기원,재무부,농림수산부,상공부)

발   신 : 주제네바대사

제   목 : UR/보조금 상계관세협상 개도국 우대문제사무국 협의

연: GVW-2068

가. 당관 엄재무관은 10.22.갓트 사무국 WOZNOWSKI 갓트 규범 국장을 접촉하고연호를 별첨 송부한 아국대안(GVW(F)-0431) 및 27.3 수정대안(현TEXT ANNEX VIII, NOTE 2를 반영한 것)을 제시하고 이에 대하여 협의하였음.

나. 동 국장은 아국대안에 대하여 다음과 같은 수정이 이루어지면 보다 설득력있는 대안이 될 것이라는 의견을 제시하였음.

- 3조에 대한 예외보다는 3.1(A)에 대한 예외에국한 시킴

- 최저 개도국 이외의 개도국에 대한 최초 면제기간은 10년 대신 8년으로 함

- 연장 협의시 검토 대상으로 경제지표 보다는경제적 필요성이 적절함

- 연장이 불허된 경우 3년간을 단순 조정기간 대신 감축기간으로 규정함

다. 아측과 동국장은 아국의 대안을 토의 자료형식으로 10.23.규범 제정 협상 그룹 회의를 즈음하여 관심 국가에 사전 배포하고 금주말 또는 내주초 이를 협의하기 위한 회의를 갖는 것을 잠정 합의하였는바 이에대한 본부 의견이 있을경우 회시 바람.

첨부: 토의자료(안)(GVW(F)-0438).끝

(대사 박수길-국장)

통상국   1차보   경기원   재무부   농수부   상공부

PAGE 1

91.10.23   08:10 DU

외신 1과   통제관

0054

GVW (石) - 0438   //022 2000
                            // GVW-2076 첨부,

KOREA
23 October 1991

DISCUSSION PAPER ON SUBSIDIES AND COUNTERVAILING MEASURES

PART VIII Developing Countries
Article 27
Special and differential treatment for developing countries

27.2 Accordingly, this Agreement shall not prevent developing country signatories from adopting measures and policies to assist their industries, including those in the export sector. In particular, the commitment of Article 3.1(a) shall not apply to developing country signatories referred to in Annex VII. The commitment of Article 3.1(a) shall not apply to other developing country signatories for [8] years from the date of entry into force of this Agreement. If subsidies are still deemed necessary beyond this period of time, the developing country in question shall enter into consultation with the Committee, which will determine whether an extension is justified after examining economic and financial needs of the country including per capita GNP, economic growth rates and balance of payments position. If the developing country obtains an extension, it will hold periodic consultations with the Committee every year to determine the necessity of maintaining the subsidies. If no such determination is made by the Committee, the developing country shallphase out these subsidies which are inconsistent with Article 3.1(a) within [3] years from the end of the last authorized period.

Annex VII, as developing country signatories to whom the commitment of Article 3.1(a) shall not be applied, countries whose GNP per capita has not reached $1,000 per annum are to be listed in addition to the least-developed

0055

country signatories.

Annex VIII, to be deleted.

27.3, Provisions of Article 4 shall not apply to developing country signatories during the period set forth in Article 27.2. However, it is recognized that a country that has reached export competitiveness in products shall be bound by the provisions of Article 3.1(a) for those products. Export competitiveness in a product consists of a country's exports of that product having reached a share of at least [4] percent in world exports of that product. Export competitiveness shall exist either (a) on the basis of notification by the country having reached export competitiveness, or (b) on the basis of a computation undertaken by the secretariat at the request of any signatory. For a country which is referred to in Annex VII and which has reached export competitiveness in one or more products, export subsidies shall be progressively reduced over a period of [10] years. For the purpose of this Article, a product is defined as a section heading of the Harmonized System nomenclature.

0056

외　무　부

종　별 :

번　호 : GVW-2172　　　　　　　　　　일　시 : 91 1029 1120

수　신 : 장관(통기,경기원,재무부,농림수산부,상공부)

발　신 : 주제네바대사

제　목 : UR/보조금.상계관세 협상 개도국우대문제 회의

　　연: GVW-2096

　　가. 아측은 연호 별첨(GVW(F)-0438)으로 송부한 아국의 대안(토의자료 형식)을 10.24.부터 MACIEL협상그룹의장, 사무국, 선진국 및 주요 개도국에 배포하고 개별적 접촉을 통한 설득 노력을 기울었는바, MACIEL 의장은 10.28 아국대안을 토의하기 위한협상 그룹 특별회의를 소집하였음(엄재무관 참석)

　　나. 아측은 제안설명을 통하여 아국은 80년에 이미 수출보조금 불사용을 위원회에 약속하였지만 개도국 우대와 관련하여 개도국을 임의적으로 재분류하려는 현 TEXT의 ANNEX VIII 을 정치적 이유로 받아들일수 없다는 아측의 입장과 동재분류 방식은 이를 시행함이 불가능할 정도의 기술적 문제점을 지니고 있음을 언급하고 아측대안이 종래의 갓트등 국제관행과 부합하여 매우 단순한 형태로 개도국의 관심사항을 보호할수 있는 방안임을 설명하였음.

　　다. 이에 대하여 개도국중 싱가폴, 브라질,말레이지아, 이스라엘, 멕시코등이 적극적 지지를 표시하였으며, 콜롬비아, 칠레, 파키스탄도 동의할 수있는 제안이라고하였음. 종래 소극적 입장이던 인도, 이집트도 현 TEXT 에 보장되어 있는 자국의 이익이 감소되지 않으면 이를 지지한다고 발언함. 그중 파키스탄은 수출경쟁 상품에대한 개도국 우대 제외 규정을 ANNEX VII 국가에 적용하지 말것을, 말레이지아는 개도국에 대한 의무면제 규정에 3.1(A) 뿐 아니라(B) 도 포함시켜야 함을 첨가하여 주장하였음.)

　　라. 선진국중 EC 는 현 TEXT ANNEX VIII 이 시행가능한 방안이며 아국제안이 단순히 개도국 재분류 개념만을 제거하는 것이 아니고 최초 의무비율의 삭제, 점진적 감축의 폐지등 실질적 내용의 여러가지 변화를 초래한다고 반대하였음.

　　아측은 최초의무비율 및 점진적 감축등이 개도국 재분류 방식의 핵심내용이기

통상국　　2차보　　경기원　　재무부　　농수부　　상공부

때문에 이들이 삭제되는 것은 당연하다고 반박하고 현 TEXT 27.2조 및 27.7조가 개도국의 모든 수출상품에 대하여(EACH AND EVERY PRODUCT) 위원회로 하여금 동 의무비율준수여부를 조사하도록 규정하고 있는바 이를 시행가능한 방안이라고 생각하는데는동의할 수 없다고 주장함.

미국은 아국제안이 긍정적 측면과 부정적 측면을 함께 포함하고 있으나 이를 협상의 기초로 검토하겠다고 전제하고 싱가폴에 대하여는 현행 CODE 14.5조에 의한 수출보조금 불사용 약속에 대한 의사여부를 질문하였고 아측에 대하여는 아국이 27.6조(최소 보조금 및 시장 점유율)에 의한 혜택을 받고자 하는지 질문하였는바 아측은아국이 개도국으로써 당연히 동 조문의 적용대상임을 답변하였음. 한편 미국과 EC는 27.6조를 개도국 우대문제와 관련하여 재론할 의사가 있음을 언급하였음.

북구, 스위스, 카나다, 일본등은 아국대안에 전적으로 동의할 수는 없으나 이를협상의 기초로 삼을수 있다고 발언하였음. 마. EC 측이 거듭 반대의견을 주장하자 브라질,싱가폴, 멕시코등은 EC 가 옹호하고 있는 현TEXT 8조 허용보조금의 규정이 개도국은 별로 소용되지 않는 내용들을 담고 있으며 이를 재검토하여야 한다고 반격하자EC측은 매우 당황한 반응을 보인 반면에 허용보조금 축소를 주장해오던 미국은 이를반기면서 자국도 전적으로 생각을 같이한다고 발언하였음. 의장은 회의를 종결하면서 아측에게 금번회의에서 논의된 각국 입장들을 반영하여 27조 전체를 망라하는 조문을 작성하고 이를 협상참가국과 협의한후 자신에게 보고하여 줄것을 요청하였는바, 아측은 이에 동 의하였음.

바. 아측은 상기 회의 종료후 주요개도국 대표들을 별도로 소집하여(인도, 브라질,멕시코,파키스탄,이집트,싱가폴,말레이지아,우루과이참석) 다음과 같이 공동보조를 취할 것으로 합의하였음. 즉 아측은 10.29 오전중으로 의장이 요구하는 조문(안)을작성하고 점심기간을 이용하여 개도국들과 협의한후 사무국과 논의를 거쳐 아국이주재하는 주요개도국 및 선진국간 협의일정을 정하도록 하되 동협의 과정에서 EC가계속 반대하는 경우에는 개도국들이 EC 의 8조 허용보조금과 관련된 입장을 공격하여 이를 봉쇄 하는 수단으로 활용함.끝

(대사 박수길-국장)

외 무 부

종 별 :

번 호 : GVW-2196   일 시 : 91 1030 1800

수 신 : 장 관(통기,경기원,재무부,농림수산부,상공부)

발 신 : 주 제네바대사

제 목 : UR/보조금,상계관세 협상 개도국우대 문제

연 : GVW-2172

가. 아측은 연호로 보고한 계획에 따라 별첨과 같이 보조금,상계관세 협정(안) 제8부 27조 전체를 망라하는 아국의 대안을 토의 자료형식으로 작성하여 10.29. 주요개도국들을 소집하여 협의를 가졌음. 당관 엄재무관이 주재한 동 개도국간 협의에는 브라질, 인도, 이집트, 싱가폴, 말레이지아, 태국, 파키스탄등이 참석하였는 바, 이집트만이 아직 본국으로 부터 회시훈령을 받지 못하였다고 하였고 기타 개도국들은 아국제안에 적극 지지를 표명하면서 이의 관철을 위해 공동보조를 취할 것을 다짐하였음.

나. 아측은 이어서 10.30. 11:00 에 예정된 보조금회의에 앞서 9:00 에 동 문제를 협의하기 위한 선진국 및 개도국간 협의를 소집하였음. 당관 엄재무관이 주재한 동협의에는 상기개도국이외에 미국, EC, 카나다, 일본, 호주, 북구등이 참석하였는 바, 동 선진국 들은 공히 아국제안을 협상의 기초로 수락한다고 하면서 점진적 감축, STAND-STLL 등 이 반영되지 못한점이 불만족스럽다고 언급하였음. EC는 아국, 싱가폴,홍콩등에 대하 여는 특별히 적용을 배제하는 조문을 두는 것이 필요하다고 주장하였으나 대부분의 개도국들이 이는 지극히 불합리한 발상이라고 반박하였음.

다. 표제협상 그룹 MACIEL의장이 주재한 협상그룹 비공식회의에서 아측은 그동안의 협의결과를 보고하였음. 동의장이 아측제안에 대한 토의를 요청하자 EC를 비롯한대부분의 선진국 및 칠레는 아국제안을 협상의 기초로 수락한다고 하면서 점진적 감축개념의 반영이 필요하다고 언급하였음. 협의에 참여한 개도국 및 홍콩, 아르헨티나는 아국제안에 대한 적극적지지를 표시하고 태국 및 말레이지아는 수출경쟁력 개념의 적용 반대, 의무부적용 규정에 3.1조(A)항 외에 (B)를 추가시켜야 함을 첨언하였음. 아측은 금일 아국제안이 27조전체를 포괄하고 있으나 아국의 의도는

통상국   2차보   경기원   재무부   농수부   상공부

개도국재분류 개념의 제거에 국한하여 작성된 것이라고 부연하여 설명하였음

라. 의장은 보조금협상과 관련하여 참가국들의 기타 관심사항으로 2조(특정성), 8조(허용보조금), 28조, 29조(경과조치등) 외에 어떠한 사항이 있는지 발언하여 줄것을 요청하였음. 브라질은 1조 및 14조와 관련하여 보조금의 산정을 정부비용기준으로 할 것으로 주장하였는 바, 아국, 싱가폴은 이를 지지하고, 3.1조(A) 및 각주에 'INLAW OR IN FACT'의 문구가 자의적으로 해석될 우려가 있으므로 삭제되어야 함 및 2조(D)의 규정이 매우 중요한 사항이라는 점을 함께 주장하였음. 미국은 동 문구를 존치하여야 한 다고 반대하였으며 일본은 ANNEX IV 및 V 에 대한 관심을 표명하였음.

마.(관찰 및 평가) 개도국 재분류와 관련된 아국입장 관철을 위한 금번의 시도는 많은 개도국의 지지를 바탕으로 선진국의 종전반대를 극복할 수 있는 가능성을 마련하였다고 판단됨. 아측은 개도국 재분류문제의 정치적 의미뿐 아니라 향후 농산물 협상에의 영향등을 감안하여 아국제안이 실현될 수 있도록 최대한의 노력을 기울일 예정임.

첨부: 개도국 우대에 관한 아국제안(토의자료)

(GVW(F)-0464).끝

(대사 박수길-국장)

GVW.(T)-046 ✓   1030 1800

" GVW - 2176 첨부,

DISCUSSION PAPER ON SUBSIDIES AND
COUNTERVAILING MEASURES

PART VIII Developing Countries
Article 27
Special and differential treatment for developing countries

27.1 Signatories recognize that subsidies may play an important role in economic development programmes of developing countries.

27.2 Accordingly, this Agreement shall not prevent developing country signatories from adopting measures and policies to assist their industries, including those in the export sector. In particular, the commitment of Article 3.1(a) shall not apply to:

(a) developing country signatories referred to in Annex VII.

(b) other developing country signatories for 8 years from the date of entry into force of this Agreement. If subsidies are still deemed necessary beyond this period of time, the developing country in question shall enter into consultation with the Committee, which will determine whether an extension is justified after examining economic, financial and development needs of the country including per capita GNP, economic growth and balance of payments position. If the developing country obtains an extension, it will hold periodic consultations with the Committee every year to determine the necessity of maintaining the subsidies. If no such determination is made by the Committee, the developing country shall phase out these subsidies which are inconsistent with Article 3.1(a) within 3 years from the end of the last

1

0061

ト 1

authorized period.

27.3 However, when a country, except those referred to in Annex VII, has reached export competitiveness in products it shall be bound by the provisions of Article 3.1(a) for those products. Export competitiveness in a product consists of a country's exports of that product having reached a share of at least [4] percent in world exports of that product. Export competitiveness shall exist either (a) on the basis of notification by the country having reached export competitiveness, or (b) on the basis of a computation undertaken by the secretariat at the request of any signatory. For a country which is referred to in Annex VII(b) and which has reached export competitiveness in one or more products, export subsidies shall be progressively reduced over a period of [10] years. For the purpose of this Article, a product is defined as a section heading of the Harmonized System nomenclature.

27.4 The provisions of Article 4 shall not apply to developing country signatories during the period set forth in paragraph 2 above. The relevant provisions in such a case shall be those of Article 7.

27.5 There shall be no presumption that a subsidy not inconsistent with this and other Articles of this Agreement (including those referred to in Article 6.1) granted by developing country signatories results in serious prejudice, as defined in this Agreement, to the trade or production of another signatory. Such serious prejudice, where applicable under the terms of paragraph 6 below, shall be demonstrated by positive evidence, in accordance with the provisions of Article 6.3 through 6.9.

27.6 With respect to any actionable subsidy, other than those referred to in Article 6.1, granted by a developing country signatory, action may not be authorized or taken under

2

0062

Article 7 of this Agreement, unless nullification or impairment of tariff concessions or other obligations under the General Agreement is found to exist as a result of such a subsidy, in such a way as to displace or impede improts of like products into the market of the subsidizing country or unless injury to domestic industry in the importing market of a signatory occurs in terms of Article 15 of this Agreement.

27.7 No countervailing duty action shall be taken against any product originating in developing country signatories if:
   (a) the overall level of subsidies granted or bestowed upon the product in question does not exceed [X] per cent of its value/calculated on a per unit basis/;
   (b) the volume of the subsidized imports represents less than [X] per cent of the domestic market for the like product in the importing signatory, unless imports from countries whose individual market shares represent less than [X] per cent collectively account for more than [X] per cent of the domestic market for the like product in the importing country.

27.8 The Committee shall, upon request by an interested signatory, undertake a review of a specific export subsidy practice of a developing country signatory to examine the extent to which the practice is in conformity with the terms set forth in paragraph 2 and paragraph 3 above.

27.9 The Committee shall, upon request by an interested developing country signatory, undertake a review of a specific countervailing measure to examine whether it is consistent with the provisions of paragraph 7 above.

ANNEX VII

The developing country signatories that are not subject to the commitment of Article 3.1(a)

(a) The following least-developed countries that are contracting parties to GATT: Bangladesh, Benin, Botswana, Burkina Faso, Burundi, Chad, Central African Republic, Gambia, Haiti, Lesotho, Malawi, Maldives, Mauritania, Niger, Rwanda, Sierra Leone, Togo, United Republic of Tanzania, Uganda, Union of Myanmar. Least-developed countries applying the GATT on a _de facto_ basis are: Cape Verde Islands, Equatorial Guinea, Guinea-Bissau, Kiribati, Mali, Mozambique, Sao Tomé and Principe, Yemen Democratic Republic and Tuvalu.

(b) Each of the following developing countries shall undertake commitments which are applicable to other developing country signatories according to Article 27.2(b) when GNP per capita has reached $1,000 per annum: Bolivia, Cameroon, Congo, Côte d'Ivoire, Dominican Republic, Egypt, Ghana, India, Indonesia, Jamaica, Kenya, Madagascar, Morocco, Nigeria, Pakistan, Philippines, Senegal, Sri Lanka, Zaire, Zambia and Zimbabwe.

4

0064

Annex VIII, to be deleted.

5

외 무 부

종 별 :

번 호 : GVW-2384　　　　　　　　　일 시 : 91 1120 1830

수 신 : 장 관(봉기, 경기원, 재무부, 농림수산부, 상공부)

발 신 : 주 제네바대사

제 목 : UR/보조금, 상계관세 비공식협의

11.19(화) MACIEL 의장 주재로 개최된 표제협의 토의내용 아래보고함.

(재무부 조건호 국장, 엄재무관, 김재무관보 참석)

1. 개도국 특별 우대 및 분류문제

0 의장이 아국제안을 중심으로 그간 논의된 내용을 아국으로 하여금 보고토록 함에따라 아국은 다음 요지로 그간의 경위를 보고함. (보고전문: 별첨)

1) 협상의 기초로 하는데는 합의가 있었음., 2) 대부분의 선진국은 STANDSTILL 또는 PHASE OUT조항이 도입되어야 한다고 하였으나, 구체적인 제안은 없었음.

3) 동 조항 도입시 기술적으로 또다른 운용상의 어려움을 야기 할 것이나 구체적인이 있을경우 협상 가능함.

4) 일부 국가는 아국제안중 27.7조의 수정을 제의하였으나 아국제안은 개도국 졸업 또는 재분류개념의 삭제에 국한됨

5) 일부 개도국은 기존 TEXT NOTE (아국제안의27.3조)의 수출경쟁력에 대한 품목별졸업 개념을 삭제하자는 주장이 있었으나 그이외의 부문에 대해서는 모든 참가 개도국들로 부터지지가 있었음.

0 이에대해 각국의 반응은 다음와 같음

1) 미국

- 기존 TEXT와 한국제안은 동시에 각각 장, 단점을 가지고 있으며 둘다 협상 가능한 안임

- 개도국 우대문제에 기본적으로 긍정적이나 이는 경과기간의 부여 관점에서 논의 되어야 하며 이러한 관점에서 STANDSTILL, PHASE OUT, SPECIAL DIMINIMUS, SPECIALREMEDY 등이 고려되어야 함.

2) EC

통상국　　2차보　　경기원　　재무부　　농수부　　상공부

PAGE 1　　　　　　　　　　　　　　　　91.11.21　　09:35 WH

외신 1과 통제관

0066

- 기존 TEXT 를 지지하나 한국안도 협상의 대상에서 배제하지 않음
- 개도국 우대문제는 모든 참가국이 동의 가능한 내용이어야 하며 <u>특정개발정도의</u>
<u>개도국(CERTAINDEGREE OF DEVELOPMENT)은 협정상의 모든 의무를 이행하여야 하는</u>
<u>것이 자국의 입장임</u>

3) 일본, 북구(핀랜드), 스위스, 카나다, 뉴질랜드등
- 시행 가능한 측면에서 한국안이 많은 장점을 가지고 있으나, STANDSTILL 및
PHASE OUT 조항이 추가되어야 함

4) 태국, 말레이지아, 파키스탄
- 한국안중 수출경쟁력 기준에 의한 품목별 졸업개념 조항은 삭제되어야 하며 여타
부분은 전폭적으로 지지함

5) 인도, 이집트
- 한국안을 지지하며 저소득 개도국의 이익이 침해되지 않는 어떠한 안도 협상 가
능함

6) 싱가폴, 멕시코, 브라질등
- 한국안을 전폭적으로 지지함

0 의장은 추가협의가 더 필요함을 언급하고 동부분의 논의를 중단함.

2. 보조금 계산(기존 TEXT 제14조)

0 의장이 '수혜자 수혜기준에 의하여 보조금을 계산할 경우에만 국내법에 이를 규
정하여야 한다'고 수정 제의한바, 미국은 동 내용을 구체적으로 서면으로 제시하여줄
것을 요청함.

0 이에 브라질은 기존 TEXT 제1조의 보조금은 정부 또는 정부기관이 부여하는 특
정 정부 조치를 규정하고 있으므로 보조금의 계산 방법도 동규정에 일치하여
규정되어야함을 지적한바 아국도 이를 지지하였음

3. 향후 일정

0 의장은 금주중 개최 예정인 참가국간 고위급 협상 결과를 기대하며 동 협상
결과에 따라 내주의 회의 일정이 결정될 것인바 금주중에는 의장 주재 회의는 없을
것임. 그러나 참가국간 주요쟁점에 대한 협의 계속을 촉구함.

4. 관찰 및 평가

- 개도국 우대 문제에 대한 아국안이 모든 개도국의 지지를 받고 있고 EC 를 제외
한 대부분의 선진국도 시행 가능성 면에서 아국안에 긍정적이므로 선진국이

공통적으로 요구하는 STANDSTILL 및 PHASE OUT 조항을 아국안에 적절히 반영하는
선에서 새로운 의장 TEXT가 만들어질 가능성이 커지고 있다고 보여짐.끝

    첨부: 아국보고 전문 1부(GVW(F)-0519)

    (대사 박수길-국장)

Since the last meeting in October, I have exchanged views with several delegations regarding the Korean proposal on Special and Differential Treatment for developing countries. At the outset, I would like to report to you that no one has raised objection to taking the Korean proposal as the basis of further negotiation. I think there is a consensus among us in that regard. Many developed country delegations expressed their concern about the lack of a standstill or phasing out mechanism in the Korean proposal. However, nobody has suggested any specific alternatives so far. We have also reflected on this matter very seriously and the following view is the result of our study.

If such a standstill or phasing out scheme is introduced, some kind of computation work should accompany it to ensure compliance with the commitment of concerned developing countries. According to the present code which allows developing countries to use export subsidies virtually without any limitation, no computation work has been required. The Korean proposal would force developing countries, except very low income countries, to eliminate the export subsidies they are using within a certain transition period. Therefore, it is not so convincing that we should have such a cumbersome additional monitoring procedure during this transition period.

Besides, developing countries are not likely to increase the use of export subsidies during this transition period simply because it would be harmful to their export industries. No exporter would base their long term business plan on such a temporary subsidy as it would merely cause serious distortion to their industry.

Nevertheless, if any delegation comes up with a specific alternative, we are prepared to give it serious consideration. Some delegations, suggested modifying other paragraphs of Article 27, including 27.7 of the Korean proposal. As clearly stated previously, the objective of the Korean proposal is strictly confined to Article 27.2 and Annex VIII to eliminate the concept of recategorization or graduation of developing countries relating to special and differential treatment. Therefore, we are not in a position to deal with other provisions which do not have direct relationship with that objective in discussing the Korean proposal. I have consulted with a number of developing country colleagues. Some developing country delegations expressed their concern on the whole Annex VIII of the Cartland text including Note 2 which is transplanted to 27.3 of the Korean proposal and that it should be eliminated because it is a kind of product graduation concept. But the remaining part of the Korean proposal was supported very strongly by almost all developing countries.

Mr. Chairman, this is what I would like to report to you at this stage.

외 무 부

종 별 :

번 호 : GVW-2419

일 시 : 91 1122 1700

수 신 : 장 관(통기, 경기원, 재무부, 농림수산부, 상공부)

발 신 : 주 제네바대사

제 목 : UR/보조금.상계관세 주요국 회의

　　　표제 협상 그룹 MACIEL 의장은 11.21. 주요국가를 초청하여 협상을 진행하였는바 토윙지 아래 보고함(미국, EC, 일본, 북구, 브라질, 인도, 이집트 및 엄재무관 참석)

　　가. MACIEL 의장은 아국제안에 대한 토의를 요청하였는 바, 아측은 대다수 선진국이 주장하는 동결 또는 점진적 감축을 필요로 한다고 생각지 않으나 관심국가가 대안을 제시하면 이를 검토할 용의가 있다고 발언하였는 바, 미국, EC, 일본, 북구가 그필요성을 재차 강조하였음. 의장은 개도국의 재량을 허용하면서 점진적 감축을 규정하는 방안으로 타협이 가능할 것이라고 언급하고 사무국은 가까운 시일에 의장제안을 구체화하는 문안을 작성제시 하겠다고 함.

　　나. 의장은 동 그룹회의를 11.29 경 다시소집하겠다고 하였는 바, 차기 회의에서는 동협상의 주요현안인 허용보조금 및 보조금 규율문제가 논의될 가능성이 크다고보여짐. 이와관련하여 브라질은 별첨 협상 초안 8조 수정안을 아측이 검토하여 줄것을 개별적으로 요청하였고 미측은 근일내 아국과의 양자협의를 제의하였는바 동 사항과 관련된 미측입장의 지지를 요청할 것으로 예상됨.

　　첨부: 브라질측 8조 수정(안)

　　(GVW(F)-0528).끝

　　(대사 박수길-국장)

통상국　　2차보　　경기원　　재무부　　농수부　　상공부

PAGE 1

91.11.23　　08:49 WH

외신 1과 통제관

0071

GVWC제)-0528 · 1/22 17 00

"GVW-241p 첨부.

20.11.91

DRAFTING PROPOSALS FOR ARTICLE 8 OF THE DRAFT TEXT ON
SUBSIDIES AND COUNTERVAILING MEASURES

(Language that has been added is underlined.Deletions are
in brackets with a line. The dotted lines replace texts
without suggested change)

(8.2) Notwithstanding other provisions of this Agreement,
a subsidy may be non-actionable if it is one of the
following:

. . . .

(b) structrural adjustment assistance (to reduce
capacity) provided that such assistance:

(i) is conditioned on: (a) the permanent (and
irreversible closing) closure of the relevant production
facilities of a producer; (b)(or) the reduction of
capacity of a producer; or (c) the privatization of
Government-owned facilities;

(ii) is given to a producer that has been
engaged in relevant production (the capacity of which is
being reduced) during the two (four) consecutive years
preceding the assistance;

(iii) is granted during (given for) a
(limited) period of no more than (time up to a minimum
of) five years;

(iv) does not result,in the case of permanent
closing. in the use of the producer's plant or equipment
for subsequent same production by any entity within the
subsidizing signatory, unless the plant or equipment was
sold at market prices;

(v) is limited to (x per cent of) the
(minimum) actual costs necessary for orderly closing,
(or) reduction of capacity or privatization,(such as the
costs of sustaining employment) provided that such costs
are reasonable.

(c) assistance to promote: · · 15
(1) adaptation of facilities to new environmental
. . . .

(ii) (is limited to (20) per cent of the cost
of adaptation;and)
. . . .

(2) adoption of new equipment and/or production
. . . .

(3) the adoption of equipment and production
processes that promote conservation of energy and
natural or other scarce resources.

(d) assistance to disadvantaged regions within the
. . . .

0072

ㄱ-1

(ii) the region is considered as disadvantaged on the basis of neutral and objective criteria (footnote),clearly spelled out in law or regulation and capable of verification.

(footnote)
the criteria shall,in principle,include a composite (*)

* the remaining text for the footnote is the text of present (iii),(iv) and (v) of Article 8.2(d)

0073

외 무 부

종   별 :

번   호 : GVW-2490   일   시 : 91 1129 0900

수   신 : 장 관(봉기,경기원,재무부,농수부,상공부)

발   신 : 주 제네바대사

제   목 : UR/보조금 상계관세 주요국회의

연: GVW-2419

표제 협상 그룹 MACIEL 의장은 11.26 주요국 소규모 그룹회의를 소집하여 개도국우대에 관한 아국 제안에 대하여 토의하였는 바, 요지 아래보고함.(엄재무관 참석)

가. 의장은 27.2 (B) 에 관한 별첨 수정(안)을 제시하였는바

- EC, 일본은 동 의장 수정안에도 STAND-STILL및 점진적 감축의 개념이 불충분 하다는 지적을 하였으며, 특히 EC 는 구체적인 수출보조금의 감축 방안을 제시토록 하여야 한다고 주장함.

- 아국은 동 수정안에 보조금 위원회가 기간연장을 불허한 경우 조정기간 부여 조항에 관한 부분이 삭제되었는 바, 이는 꼭 필요한 사항이며 이를 선진국측이 수용하는 경우 점진적 감축등에 관하여 동 조항 두째 문장에 ' IN PROGRESSIVEMANNER' 등의 용어를 삽입하여 이를 반영하는 방법도 고려할수 있다고 발언함.

나. 의장은 CARTLAND TEXT 27.4 에 관한 별첨 멕시코 수정제안을 배포하였는 바,이에 관한 본격적 토의는 이루어지지 못하였음.

- 아측은 동 회의후 멕시코 대표와 별도 로 접촉하여동 수정제KED 취지를 문의한바 현재의 규정(안이) 개도국에 6.1조 각 항의 적용을 면제하는지 여부가 불분명하기 때문에 이를 명확히 하기 위한제안이라고 하였음.

다. 미국은 아측에게 8조 허용 보조금에 관한 미국입장을 설명하기 위한 별도 협의 요청하였는 바, 11.29 오전 이를 위하여 접촉예정임.

첨부: 1. 아국제안에 대한 의장 수정안

2. 27.4 조에 관한 멕시코 수정안. 끝

(GVW(F)-555)

통상국   2차보   경기원   재무부   농수부   상공부

첨부 1. 의장수정안

GVW - 355   1112
  GVW - 2

27.2 (b)   other developing country signatories for 8 years from the date of
entry into force of this agreement.   Any such developing country signatory
shall phase out its export subsidies within this period.   Time-limited
extension of this period may be granted by the Committee to a developing
country signatory after examining its economic, financial and development
needs including per capita GNP, economic growth and balance of payments
position.

0075

STT-2-1

붙복2. 명시료 수정안

19.11.91
(Mexico)

SUBSIDIES AND COUNTERVAILING MEASURES NEGOTIATION
Editorial clarification of art. 27.4

1. Article 27.4 (MTN.GNG/NG10/W/38/Rev.3) is an important element of the Subsidies negotiation, as it releases developing countries from the "presumption rule" provision of Article 6.1.

2. However, the current drafting of this point in Article 27.4 is obscure and potentially inaccurate: "There shall be not presumption that a subsidy <u>not inconsistent</u> with this and other Articles..."

3. An alternative language can clarify this important provision, in order to avoid future misinterpretations:

    "In the application of Part III of this Agreement there shall be no presumption that a subsidy granted by developing country signatories results in serious prejudice, as defined in this Agreement, to the trade or production of another signatory. Such serious prejudice, where applicable...with the provisions of Article <u>6.3</u> through 6.9."

0076

55T-2-2

외 무 부

종 별 :

번 호 : GVW-2571

일 시 : 91 1206 1730

수 신 : 장관(통기,경기원,재무부,농림수산부,상공부)

발 신 : 주제네바대사

제 목 : UR/보조금 상계관세 주요국 회의

연: GVW-2490

표제협상 그룹 MACIEL 의장은 12.5 소규모 그룹회의를 소집하여 아국제안(협정 초안 27조)에 관하여 토의하였는바 요지 아래 보고함.

가. 의장은 27.2조(B)항에 관하여 별첨과 같은 절충안을 다시 제시하였는바 아측이 전번회의에서 제시한바와 같이 '가급적 점진적 감축'및 '연장 불허시 조정기간 부여'가 각각 반영되어있음. 이에 대하여 EC,일본은 STANDSTILL 개념이 반영되어야 함을 , 미국, 북구는 결과적으로 11년의 기간이 너무 장기간임을 언급하였음.

나. 아국제안 27.3조의 수출경쟁력 달성 품목에대한 의무적용 문제는 이를 시행함에 있어 통제상의 문제점이 있는 것을 사무국측이 설명하고 이에대한 해결 방안을 논의하였으나 아무런 결론을 도출하지 못하였음.

다. 협정초안 27.4조(아국제안 27.5조)와 관련한 멕시코 제안(연호 별첨 기송부)과 관련하여 사무국측은 현 협정초안이 멕시코 제안과 같은 내용이라고 설명하였으나 미국,EC등은 개도국에 대하여 6.1조의 의무를 영구히 면제하는 것은 불합리 하다는입장표명이 있었음. 아측은 선진국의 이러한 견해가 멕시코 제안의 필요성을 입증하는 것이라고 강조하고 멕시코 제안의 채택 필요성을 지지하였음.

라. 12.9(월)에는 표제협상 비공식 회의를 소집하여 전반적인 토의를 가진후 12.10(화)에 다시 주요국 회의를 소집할 예정임. 협정초안 8조와 관련한 미국과의 접촉은 12.6로 연기되어 갖게될 예정임.

첨부: 의장 수정안(2차) 1부

(GVW(F)-0584).끝

(대사 박수길-국장)

통상국   2차보   경기원   재무부   농수부   상공부

PAGE 1

91.12.07   08:59 DQ

외신 1과 통제관

0077

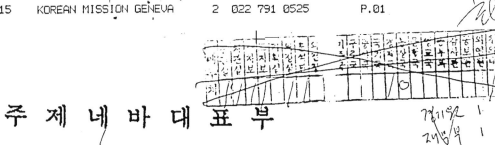

주 제 네 바 대 표 부

번 호 : GVW(F) - 584   년월일 : 11206   시간 : 1800

수 신 : 장   관 (통기, 경기원, 재무부, 농림수산부, 상공부)

발 신 : 주 제네바대사

제 목 :   GVW-2571 첨부

총 2 매 (표지포함)

보 안 통 제	

외신과 통 제	

584-2-1

0078

Chairman, 12.5

27.2 (b) Other developing countries signatories for 8 years from the date of entry into force of this Agreement. Any such developing country signatory shall phase out its export subsidies within this period, preferably in a progressive manner. One year before the expiry of this period, if a developing country signatory deems it necessary to apply such subsidies beyond the eight year period, it shall enter into consultation with the Committee, which will determine whether an extension of this period is justified, after examining all the relevant economic, financial and development needs of the country. If the Committee determines that the extension is justified, the developing-country signatory in question should hold periodic consultations with the Committee to determine the necessity of maintaining the subsidies. If the Committee determines that no extension is justified, the country shall nevertheless phase out these subsidies inconsistent with Article 3:1(a) within [three years] from the end of the last authorized period.

RMS/27.2 584-2-2 0079

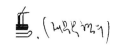

관리 번호	91-903

원 본

외 무 부

종 별 :

번 호 : GVW-2578   일 시 : 91 1209 1500

수 신 : 장관(봉기,경기원,재무부,농림수산부,상공부)

발 신 : 주 제네바 대사

제 목 : UR/보조금 상계관세 협상 한.미 양자 협상

연: GVW-2571

표제 협상 관련 당관 엄재무관은 12.6 미국 동협상 담당관 PARLIN 과 만나 양국입장에 관한 의견을 교환하였는바, 요지 아래 보고함.

가. 협상 초안 8 조(허용 보조금) 관련 사항

- 아측은 3 본 사항과 관련된 선진국간 의견 조정 진전 여부와 미국의 별도 제안 제출 예정에 관하여 문의한바, 미국은 별도 제안을 준비하지 않고 있으며, 여타 선진국과의 협의가 별 진전을 보이지 못하고 있으나 다른 국가가 대안을 제시하는 경우 이를 적극 검토할 예정이라고 답변

- 미국의 현재 입장은 협정 초안 제 8 조에 제시된 4 가지 허용 보조금의 범위를 가능한 한 축소하되, 그중 구조조정이 가장 받아드리기 어려운 분야이며 연구 개발도 상업적 기술개발과 관련된 보조금에 대하여 부정적 입장이 많다고 함. 그동안 미국이 여타 선진국들을 접촉한 결과 EC, 카나다는 지역 개발을 일본은 구조조정 및 연구 개발을 가장 중요하게 생각하고 있고 환경은 이를 강조하는 국가가 별로 없다고 하면서 이를 축소하는 방안에 대한 아국입장을 문의

- 이에 대하여 아측은 가능한한 허용 보조금의 폭넓은 규정이 바람직하며, 구조조정은 산업 구조의 노동집약성 탈피를 필요로 하는 아국의 입장에서도 매우 중요한 것이라고 답변함.

나. 개도국 우대(아국제안 및 협정초안 27 조)관련 사항

- 협정초안 27.6 조(개도국 특별 DEMINIMUS 규정)와 관련, 미측은 개도국의 수출 보조금 사용 억제를 위해 수출 보조금 불사용 약속국가에 한하여 이를 적용하는 방안에 대한 아측 견해를 문의한바 아측은 아국이 이미 불사용약속을 하였으므로 특별히 반대할 이유는 없으나 ANNEX 7 에 게기된 저 개발국가는 예외취급하는 것이 바람직할

롱상국   차관   2차보   분석관   경기원   재무부   농수부   상공부

PAGE 1   91.12.10   00:39

                                         외신 2과 통제관 FM

                                         0080

것이라고 답변

- 미측은 아국제안 27.3 조(수출경쟁력 달성품목)과 관련하여 아측의 견해를 질문한바, 아측은 동조항이 시행하기 어려운 기술적 문제점을 안고 있을 뿐만아니라 선진국에 실질적 도움이 되는지에 의문을 가지고 있다고 답변한바 미측도 이에 동감을 표시함.

다. 관찰 및 평가

- 허용 보조금을 축소하는 협상이 진행될 경우 아국은 가능한한 이를 폭넓게 규정토록 협상에 임하되 불가피한 경우 아국에 중요한 우선 순위가 높은 보조금을 협상안에 존치토록 노력하는 것이 바람직하다고 사료됨.

- 협정초안 27.6 조 관련 수출 보조금 불사용 국가에 한정된 개도국 우대 조치는 아국으로서는 여타 개도국과의관계를 고려하여 적극 지지할 수는 없으나 다른 개도국의 수출 보조금 불사용 약속은 아국 수출의 국제 경쟁력유지에도 바람직하다고 사료되므로 이를 반대하지 않을 예정임.

- 위 각 사항과 관련 본부의견이 있을 경우 조속 회시 바람. 끝

(대사 박수길-국장)

예고 91.12.31. 까지

관리 번호	91-917

외 무 부

종 별 :

번 호 : GVW-2595   일 시 : 91 1211 1130

수 신 : 장관(통기,경기원,재무부,상공부,농림수산부)

발 신 : 주 제네바 대사

제 목 : UR/보조금 소그룹 협의   접 수 필(1991.12.31. 稿)

연: GVW-2571, GVW-2490

12.10(화) 표제협의가 속개되어 연호 송부한 의장 조정안에 대한 토의 내용 아래 보고함.(김재무관보 참석)

1. 각국의 반응

- 아국은 협상의 기초가 될수 있는 적절한 안이라고 하고 의장안을 지지한바, 참가국중 개도국 대표 전원인 브라질, 멕시코, 인도, 이집트가 아국 입장에 동의함.

- EC 는

O CATERLAND TEXT 의 ANNEX VIII 의 삭제에 반대하지 않으나 일정 개발 수준 이상인 특정 개도국(아국, 싱가폴, 홍콩, 이스라엘 지칭)은 수출 보조금 사용과 관련된 S AND D 적용에서 배제되어야 하며

O STANDSTILL 조항이 반영되어야 하고

O PHASE OUT 기간 및 조정기간까지 합할 경우 11 년이므로 지나치게 장기간이며 특히 "IN A PROGRESSIVE MANNER" 보다는 "GRADUALLY"의 용어가 적절하다는 이유를 들어 의장안에 반대의견을 표명하였음.

- 미국은 워싱톤으로 부터의 반응이 의장안에 매우 부정적임을 전하면서 특정 개발 수준 이상의 개도국(아국을 공개적으로 지칭)이 S AND D 의 적용을 받아 수출 보조금을 사용할수 있도록 되어 있는 현 의장안은 받아들일수 없다고 함.

- 일본, 북구는 STANDSTILL 을 재차 강조함.

- 이에 의장은 자신의 안을 기초로하여 특정 개도국은 수출 보조금을 지급하지 않겠다는 COMMITMENT 를 첨부토록하는 방안을 조정안으로 구두제시하였는바, 각국으로 부터 아무런 반응이 없었음. 또한 의장은 앞으로 동 문제 토의를 위한 의장 주재 협의는 없을 것이라 언급하고 참가국간의 협의를 촉구함.

통상국 경기원	장관 재무부	차관 농수부	1차보 상공부	2차보	외정실	분석관	청와대	안기부

PAGE 1

- 연호 송부한 멕시코안은 아국등 개도국이 지지하고 선진국으로 부터는 아무런 반응이 없었음.

- 브라질은 별첨과 같은 개도국의 민영화 사업 부문등에 대한 상계관세 부과를 면제토록 하는 자국의 안을 배포함.

2. 관찰. 평가

- 그간 미국이 비교적 중립적인 입장을 취해왔던 지난 회의까지의 태도와는 달리 워싱톤의 반응이라 전제하면서 의장안에 분명한 반대의사를 표명한 것이 금번 협의 특징이나, 이는

O 협상 마지막 단계에서 허용 보조금의 범위등 미국과 EC 간의 주요 쟁점에대한 타협과정 및 아국안, 27.0 조의 DEMINIMUS 협상 과정에서 아국등 개도국의 지지를 확보하기 위한 방안으로 보여짐.

- 의장 조정안이 그대로 반영될 가능성은 현재로서는 불투명하나, 그러나 기본적으로 EC 도 CATERLAND TEXT 의 ANNEX VIII 의 삭제에는 동의하고 있고 협상 마지막 단계에서 주요 선발 개도국이 현행 CODE 에서와 같이 수출 보조금을 지급하지 않겠다는 COMMITMENT 를 하는 여부가 논의될 것이나 적어도 개도국을 재 분류하는 방안의 도입은 저지할수 있을 것으로 전망됨.

첨부: 브라질 안 1 부 끝
(GVW(F)-594)
(대사 박수길-국장)
예고 92.6.30 까지

PAGE 2

0083

주 제 네 바 대 표 부

번 호 : GVW(F) -5P4   년월일 : 112/11   시간 : 1800

수 신 : 장   판 (통기·경기원·재무부·상용부·농림수산부)

발 신 : 주 제네바대사

제 목 : " 천부 "

총   2 매 (표지포함)

<table>
<tr><td>보 안
봉 재</td><td></td></tr>
</table>

<table>
<tr><td>외신과
봉 재</td><td></td></tr>
</table>

5P4-2-1

27.7(bis)   No countervailing duty action shall be taken against any product originating in developing country signatories if:

a) the subsidies were granted or bestowed upon the product in question within the scope of programmes to privatize state-owned facilities or to promote conservation of energy and natural or other scarce resources.

b) the programmes referred in (a), above, have been established in the national legislation and implementing regulations of the developing country signatory concerned; and

c) the subsidies were granted or bestowed strictly within limits to allow for the viability of such programmes.

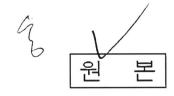

외 무 부

종 별 :

번 호 : GVW-2667   일 시 : 91 1216 1200

수 신 : 장 관(봉기,경기원,상공부,농림수산부)

발 신 : 주 제네바대사

제 목 : UR/보조금.상계관세 비공식 협의

　　12.15(일) MACIEL 의장 주재로 개최된 표제협의내용 아래 보고함.

　　- 의장은 마지막 협의임을 강조하면서 CATERLANDTEXT 를 기초로 하여 그간 각국이 서면으로 이의개정을 요청한 사항을 중심으로 토의를 진행함.

　　- 2.1(B) 중 마지막 문장 REGULATION 다음에 OROTHER OFFICIAL DOCUMENT 를 추가함.

　　- 3.1(A)의 FOOTNOTE 를 EC 의 제안에 따라 별첨 1과 같이함

　　- 14조의 제목을 삭제하고, 14(C)의 둘째문장 DIFFERENCE 뒤에 IN FEES를 추가함.

　　- 제27조(개도국 분류) 문제

　　0 의장은 한국안을 중심으로 집중적 협의가 진행되어 상당한 진전이 있었음을 설명하면서 다음과 같은 내용에 참가국간 의견을 같이하였으므로 이러한 내용이 새로운 의장안에 반영될 것이라 설명함.

　　(1) LLDC 및 1000 불 이하 저소득 개도국은 3.1(A)를 적용하지 아니함.

　　(2) 기타 개도국은 8년에 걸쳐 수출 보조금을 줄여나가야 함.

　　(3) 수출경쟁력을 갖춘 특정분야는 상기 보다 짧은 기간내에 수출보조금을 줄여나가야 함

　　(4) 6.1은 개도국에 적용되지 아니함

　　(5) PHASE OUT 기간동안 개도국에는 HIGHERDEMINIMUS 가 적용됨

　　0 이에 대부분의 참가국은 지지를 표명하였고 특히 브라질은 민영화에 대한 특별고려를, 태국은 수출경쟁력 갖춘 부문에도 동일적용을 말레이지아는 3.1(B)까지 포함을 각각 주장하였고, EC는 의장의 접근 방식에 지지를 표명하면서 선발개도국은 협정상의 일반의무를 부담하여야 함을 기록용으로 언급함.

　　0 아국의 의장의 노력에 사의를 표명하고, 추후 고려사항으로 민영화,

통상국　　2차보　　경기원　　농수부　　상공부

PAGE 1   91.12.17   08:10 WH

3.1(B)의포함문제, 수출경쟁력 갖춘 부문의 취급문제등이 있음을 언급함.

- 29조는 항가리가 월요일까지 대안을 제시함

- ANNEX I 의 (H),(I),(K) 에 대해서는 인도가 관심국가간 협의후, 월요일까지 대안을 제시함

- 제8조(허용보조금의 범위)는 미국과 EC간에 계속 협의하여(정치적 결정을 할수 있는 수준에서의 교섭을 의미) 타협을 모색키로 하고 본협의에서는 논의하지 않기로 함.

- 의장은 화요일 저녁까지 자신의 안을 제시할것이라 언급하고 협의 종료함.

첨부: EC 의 FOOTNOTE

(GVW(F)-0629).끝

(대사 박수길-국장)

PAGE 2

0087

첨부 1   3. `1. (다)의 footnote (른(제)반)

15.12.91

[3]This standard is met whenever the facts demonstrate that the decision
to grant a subsidy, without having been made legally contingent upon export
performance, is in practice tied to actual or anticipated exportation or
export earnings. The mere fact that a subsidy is accorded to an enterprise
which exports a large part of its production shall not for that reason
alone be considered to be an export subsidy within the meaning of this
footnote.

A:FOOTNOTE
SCMT

62P_근글

0088

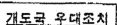

개도국 우대조치

- ## 협정안 비교

브랏셀 의장안 ('90.11)	Dunkel 의장안 (91.12)
- 수출보조금의 지급 혜택 o 개도국의 발전정도에 따라 5구분하여 금지보조금인 수출보조금의 지급혜택 을 상이하게 함. . 최빈개도국 → 지급 허용 . 기타 개도국 → 8~11년내 감축 . 선발개도국 → 지급 금지 - 소액보조금의 상계관세 부과금지 o 물품금액의 [X]% 이하의 보조금 시장점유율이 [X]% 이하인 물품에 대한 보조, 단 이러한 국가들의 누적 시장점유율이 [X]% 이하일 것 - 심각한 손상 추정, 수량기준 규정의 예외 인정	- 수출보조금의 지급혜택 o 개도국 규제 미적용 o 최빈개도국 및 기타 일부 개도국은 적용배제 - 소액보조금의 상계조치 조사 개시 (de minimis 규정) o 물품총액의 2% 이하 단, 수출보조금 실시된 국가는 3%이하 o 시장점유율이 4% 이하, 단 이들 국가들의 누적시장 점유율이 9% 이하 일 것 - 적 용

평가 : 아국입장 반영 → 수용 가능

o 개도국의 발전정도에 따른 재분류 및 차별대우에 관한 아국입장이 대부분 반영됨.

아국의 개도국으로서의 우대 내용

o 수출보조금의 지급 평가

  . 아국은 '80년 Tokyo Round 에 의한 보조금 상계관세협정에 가입시 6년의

  유예기간을 받는 조건하에서 수출보조금의 평사용을 약속함.

  . 따라서 86년부터 수출보조금을 지급할 수 없도록 되어 있음.

o de minimus 혜택

  . 아국은 수출보조금 평사용 국가로 물품금액대비 3% 이하의 보조의 경우

  상계조치가 적용되지 않음.

o 심각한 손상 추정 및 수량기준 규정에 적용받지 않음.

0089

80년 가입당시 약속

Proposed commitment of the Republic of Korea

1. With regard to the provisions of Article 14 of the Agreement on Subsidies and Countervailing measures, Government of the Republic of Korea grants no aids to domestic producers or exporters which are generally incompatible with the commitment of Article 9, nor does it intend to establish such aids.

2. The Government of the Republic of Korea understands that, in the light of the above, it will not be subject to the review procedures mentioned in paragraph 8 of Article 14 of the Agreement on Subsidies and Countervailing measures, as regards export subsidies for a period of six years from the date of the acceptance of the Agreement by the Republic of Korea.

3. The Government of the Republic of Korea also understands that, if extraordinary economic conditions lead it to reconsider its position, the signatories would give sympathetic considerations to the establishment of programs consistent with the change in competitive and development needs of the Republic of Korea.

4. The Government of the Republic of Korea further understands that as its official export credit rates are above those of the international undertaking mentioned in paragraph(k) of the illustrative list of export subsidies, the present system of shortterm export credits of the Republic of Korea is compatible with the commitment of Article 9.

0090

UR협정 초안에 대한 주요 쟁점 및 아국 입장

1. 시장접근분야

주요쟁점	의장 협정문 초안	우리입장 반영 여부 및 대응방안	비 고
- 관세인하 이행기간	- 5년 * '91년 협정초안 에는 8년으로 명시	- 아국입장 반영 o '86.9 UR협상이 개시된 이래 협상이 장기화 되었고 UR 관세 협상의 성과를 조기에 거둔다 는 측면에서 5년의 이행기간 은 타당시됨.	
- 관세인하 이행기간 에 대한 예외인정	- 양허표에 특별한 언급이 있을 경우 에는 상기 이행기간 에 불구하고 예외 허용	- 아국입장 반영 o 농산물 관세 양허, 무세화 · 관세조화제안의 수용이 불가피 해지는 경우에 민감품목 및 분야에 대한 장기 이행기간 확보 필요	
- 비관세조치	- 비관세 조치의 양허 표 작성 o 양허의 수정 · 철회 의 경우에 GATT 28조 적용	- 시장접근그룹 합의 결과에 따름 o 양허표에 게기 가능한 비관세 조치의 <u>선별</u> 필요	

0091

2. 보조금/상계관세 분야

주요쟁점	의장 협정문 초안	우리입장 반영 여부 및 대응방안	비 고
개도국 우대	- 최빈개도국을 제외한 개도국은 8년내 수출보조금의 점진적 감축 o 기존의 소득수준에 따른 개도국 재분류 및 차별대우 삭제 - 개도국에 대한 특별 de minimus 인정(2%) o 수출보조금 불사용 국가는 3% 인정 - 민영화사업에 대한 보조금 지급허용	- 아국입장 반영 o 단, 수출보조금과 관련 '80 동경라운드 보조금 협정 가입시 6년 유예기간을 인정받는 조건 하에서 수출보조금 불사용 약속을 하였으므로 수출보조금 사용 혜택 없음.	아국입장 - 수용 가능
허 용 보조금 범 위	- 허용보조금의 범위 대폭 축소 o 기존의 4가지 허용 보조금(연구,구조 조정,환경보호, 지역개발보조금) 중 연구, 지역개발 보조금만을 허용 보조금으로 인정	- 아국입장 반영 안됨. - 기존의 4가지 보조금이 모두 허용 되도록 아국 입장 반영 필요 o 특히 <u>구조조정</u> <u>보조금 반영</u> <u>필요</u>	아국입장 - 수용불 가 아국대책 (1안) 구조조정 환경보호 보조금의 허용인정 (2안) 구조조정 보조금의 허용인정

0092

주요쟁점	의장 협정문 초안	우리입장 반영 여부 및 대응방안	비 고
상계조치 남용방지	- 제소권자인 국내 산업의 Major Proportion 개념의 계량화 삭제 o 기존협상안에서 국내 산업을 생산가액의 [X]%이상으로 규정, 제소자격을 제한하여 상계조치남용을 방지하려던 규정 삭제 (반덤핑협정안의 내용이 그대로 반영됨) *ADI* *SG 라드에게*	- 아국입장 반영 안됨. o 제소자격에 대해 기존 협정에서와 같이 자의적 해석이 가능해지므로 상계조치 남용 우려 o 따라서 반덤핑 협상에서 국내산업의 계량화 입장 반영 필요	아국입장 - 수용 불가 아국대책 (1안) 계량화하여[X]의 50% (2안) 계량화하되, 구체적 수치는 신축적 대응

0093

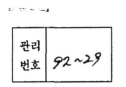

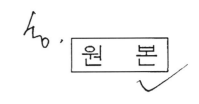

외 무 부

종   별 :

번   호 : GVW-0032   일   시 : 92 0109 1200

수   신 : 장관(봉기, 경기원, 재무부, 농림수산부, 상공부)

발   신 : 주 제네바차석대사

제   목 : UR/보조금.상계관세 협상

검 토 필 (19 . 12.31.) 九

　　당관 재무관은 1.8 표제 협상 DUNKEL TEXT 와 관련, 갓트 사무국 WOZNOWSKI 갓트규범 국장 및 일본, 싱가폴, 브라질대표등을 각각 접촉하여 의견을 교환하였는바 요지 아래 보고함.

　　1. 아측은 WOZNOWSKI 국장에게 그동안 각국의 반응 및 앞으로의 협상진행 전망을 문의하는 한편, 특히 보조금. 상계관세 TEXT 에서 허용보조금의 범위가 공개적인 토의없이 대폭 수정된 점을 지적하고 이에대한 해명을 요청하였는바 동인은 다음과 같이 답변함.

　　가. 보조금. 상계관세 분야를 포함하여 갓트 규범분야의 TEXT 에 대하여 여러협상 참가국이 많은 불만을 제기하고 있음. 그러나 동 협정안은 의장이 협상에 판단되는 절충안을 제시한 것이기 때문에 협상 참가국간의 전체 합의가 없는한 이를 수정하기는 곤란할 것임.

　　나. 허용 보조금 범위에 관하여는 그동안 동 사안이 주요 협상참가국간 첨예한 의견 대립을 보이고 있는 분야로서 공개적인 협상을 봉한 합의도출이 어렵다고 판단하여 의장 자신의 책임하에 이를 제시하였는바, 삭제된 허용보조금중 구조조정 보조금은 사양산업의 폐업 및 감축을 그대상으로하고 있어 철강등 예외적인 분야를 제외하고는 실제로 수출산업으로 상계관세 대상이 거의 존재하지 않으므로 커다란 의미가 없다고 보았으며, 환경설비는 이에 심각한 관심을 표시하는 국가가 적었기 때문에 삭제되었으나 OECD 등에서 세계환경 보존을 위한 기본정책 방향에 위배된다는 항의가 있었음.

　　2. 한편 일본은 자국이 가장 관심을 가지고 있던 구조조정 보조금이 삭제된데 대하여 유감이긴 하지만 그동안 미국의 강령한 입장표명에 비추어 이를 예견하고 있었다고 언급함. 싱가폴, 브라질등은 동 허용 보조금이 실질 협상없이 수정된데

─────────────────────────────

통상국　　장관　　차관　　1차보　　2차보　　외정실　　분석관　　정와대　　안기부
경기원　　재무부　　농수부　　상공부

PAGE 1   92.01.10   04:31
                          외신 2과 통제관 FM

0094

대하여 TRANSPARENCY 가 결여된 점이 불만이나 삭제된 보조금 항목들이 개도국들이 활용하기에는 크게 적합한 것이 아니기때문에 개도국들이 일반적으로 큰 관심을 갖고 있지 않는 것으로 보인다는 협상담당자 차원의 분석이 있었음.끝 (차석대사 김삼훈-국장)

예고:92.6.30 까지

외교문서 비밀해제: 우루과이라운드29

우루과이라운드 제도 및 기타 분야 협상 1

초판인쇄 2024년 03월 15일
초판발행 2024년 03월 15일

지은이 한국학술정보(주)
펴낸이 채종준
펴낸곳 한국학술정보(주)
주 소 경기도 파주시 회동길 230(문발동)
전 화 031-908-3181(대표)
팩 스 031-908-3189
홈페이지 http://ebook.kstudy.com
E-mail 출판사업부 publish@kstudy.com
등 록 제일산-115호(2000. 6. 19)

ISBN   979-11-7217-111-7 94340
       979-11-7217-102-5 94340 (set)